FIRE

AND

AIR

A LIFE ON THE EDGE

PATTY WAGSTAFF

WITH ANN L. COOPER

CHICAGO
REVIEW
PRESS

Library of Congress Cataloging-in-Publication Data

Wagstaff, Patty.
    Fire and air: a life on the edge / Patty Wagstaff, with Ann L. Cooper.
    p. cm.
    Includes bibliographical references.
    ISBN 1-55652-310-6 (alk. paper)
    1. Wagstaff, Patty. 2. Women air pilots—United States—Biography.
3. Stunt flying—United States—Biography. I. Cooper, Ann L. (Ann Lewis)
II. Title.
TL540.W243A3 1997
629.13'092—dc21
[B]   96-52069
                                                                      CIP

©1997 by Patty Wagstaff and Ann L. Cooper
All rights reserved
Published by Chicago Review Press, Incorporated
814 North Franklin Street
Chicago, Illinois 60610
Printed in the United States of America

ISBN 1-55652-310-6

5 4 3 2 1

Contents

Thank you to Ann L. Cooper for her patience and insight. Thank you to Bob Wagstaff for the gift of flight. Thank you to Grandma and Uncle Jack for their unconditional love. Thank you to my competitors for inspiring and helping my desire to win.

To All Pilots

I sat upon a cold stone steed,
steel black bit in hardened mouth.
My spurs sink in but steel doesn't bleed,
I turn my head to the wind from the south.
But fools cannot fly, cast nostrils don't snort
nor whinny nor howl. I sit there 'til night.
The reins held loosely, I hold my court
with dreams, until dawn dies with the light.
You who put wings on steel spun sides
and wires and strings between your thighs.
A nudge with a knee, mouth comes into life,
giving some rein, your steel steed flies!
Fools, those blown by the wind, they have no wings.
What are their dreams, if life is only birth?
Your vestal white steed's propeller mane brings
and breathes life from air, water, fire, and earth.

—*Patty Wagstaff*

Foreword

Flying is a unique and exciting opportunity, whether you fly as a pilot or a passenger. Flying places you in three-dimensional space, allowing you to view the world from a new and different perspective, one to which many people are not accustomed. It gives you a whole new appreciation for our world when you have a chance to see large cities, tall mountains, green valleys, and deep blue lakes from high above.

Within the world of flight, pilots look upon aerobatics as something special. It is an activity that takes the airplane's capabilities and pilot's skills to the limit. I have found, through personal involvement in aerobatics, that I have learned more about myself as a pilot than almost anything else I have done in aviation.

Aerobatic flying requires complete focus, skill development, confidence, hard work, and practice. It takes a unique individual, such as Patty Wagstaff, who can utilize his or her abilities to perform difficult maneuvers under stressful conditions, with the ultimate goal of becoming the best—a champion!

I got my start in aerobatics by watching other pilots perform their routines at air shows and fly-ins. For me, it was entertainment. But it was the excitement I felt that made me want to try it. Gene Soucy, a close friend who was already an aerobatic competitor, served as my mentor. On the ground, he described the maneuvers. Then I would make the airplane climb to high altitudes and practice under his watchful eye.

I entered my first competition and experienced firsthand the pressure of performing maneuvers under the close scrutiny of five judges who are looking for very specific things. If your lines and angles aren't precise or if the wind drifts you out of the aerobatic competition box, you are penalized. There are so many things to think about, and, all the while, G forces affect your body as you pull and push the airplane through its maneuvers.

As I moved up through the ranks, I could see the competition between pilots build as they matched their skills against each others'. You are up there all alone, flying only for the judges who score each of your maneuvers. Your abilities are totally exposed. But it comes down to the simple fact that the pilot with the most points wins. Nothing else counts.

I was fortunate to be a member of the U.S. Aerobatic Team that won the World Aerobatic Championship in Salon, France, in 1972. Having been there, I know what it takes to get to the top. Today, the amount of commitment necessary to win is even greater because the equipment is better and there are more competitors who are training longer and harder. If you are going to be the best, you must have the skills and the dedication to do so.

Patty Wagstaff meets and exceeds those requirements. She is a superb competitor, and has the mental outlook, work ethic, and flair to be a national and international champion. This is confirmed by the fact that she won the National Aerobatic Championship three times, was a member of the U.S. Women's Aerobatic Team that won the World Aerobatic Championship in Red Deer, Canada, in 1988, and has competed in numerous world competitions. Aerobatic competition is an individual sport in which your success is dependent totally upon your performance. Patty has developed a mental toughness to be able to perform at a consistently high level. That is the mark of a winner.

But aerobatics is more than just competition. To many, it is entertainment. Air shows have become one of the largest recreational activities in the United States, and Patty has been one of the leaders. She flies with confidence and at the same time adds a flair that makes her performance highly entertaining and appealing to the public.

Air shows are fast becoming the public relations arm for aviation. They offer an opportunity to bring aviation to the entire family. Patty has combined her superb pilot skills with the ability to communicate to become an ambassador for aviation, at aviation events across the country, and representing the United States in world competition. She understands the importance of spreading the message of flying for fun and has done this well.

Patty has brought a unique style to aerobatic competition and air shows. She has been a trailblazer. She can move from the cockpit to the flight line with grace. She is a hard charger and a fierce competitor. When she is in the cockpit, you know that Patty is in charge of the airplane, but at the same time, she can be a gracious air show performer when mixing with the audience.

She has dedicated her life to be the best in her field—male or female. Aerobatics is physically demanding. You are constantly operating under tremendous mental pressure, having to execute maneuvers in a variety of conditions. To do this you must be experienced, a quick thinker, and focused. That describes Patty. Over the past two decades I have seen the best air show pilots and aerobatic competitors. I know what it takes to get to the top and stay there. I understand what kind of sacrifice has to be made. Patty Wagstaff has earned all the recognition she has received as one of the leading aerobatic pilots in the world today.

Tom Poberezny, President, Experimental Aircraft Association
Former U.S. National Aerobatic Champion
For twenty-five years a performing air show pilot with
the Eagles Aerobatic Team

Prologue

Few ever have the opportunity to "hang on the perch," orbiting above a spectacular array of faces in a huge crowd, their eyes searching upward as one. Few have arrested an entire human tide, one tingling with expectancy, preparing to create an excitement for each upturned face. Patty hangs on the perch, her aircraft a metallic cocoon into which she is snugly placed, and looks out of her glistening bell jar feeling larger than life. The rest of the living have been reduced to miniatures in a Lilliput world, to Patty a fishbowl of primary colors, striped awnings, colorful tents, minuscule parked airplanes and automobiles, and shiny reflective buildings that return to her the rays of the golden sun that hangs above her head and bathes the scene in light and shadow.

Her bell jar does nothing to hush the thunder of her snarling, pulsating engine. Her propeller whirls into a blur, its rpms tuned to the cadence of power. An upward tip of the wing and the noise alters from a growl to a whine, then resounds again as speed builds and the nose of the aircraft dips toward air show center. The sounds of the human world are reduced to a few crisp voices crackling over the modern, cushioned headpiece clamped over her ears. She has a tiny boom mike projecting before her lips.

The air boss reports, "One minute to go, Patty. Are you ready?"

"Ready," is her crisp reply and she turns up the volume of her stereo music to psych herself further and to get a beat throbbing to a rhythm, the beat of her aerial dance. She runs rapidly through her preshow check once more, touching the connections of her five-point harness and clicking the ratchet one more notch and, glancing to see that the oil pressure is right, that the fuel tank is selected to akro (aerobatics), that the prop is all the way in, and that the mixture is rich. Retightening the strap of her headset, she's ready to flick her smoke oil on, ready to dive toward center stage, ready to dazzle.

She knows that the crowd below is listening to the patter of a good announcer revving them up via the strategically placed loudspeakers and that the musical beat has begun to drum in their ears. All of them turn to watch the sky for her appearance, the eagle-eyed among them pointing, calling out, "There she is!"

Smoke oil on, throttle forward, the act begins.

Although to Patty the crowd is silenced by the immediacy of the throaty engine and the stereophonic staccato, she will rejoin that throng within ten to twelve minutes and will be inundated with the sounds of catcalls, whistles, thunderous applause, and occasional shouts of "Way to go, Patty!" "Fantastic, Patty!" and "I love you, Patty. You're the girl of my dreams!"

She'll hear squeals of delight from thousands of children, their cherubic faces tilted up to view her with awe and with joy. Some will be jumping up and down, clapping and yelling, unable to contain their delight. Some will push forward, wriggling through the labyrinth of arms, legs, cameras, beach chairs, and blankets to reach for a proffered glossy brochure, to stroke the sleeves of her flight suit, to put tentative fingers toward her hair, a mahogany halo; and to beg for an autograph, a chance to be the most important child in Patty's life, if only for the moment.

An inspiration to young and to old, to anyone who has ever held a dream, Patty symbolizes the realm of possibility for those willing to pursue, to commit. As her aircraft has just tumbled through unusual attitudes, so, too, does she incorporate the unusual in her own can-do spirit. With her special effects, she has made an impact on all who have seen her and known her.

This book is dedicated to Patty, about whom Ian Groom, her fellow pilot in precision aerobatics, has said, "Patty has a confidence of her own. You can't be successful in a highly competitive environment without a confidence such as hers. Patty answers any critics by demonstrating with substance."

It has been my privilege to work with Patty in the creation of this, her first book. She is a complex woman of intelligence and sensitivity. I thank her for her candor, for her generosity, and for her trust. Hang on that lofty perch, Patty.

Ann Cooper
October 1996

In appreciation:

Charlie Cooper, my best friend; and my family, all of whom understand that I'm impulsive and hopefully will learn that I am centered.

Lisa Swayne and Bill Adler, literary agents who know the meaning of service and the edgeless joy of piercing the blue.

Cynthia Sherry and Lisa Rosenthal-Hogarth, editors with whom I hope to have established an ongoing relationship.

Karen Roberts, for giving of her time and friendship.

This book is for all who yearn to know one woman's answer to the mysteries and magic of life and how to live every day to its fullest.

Introduction

The urge to take flight like the birds dates to earliest history. There are accounts in the Bible by Ezekiel, a Hebrew prophet of the sixth century B.C., of flight in ancient times. And, of course, we have the mythological story of Icarus falling into the sea when the wax on his wings melted. The thought of flying has so intrigued humans throughout history that even Leonardo da Vinci applied his great talent to the idea. He designed a flying machine in 1495 that looked very much like the present-day helicopter. There is a certainty that what we dream of will become reality in time. So, it was left to practical men who also had the dream to make flight a reality. The Wright Brothers were inspired by glider pioneers Otto Lilienthal and Octave Chanute. They built and flew their own glider in 1900. By 1902 the Wright Brothers were gliding regularly, using vastly superior airfoils of their own design and, in the process, correcting the aerodynamic tables that were first developed by Lilienthal. All that remained to achieve sustained flight was to add an engine and propeller. History records that feat as having been accomplished by Wilbur and Orville Wright in 1903 at Kitty Hawk, establishing that location as the proving ground for the first powered flight of a heavier-than-air machine. They went on to explore turning flight in numerous test flights at Huffman Prairie on present-day Wright-Patterson Air Force Base in their hometown of Dayton, Ohio—the birthplace of aviation.

In a few short years after the demonstrated flight by the Wright Brothers, the value of the airplane as an instrument of war was recognized. The Germans and Allies alike developed airplanes as fighting machines to help their causes during World War I. We can only imagine today what it must have been like in those heady days of "gentlemanly" combat. The sky became the battlefield for noisy swooping, turning, and looping airplanes, each attempting to maneuver into a firing position and seeking desperately to gain an advantage. This was a deadly serious business, and the most imaginative, adventurous, and fearless pilots became the heroes on both sides of the Atlantic.

Some of the most famous pilots, those we continue to recognize to this day, were engaged in that war, on both sides of the effort. Manfred von Richthofen, the "Red Baron," is known as the leading ace of World War I for shooting down eighty Allied airplanes. Eddie Rickenbacker is still renowned as the leading American combat pilot for scoring twenty-six victories before the Armistice. The Great War provided the motivation to develop airplanes—fighters and bombers—that would set the stage for an explosion in aviation during the 1920s and 1930s. Many pilots bought war planes for next to nothing and toured America as barnstormers. Demonstrating the maneuvers that were used in aerial combat, they developed aerobatics routines that delighted the crowds and firmly fixed the idea of flying into the American psyche. From those early days of barnstorming, aerial circuses, passenger carrying, and mail delivery came the mighty aviation industry as we know it today.

A most daring event in aviation occurred in 1927. Early in the morning of May 20, Charles Lindbergh climbed into his Ryan monoplane at Roosevelt Field on Long Island for an attempt to fly across the Atlantic Ocean. He had entered the competition to be the first pilot to fly nonstop across the ocean; to land in Paris, France; and to claim the prize of $25,000. After thirty-three hours and thirty minutes of flight, he came down at Le Bourget Field outside of Paris as a world-famous person. He was decorated by many countries and received a hero's welcome wherever he went. He had not only succeeded at something where many had failed, but he had provided worldwide attention for aviation.

A history of flying would not be complete without the inclusion of the role that women have played. As early as 1928, Amelia Earhart was making news by becoming the first woman to cross the Atlantic Ocean in an airplane—as a passenger. Determined to prove that she could perform the same feat at the controls of an aircraft, she flew solo across the

Atlantic in 1932 and completed many solo long-distance flights around the United States. In 1935 she made a solo flight from Hawaii to California. Sadly, she disappeared while on a round-the-world flight in 1937 with her navigator, Fred Noonan. No trace has ever been found of the plane where it vanished near Howland Island in the Pacific Ocean. Even though she was lost fifty-eight years ago, Amelia Earhart still provides inspiration for the thousands of women that fly today.

Jackie Cochran was another fearless pilot and record-breaking aviator. Having won the Bendix Transcontinental Air Race in 1938, she went on to become the first woman to fly faster than the speed of sound and to set new speed and altitude records for women. During World War II, Jackie Cochran spearheaded the formation of the Women Airforce Service Pilots (WASPs). More than 25,000 women applied for training, with 1,830 accepted and 1,074 graduating from the program. The WASPs flew more than 60 million miles for the Army Air Force and flew nearly every type of airplane, from trainers to fighters and bombers.

All that you have just read is merely an introduction to the best of the best. Patty Wagstaff is a pilot in the tradition of Amelia Earhart and Jackie Cochran, yet she is much more than simply a female pilot. Patty regularly competes and wins against men in what has always been a man's world—aerobatics. Not content to merely fly airplanes, Patty is an exceptional stunt and aerobatic pilot, winning the National Aerobatic Championship three years in a row: 1991, 1992, and 1993. She has won so many honors and awards that it would be meaningless to list all of them here. Suffice it to say that one of her airplanes, the unique Extra 260, is on display in the Smithsonian Institution's National Air and Space Museum alongside the airplanes flown by the Lindberghs and Amelia Earhart. Patty also received the Smithsonian Award for Current Achievement in 1994.

Here is a gal who has made all pilots proud. She competes with the best—and beats them! I am proud to have her as a friend.

Al Worden, U.S. Astronaut
Apollo 15

ONE

Elements

I am in my element—the air. I am suspended, surrounded by that which claws at my every sense: swirling clouds and an acrid mixture of lubricants, outside air, faint exhaust fumes, and, occasionally, a whiff of something sweet and pungent that I can't identify. The control stick is molded to my fingers. I squeeze tightly, then my touch is light; my hands are inquiring yet positive. My feet, never still, respond to every pressure of my toes—pressing, relaxing, rhythmic like those of a dancer. I sight the horizon, envisioning a distinct line even when it is faintly obscured with blurred stands of evergreens and mauve-colored hills. I choose section lines on the surface to choreograph my routine, never losing sight of where I am in space the way a twirling ballet dancer focuses on a single spot on a stage to maintain balance.

This is where I belong and where I feel alive, even joyous. Each time I fly aerobatics, I feel more at home in my machine and in the air. I believe in the elements: air, earth, water, and fire. I believe that people are basically elemental, drawn instinctively and specifically to one or two of them, like the animals that we are. Air and fire are seductive to me. I *feel* them. Air and fire—my equation for the airplane.

It is my rare fortune to make flying my business, my pleasure, my challenge, my delight. In Alaska in 1979, Bob Wagstaff, an Anchorage attorney and flight instructor and later my husband, first turned over to me the controls of his Cessna 185. Five years later, four years after having received my license to fly as a private pilot and a scant two years after my first aerobatic flying lesson, I put my airplane, a Decathlon registered as 1118E (one one one eight Echo), through its paces over Minnesota's patchwork quilt of woods, land, fields, and lakes; a puffy eiderdown of greens, beiges, golds, browns, and blues.

Tumbling beneath high, lacy clouds—"mare's tails," they are called, for their streaming horsehair curves—I knew the wispy layers were made of tiny ice crystals, but I pretended they were scattered diamonds. One with my machine, I concentrated, part of me frolicking like a child, below diamonds and above a colorful tweed carpet, and another part of me cold and calculating as I perfected maneuvers. I pushed myself to excel. It was late July 1984, and I had flown alone more than three thousand miles from the skies of Alaska to compete in my first aerobatic contest in Fond du Lac, Wisconsin. Keyed up with feelings akin to stage fright, I rehearsed my routine over and over again for what, at that time, loomed as the biggest event in my life.

Knowing full well that the busy skies around Fond du Lac and Oshkosh precluded practice—it was the week following the huge convention that annually attracts more than twenty thousand airplanes and nearly a million people to Oshkosh—I had flown to the boonies outside of Hibbing, Minnesota. I needed a place with skies free of aerial congestion and chose Hibbing simply because it was the birthplace of singer Bob Dylan.

I kicked my airplane into a spin and twirled downward, whipping the squares of farmland and nearby lakes into concentric circles, a whirling kaleidoscope of earthy browns and greens and watery blues. Stopping the rotation as suddenly as it began, I momentarily leveled the airplane before starting a new maneuver, a slow roll. Fully alive, I felt keenly aware of my relationship with the earth and the horizon—my position in the sky.

As I rolled over into the inverted position, my hair streaming over my head in response to the negative G forces and turning me momentarily into a modern Medusa, the controls suddenly stiffened. The stick was jammed! The elevator, the surface that allowed me to climb or to dive, to pitch the aircraft around its lateral axis, was rigid! Useless! A *control* failure! Was this my Perseus, determined to slay me? Few things terrify pilots, and this was one of them—feared just slightly less than a fiery explosion, an in-flight fire! "God! What'll I do?"

My mind raced over the immediate past. The year had been so incredible to me—one in which I competed in my first aerobatic contest *and* performed in my first air show. In 1982 Bob had given me a series of ten lessons in aerobatics with Alaska's Darlene Dubay—my first heady sip of what would become an intoxication. My wild side took to aerobatics like one who had been kept in darkness and was suddenly led into blinding light. Colors that had been blurred and pale were suddenly vivid and psychedelic. Paths that had been undefined sharpened acutely. With a passion that consumed me, rushing the sweet taste of adrenaline to my tongue, aerobatics brought purpose to my life. I found ecstasy. I found a new world.

I began to get air show requests, and, in July 1984, I was invited to do an air show routine in the town of Soldotna on the Kenai Peninsula southwest of my Anchorage home. Jim Eshenhower, a friend, had flown to Soldotna as a passenger in my Decathlon, a two-seat, single-engined aerobatic airplane. I recalled our return after that air show.

The high of having performed was still with me, and halfway home, I shouted, "Hey, Jim, want to see a roll? A loop?" Jim had never flown aerobatics. After a quick glance over my shoulder to make sure he was nodding, I grinned at him, then glanced outside to see that we were alone in our chunk of sky. I rolled the Decathlon sharply to the left, reversed and rolled to the right, then pulled up into a smooth loop in the dusky skies over the Kenai Mountains. At the completion of the loop, I threw in a spin for good measure.

After we taxied to a stop at Anchorage's Merrill Field, Jim reached into his pockets for the key to his car, one among several that formed a wad of heavy metal on their ring. Jim felt around in his pocket, looking at me quizzically. He said, "My keys?! Where in heck could I have lost them?" He checked his pockets again, then leaned to feel for them under the seat and on the floor of the airplane near the rudder pedals.

"They probably came out of your pocket when we were doing aerobatics."

"I don't even know if I had them when I climbed into your airplane, Patty. In fact, I can't quite picture where I had them last. Obviously, I drove here to the airport. But I don't remember even thinking about them at Soldotna."

Bob had joined us at Merrill and the three of us looked everywhere. We used a flashlight to search every crevice in the airplane, even taking off the inspection plate covers in the tail. A Decathlon has an enclosed cabin, which made it hard to imagine that the keys had gotten into the tail, but we searched every accessible inch of the interior, finding nothing.

"I must have dropped them on the ground at the air show," Jim said. "Damn! That means I'll have to fly my airplane back to Soldotna. Maybe someone has turned them in."

"Do you want to jump-start your pickup?" asked Bob.

Jim shook his head. "That wouldn't help much, Bob. There are about ten keys on that ring and I can't get far on Monday morning without them. Hell, I can't even get into my house tonight. I'd better fly back to Soldotna in my Cessna 140. See you guys later. Thanks for the aerobatics, Patty."

No sooner had Jim left than I started packing one-one-one-eight-Echo for the long flight to the States for my first aerobatic contest in the lower forty-eight.

I arrived in the States a few days prior to the start of the 1984 International Aerobatic Club (IAC) Championship in Fond du Lac. I headed for Hibbing to practice my maneuvers and my freestyle routine. About three or four maneuvers into my freestyle was a slow roll—*the* slow roll. When the stick stiffened—the elevator jammed—I knew immediately that I had little or no control of the pitch of the plane. I felt numb and an icy rush sliced through my body.

I was upside down, my head pointed toward the ground. I carefully eased the stick to the right, testing the amount of failure. Luckily, the ailerons were free. The airplane responded and rolled upright.

The stick was jammed close to neutral—one lucky break. I wasn't pitched downward toward the ground or upward into a stall. I handled the plane very gingerly while I sorted out my options.

"Trim. Use the trim!" I could hear instructors' voices in my head. A Decathlon has a powerful and sensitive trim control—a connection to a small tab on the tail that enables a pilot to reduce elevator pressures during diving or climbing—so I rotated that lever in the cockpit, moved the tab, and managed to hold the nose straight and level. Once upright and straight and level, I thought, fleetingly, about Jim Eshenhower's keys.

I turned slowly for the airport, using the trim lever with every power change, and by strategically cranking it, I worked the elevator and controlled 1118E to a safe landing.

Several things contributed to making the outcome successful. It was a small airport without a lot of air traffic, for one. I shuddered to imagine what might have happened in the high-traffic area of Fond du Lac or Oshkosh. Also, the winds were light and the weather was crisp and clear. Credit, too, was due my flight instructors, Darlene, Bob, and Tom Robinson. While training me, they all had insisted that I practice handling landings strictly by use of trim.

"This is excellent practice for an emergency," Bob had said. "You never know, in aerobatics, when you will have pushed your machine or yourself too far. Be ready for the unexpected."

I had consistently practiced climbing and descending strictly via the use of trim. Now I had reason to be thankful!

Once safely on the ground, I searched for the cause. I had flown the equivalent of crossing the entire United States at its widest point, and, until I did the slow roll, I had no inkling that a wad of keys wrapped in a vicious tangle around the elevator stops waited to kill me.

I called Jim in Alaska. "Hi. This is Patty. Are you still looking for your keys?"

"Where are you, Patty?"

"I'm in Hibbing, Minnesota. Bob Dylan's karma must be taking good care of me."

"Bob Dylan? What?"

"Your keys got all the way back to the Decathlon's tail and tangled in the control cables."

"You found them! Needless to say, they weren't at Soldotna. That's good news! I—"

"You bet it's good news! I'm really lucky to be here telling you about it. I can't imagine where they've been or why I haven't heard them rattle around back there!" I filled him in on the rest.

"Fantastic, Patty. I'm sorry they caused you trouble. . . . Uh, glad to hear you're OK."

Jim wasn't nearly as glad as I. The more I thought about it, the more I realized how close I had come to a fatal accident. If I had been in a spin or some maneuver that required the use of the elevators for recovery, the outcome might not have been so pretty. I was damned lucky!

It wasn't keys or extraneous clutter but elevator failure and a trim problem that added up to trouble for a friend and another member of the U.S. Aerobatic Team, the late Rick Massegee. Rick, who had put his heart and hundreds of hours into the building of his own airplane, had to bail out of that stricken craft when his trim proved to be unusable. It was dramatic—and scary!

We were in El Reno, Oklahoma, in 1989, the practice site for a few of us with plans and dreams of making the U.S. Aerobatic Team. In preparation for the nationals, the annual National Aerobatic Championships, which are held in the Sherman-Denison area of Texas on the site of what was Perrin Air Force Base, we convened annually at El Reno and put forth a joint effort. We competed with one another, trying to the best of our abilities to outfly each other and to be successful as individuals. As members of the nation's aerobatic team and representatives of our country, we also tried to pull together to form a cohesive unit to vie against the teams of other countries in world competition.

Just before he flew, Rick, who knew I was seriously thinking of replacing my four-cylinder-engined airplane with a more powerful model, said to me, not for the first time, "You really ought to fly a plane with a six-cylinder engine and get the feel of it."

I admitted that I'd like that but didn't commit myself.

Rick added, "OK, look. I've got you on the insurance. Today's the day you are going to fly my airplane."

"OK, Massegee, but you go ahead and fly it first. I'll fly it later," I said.

Newly arrived after having flown cross-country in his Rebel, it was important that Rick check out his plane first. Rick took off. His second maneuver was an Avalanche with double snap rolls on top of a loop. Right after the second snap, he broke off his routine. From the ground, we could see that he was struggling to get the airplane stabilized. Then he radioed down and said, "I got a problem. I don't have an elevator. Something broke."

"Oh, God, Massegee."

Clint McHenry, Bill Larson, Bill White, and I were on the ground with local people like Rick Mulaney, the airport manager, and others. I glanced over at Massegee's parents, knowing they understood an aircraft's flying characteristics. Their faces showed their anxiety. To compound the problems, adverse weather, which can so often be one of the biggest problems for pilots, loomed on the horizon. The skies, relatively trustworthy when he took off, had darkened with a rising blackened toadstool of a thunderstorm to the southwest.

Rick circled, making four careful approaches to the grass runway, all without success. Those of us attached to the handheld radio, the umbilicus, were riveted to the ground between the two runways. The tension was palpable. The wind started to pick up, gray scuddy clouds moved toward us, and skies to the southwest turned from dark gray to black, in an ominous, sinister drama. His mother looked at me and said, "Tell him to jump. He can replace the airplane."

Having responded to our call, an ambulance arrived and I talked to the medical volunteers and warned them of some of the possibilities. "If he touches down and he isn't in the right attitude, his airplane might flip over. If the wing is crushed, the spar might break his legs. He might have to be cut free of his harness and seat belt. And you will have to watch— he could be dangling, and when you cut him free he might fall and hurt himself seriously unless you catch him as you release him. You have to think about back injuries." I thought to myself, "Dare I mention fire?"

An Army National Guard helicopter flew by, a big red cross decorating its side. They had heard our radio transmissions and called to offer help.

Rick did everything right. His fourth approach was almost his last. The plane pitched up violently. Everyone held their breath. It was horrible! With fantastic effort, he got it under control and all of us breathed a collective sigh.

He finally radioed, "I'm getting out."

The winds had picked up and we knew he was dealing with increased turbulence. By our calculations, he had one gallon of fuel remaining. Rick opened his canopy. We saw the Plexiglas blow away from the fuselage and flutter down. He climbed out onto the wing and we saw him jump, his arms outstretched. The popping open of his emergency parachute was a beautiful sight. Big, round, and cumbersome, it was subject to drift but sturdy and safe. We watched him descend, carried away from us by the slow wind that was energized by the coming storm. We later learned that a piece of the push-pull tube had broken and caused the loss of his elevator.

Having sunk hours into creating and flying his own airplane, he told me later, "God, standing on the wing and letting it go was hard. It was really painful."

It hurt us all and I felt it especially keenly, since Rick had asked me to fly his airplane. It was sobering to look at the wreckage of an otherwise fine airplane. You never get used to that. He told me, "That could have been you. God, I'm glad you weren't in that plane."

Later, much later, when the wing of his Russian aerobatic airplane broke and folded, Rick didn't get another chance. It happened very quickly. I appreciated what he had taught me and grieved for him and for his parents' pain.

Watching Massegee at El Reno brought back memories of a near accident that I had in 1986 while flying my Pitts S-1T, N200ST, at an aerobatic contest in Eloy, Arizona. I wanted extra performance and decided to reduce the weight of the airplane by removing an aft-mounted battery. When removing the battery, however, I did *not* remove the wooden tray that held it. I thought that it was glued or tie-wrapped to the steel tubing against which it was fitted. I assumed—*a dangerous mistake*—that it was secure. In flying, assumptions can kill.

I took to the air for my compulsory flight and climbed to altitude, ready to go. My fifth maneuver was a Tail Slide. I intended to climb vertically, cut the power to idle, and hold the airplane in that nose-high attitude until it slid backwards. I planned to further urge the airplane into a downward vertical line just after it flopped over, having run out of upward momentum. The airplane flopped as I expected. Then, to my surprise and horror, the elevator controls jammed! When I tried to push forward on the stick, it wouldn't budge! "Oh, shit!" I said.

There is a saying popular with fighter pilots: "Sheer luck beats skill and cunning every time." I was lucky. I couldn't push forward, but I was able to ease back on the stick and, with the power at idle, to level off. I finessed through an entire circle, flying in a wide arc, descending in a gentle approach, and landing. I forced my hands to be light on the controls.

It didn't take a genius to figure that the battery tray had jostled out of position and into the tail of the airplane. It was careless of me to assume the tray was secure. I was *very* lucky that the elevator jammed in a nose-down vertical dive—a recoverable situation—rather than in the midst of, say, an inverted spin.

I take exception to Ralph Waldo Emerson who in 1860 wrote in his *Conduct of Life*: "Shallow men believe in luck." Although I guess he can be excused; in 1860 aerobatics didn't exist. One hundred and twenty-some years later, however, I am thankful for several doses of good luck.

Along with preparation, determination, and hours and hours of practice, I can't help but appreciate a bit of good fortune.

"How long are you going to fly aerobatics?" I've been asked.

I want to answer with a question, "How long are you going to be a dentist? A newspaper writer?"

I can respond to children's questions for as long as time will permit. I love to encourage youngsters toward aviation and make them aware of aviation careers and opportunities. Adults press, asking: "What makes you drive yourself to excel?" "When so many others are killed at it, why do you *do* aerobatics?"

Another air show star and friend, wingwalker Cheryl Littlefield, had answers to the questions she was most commonly asked printed on the back of her T-shirt.

Yes, my mother knows I do this.
Yes, I trust Gene, my pilot.
No, you can't do it.
Yes, it's windy.
No, I'm not crazy.

Perhaps I should resort to that, too.

When people ask if I get frightened, I shake my head. "No" is the simple answer. The more complex, and unspoken, response is that in the air, I let myself go. It is cosmic, a Zen mode. I don't think about anything but symmetry and dancing, lines and pirouettes. I indulge myself.

I believe that before any *real* moment of impact, there is no fear, no *time* for fear. Only close calls afford the luxury of succumbing to the slow rise of adrenaline into the solar plexus where it explodes into real fear. Fear is paralyzing, totally counterproductive. I have been told that I have a death wish. I think it is just the opposite. I think what I do is the ultimate in living.

I love what I do. I have never regretted my choices. I have never even wondered why it is that aerobatics is what I do. I think I was meant to be here. Fire and air are my elements. In retrospect, they are my destiny.

TWO

Genesis

My earliest memories have been sharpened and enhanced by photographs and have evolved from the recollections of others. I was told that, as a newborn, my dark hair was highlighted by a streak of blonde hair. The nuns told my mother, "Look. God couldn't decide whether to make her a blonde or a brunette. He gave her a little of each!"

I think there were a lot of things that God couldn't decide about me.

I was born Patricia Rosalie Kearns Combs in St. Louis, Missouri, in 1951 in the month of September, a Virgo in the year of the rabbit. According to the Chinese, people born in the year of the rabbit are the most fortunate. I was lucky to have entered a family with a legacy of patriotism, of service, of accomplishment, and of adventure.

My father, Robert Thomas Combs, served as an Air Force pilot based at Scott Air Force Base in Illinois. My mother, Rosalie Patricia Dorey Combs, gave birth to me in St. Mary's Hospital in St. Louis. Almost immediately my father was reassigned and we traveled to Mather Air Force Base in Sacramento, California. Less than three months later, we retraced our trek, driving from California to New York. We lived for a while in Roanoke, Virginia, then returned to New York. Travel agreed with me. My mom told me repeatedly that I was a happy baby who loved to be on the road.

My father's father, William Harry Combs, was a graduate of the U.S. military academy at West Point. He served as a lieutenant colonel with the famous Merrill's Marauders until killed by the enemy in Burma. His wife, my grandmother, Anthonette "Antho" Combs, was especially proud of the family's patriotism and military service. Uniquely, my father's three brothers, Jack, Dick, and Bill, attended West Point at the same time— the first three brothers to do so. One month after my grandfather's death, Dick was also a casualty of war, killed in Bougainville, one of the Solomon Islands. Despite the sacrifices she endured, Antho kept alive in her family the proud tradition of service to one's country.

Dad learned to fly as a cadet in the U.S. Army Air Corps, flying all the trainers that led him up to the B-25s with which I associate his military flying. When I was small, Mom took me to the airfield to see his heavy, noisy, smoky beast that simultaneously scared and thrilled me. I remember his hands reaching out to me as I crawled onto a huge metal wing and joined him in the cramped cockpit.

When Dad was an airline pilot for Japan Air Lines (JAL)—and airline rules were more relaxed and unstructured—I sometimes moved from a passenger seat into the cockpit of his beloved DC-4s, -6s, -7s, and -8s.

As I grew older, I was the one to quiz Dad when he prepped for his required check rides, and I spent time updating his flight manuals. I also bugged him to tell me about flying and about aerobatics whenever he mentioned them. "What's it like to do a loop, Dad? What's it like to do a roll?"

He generally shrugged and said, "It's no big deal."

I didn't know then that the curiosity was sowed. Like a small seed that lies quietly in dark soil waiting for just the right combination of moisture, nutrients, and temperature, my curiosity about flying remained dormant, ready to be nurtured, ready to burst into full bloom.

Pilots tend to maintain a close fraternity, so it wasn't surprising that most of my parents' friends and acquaintances were pilots. When surrounded by them, I heard some of their conversations that touched on football scores or golf tournaments, but generally focused on flight and flying. Fragments of information about aviation stayed with me, and from my earliest memories I stored mental images of my dad—in his uniform, with other crew members, in and around his airplanes. Our family life, later torn to shreds by alcohol abuse, fell far short of idyllic, but some of my best and most vivid recollections are of the times in the cockpit that I spent with my father. He was happiest there, and the special moments we shared were always about flying and airplanes.

When I was almost nine, my mom gave birth to my sister, Toni. Mom had been trying, unsuccessfully, to get pregnant for several years and had even suffered at least one difficult miscarriage along the way. I prayed for her to give me a brother or sister, but it wasn't until my dad's sister, Aunt Carol Syversen, who by that time probably had six or seven of her eventual twelve children, gave us two statues of St. Gerard, the patron saint of motherhood, that my mother became pregnant. St. Gerard answered our prayers and Toni came along.

Toni was not premature, but she was tiny, weighing only three pounds at birth. Kept in an incubator for a month, she seemed to me to be a mythical creature until Mom brought her home. Then I loved Toni right away and I felt blessed and lucky to have her as my sister. She made me feel less alone in the world. To this day, Toni continues to be an inspiration and one of my best friends.

Before I began flying airplanes, I barely understood why a person would even *want* to be disciplined. I wondered, what could be worth the investment of complete ego and soul? I knew that Dad was successful at piloting and that his happiest times were spent at the controls of his airplanes. He was admired by others and I respected his skill and courage, but I didn't particularly appreciate the effort that he had put into his career, the persistence that it demanded.

Toni always seemed directed, establishing goals right from the start, but I sought to experience *everything*. I fantasized about becoming an astronaut, a code breaker and spy for the government, or the owner of a gypsy circus troop, but I wasn't sure how to create my own reality. I wasn't even allowed to choose my own clothes, so I barely recognized my innate ability to make things happen. I thought life was controlled by outside forces. Like a leaf in the wind, I gave people and situations the power to decide my fate. It took a long time for me to discover that I had a choice.

Toni always knew about choice. She wanted to be a pilot like our father. Part of our differences in focus was generational, part personality, part nature, and part nurture. Dad never encouraged or discouraged either of us, but Toni set her sights on airline piloting. Neither of our parents envisioned us in a career, especially an aviation career because we were women. It wasn't even discussed until Toni had the drive, the dedication, and the perseverance to make it happen. I couldn't have stuck with the same program that appealed to her. I took *years* to discover what I wanted to do and to get a glimpse of life's possibilities.

Today Toni is an airline pilot with Continental Airlines, flying over the same oceans as our father flew. Based in Guam and flying commercial jets throughout Micronesia, she is well-respected and, most importantly, she is happy. One of her captains, Sherman Smoot, said, "I like flying with Toni because I know that everything is done correctly. She is completely thorough and competent. Plus that, we have a good time because she has a great sense of humor!"

Toni mirrored Dad. He wanted only to fly. His Westchester County, New York, family members, primarily bankers and businessmen, failed to fully understand his dream. They were proud of his military service record, yet they waited patiently for him to tire of flying airplanes and to return to the world of briefcases and gray flannel suits.

My father clung tenaciously to the cockpit. After his military service, he was hired to fly with the "nonscheds," unscheduled airlines like World Airways and Flying Tigers that circled the globe, charter or cargo, whenever and wherever. Those flights were challenging, arduous, and ever changing—right up Dad's alley. He rarely knew before takeoff where a flight was headed or how long he would be traveling. Dad later opted to go to the major airlines, the "majors." It was probably for solid career reasons—a steady pace and more predictable schedule and salary—but I bet the varied destinations and the unpredictability of the nonscheds held a special fascination for him. Like most pilots, he wasn't in the flying game for the big bucks.

One major reason that he wasn't hired immediately by the majors was his hearing. It was a big family secret that he had hearing difficulties, one that was never discussed. Born with a congenital hearing condition, Dad underwent an ear operation that was designed to improve his hearing, but it wasn't a great success. When we went to the hospital, my mother told me to keep his operation a secret. I was too young to comprehend that ear trouble would keep Dad from being hired as an airline pilot. His hearing continued to worsen with time but never seemed to affect his piloting ability.

Today, in his seventies, my dad is an aviation legend of sorts. His commercial flying experience covered more than forty years, and when the threat of his leaving the cockpit reared its ugly head on his sixtieth birthday, Dad beat the system for a while by flying out of the Dominican Republic with a Dominican Republic pilot's license. As recently as 1995 he was hired to fly out of the Sudan. Other airline pilots who have been forced to retire at age sixty might be envious that he occasionally flies as a commercial pilot. The rule about retiring at age sixty is being contested, and Dad is a sterling example for the defense.

My mother, Patty Dorey, was an only child who grew up in a home that was divided by divorce, uncommon for the time. Mom was raised primarily by her mother, Rosalie Dorey, my other beloved grandmother.

A beautiful brunette, my mother was a photographic and fashion model in New York City when she and my father met. They made a strikingly handsome couple when they were married in 1950. Dad was in the military and they, like other newlyweds, were uprooted often before settling into a career. By the time we had moved to north Hollywood when I was almost five, we had crisscrossed the United States five times by car and by train.

On long trips, my mother was quite the teacher. By the time I was four, she had spent a lot of time with me and had taught me to read pretty well. I appreciate that she gave me the beauty of letters and words and I really favorably anticipated school, thinking it would be a glorious world of letters, numbers, words, and other kids. I liked to learn and I thought kindergarten was fun.

Life was good in southern California, maybe because my mother loved it and was happy there. She and I visited the Farmer's Market on Fairfax Avenue; Olivera Street, the famous main street of the historic Spanish district; and the beach, with its sun, surf, and sand. Things were basically smooth, yet some minor thing must have erupted because it was in Hollywood that I ran away from home for the first time. It wasn't the last. Like a sudden scurried flight of a frightened bird, my reaction to confrontation was to run. My memory of the specific argument has evaporated, but I remember rushing to escape, feeling closed in and alienated.

"I'm leaving," I announced to my mother, having packed a small bag filled with my favorite things and topped with my teddy bear. I left, walking quite a distance until I came to an intersection that I had been forbidden to cross. I remember standing on the curb, as swamped as any little child can be. What will happen if I cross this street? What if my mom catches up with me? I finally must have decided that the risk of discovery and punishment outweighed all. I dragged myself home slowly and crept up the stairs into my bedroom to curl up with some of my books.

Not long after my first attempt to run away, we moved again. This time our home was San Mateo, California. I finished kindergarten with Miss Rose, and it was then that more of my rebellious streak emerged. I was full of curiosity; I was adventurous and independent. Miss Rose was older than my teacher in Hollywood and, although she wanted complete discipline in her class, she didn't have a clue how to motivate kids. The more boisterous the kids—especially mischievous kids—the louder and more shrill her voice and the less control she could muster. I wasn't much help. Whenever she tried to get the kids to form a circle, I wanted to go the opposite way. I was the same when my mother took me shopping with my cousin Cindy. Competitively, I dashed out of sight, scrambled into the midst of clothes racks, or rushed to be way out in front.

When I was five, my mom took me to the boardwalk in Santa Cruz, California, and for my first ride on a roller coaster—an experience I have never forgotten.

"I don't think a little girl that young and small should be on the Giant Dipper," warned a ride attendant. "She should wait a few years and come back when she's older."

My mother stuck up for me. "She wants to go. I'm sure she'll be all right."

I was begging, "Please. I want to go on. Please!"

Reluctantly, they fastened us into our seat and I wiggled with anticipation. The ride was great. When we came back down, I had bitten my lip, hard, and my mouth was bleeding. I was crying a bit, but more from joy than pain. I begged to ride it again.

Something similar happened when Mom took me to San Francisco to see Barnum and Bailey's Greatest Show on Earth. Throughout the entire show, I felt as if I were on the wrong side of the fence. I wanted to join the circus performers and the animals. I wanted to be part of the noise and the glamour, to be surrounded by the bold colors and the noisy calliope. It was frustrating. I didn't want to watch; I wanted to be in the ring. I wanted to swing from the highest trapeze, ride the whitest horse, or balance a bicycle across the highest wire. For months afterward I longed for a band of gypsies to show up in my backyard and spirit me away.

While we lived in San Mateo, Dad flew as a charter pilot out of Oakland for U.S. Overseas Airline. He was on call to fly whenever and wherever he was needed, sometimes in the middle of the night, lengthy distances, and for days at a time. When I was six, my father flew my mother and me to Hawaii—my first flight on a big airliner and the first vacation that I remember. The plane seemed huge and it frightened me. Mom, whose own mother had been timid, reassured me, determined to help me face the unknown.

She must have had to face her own fears as well. There were times when Dad's trips lasted for as long as a month. Long separations were probably hard for her. She must have been relieved when her mother came from New York City to live with us. I loved Grandma Rosalie and loved her name, my middle name, wishing that it were my first.

I attended first, second, and third grades at the Beresford Park School in San Mateo, where I felt school was worthwhile and stimulating and I did very well. My first-grade teacher, Miss Jelly, was pretty and nice. I was her best reader, and she made me feel like a star when she sat me in the front of the classroom to lead the rest of the class in reading. Not too many years later I was called to sit in front of the class for other reasons.

Discipline wasn't much of a problem for me in grades one and two. I continued to thrive when I was put into Mrs. Basini's gifted class in second grade. I learned to ride a bike and, with friends, made a jungle out of a vacant lot, explored the creek behind the house, caught tadpoles, and took turns tying one another up pretending to torture each other. We visited each others' houses and had a lot of time to play games like *Monopoly* and *Scrabble.*

Yet the older I grew, the more I resisted rules and restrictions. It chafed to have adults threaten to squelch the independent person I was becoming. I resented mindless conformity, like the kind Malvina Reynolds lampooned in her folk song "Little Boxes." Nobody was going to stamp me out like a cookie-cutter person. If I could help it, I was never going to be somebody else's clone.

Was there something mysterious about third grade? I don't recall, but I started to struggle. It became more of a challenge for my parents to convince me that school was a great place to be. The more structured and regimented the system and the more we were expected to sit still, the more restless I became. I had trouble with concentration and probably demonstrated a classic case of attention deficit disorder; however, ADD had not yet been identified or diagnosed.

My problems intensified when home became as equally unattractive an option as school. Trouble had been brewing, and it erupted when I entered fourth grade, the first school year that I was separated from boys. My parents decided, despite my objections, that I should attend Notre Dame Catholic School in Belmont, California. They had expected me to remain the smart, sweet, responsive daughter that I had been as a baby, and when I showed my own adventurous spirit, they were at a loss. They honestly thought that a strict Catholic education would not only offer discipline but would be superior to that offered in the public schools. They believed Notre Dame was a more prestigious academy.

I wanted a coed school education. I wanted to be with kids from my neighborhood, girls *and* boys, the friends that I was making. My parents—probably no different than most parents of the late 1950s and early 1960s—never asked my opinion on schooling. Fearful of losing control, they insisted on a strict parochial girls' school. Hoping for help in discipline, they looked to nuns. From that point on, my formal schooling started a long, slow, rolling, downward slide.

Like one who had been churned in the surf by a monstrous wave, I started tumbling, not sure which way was up. Too independent to blindly accept rigid discipline, I started to buck the system. I felt if I compromised, I would be swallowed up, robbed of artistic creativity and imagination. Formal schooling became my nemesis. I was too free a spirit, too blithe—and too strong—to be restrained in a rigidly disciplined school. The more restrictive and narrow that I found Notre Dame, the more rebellious I became. The combination was volatile!

THREE

Tokyo Rain

Not long after Toni's birth, my dad came home one night with a big grin on his face. "I landed a flying job with one of the majors. I'm going to fly with JAL, Japan Airlines," he announced. "This is a great opportunity for me—for all of us! I'll be hired on contract to fly for IASCO, the International Air Service Corporation, and we'll find a place to live in Japan, in Tokyo."

He reassured us that once we left California, we would be able to visit the States. One big advantage of piloting for a major airline is that family members are able to deadhead on flights; relatives can obtain free tickets, on a space-available basis, to fly to any location served by JAL.

Toni was tiny. It made no difference to her where she slept and ate, but it made a great difference to me. I was only nine, but I figured instantly that if we were to move to Japan, I could leave Notre Dame Catholic School. I was elated. To be moving to an exotic foreign land seemed like a fantastic adventure.

We moved to Tokyo in the early 1960s and found temporary housing in a downtown hotel, the Ginza Tokyu, while we waited for a house to become available for us. In a dramatic beginning to my peripatetic life, I was eventually to live in Tokyo, Yokohama, New York, Palo Alto, Yokohama (again), Switzerland, London, San Francisco, Los Angeles,

Australia, Alaska, and Arizona. My residences rivaled a William James stream of consciousness. In *The Principles of Psychology*, James wrote: ". . . like a bird's life, it seems to be made of an alternation of flights and perchings."[1]

My "perching" in the Tokyo hotel was as if I lived in one tall playground, exciting for a nine-year-old. I made close friends with another girl and we spent our time exploring the elevators, kitchens, and fire exits of our new and exotic locale. We got to know many of the employees, who treated us kindly. We hung around the kitchens where cooks and waiters fed us, introduced us to their ethnic dishes, to their unusual cookware, and to some of the intricacies of preparing Japanese food.

We roamed freely in the nearby streets of downtown Tokyo, getting lost and then finding our way without any of the fear associated with being lost in the United States. Restrictions fell away in Japan. Japanese society in the 1960s didn't seem to breed petty thievery or dishonesty. Crime was virtually unknown. People parked bicycles on streets with no thought to chains and locks, and if a wallet was left in a public restroom, the owner counted on finding it where it had been left or turned in to a responsible party for safekeeping.

It is no secret that children are adored in Japan, and, on the one hand, that translated to more freedom and to more independence for me. From the start, as I headed for school each morning, I walked alone about a mile to the bus station. From there, I traveled by bus to catch a train. I must have been a curious sight: a wide-eyed, petite, brown-haired American girl in a woolen Japanese school uniform. People stared at me and tried to converse with me. They wanted to learn to speak *eng-rishu*. I became interested in the Japanese and grew to respect the ambition of the intelligent people I met. I reveled in the hours that were mine when I wasn't required to be in school.

The school itself, however, was another bitter disappointment. My parents repeated their mistake and, against my wishes, enrolled me in another restrictive all-girls' Catholic school, Sacred Heart Academy of Tokyo. Although I didn't like them, I didn't object too strenuously to the uniforms. Every schoolchild in Japan wore a uniform. But I became increasingly restless and frustrated by our stoic regimen, the harsh discipline, the interminable marching to assemblies, and the colorless, sterile, dark,

---

[1] Beck, Emily Morison, ed. *Bartlett's Familiar Quotations*. Boston: Little, Brown, 1980.

stifling rooms in which we were taught. I was becoming more intellectu-
ally aware, and I felt that schooling was an attempt to control both mind
and body with no room for creativity or spontaneity. Every lesson became a religious exercise. Some girls went along with it and, if they had
expectations, they never voiced them, but the American girls were generally the most rebellious and outspoken.

English was the primary language of my new prison and, although
the curriculum also concentrated on French, Japanese wasn't taught at
all. To compensate, I studied books, met and cultivated some Japanese
friends, and studied signs on buses, in storefronts, and in train stations.
Gradually, I taught myself to read and write the Japanese phonetic alphabets of hiragana and katakana. On my own, at home or on the train,
I studied kanji, the more complex system of writing based on Chinese
characters. I learned enough street slang to get along. I was a quick study
when subjects interested me.

My memories of school at Sacred Heart are steeped in a medieval air.
Nuns fresh out of training in Ireland or France seemed as if they were
ghostly figures, black shadows gliding down dark marble hallways, poised,
suspicious, and ready to pounce. The school rooms were austere and the
uniforms were unattractive and uncomfortable. I didn't believe that it
was a matter of religious philosophy in which I was being schooled; I
thought it was all about being disciplined and controlled. Some of the
teachings were strange, too, filled with spiritualism and animism. The
stories were creepy. I was told repeatedly of the devil coming at night in
the form of a rat trying to tempt me and of "conscious nuns, smelling
their burning flesh while being carried bodily off to Hell."

I hated school. Since I was taught that the holier the person, the more
the devil would try to tempt you, I figured it didn't pay to be too holy.

I was confirmed at age ten and, without an understanding of the meaning of confirmation, I picked a catchy name, one that might come in
handy someday. I took my father's name, *Roberta*. Most of the other girls
took the names of saints, like Theresa or Bernadette, but I wasn't interested in sainthood.

I ran away from home for the second time when I was eleven years
old. After an argument with my mother, she locked me in my bedroom
and told me that I couldn't go to school. That was an indication of the
unpleasantness of the situation at home if school, or the *idea* of going to
school, became my escape. Despite how I felt about school, I had a perfect attendance record. Locked in my bedroom, I fumed.

Finally, I took my coat and all the money I had saved, probably about one thousand yen (worth about three American dollars), and crawled out on my upstairs balcony. The neighbor's wall, cemented with upright shards of glass, was my second obstacle, but I jumped over that, landing in their yard. I ran along narrow alleyways about a mile and headed for the Shibuya train station. I ignored the fact that it was pouring rain, which deepened the cold.

There was freedom in the streets of Tokyo, but a dichotomy existed between my freedom as an American kid in Japan and the strictness of my schools and my home. Another factor, too, was important. Foreigners in Japan were held up as representatives of their respective countries. My parents had drummed into me that our presence in Japan carried with it a responsibility for my actions and my behavior.

Imagining that I could live on the beach at Hayama, I stopped in a shop to buy a cigarette lighter. I figured that I needed a way to start a fire to keep myself warm. On the way out of the shop, I caught sight of my mother with my three-year-old sister in hand, searching the Shibuya streets to find me. Poor little Toni was washed with cold rain that streamed from her hair. I felt a wave of pity for her and worried that she would catch a cold. I was struggling with a combined dose of Catholic guilt and some reality therapy. I thought, "*Who could live on a beach with one pathetic lighter for light and warmth?*" I made myself visible to my mother. She frowned, grabbed my arm, and dragged me home. I was temporarily resigned and discouraged and, after my mother had punished me, my resentments increased.

I did have two special friends with whom to share my life in Tokyo. Susie Hutt lived on the outskirts of the city and I loved going to her home. She and I spent hours searching for horses to ride. Elena Bolini, an Argentinian, was the second. Friends made the after-school hours bearable, though no one could help to make incarceration in the Sacred Heart Catholic School tolerable. That simply had to be endured.

Reluctantly, I attended Sacred Heart through most of seventh grade, but after a few skirmishes with teachers, some detention, and a general inability to keep from being considered a troublemaker, I found it increasingly difficult to tolerate school. I became nonconformist, unable to function to the administration's expectations, to be limited by the boundaries that were devised (I was sure) to keep us in line.

After several meetings with the Mother Superior, I was expelled from school. The final blow, according to the nuns, was when I started a little sales operation, selling white mice that I raised in my desk to my friends to raise money for candy bars and the art materials that I wanted to buy after school. The nuns leaped at the sale of the mice as the perfect excuse to get rid of me (like I was hurting anybody!). It was a kid thing to do that turned into a profit-making business. If I had been a boy, would I have been treated in the same way? Boys were expected to sow their wild oats. It was accepted that "boys would be boys!" Although I didn't fully understand it all at the time, the more the nuns tried to train me to become docile and submissive, the craftier and more rebellious I became.

My initial rebellion was pitted against the mindless conformity and the strict regimen of formal religious schooling, but alcohol abuse began to take its toll at home and exacerbated my feelings of restlessness and isolation. I was alienated at school and it became apparent that I was also increasingly alienated at home.

Alcohol use was part of my parents' social scene in the 1960s. It permeated their entire generation in the United States, and the social custom followed them to Japan. Just as in the States, when a couple called upon another couple, the expected courtesy was an offer of hard alcoholic beverages. Dinner parties began with cocktails and hors d'oeuvres, proceeded with carafes of red, rosé, or white wines with the meal, and concluded with after-dinner liqueurs. Virtually gone were old-time ice cream socials or any practice of offering coffee and cake or lemonade and cookies.

Alcohol abuse was a predictable result, and it tore at the fabric of our family as it did so many others. Like other kids in what are now labeled dysfunctional families, I became the barometer of my parents' unhappiness and deteriorating relationship. As both of them escalated their drinking, their own relationship suffered, as did their relationship with me. Minor squabbles blew up into major verbal battles. Angry words that were screamed in the dark of night were often forgotten in the dawn of the next day, though they continued to ring in my ears. Sometimes evenings that passed with my parents' drinking too much alcohol ended with almost obsessive anger toward me. My mother, especially, got so angry and so vitriolic that it was scary. Undoubtedly in the traditional tensions between parents and child, there were times that I deserved to be punished, but, too often, I was punished severely for minor things. I was still a little kid, easily confused by tirades I couldn't understand. One time, my mother, angry with me for something, told me that my father would punish me. I put a plastic clipboard in my pants for protection, but still my father whaled into me with a large wooden paddle until the paddle broke in two. It was no wonder that any confidence and trust that I felt unraveled.

Did my family's lifestyle create an atmosphere conducive to alcohol abuse? We lived in a cosmopolitan community. My friends were a pretty sophisticated group. Some of their parents were in the foreign services of their countries. One of my friends, Elena, was the daughter of the Argentinian ambassador. Another of my friends was the daughter of the ambassador from Lebanon, another from Sofia, Bulgaria. I had friends from India and Pakistan, too. Some of our mothers volunteered their time in worthwhile ventures, but few of them worked outside of the home while in Tokyo and most had live-in maids. Regular chores such as grocery shopping were difficult and many wives depended upon their maids for help in coping with language differences.

Although my parents fought when Dad was home between trips, troubles didn't ease when he was away. I became wary, as Mom could be fun and friendly and then, altered by alcohol, she could be the Madwoman of Chaillot. I never knew which face I'd see, which voice I'd hear. This unpredictability was awful and I mostly tried to stay out of her way. I wanted to protect my sister, but, luckily, no violence was ever directed toward her. I was the one both parents came after and we had no intervention or counseling for help. All of our relatives were six thousand miles away. Other than my friends, I had no one to talk to.

I lost myself listening to music, sprawled on my parents' bedroom floor near the record player. I spent hours lulled by Johnny Mathis and Frank Sinatra, especially his "*Come fly with me, let's fly, let's fly away. / If you could use an exotic cruise, we could fly to far Bombay.*" My favorite singer was the blonde, glamorous, and soulful Peggy Lee. Inspired, I designed an evening gown for her and mailed a drawing of it to her. In return, I received a beautiful black-and-white, eight-by-ten picture signed "Fondly, Peggy Lee," one of my most prized possessions for many years.

I don't pretend to understand the complexities of my parents' relationship or the struggles between parents and their children, but I saw that many women of my mother's wartime and postwar era achieved identity primarily through their appearance, their homes, and their families— through form, not content. Much later, it was a painful reminder to see the movie *The Days of Wine and Roses*, with Jack Lemmon and Lee Remick.

My mother seemed to despair. Despite her good health, decent husband, two healthy kids, and enough money to live well, she couldn't find happiness within. Where was her sense of fulfillment?

The older I got, the more unhappy and difficult my mother seemed to become. Was she ravaged with insecurity that worsened with alcohol abuse? I wondered if she dreaded aging, felt threatened as I grew to be the young woman she once was and wanted to remain. Was it hard for her that her own daughter was growing prettier? Her beauty was such a big deal in her life, such a big part of who she was.

My feet—or public transportation—became my escape mechanism, my magic carpet, my passkey to Japanese shops filled with all sorts of goodies and to movies, further escape in themselves. I formed friendships with several Japanese people and visited with them as often as I could. In the winter we sat on tatami mats, our feet dangling over a heater at the bottom of the customary opening in the floor, our arms resting on tables covered with quilts. Over brewed tea, we shared our cultures, our languages, our similarities, and our disparities.

Not long after being expelled from Sacred Heart, I was happy when my dad told me that we were moving to Yokohama. It was the spring of 1964 and, again, I looked forward to leaving school behind.

FOUR

Harbor Lights

The move to Yokohama seemed a good one. I escaped Sacred Heart and found rural and uncongested Yokohama a more pleasant place to live than Tokyo. From the cockpit of his airplane, Dad found a house for us. He came home to tell us of a beautiful home perched on a cliff overlooking Tokyo Bay.

He made the necessary arrangements. No sooner had we moved in than the view of the ebb and flow of the water traffic started me dreaming. The windows of our house faced the main channel of the harbor. I was the only family member living upstairs, and I had an unobstructed view of all the shipping activities in Tokyo Bay. By the hour, I watched ships cruise the waterways and knew that people were constantly coming and going, sailing away. I was twelve years old and my imagination was invited to run wild. I pictured myself on a myriad of vessels, each bound for an exotic port. At the stroke of midnight on New Year's Eve, the ships in the harbor simultaneously sounded their fog horns making a marvelous ruckus. I waited up to hear them and wished that New Year's Eve came more often.

Two girls, Debbie Corroone and Carolyn Schweizer, became my best friends. As in Tokyo, none of our mothers worked outside of the home, and with full-time help, our mothers' time was their own. Luncheons, bridge, and shopping filled many of the hours that children spent in school, and cocktail and dinner parties enlivened their evenings. Volunteer work also occupied their time. Some taught English to Japanese children and adults. My mother volunteered at Kishine Barracks in Tokyo, and I felt proud of the time that she gave to the soldiers wounded in Vietnam. Some stories she brought home about the guys really tore me up.

My memories of Yokohama are fragments like the tiny bits of colored glass in a kaleidoscope. Pungent odors of fish and the sea mixed with delicate flavors of oriental spices, and metallic gongs of religious festivals linked with lush silken kimonos that glimmered with golden threads. My mother dressed Toni in kimonos to take her to festivals for children and joined the iridescent scene.

Below our house at the base of the cliff, a hundred yards off the shore of the rocky beach, sticks protruded above the water and defined individual *kombu,* or seaweed farms. *Kombu* farmers harvested crops of seaweed the way rice farmers harvested their rice. Most of our Japanese friends pronounced my father's name Combs as *kombu.* He became "Captain Seaweed" and my friends and I loved that.

Yokohama held a little hope for me for a while. There was an American school, the Nile C. Kinnick High School, or Yo High as we called it, attended by most American kids, including my best friends, Carolyn and Debbie. Navy-run, it was a coed public school. I begged my parents over and over, "*Please* send me to the American School. *Please!*"

Though discord had become the rule of their marriage, on my schooling my parents vehemently agreed. They said, "Oh, no. You'd go wild there."

Instead, they picked out another winner for me—St. Maur's, run by Our Ladies of Perpetual Discipline. Convent nuns, strange to the ways of the world and swathed from head to toe in black, were primarily straight from convents in Europe. Some were Irish and some, like the Mother Superior, were French. An ominous spectacle, the Mother Superior was ancient and rotund. She wobbled around the school peering into the upper windows of our classrooms with only her great French nose visible. No one ever spoke to her; she was merely a figurehead. Mother Superior may have been the queen, but the tall, humorless, and intimidating Sister Veronica was the real power behind the throne, and, from the start, she looked down her nose at rambunctious me, the class clown.

Immediately adjacent to St. Maur's, but off-limits to us girls, was a boys' school. It was forbidden that any girls fraternize with any of the boys. Separated only by a big row of trees and a fence, I found it impossibly frustrating that we were isolated, the very worst. The girls were fun, but I liked being around boys, too. Before we had moved to Japan, more than half of my neighborhood friends had been boys. I missed male energy. The double standard was not only stupid, but it was transparently designed to keep us pure and virginal. At lunchtime my closest friends and I sat under the trees watching the boys playing in the next field, envying their freedom and that they didn't have to take sewing class.

St. Maur's was cold and frightening for me. We were watched, inspected, and injected hourly with massive doses of Catholic guilt. We had to do the old kneel-down-to-see-if-your-hem-reaches-the-floor routine. If it *didn't*, then the uniform, designed to make everyone look like a nun-in-training, was too short! If we wore makeup, we were made to wash it off.

Even though my parents turned deaf ears to my begging to change schools, I did manage to meet a lot of kids after hours at Yo High and to get involved with a wide variety of people. Yokohama's American kids hung out at the Navy Base, where there was a teen club, a bowling alley, and a cafeteria. In the summer, we swam at the Navy swimming pool. Sometimes we snuck into the Post Exchange, the Fort Knox of the base and the only place that military ID cards were checked, just to feast our eyes on American things. We were crafty about getting in, sometimes swapping pictures and sometimes borrowing ID cards from friends.

Japan was an interesting place to live in the 1960s. Cities were rapidly rebuilt in the aftermath of World War II but still bore some of the horrors of war. Although the country was comparatively well-off, the war's wreckage was still evident. Veterans, the only beggars allowed, stood out, dressed in white. They worked the train stations, walking through trains to beg for money, and that was scary because after a number of anti-American demonstrations, I was terrified they would recognize me as an American. I spoke *loudly* to my friends in another language hoping to defuse the issue of my nationality. But any demonstrations by the Japanese that I saw were very orderly. The participants stayed in line and rioting was unknown. No one ever threatened me, though it took a while to learn that the Japanese don't react that way. I learned to admire that even in their angry riots, they were able to voice their political views without making personal attacks.

In many ways I loved being in Japan. It was a wonderful place to grow up—exciting, exotic, and interesting. I could freely take long walks and explore the cities and towns and watch the people, their faces, and their dress. I took in exotic odors and the intrigue of tiny shops tucked into corners of tiny streets and entered Shinto shrines and Buddhist temples shrouded in mist. I liked the green, feathery branches of unusual trees and, in the smallest of gardens, tiny triangles of brilliantly colored flowers. Yet, like a captive bird, I dreamed of escape to America.

In Yokohama, my friends and I hung out at Haseidan and Sankeien, two local temples. Haseidan, the domed Temple of Eight Gods, stood poised on a cliff high over the ocean. We spent a lot of time exploring the cliffs, but sometimes we took off our shoes and entered the temple, tiptoeing quietly up wide stairs to its inner sanctum. There stood eight life-sized sculptures, among them Buddha and Jesus.

As we got older, we hung out in shops, movie theaters, and eventually in nightclubs and bars on Motomachi Street and Izezaki-cho. Movies were our main pastime, but we also searched for new and interesting things to do. We cruised Chinatown, one of Yokohama's roughest areas, hanging out in some of the bars and staying out as late as we could. The thought that our parents or their friends might see us was just scary enough to make it exciting. The minimum drinking age for *gaijins* (foreigners) was enforced, but there was truly little in the way of danger. In the streets, our greatest threats came from wild American sailors and we avoided them. We hung out with an international group of merchant seamen and other kids from school. We smoked cigarettes and practiced speaking different foreign languages. For me, formal education held no great mystique, but informal education went on all the time.

My parents' drinking and party-going escalated. Our house was becoming a real battleground. Their tongues loosened by alcohol, my parents had ugly fights with each other, and, as those worsened, the more they fought with me. They were out of control. Between my weird education from the nuns and my parents' unpredictability at home, I became a nervous wreck. My status hinged on my parents' relationship and that was unreliable at best. I never knew what might happen when, what the prevailing mood might be at any given time. I felt as if they picked on me endlessly, running the gamut from being friendly, to lecturing, to wanting to hit me, and to threatening to stab me. Shivers swept through me to hear, "Patty, come down here!"

When my mother was totally out of control, she chased me around and out of the house, brandishing a knife. It was terrifying. I was utterly convinced that, out of their minds with drunkenness, my father or my mother could kill me.

Debbie Corroone recalled, "Patty was nervous and a little reckless. She got in trouble by knocking over a lamp that hit a wooden chest and made a small dent. Her mother was very angry and said, in front of me in an eerie voice, 'Patty has been a bad girl and needs to be punished.' Patty immediately started crying, 'No, Mommy. No, please.'

"Another time, I spent the night at her house when we were in high school. Patty's dad was away, and suddenly we heard Patty's mother calling her to come downstairs, that she 'was going to get her.' Patty and I locked the bedroom door and waited. Her mom came up the stairs, lifted the door off the hinges, and threw it down the stairs. She came in carrying a big knife. Patty was terrified and hid behind me. Her mom rambled about all the grief that Patty caused and kept coming toward us. I said, 'Mrs. Combs!' and she started rambling about our fathers in Chinatown. Patty and I escaped through the door and ran down the stairs. Outside, we hailed a cab and went to my house. Mrs. Combs got Toni out of bed, wrecked the car trying to make it to my house, and then caught a cab. When she knocked at our door, my mother told her, 'Patty can't go back with you unless Debbie goes with her.' We all piled into a cab, Patty and I in the front. During the entire drive, Mrs. Combs kept trying to get at Patty. The next morning, Mr. Combs came home and everyone acted normal."[1]

My friendships were my salvation. My father probably stayed away on purpose. He escaped into his flying, avoiding vicious scenes rather than trying to play the role of referee. He wasn't communicative and, besides, he expected my mother to raise the children. He did as she bid when she told him that I needed to be punished. I walked on eggshells and discovered that any time I confided in them, it might be turned against me.

When I was thirteen, I ran away for the third time. I headed for South Pier—a gateway to freedom. I had every intention of stowing away on a ship bound for San Francisco. I figured that I could live there, join a

---

[1] Corroone, Debra, personal letter, 1996.

circus, find some friendly relatives. I'd been dreaming and scheming about it for what seemed like ages. I figured that I could sneak aboard a French, Liberian, or Japanese ship and chose the latter, figuring that the Japanese were trustworthy. I knew not a single person aboard would lay a hand on me as we crossed the ocean.

Getting on board was easy. I snuck between cartons and boxes on the dock and, when no one was looking, crept aboard ship. I even said hello to some people who, curious about me, invited me into the dining room. Everyone was quite pleasant and friendly to me. It took about a half hour for the old guilt feelings to start. I couldn't help but wonder how my parents would feel, what they would do when they found I was gone. Guilt turned to panic when I saw the pictures of nude *Playboy* pinup girls tacked on a wall. My puritanical upbringing cropped up. "Anybody who would tack up a picture like that in public has to be weird," I decided, and I went back down the gangplank the way I'd come. Then, to avoid getting into trouble with my parents, I dreamed up an excuse for being late. I threw my book bag into a canal and called my parents from the New Grand Hotel to tell them a story about having been kidnapped. They brought a policeman with them when they picked me up at the hotel, but all three of the adults decided quickly that I was making the story up. I wasn't making it any easier on myself. I had a tough enough time getting along with them as it was.

One boon to my sanity was my loyal dog, Heddy, a black mutt that had come with us from San Mateo. Dogs' love is so unconditional. Heddy slept with me every night and made me feel protected. As our wood house had no central heating, she kept me warm during the winter. Moonlight had a way of playing with the twisted branches of the Japanese pine trees outside my room, casting crooked shadows and swaying shapes that moved across the walls night after night. I snuggled with Heddy and closed my eyes as tightly as I could, yet I still had a lot of nightmares. Trouble at home made life hard and at school dire warnings were still being drummed into my head, like, "If you hear noises in the middle of the night, it is probably the devil trying to tempt you." Even Heddy couldn't dispel my nightmares.

When I wasn't in school, I escaped into music, art, sketching, and reading hundreds of books. By encouraging me to love books, my mother had knowingly *and* unknowingly prepared me well for my future. I picked up books at the library and from my dad's bookshelf, some of them about flying—an ultimate escape—and all of them offering transport. At fourteen, I read my dad's copy of *Fate Is the Hunter* by Ernest Gann and found it to be a most romantic book on flying. Gann, an airline pilot, eloquent writer, and magical storyteller, helped me to see that everything in life is interconnected. He wrote of thunderstorms with their devilish dispositions and echoing fury and of being airborne and surrounded by the blackness of night with little reference above or below. He wrote of not knowing if he and his airplane were lost but of knowing that hundreds of miles of unforgiving sea waited below and that airborne, he was not lost but found. Gann's words were artists' brush strokes painting flying as a beautiful thing, larger than life. He made aviation noble, heroic, the ultimate escape!

His autobiographical book was all about men, but I never let reality—the dampener of good dreams—get in the way of a good fantasy. Gann drew me into the cockpit and gave me material for dreams of flying, skimming low over cities brilliantly dotted with eerie and magical lights and bathed in crimson as the sun dawned on silhouetted skylines. He began his flying career in 1935, when commercial flying was almost exclusively up to the men. But I focused on the experience, not the details. Still dreaming of sailing out of Yokohama harbor, still longing to be transported, I was ripe for his romantic, inspiring words. He gave wings to my mind.

During tenth grade there was no way to convince my parents that the single thing I hated the most about going to religious girls' schools was that there were no boys! How many studies have to be completed on the psychosocial consequences of segregation of the sexes before brilliant minds discover what I knew instinctively to be true—that the atmosphere is out of balance in single-sex schools.

Things at home continued to deteriorate. My parents were individualistic and I couldn't depend on the reactions that I would get. Once my mother caught me smoking. She hissed, "Just wait until your father comes home. He's going to kill you." That time, my sin went virtually unnoticed by my father. But I lived in dread. Bad dreams punctured my sleep, wakening me with cold sweats and throbbing, stomach-clenching fear.

My performance at school mirrored the deterioration at home. I wasn't inspired with schoolwork. Classes were truly dull. It was hard to cut class because we were watched by hawks, but I skipped class mentally and was accused of daydreaming. Also, I started openly questioning some of the

Catholic doctrines, specifically the concept of the Immaculate Conception. "I don't understand," I told a friend. "How can you just take on faith what doesn't happen in reality?"

My heresies got back to the oppressive and oppressed Sister Veronica. Called into her office, she said that I must repent. She told me that I had to go before the whole school to ask for forgiveness and threatened to tell my parents. I didn't want the problem sent home. I knew my mother and father would just take the nuns' side. I had no choice but to go along with the unusual demands. During Benediction, a form of High Mass, I was made to face the faculty members and the student body, kneel, and say the Act of Contrition. It was supposed to cause acute humiliation, but I didn't let it get the best of me. I steeled myself, thinking, "There is no way they're going to get the best of me. I won't give anyone that satisfaction!" My resolve and my class-clown persona were my saving graces and I remained true to form. I said the Act of Contrition out loud in front of everyone in my school—my penance. Then I rolled my eyes and made the other kids laugh. I was sure that unquestioning devotion wasn't what religion or God was all about.

At about the same time, I had some of my own questions influenced by our school bus driver, a quintessential hippie. He was fascinating, with beautiful, long hair and gentle ways. He was really cool, one of the first hippies that I met as the counterculture started to flourish. During our bus rides, we asked him questions. "Are you a Catholic?"

And he said, "No, I'm an atheist."

"What's an atheist?"

"Well, I don't believe in God." His manner was casual, offhand.

"Wow," we said to each other. "He says he doesn't believe in God." I was intrigued. He doesn't believe in God! After I had chewed on his words a while, it dawned on me that he wasn't afraid to say that he didn't believe in God. I thought, "That's cool. That's an option!" I decided right then and there that I was an atheist—mostly because our avant-garde bus driver was so cool. I began to skip church as often as I could. On the occasions that my parents were too hungover to attend church on Sunday mornings, an increasingly common situation, they sent me off by myself. But, instead of going to church, I generally went to a bowling alley, drank milk shakes, or checked out the ships in the harbor. I wasn't sure that atheism was the answer, but I had discovered that other options existed.

I wasn't the only one who wandered in search of freedom. Travel, its own form of escape, was especially exciting, and exotic places filled me with romanticism and sensuality. During some of our happier times, my family sailed on cruise ships to Hong Kong, Taiwan, and Manila. We flew to Hong Kong, Malaysia, and Thailand and cruised south from Yokohama through the Formosa Strait, passing the forbidden shore of Red China as Chinese junks and fishing boats bobbed within a few feet of our ship. At night, eerie phosphorescence in the water glowed, surrounding our ship with a wreath of turquoise light. Hundreds of dolphins, sleek, shiny, and silvery, swam just below the surface, occasionally leaping out of the water. And reflected in the water from tangled tree branches were unusual and colorful Chinese birds. Debbie Corroone and her mother, Norma, joined us, and Debbie and I delighted in roaming the streets of Kowloon. We visited Red Chinese bookstores and bought books on Mao Tse–tung and Tao. In herb stores, we sampled foods we never believed existed. We saw skinned dogs hung for sale in butcher shops and we ate shark's fin soup, cat meat stew, and whole cooked pigeons sliced exactly in half, the entire digestive tract visible as if in a biology class. It was later that we learned what we had tasted.

During the summers, Toni, my mother, and I returned to the United States for a month's stay with my grandmother, Rosalie Dorey, in California. We wanted her to come live with us in Japan, but a fearful woman, she refused to fly. My mom told of being a child herself, saying, "Your Grandma Dorey was terrified of thunderstorms. At the hint of a storm, she ran through the house hiding anything metallic. Then she grabbed me and we hid in the closet until the storm passed. She wouldn't go in elevators, either." Many of her fears were transferred to my mother, yet she caused my mother to try to be strong with me. Once, when I was small, we were in the midst of a violent storm, the day turned to the blackness of night, terrifyingly loud. My mother, in what was probably a great display of courage, said, "It's beautiful. There isn't anything for you to fear. Sit here and look out the window. Watch the beautiful storm." She had to overcome a lot to handle me that way, and I can trace some of my love for thunderstorms to the way my mother raised me when it was possible for her to be stable and strong. Those were our good times.

On the opposite end of the spectrum, our wars escalated as I rebelled. Both of my parents aimed to control me; they felt they *needed* to control me. But the more they tightened the vise, the more impossible life became. They had little confidence in their own parenting abilities and found it impossible to allow me to make any choices of my own.

In spring of my sophomore year, the officials at the dreaded St. Maur's finally got rid of me. It wasn't because of anything heinous or any one specific incident; I was just classified as a troublemaker and the class clown.

I was fifteen years old and, that same spring, my dad's mother, Antho Combs, came to Japan to visit us. All of my cousins (Antho had thirty-one grandchildren!) and I simply adored her. One of the most perceptive and caring persons that I have ever known, Antho taught me important lessons. I was almost impossibly inquisitive, asking questions incessantly and thinking nothing of butting into a conversation when a question popped into my head. My grandmother said, lovingly, "Patty, if you stopped asking questions all the time and listened, you would discover answers. You would get more information that way."

Coming from Grandma, those words hit home.

She couldn't help but be aware of the tension in our family and the fireworks that sparked between my parents. She knew that they were having trouble getting along and saw that they picked on me. I couldn't sit and read a book without one of my parents criticizing, "Stop biting your nails" "Sit up" "You're slouching." It all distressed Grandma.

I was a wreck and my parents, thinking I had a nervous condition, put me on Valium. They didn't recognize that they were the cause of the symptoms they were trying to cure.

Grandma, knowing that I had been expelled from school and aware of the many times that I had tried to run away, said to my dad, "You have to get her out of here or you are going to lose her."

With those words, Grandma rescued me; perhaps she even saved my life.

She suggested that my parents let her take me to New York to live with my dad's sister Carol and her husband, Hjalmar "Uncle Jimmy" Syversen. They had twelve kids—a huge, boisterous, loving family, living in Yorktown Heights, New York. Desperate for some answers, my parents let me go. They were probably relieved, glad to get rid of me. I was ecstatic about going.

I spent an idyllic summer in their large home, away from school and away from the sparks that burst into flames in our family. Charged with the care of two ponies, I was in heaven. Horseback riding had been one of my salvations in Japan. I was as horse crazy as most girls, and threatening to keep me from riding and jumping horses at the Navy riding facility had been the only leverage my parents could use against me, the one card they could play that truly hurt. Being told that I couldn't ride horses on a special weekend was agony, one of the few threats that kept me in line. To have two horses to feed and exercise was beyond my wildest dreams.

Topping it off, in the fall, my aunt and uncle enrolled me in John F. Kennedy High School, a public school. I could hardly wait.

But my parents came to visit and brought everything to a standstill. They complained that I had to do too much housework. (Did they imagine that I was being treated like Cinderella?) Of course I had to help make beds and cook. Everyone had to work in a big family. I even enjoyed it. But I think beneath that complaint was a different and more honest reason—friction and jealousy between my aunt and my mother. No one wants to think that someone else can do a better job of raising her child.

Whatever the truth, my objections were overruled. They took me to California and enrolled me in another school, this time a strict girls' boarding school in Palo Alto, California, Castilleja—my third prison.

The institution rules were plainly posted and vigorously upheld: **Students do not leave the school grounds during the week. On weekends, students may leave campus, but their time away is limited to three hours.**

Like the proverbial straw and camel, my secondary education squealed to a halt.

The counterculture of the sixties was in full bloom, nowhere more prevalent than in nearby San Francisco. I finagled ways to get off campus and, on my trips to the city, I met intriguing people and quickly rejected formal education.

As I had once cruised Tokyo and Yokohama, I cruised San Francisco's Haight-Ashbury district with my friend Liz Murdoch. I learned about the metaphysics of Zen Buddhism and teachers like Krishnamurti. I was introduced to the music of the Grateful Dead and Janis Joplin, to contemplation and meditation, and to the lessons of the drug culture and psychedelics.

Life was more compelling and dangerous for me in San Francisco than with my aunt and uncle in New York, but I have no regrets about the directions I took. Along the route, I uncovered other methods of escape and even more tools to save my sanity.

FIVE

Revolution

In opposing the power structure and denying the status quo of the post-war society, I joined thousands of others who searched for meaning in the streets of San Francisco during the late 1960s. We were all experimenters yearning for truth and beauty, simplification, and a denial of outdated social mores. I reached in every direction to learn all that I could about life, immersing myself in the overwhelming atmosphere of the streets. It was a mind-set more than a place, an adventure taken on by people breaking new barriers to freedom and honesty. I wanted to lose myself in it.

I was physically present at Castilleja for most of my class requirements, but psychologically and emotionally, I was in downtown Haight-Ashbury. Not overly concerned with the expectations of my parents or my teachers, I scraped by in school, barely lasting through junior year. Castilleja offered an excellent academic program, for other students. I never took advantage of it. I rejected mindless conformity and resented the institutional environment, a resentment exacerbated by the knowledge that directly outside the walls, there existed a world of freedom and higher ideals. I endured class and, whenever possible, spent my weekends exploring the fascinating world of the city, a commune at Half Moon Bay and the Panhandle in Golden Gate Park, learning about a whole new dimension of existence. I found solidarity, a feeling of family with the city kids I met, many from difficult homes and unbelievably abusive or neglectful backgrounds.

At sixteen, I was literally worldly wise, and, like so many other young people, I thought I knew everything that I needed to know. I found formal education as stultifying as chains and shackles and, unfortunately, school officials had little recourse but to urge me not to return.

I headed for Japan in the summer of 1968, dreading the thought of spending the summer with my parents. But I had no other choice. I had no other place to go.

I did have work waiting for me. Three years before, a man had approached me on a Tokyo street and offered me modeling work. I'd been intrigued. Foreign girls were desirable to most modeling companies, so, after checking on the reputation of the firm, I accepted. I modeled for him and worked in movies and television as an extra and occasionally as an actress. I saw my likeness on calendars and billboards all over Tokyo as well as on television ads, in a long, blonde wig pouring Kirin beer for Japanese *bishunisu-men*.

The return to work promised to make the summer more tolerable, although the situation at home still spiraled downward. I got violently sick and before I could take any modeling assignments, I had to be cured of a nasty bout of jaundice. Confined to my room for a couple of weeks, I couldn't eat and did little more than read, smoke cigarettes, and try to stay out of my mother's way.

My mother's mood vacillated widely, like a metronome with the weight at the top of the pendulum, and was made vastly more unpredictable because of her drinking. Influenced by my mother, my father got into some of the battles. My father mainly resorted to endless lectures, his voice droning on and on. I sometimes wished he'd just smack me and get it over with.

My mother often hit me and I was terrified when she chased after me, her voice reaching a screeching pitch, or, even more soul-numbing, dropping to an eerie singsong that made her sound possessed. Jaundiced and confused, I alternated between angrily blaming my parents and feeling stabbing guilt directed at myself for the unbelievable stress with which we lived.

Once again, I was the scapegoat for much that was unpleasant at home, and escape continued to be my motto. Yearning to be healthy so that I could literally run away, I disappeared into books, voraciously consuming as many as five or six novels a week. I lived vicariously through every one of them, identifying with characters that touched my psyche. Equally lost in music, I escaped with the help of Bob Dylan's songs, Joan Baez's Vanguard recordings, and the music of the Jim Kweskin Jug Band.

When I recovered sufficiently to return to modeling, that and reading, music, friends, and cruising the city were all that made the summer bearable.

By fall, my parents were adamant that I receive my high school diploma, but they were opposed to sending me to a coed school. They enrolled me in still another single-sex institution, this one in Switzerland. I was entering my senior year, and, apathetically, I no longer cared where they sent me. Switzerland? I figured that I'd be as happy on the opposite side of the world as my parents would be to have me there.

They selected La Chatelainie, never seeming to learn that my elements were fire and air or that each of us is more complete with yin *and* yang, male *and* female. Perhaps if they had shown signs of trust, the burden of responsibility would have rested on my shoulders. If they had relaxed my reins as a high-strung thoroughbred racehorse instead of curbing me with a firm bit, I might have tempered my rebellious nature and acquiesced more gracefully. I *might* have.

Despite the fact that La Chatelainie was a girls' school, I loved being in Switzerland. La Chatelainie, a beautiful, classic chalet in Saint-Blaise, was located near Neuchâtel and the shores of the beautiful lake that bears the same name. It was in a quaint little village in the northwest, not far from the country's border with France. In the far distance, the Matterhorn rose majestically and, nearby, the mountains were snow-covered and awe-inspiring most of the year. We spoke French, we played the Moody Blues's "Nights in White Satin," and we ate homemade soup in the dining hall. School was better than it had been since third grade. It had an interesting international mix of students and I made friends with kids from all over Europe. I got good grades and found the small classes of four or five students stimulating.

Not surprisingly, though, I still found confinement unbearable. I discovered that I was a leader, that other girls were eager to escape from school and trailed easily when I suggested ideas that might have occurred to them but that they wouldn't try on their own. My senior year capped the chaos that was my high school career. What my parents and school officials wanted for me and what *I* wanted became a mad tug of war, a vicious triangle that had to do with control, necessary or unnecessary. It had to do with trust or the lack of it. It had to do with fear, real or imagined. My parents were lost in a world of pain with a disintegrating relationship, alcohol, and anger, and the school's faculty was burdened with a mission of enlightenment. I felt like a modern girl being raised with the attitudes of the Dark Ages. The 1960s were difficult for a lot of families, but I was sure that had I been a boy, things would have been different. I would have been granted greater freedom to be myself, to let my inner self emerge.

My being sent to school in Switzerland was certainly one answer to our family dilemma. It got me out of my parents' hair and vice versa. Yet however beautiful a site and as free as I felt from parental eyes, life in Saint-Blaise meant another year in a cloistered and restless existence in another girls' school. I considered myself lucky, yet other shadows reached teasing, inviting fingers to me—boys, dancing, partying, hanging out, *getting* out. Escape became a challenging game. Circumventing the rules challenged my ingenuity, and I sought methods by which I could get my own way. I searched for and discovered a locked window that wasn't as secure as school officials thought. Once I had mastered the art of sneaking out of our chalet at night, it became almost easy.

I would probably have made an intriguing subject for a psychologist. Even I didn't know if I got into trouble so that someone would put a curb on me, so that discipline could follow, which I would equate with love. I did enjoy the role of ringleader. Defiantly, I thought, "Why shouldn't teenagers go out? Why shouldn't there be something social for us to do?" When events were planned—and those were rarities—they were confined to the girls at the school and to little tours. Picture Ludwig Bemelman's *Madeline* and the "twelve little girls in two straight lines." *God!* There we were.

In Japan, I had had freedom to roam after school hours. In Europe, when classes were over, confinement was stifling. We were virtually prisoners during the week, only allowed off campus to go to the nearby town of Neuchâtel on the weekends, and, in the French tradition, drink a little wine.

When we snuck out at night, we generally went to chips and coffee houses. Once in the cover of darkness my girlfriend and I went to a German beer hall, by far one of the raunchiest places ever. You could feel the illicit undercurrent, and we watched truck drivers suggestively licking greasy frog legs while eyeing buxom, Germanesque barmaids. Once I had discovered the way, another American girl and I went on our evening trips. Our escape route, after we climbed through the window, took us out onto a roof. We rigged a ladder to get off of the roof, making sure that it was long enough so that we could reach it to climb back up. *That* was the challenge!

Like second-story men, we were cautious on the roof. Anyone in the neighborhood could have seen us and blown the whistle. Everyone in the little village knew of the girls' school and were wise to some of the tricks. If anyone saw two *girls*, a report was fired to the school *tout de suite*, so one of us dressed like a boy, and, if a car or passersby came along, the "boy" sort of swaggered and put an arm around the other girl. We laughed the whole way.

Out of range of the school, we hitchhiked, or *autostopped*, as it is called in Europe, to town to some of the clubs. We tried to stay semi-inconspicuous, not drinking much or anything. We were looking for knowledge as much as amusement. In Neuchâtel, a college town, we met kids from all over the world—France, Italy, Germany, Switzerland, and Scandinavia. We discussed music and politics over wine while smoking Galoises cigarettes or my occasional pack of Hi Life from Japan.

Inevitably, I got caught. I usually got caught. Eager to get to a party to which we'd been invited and probably a little brazen because of previous escape successes, I was careless. The boys who had invited us to the party rigged a ladder in front of the school. We should have used our own in the back.

I didn't look around very carefully before starting down the ladder and was perched on it in full view of the whole world when a woman came out of a little pub across the street. My timing was terrible. There might as well have been floodlights, sirens, and photojournalists with cameras. I was caught red-handed.

The woman yelled at the top of her voice, "*Au secours! Il y a une fille au dehors. Il y a une fille au dehors!*" ("Help! There's a girl outdoors!") Her voice rivaled that of a fishmonger.

The next thing I knew, I was answering questions from the local gendarmes called in, no doubt, to scare me out of my errant ways. Then I was paraded before school officials. There wasn't much I could say in my defense. I was guilty.

I learned one valuable lesson. It was stupid to let others lead. I should have relied on my own instincts and depended on methods that had worked in the past. I learned, again, that I was ultimately on my own, a life lesson that became more important with time when life itself was at stake and under my sole control.

At first, I thought the school officials might punish me yet keep me in school. My hopes fell like a ton of bricks when they ordered me to inform my parents. The superintendent said, "Write a letter to your parents explaining exactly what it is that you did. We want them to know what has happened. We'll wait for their reply."

Christmas vacation was imminent and I was scheduled to fly to Japan. I knew that if my parents had a letter that admitted my troubles at school, our next meeting would literally be the death of me. I believed my life was truly in danger, my parents' resilience long gone. *I was convinced that my parents would kill me.*

Picturing the worst from the distance of Switzerland, I decided not to go to Japan. As I had done many other times in my life, I ran away from them and toward a more certain freedom.

I knew that I could take care of myself. Being on the streets didn't scare me, nor was I afraid of the darkness of city concrete. The adage: "If you don't like the circumstances you're in, then change them" was my mantra, then and now.

This time I discovered that a school friend's brother, an American kid, was spending the Christmas of 1968 in a rented flat in London, England. He agreed to let me stay there for the holidays. So, off I marched to the beat of Jim Morrison, Jimi Hendrix, and Bob Dylan, their messages pulsating and echoing in my ears. Dylan got to me with his: "If dogs run free / then why not me? . . ." Dylan understood.

I was scheduled to fly to Yokohama for the holidays. Instead I made my way, via plane and train, to Calais, France—the seaport town twenty-five miles from the landing site of Harriet Quimby, the first woman to pilot an airplane across the English Channel, in 1912.

Quimby was remarkable—a vivacious beauty who stunningly wore a unique, gleaming purple flying suit in an era that well preceded women having an opportunity to vote and in which women rarely were seen in anything that resembled slacks or knickerbockers. She was an example of how publicity and fame are not only fleeting, but they are a matter of timing. She undoubtedly would have gotten much more attention for her heroic feat if it hadn't occurred the same day as the tragic sinking of the *Titanic!*

On the train, it was obvious that I was traveling alone. An older Hungarian man, seated opposite me, "befriended" me. It started out innocently enough. He told me that he was a professor who specialized in linguistics. He told me that my accent fascinated him and that he was fluent in eighteen languages. When he asked if languages interested me, I saw no reason to ignore him. I *was* interested in languages and he was someone to talk to. I knew that it wasn't unusual for Europeans to speak four or five languages—their nations are in such close proximity—but eighteen languages was an impressive list.

He chattered on—mostly unintelligibly—until it came time for something to eat. Then, he followed me through the train, offering in English to buy my lunch and later, my dinner. He seemed fatherly until he abruptly reached out across the seats and put his hands on my breasts. I pulled away. "What are you doing?!"

He leered at me and said, "Oh, I just wanted to check to see if you had any."

I kept a comfortable distance from him until we reached Calais. At that point, we left the train to board a ferry for England. I tried to lose him, but he followed me around the ferry, even to the bunks on the lower level.

"It's going to be a long night," he said. "We don't get to London until the morning. Let's sleep together. I won't do anything."

In a scene reminiscent of the song, "Have Some Madeira, My Dear," popularized by the Limelighters in the 1950s, he tried to force me into one of the bunks. I managed to slip away.

We had picked a rugged day to cross the channel. The day was bitter with cold, and low clouds scudded just over our heads, pushed by an angry wintry wind. The water swelled and rolled, rocking the ferry violently. As one after another of the passengers succumbed to seasickness, some were sickened more by the retching sounds and odor of vomit around them than by the pitching deck and the rolling sea. I was the only person on the boat who did not feel queasy or throw up—without exception, the only one. Several people, holding bags to their faces, asked my secret. I should have pulled out my Tarot cards and charged them for a reading. I had no special secret. I simply had a strong stomach—for roller coasters, for ferry boats . . . and for lecherous men. But the old fart reinforced one lesson that I needed to remember: as nice as men may appear to be, all aren't to be taken at face value, especially for a young woman alone. I owed him for strengthening my wariness and my self-protective edge.

Arriving in London with exactly one English pound, or about U.S. $2.50 at that time, I took my first step inside a classic red British telephone booth and made a call. My friend's brother told me how to get to his flat in Covent Garden and, following his directions, I hopped on a bus. I was free—as free as is possible without money—but still chained with feelings of guilt. I tried to figure out what time it was in Yokohama. I knew that since I hadn't arrived in Tokyo's Haneda Airport as planned, my folks had figured that I wasn't coming home. I wondered what they thought and what they might do.

I hoped that my sister wouldn't be put in the middle of anything and that she wouldn't suffer in any way because of me, but my survival instincts outweighed my worry. I pressed on.

I took advantage of having a place in Covent Garden, to hang out while looking for something more lasting. I wrote a note to my parents to let them know I was alive, avoiding the subject of school and omitting any address or phone number at which I could be reached.

Everyone in England was on holiday. Christmas was lovely and it was a blast to see the decorations of another country—entirely different from Japan and interestingly reminiscent of pictures I'd seen of quaint old New York. The spirit was festive and people were kind.

My friend's brother's flat lacked a radio or stereo, so I became a familiar figure in the record shop across the street listening to my favorite Dylan song, "All Along the Watchtower." I was such a steady customer that at my appearance, the short Indian man who ran the store greeted me and automatically reached for a pair of earphones, fitted them to my head, and turned on "my" record. Daily I listened to the recording of Dylan perform the song once or twice, then thanked the attendant and left.

I landed a job of sorts. Nicky and Fuzz, two musicians from Scotland, gave me a room in their big house in Knightsbridge in exchange for driving them around London in their old Bentley—me, sans driver's license. But to play the part, I wore an old uniform jacket complete with a matching chauffeur's cap and velvet that I sewed on the sleeves.

Money was never the end; it was always my means. I often took my entire paycheck and blew it on one good dinner, entertaining friends. Nicky and Fuzz, who seemed to know everyone, introduced me around. We spent our evenings hanging out at the Arts Lab, a meeting place for international travelers in Covent Garden, owned in part by John Lennon. We also went to the Roundhouse, a concert hall, where I got to meet the members of bands like Cream and Ten Years After. I met some Londoners on my own and discovered that they knew how to enjoy the holidays. Pubs, great smoky scenes, were crowded with rockers. Music pounded and voices rose to outdo one another. Dancers moved through the fog created by smokers who blew billowing puffs toward the ceiling. Everyone tipped their glasses and found reasons to laugh.

School was the farthest thing from my mind. My black-and-white yin and yang blended into muddy brown. I knew I didn't have to be part of my parents' generation nor conform to their rigid role models and stereotypes, but I also lacked the financial resources to survive outside of their world.

I decided to quit school and created a detailed rationale. I didn't see the importance of a high school diploma. I knew I could land a modeling job and figured that I wouldn't need a diploma to be a model. Besides, I thought, who needs a degree to be educated? I thought I'd never lead a life that required a piece of paper to prove who I am. Yet were it ever to matter, I could get my diploma for a specific need and from a school of my own choosing.

I extended my holiday as long as possible, eking out two months in London. It was two months of fun—odd jobs, hanging out, and making new friends. Guilt feelings edged slowly upward and I ultimately wrote to my parents again.

I was confused, tangled with mixed emotions. Running away would have been wrong in a normal family existence, and I vacillated between worry about what was happening at home and a growing awareness that I was drifting, that I wasn't really getting anywhere. It unsettled me that the longer I distanced myself from home, the wider the gap between myself and my entire family grew. I truly missed my grandmothers.

I knew that my dad and mother felt a sense of duty toward my education and imagined them finding it unthinkable that I was a high school dropout. During my time in England, Dad hired private detectives to find me. My hiatus lasted until they were able to track me down.

That day one of my friends woke me saying that someone from the Arts Lab had come to offer me a job distributing posters. I shrugged into some clothes and went out to a waiting car. My father and Scotland Yard look-alikes jumped me from behind the car, grabbing my arms.

I screamed, but the three dragged me to a hotel room where my mother waited with my sister.

It wasn't exactly a joyous get-together. My parents had traveled a long way to drag me back with them. They continued to struggle with their relationship and I was distinctly no asset to their program. My father lectured some, and they kept the evil eye on me until they could get me onto an airplane bound for Japan. My return made their rocky situation even rockier. What little truce I could muster with my parents barely lasted for a week. During this time, they discussed my fate.

In desperation, my father put me on another airplane, this one destined for San Mateo, California. He said, "You're going to live with your grandmother Rosalie, Patty. She'll get you enrolled in high school and, by God, you're going to get a high school diploma."

It was 1969. That year New York's Woodstock music and art fair drew more than 300,000 fans. I would have loved to have been there. Popular songs were "Hair," "Aquarius," and "In the Year 2525." Hundreds of thousands of people gathered in our country's cities to protest the war in Vietnam, and U.S. troops began a withdrawal. James Earl Ray was sentenced to ninety-nine years in jail for the murder of Martin Luther King, Jr. and Senator Ted Kennedy plunged into dark waters of Chappaquiddick Island with Mary Jo Kopechne, later found drowned in his car. Student disorders closed the London School of Economics and Political Science, a Czechoslovakian student publicly burned himself to death to protest Russian occupation of his country, and relief airlifts were sent to take supplies to Biafra. With increasing unrest erupting all over, it was as if the molten lava in the core of our globe was giving a hot seat to human inhabitants in all quarters.

In my own little world, I reveled in being in a public school at long last and in being different, appearing straight from London in velvet, leather, and lace. When I spoke, my accent was an unusual medley of all the different places and influences that I'd absorbed. Kids asked where I was from.

I made a lot of friends very quickly, more interested in the social scene than in the classes. They continued to be uninspiring. My friends and I attended classes but attended most of the concerts in San Francisco as well. I hung out at La Honda up in the mountains and swam in the creek at Huddard Park. I went to the commune on the beach at Half Moon Bay and played in the surf when the setting sun turned the western sky crimson and long, flamelike tongues of color stretched across the water. There was always something exciting to do and a cool group of people with whom to do it.

I met a large group of conscientious objectors. I had been raised with fiercely patriotic concepts, knowing the words to every military song from "Caissons" to "Off We Go into the Wild, Blue Yonder" as a kid, and feeling as if our government would never unwittingly or flagrantly conduct itself without any but the highest precepts. Then I met some particularly gentle men who had faced military induction, at which their long hair would be shaved and their principles threatened, and I palpably felt the disillusionment with our governmental decisions. Few of them could have gone to the jungles of Vietnam to kill people and most found a way to disappear into the people of the streets. Once, some cops plowed into one of our anti–Vietnam War demonstrations and, wielding clubs like claymores on the fields of Scotland's Culloden, bashed at the heads of some of my most peace-loving friends. The vision of their heads resting in their own blood in the gutter turned me against all authority for a long time.

It only took a couple of months to graduate and I know that every member of my family, including me, breathed a sigh of relief. I finished high school, just as I had always known I could, in a coeducational school. I had the precious diploma, which I promptly threw away, and I had a host of friends. It had been a long haul, but I reached a significant plateau. My mom and dad couldn't gripe that I hadn't finished school, my eighteenth birthday was just ahead, and I was back in the States where I could get lost and live my own life.

On the other hand, it was also a painful time. I lost a good friend, John Webb, a sweet guy who had been idolized by all of us—John, the mystical poet with the beautiful long hair and the gentle ways. One of my best friends, Danne Borgano, was in love with him. John died a tragic death, overdosing on a combination of drugs. We all stood at his funeral, fourteen friends minus one, saying good-bye. I didn't know it at the time, but John was the first of many friends that I would lose tragically.

I enjoyed my seventeenth summer with my Grandma Rosalie, but from an adult point of view, I was aimless. Grandma wrote to my parents saying, "Patty worries me. She doesn't seem to know where she's headed. I wish she would get some work or something." She wasn't unlike my mother as she, too, looked at me one day and asked, "Who would marry you?"

I wasn't looking to get married, but like my parents, Grandma was after me to set some goals. She wanted me to define some direction in my life. Nothing in my upbringing had influenced me toward a career or a job. I, like other girls, was raised with the "goal" of marrying a success-ful man, staying at home, and raising kids. Taught to expect a few volunteer charity and societal things in the future, most of us were encouraged to develop a have-something-to-fall-back-on-in-case-something-happens-to-your-husband type of skill. Career woman? In my family, a career woman was considered to be an oddity. But I knew I didn't want to be tied down with kids.

My dad, on a flight that brought him to the States, came to visit. He agreed with my grandma and asked about my plans for the fall.

I said that I wanted to attend art school, having taken some art lessons at age ten in Japan, and showed him brochures for the San Francisco Institute of Art. It was always assumed, at least by me, that I would have art, if not as a career, then at least as a hobby.

My father probably figured he had spent enough money and anguish on my schooling, such as it was. But it never occurred to me that I could arrange to pay for my own.

I wanted to go to art school, but neither of my parents dared send me to such a place because they were afraid I would fall in with "unsavory characters." They were totally afraid of people they didn't understand, such as artists, hippies, and their own daughter. In the tug-of-war be-tween trust and fear, we were all guilty. It was a vicious circle—the less that I was trusted, the less that I tried to earn trust; the less respect I was shown, the less I showed toward my parents. It was a lousy combination.

I had no funds and no job, so with art school out of the question, I really had no plan for the future at all. I enrolled in a liberal arts course at San Mateo Junior College to placate everyone, but my heart wasn't in it.

During Dad's visit, he bought me a car, a Volkswagen. He figured that I had to have transportation if I was going to attend junior college and get any sort of job. However, I hadn't had the Bug very long before it almost became my coffin.

In the week before my eighteenth birthday, September 1969, I headed home from an all-night party and was overcome by fumes from a minor carbon monoxide leak. I lost control of the Bug and crashed headlong into a couple of parked cars. I felt the crunching collapse of otherwise strong, well-formed metal. Thrust through the windshield, my face was slashed to ribbons! Shattered glass flew everywhere, some of it buried in pockets of my leather vest!

There isn't much about the accident that I recall, but I do remember being out of the car and seeing bystanders staring at me, horror on their faces. I remember yelling, "Don't look at me. Look at the *car!* It's wrecked. My parents are going to *kill* me!"

Blood streamed from my face. I sunk to the ground, touching my face gingerly with my fingers and staring almost blankly at the blood on them.

An unknown good Samaritan called an ambulance, and, once it had wailed its way to the scene, I was lifted into the vehicle and rushed to a hospital, sirens screaming a warning to other motorists on the road but muffled to those of us inside. Chunks of my mouth were gone and the damage done to my face required sixty stitches by a good plastic surgeon. After surgery, I slowly progressed from what had been a scratched and bloody pulp to a swollen, puffy mass of black and blue. I was put out of circulation for quite a while.

Like a recurring bad dream, my dad came to get me, again. He took me back to Japan, again. I moved back into my parents' home, *again*.

Mom said, "Patty, your beautiful face!"

It didn't surprise me that my mother's reaction to my car wreck was to be worried about my looks. At the moment, however, her concerns were justified. My entire body was black and blue. My face was misshapen and mottled. I was hurt and bruised, totally subdued.

What the future held seemed to be most compelling to my parents at the moment. They agonized over it. At night, I could hear them talking about me. My mother said, "What do you suppose she is going to do? She can't go anywhere. How long is she going to take to recuperate? Will we ever get her married off?" Even my father was appalled at her attitude.

Finally, they reached a decision and Dad told me that he was going to send me to a secretarial school in Tokyo, a business college. Pragmatically, he and my mother wanted me to have some marketable skills, some preparation for earning a salary.

I tried to argue for an art course, but that argument was useless. A career was never the issue. Besides, they saw no earning potential in a career as an artist. My mother kept insisting that I needed a trade that would be insurance against the death of my eventual husband and to support any children that I might have to raise on my own.

Perhaps moving to Japan kept my parents out of touch with what was going on in the United States and left them with values that were straight out of the Dark Ages. Their ideas were those that were prevalent in the late 1940s as World War II ended. At that time, women who had performed admirably in the workforce during the war and had more than proved their capability to contribute were urged *back* into the home, *back* to a Victorian concept of women doing diapers and dishes. Men were coming *back* from war and women were pointed *back* out of the workforce. There was a reverse thrust and it was global. In Germany they called it *"Kinder, Küche, Kirche"* as women were urged to return to "children, cooking, and church." My parents were believers. Besides, the 1960s had been as frightening to them as it had been to a host of others. The entire decade had terrified many.

I spent another year in Japan, a year of highs and lows that seemed characteristic by now. Part of it was spent undergoing minor cosmetic surgery and gradual recovery. I tiptoed around the house that should have been a home, feeling more imprisoned than sheltered. I knew only turmoil with my parents, so I detached my mind and disappeared, again, into dreams, books, and fantasy. My father stayed away on trips as much as possible and my mother started seeing other men. Although the thought of divorce had been repugnant to them, they headed inexorably toward it and I had thought for a long time, the sooner the better.

When I finally enrolled in a secretarial school in Tokyo, I endured the classroom hours that I couldn't avoid. I believed I could teach myself in one weekend what they had developed into a college-level course. For the nine-month course, I dutifully rode the train to Tokyo every day, entered school for a short time to absorb something basic, and then left. Most of the classes were in Japanese and little attention was paid to attendance once the days began. Absent for most of every class, I could still outtype in speed and accuracy any others enrolled in the school. I read some of the books, whizzed through tests when they were given, then spent most of my days in movie theaters.

I met some artists in Tokyo and helped them design stage sets. I did a lot of walking in the streets. When my old friend from Castilleja, Liz Murdoch, moved to Tokyo, she performed in the local production of the famous play *Hair*. With Liz, and because of her introductions, I spent a lot of time with the cast members and spent time with a Japanese guy, Keishi, who had one of the leading parts. He was a beautiful man with shining black hair that hung to his waist.

My parents never knew about Keishi. I rarely included them in anything personal, as their response was too unpredictable, and they missed someone special. Keishi was sensitive, a wonderful artist, on stage or on canvas. He and I often met near the Statue of the Dog, a center point of the Shibuya Station that could be compared to the clock at the Biltmore Hotel in New York City. It was "the" place to meet. Erected as a tribute to a loyal pet who had followed his master dutifully to the station, and steadfastly returned to the station to meet the evening train long after the death of his beloved master, the statue was well-known and a focal point for all. After meeting, Keishi and I either walked for miles, had coffee and salted toast in Shinjuki, went to art exhibits, or visited friends. Apartments in Japan are, in general, extremely tiny, but despite the size of our group of friends, we always managed to cram into one.

When a business school opened in Yokohama, I transferred to it. There Carolyn Schweizer prowled the city with me. She and I also hung out with merchant seamen from Sweden and Germany whom we met in clubs. Four of us had a favorite haunt in Izezaki-Cho, Washington Square. That place attracted all sorts of interesting people: soldiers on rest and recuperation from Vietnam, merchant seamen, American travelers, and civilian bush pilots from Cambodia and Laos who told us stories of their adventures with Air America. It was painful to see the wounded psyches of the GIs on momentary escape from Nam. One good friend, Doc, wore the bone of a human finger around his neck. I never asked where it came from, not sure that I wanted to know.

Carolyn's and my favorite thing to do was to sit around drinking Singapore slings and absinthe fizzes made from a liqueur that is illegal in most other parts of the world, and listening to intriguing sounds of the outer world brought by the cosmopolitan chorus of adventurers and to our inner voices.

In Yokohama, I paid a bit more attention to my classes and finally completed a business degree. I was, to my parents' delight, prepared to be a secretary. I was *prepared* insofar as a graduation certificate was concerned. Mentally and emotionally, such a job held no interest for me at all.

But I had to do something. Scenes at home finally blossomed into free-for-alls that were inflamed by alcohol. Bad scenes became truly ugly. I felt as if I were caught in a whirlpool. In one particularly horrible fit of rage, my mother attacked me and kicked me in the ribs. When I had the medical bill sent to my parents for the X ray that showed cracked ribs, they gave me five hundred bucks and a one-way ticket to San Francisco and told me to get myself some work.

In California, I shared an apartment with my high school friend Sara Lyons, and things were mellow for a while. In the early 1970s, San Francisco pulsated with life. Sara and I spent hours on the streets engrossed in the sounds of street musicians, watching mimes in Union Square, or riding cable cars to the Wharf. Some evenings we stayed home with friends. We wrote poetry, drank wine, smoked, and came up with some wild ideas.

Odd jobs kept a roof over my head. I sold earrings at street-side stands, worked in a bookstore, and, dressed for the part, worked at the Marin Renaissance Faire selling mead, the alcoholic liquor made of fermented honey and water and jazzed up with spices, fruits, and malt.

Sara and I never missed a concert at the Fillmore West and we never failed to go backstage. The rock and roll scene was fun and as we got acquainted with performers, we were invited to parties all over the city and throughout Marin County. One of our heroes was a singer, Tim Buckley. Having met him once in London, I loved seeing and hearing him in the States. Like groupies, Sara and I followed him from concert hall to concert hall.

Sometimes we cruised in limos, laughing, talking, and drinking champagne. One evening, Sara and I put on wild animal skin outfits. Clicking along with our feet at least four inches off the ground on big platform shoes, we came to a street corner. A stately African man stopped his limo beside us, opened his door, and got out. He said, sweeping his arm in an arc, "You look like queens from my country. I would crown you."

We laughed. We *felt* like queens—of the jungle, of the night. Still laughing, we ran all the way to Enrico's on Broadway. There we drank cappuccino and ate turkey sandwiches while we watched the carnival of life stroll by—drag queens, hookers, and hippies. We were part of the scene and the carnival was intoxicating.

Yet, survival was a great incentive. I had to get a "straight" job to pay the rent. I worked for the National Automobile Association and made an appearance at work each day for about two months, applying my paycheck toward a roof over my head and food to eat, plus candles, books, and my favorite herbs and oils from the Mystic Eye, a shop on Broadway.

My boss, a big guy who tried to hide his creepy ways behind a dignified suit, found it amusing to "playfully" chase me around the filing cabinets. I wanted to tell the world, "You have no idea what it's like to be a young, single woman in a cloistered office with a lecherous guy. It can be humiliating. It can be scary. Women have an obligation to educate men, to refuse to be considered as objects, and to demand respect, one human to another."

I had nothing vested in the job, no family to support, so I quit and found another. I had lived with tension for too much of my life and this was one more version of intimidation I didn't need. I tried to maintain, to maintain the *appearance* of sanity and to maintain an *image* of functioning in mainstream society and the world of employment and employers. There were great generational and philosophical differences between the youth of the counterculture and the culture of those who were older.

I wrote in my journal: "A revolution is coming down around me. Are we a majority? Or are we leaping blindly into the night longing for freedom to be ourselves, free rational minds . . . opposing all who stand in our way? By opposing the power structure, can I liberate myself?"

I had to fit into a world that was not of my making.

SIX

Vortex

In northern California of the early 1970s, hitchhiking was in. College students hitchhiked. I hitchhiked. Everyone hitchhiked. It was the way to get around, especially for those who couldn't afford cars. In California, kids lined up—guys with long hair pulled back into ponytails, their foreheads swathed with sweatbands, and little hippie girls with miniskirts or dresses that brushed their ankles, sandals, or boots, and beautiful strings of glass beads or flowers. All watched the stream of cars, waiting for a driver to pull to the side of the road and stop.

When my friends and I hitchhiked, we didn't always have destinations. We just went. We ran into people that were interesting, made new friends, and found adventure. It was fun, sometimes edgy, but fun.

The first time that I took off for something other than just a local ride, I was living with my girlfriend above a racy bookstore in the Tenderloin area of San Francisco. I called my friend Becky because she reminded me of Rebecca of Sunnybrook Farm—blonde, sweet, and innocent. She was a year younger than I and I was all of nineteen.

Still plagued with some of the nasty nightmares that had so interrupted my sleep as a child in Japan, I wanted to get away for a while. I coaxed Becky into thumbing to Omaha, Nebraska, with me to see some friends. We got picked up almost as soon as we put out our thumbs, but as night started to fall, the driver suddenly turned off onto a side road. He leered at us and pulled out a bottle of wine.

I said, "Come on, Becky. We're getting out of here." The guy didn't make any move to stop us and we got out of his car and ran.

A few more drivers later, we were almost through Nevada before getting down to our last couple of bucks. Stopped momentarily in a little town, we met a guy in front of a casino who told me to put all of my money onto number seventeen red on the roulette wheel. Accepting his advice, I placed my bet on the table. When we won our money back five times over, I scooped it up, stifling my curiosity until sometime later. Becky shook her head, saying, "It seems as if things just come your way."

As if to add credence to Becky's belief, we were picked up by a nice man in his forties, dark haired, casually dressed, and comfortable to be with. He took us all the way to Omaha where we surprised our friends and stayed for a couple of weeks. After a fun visit, we headed west again.

On the return to California, a salmon Cadillac, its huge chromed fins gleaming, screeched to a stop beside us and a gem of an old man, easily in his eighties, rolled down the window on the passenger's side. "You gals goin' to Reno?"

"You bet," I answered. "Can we get in?" I reached to open the back door of his Cadillac.

"No," he said. "Don't get into the back seat. You do the drivin' and I'll sit in the back. You girls can carry me to Reno in style."

I grinned at Becky and we slid into the barge of a car. I stepped on the accelerator and the faster that old car went, the more the man leaned forward, slapping the back of the seat, urging, "Go faster. Go faster!"

We headed down the strip of asphalt toward the neon of the Biggest Little City in the World, accelerating until the needle pushing toward the upper reaches of the speedometer began to get to me. At first I worried about keeping the boat on the road. But the farther we went, the more I pushed through the wall of doubt into self-confidence. Starting to enjoy the satisfaction that comes from operating machinery precisely and well, I raced ahead of myself down the road, watching the ribbon of highway apparently swallowed by the throaty vehicle and displayed in the rear view mirror like a curving, whipping tail.

When we arrived in Reno, the old man gave us a room in his ranch house—no strings attached. He said, "And take that car and use it. I got no place to go and am in no hurry to get there."

We cruised Reno in the great pink boat. It was wild. Life was a delirious adventure and I was along for the ride, not knowing my destination.

A few months later, the thought of Mexican beaches lured us into our second long trip. Agreeing to meet friends from California, we hitched rides as far as Arizona. Monsoon rains had just passed, washing Tucson and leaving a rainbow encircling the entire town, the pots of gold hidden deep within the purple hills. It was beautiful. I fell in love with the open space, the mauve skyline devoid of buildings and decorated instead by gaunt saguaro and spiny ocotillo. It was my first glimpse of the city that I would later call home.

We ran into an old friend, a Navajo from a reservation south of Tucson. A fan of Carlos Castaneda, he showed us his magic world which was somewhere and everywhere in the mountains south of Tucson. We looked at Arizona through his wisdom, his philosophy, and his eyes.

Hoping to reach the Sea of Cortez, where we planned to catch up with our California friends, Becky and I managed to hitchhike as far as Sonoita, a nowhere border town in which we were stalemated in trying to cross the border, barred by officials. The duty officer said, "There is no way that I'm going to let you two girls into Mexico alone."

Arguments were useless, so we turned and planned to head back to California. When our money started to run out, we looked for jobs. In one instance, we were hired to clean scummy bathrooms in a service station. Becky and I worked for three hours and, to our disgust, the owner handed us each a fifty-cent piece. We had to try our hand at something else if we were going to get back to San Francisco. Becky wielded as mean a pool cue as I did, and the more we played, the better we got. In Parker, a town on the Colorado River, we challenged two guys, playing best out of three for two bus tickets. We won and the losers, with shrugs of their shoulders, honorably bought us our tickets.

Back in San Francisco, my escapes short-lived, I faced having to get a real job. I dreaded the regimen, the trappings of the establishment. Economically, however, I had no option. I simply had to find a job.

At about this time, a gorgeous man with long blonde hair and wonderful gentleness, John O'Bar, came into my life. I was crazy about John and spent most of my waking hours with him. John, who was special to me, offered me a close and valuable relationship. John was another of the conscientious objectors who found himself at odds with the purposes of the government and its military objectives. He had served in the U.S. Navy but was as distressed as many others during the Vietnam era and the ensuing decade. We bared our souls to one another, feeling equally safe and loved.

But the trust that we'd worked to develop was sorely tested when I had to be hospitalized for a recurring bout with jaundice. My mother, who traveled fairly regularly from Japan to the U.S. by deadheading, visited our relatives in San Mateo. Because I was ill, she came into San Francisco to see me as well. I remember the rest as a bizarre chain of events that shattered my faith to its roots. When my mother visited me in the hospital, I made the mistake of telling her how special John was to me, how kind, gentle, and loving he was. She met him in my hospital room, but when visiting hours were over, I was evidently out of sight and out of mind.

Had she kept it to herself, I never would have discovered that I had my own Mrs. Robinson. I don't know whether it was guilt or pride that made her confess to me, but Mother told me later that she and John had left my hospital room together. My mother invited him to have a drink, had persuaded John to have too many. (It horrified me to even think about it.) She seduced him.

I was appalled. When I confronted John, he apologized. Several times he told me that he was sorry. He said that he never had been much of a drinker, that he'd gotten drunk, that it would never happen again, that he truly loved me.

I was hurt and angry. Although I felt sick about it, I forgave John. He was only nineteen and I blamed my mother. She was forty-two and I never could find a way to forgive her.

I had felt estranged from my family for quite a while. I'd distanced myself from their attempts at domination and control and from the fury that surfaced when they were drinking alcohol. In the much more complex relationship between mother and daughter, a wall formed between my mother and me. I had avoided her and the alcoholism that altered her personality like the plague. Now, whatever bonds had tenuously remained were severed completely. If not for my love for my sister, I would have refused to admit to having a family at all. Reduced to square one, I could only depend on my own resiliency and capabilities. I was devastated. Now I was truly and completely on my own.

Adrift, for a time I moved into a big place on Polk Street with a group of gay guys who were my best friends. They were good company and guaranteed not to sexually hassle me, and they made me feel entirely comfortable. Sometimes we went to all-night dance halls all dressed to the nines in feather boas and platform shoes. It never mattered that I was the only female in the place.

Some evenings I went to the bar where Becky, who was choosing a different path, performed as an exotic dancer. Exotic dancing didn't appeal to me. It wasn't an issue of morality; it just wasn't something I wanted to do.

I had no money. I wasn't in school or college. Any jobs that I held were temporary, just something to do to earn pin money. I had no hope, nothing to look forward to. Life spiraled into a downer, and, for the first and only time in my life, in my despair I considered a painless, drug-induced suicide.

But the morning after my darkest night, I started out of my apartment and the splash of a street vendor's brilliantly colored fresh flowers shot a message to me. The flowers were beautiful. The flowers, resplendent in every color of the rainbow, were alive! In another first, I got a glimpse of my own power. Suddenly it hit me that the choice about a future, *my* future, was up to me.

I called my relatives in Marin County and leaned pretty heavily on one of my cousins, Sue Mills, the founder and owner of Sue Mills, Inc., makers of school uniforms. Sue, a friendly, outgoing, and tough woman, lived alone in a beautiful house that overlooked Mount Tamalpais. She had always said, "If you ever need anything, call me." I called, but I didn't need to tell Sue how desperate I was. She could hear it in my voice. She generously took me in and I lived with her for a year.

Ironically, the young girl who had despised the uniforms that Catholic schools forced her to wear found herself doing part-time work in a uniform factory. I even modeled school uniforms for Sue's professional brochures! This was a 180-degree change of direction. I owed a lot to Sue and I appreciated her help. She gave me attention and love just when I needed it the most. She didn't coddle me but made me feel responsible. Sue gave me a job and was firm about the fact that I had specific tasks to accomplish and a time clock to punch, and she was worth doing it for.

But my becoming productive wasn't one great triumphant climb out of the cellar. Despite her support, I had no car, no means of support, and I was emotionally and literally distanced from my family. I saw no way out, no answers. I still had to fight against a vortex that drew me toward the low level to which a person can sink. It was hard to reverse its direction. I wrote in my journal: "When you are caught in a whirlpool, you're not going to pass by a hand that reaches down. You're going to grab at it. And *then* find out what it's made of."

Sue lived in a remote area, far from everything. I was without wheels and, like a truck that high centers on a deeply rutted road, I found it impossible to progress. I was isolated from trouble but also from all the friends that I had developed and those I had learned to love.

The trust and innocence of the flower children of the 1960s were disappearing. I had turned from a family without trust to gentle souls— my city friends who meant so much to me. But even that trust was betrayed. I saw that others took advantage of us, and started to recognize that we were being used by those who were greedy and unscrupulous. The atmosphere in San Francisco altered from what I had perceived to be one of affection and love to one with a darker shadow of cynicism and doubt.

I tried to live in Marin County, but I felt as if I'd moved to the boondocks. I missed being surrounded by the electric excitement of a city and I missed being part of the action.

"Why don't you move in with Elena?" Sue suggested.

Elena Mills Foley, Sue's daughter, lived in San Rafael. I called her, and, like her mom had, she made me feel welcome. Her home was closer to civilization, closer to a bus station, which was useful when there was an emergency or a downpour. I landed a good office job in a city planner's office and generally hitchhiked to work. My job was interesting, which was a relief, and my after-work hours were spent with my best friend, Sara Lyons, who also lived in Marin and with whom I enjoyed the music and art scene in Sausalito.

Told by some friends who had relocated that there was a lot going on in Los Angeles, I decided to visit some friends who had moved to Malibu Beach and rented a house. They seemed enthusiastic, so I went down there to see what it was like. From Los Angeles, I called Sara and told her, "Come on down. Come see what you think. Maybe we should move down here."

The evening that I was in the airport waiting for Sara, I sat down in the cocktail lounge to order a drink. A good-looking guy sitting nearby noticed that the waiters weren't coming my way.

He stood up and came over. "Can I buy a drink for you?" he asked, his Australian accent unmistakable and equally attractive. He smiled and we got to talking. "The name's Bill," he said, "Bill Beck. And you are . . . ?"

"Patty. Patty Combs."

"Are you coming or going?"

I laughed. "That's a question that my parents thought would never be answered."

"I'll rephrase that. Are you arriving or departing?" He had a nice smile.

We talked a while longer, then I explained that I was in the airport to meet Sara. I glanced at my watch and stood up to leave. Bill gave me his phone number and said that he had a fishing boat, an abalone boat that he kept in Santa Barbara. He told me to give him a ring sometime.

The L.A. scene had its moments, but it didn't take very long for me to realize how barbaric it was; everyone I met seemed to be living for the chance of getting something from someone else. Like voracious human sharks, everyone was out for what they could get. I discovered that I was little more than a commodity, a pretty young thing, but just a woman. Women who hung around clubs, parties, or music gigs were shown little or no respect. I did my share of the street scene, often having too much to drink. I existed in full view of the contradictory, seamier side of the City of Angels. Yet people did flock there to make things happen for themselves and that creative, upbeat energy was contagious. Everyone that I met exuded the belief that given a chance, he or she was going to make it big.

I swam outside of both streams. I was no shark, but I wasn't an ingénue either. I was too much of a realist to be an optimist. Treading water between the two, I searched for identity and waited to see what might happen.

I had opportunities to try out for acting parts, though I was no actress. I loved music and had a lot of friends in the music business, though I was not a musician. I was artistic, but I hadn't a portfolio. I didn't know what I wanted, but I wanted something that I could claim as my own. I *didn't* want to be the appendage to another.

A small inheritance left to me by my great-grandmother, Mary Dorey, bought me a little green MGB. I made a mistake, however, and loaned it to a friend who ended up in a nasty car accident. He almost tore his thumb out of its socket and was rushed to a hospital. My car was totaled.

Not long after, while washing some dishes, I cut my finger badly. I, too, was rushed to a hospital by a friend for stitches and medical treatment. My bloody finger was symbolic of everything coming down around me.

I thought about Bill Beck. I had only met him that one time in the airport, but I remembered that he seemed sincere. He had a job as a fisherman and had built his own boat. He seemed earthy, head and shoulders above most of the men that I met in L.A.

Early one morning, while I stared at the distant horizon, the far reaches of a seemingly endless Pacific Ocean, I called Bill. Streaks of early sunlight filtered out over the water from behind me, sparkling in the distance and edging each wave with lace. Inside I churned as restlessly as the huge sea. When Bill answered, I told him who I was. I said, "Do you remember me?"

He said, "Who could forget you? What's up?"

"Oh, I'm just looking out at that ocean that you seem to like so much. How's it going?"

"Why don't you come to Santa Barbara for the weekend and see for yourself? I'll show you my abalone operation and you can soak up some rays."

I didn't have to be asked twice. I took a bus to Santa Barbara. Like a chameleon, I shed one life for another. I left the city night scene for the sunny, athletic, and outdoor daylight. Instead of crowding into small, smoke-filled rooms to hear a guitarist strain to be heard over conversation and the clink of glasses, I swam, lay on the beach, and helped Bill with his boat. Bill was like a breath of fresh salt sea air. Clever with his hands, he was confident in his abilities. He worked hard, appearing to know the value of good honest toil and he had a vast knowledge of the sea and ships. In comparison to the men I had been meeting, Bill seemed to exude stability in the midst of my own uncertainty and instability.

At certain times in life, puzzle pieces start to fit. Meeting Bill Beck at a time when I was searching seemed to give me an anchor that I'd been missing. Though I hardly knew him, I found that the chemistry was right. I found him attractive; he was an athletic, great-looking blonde. Sharp and witty, he had a good sense of humor. He had a lot to teach me and seemed to be happy to share his knowledge and lore of the sea. He seemed straighter than the rest.

Was that because he was a fisherman? At the very least, he worked, finding something useful to do with himself each day. That was more than most of those who peopled the shark frenzy I'd just escaped.

I was impressed that he was clever. He could build almost anything, and when I got to Santa Barbara he was still making improvements on his self-built fishing boat. He had ambition, a quality that I greatly admired, though I would later discover that his ambition was limited to get-rich-quick schemes.

Ours was a whirlwind relationship. I went for a weekend and stayed weeks. I went for a few days of sun and six weeks later, in June of 1973 at the courthouse in Santa Barbara, we were married. I became Mrs. Bill Beck. I was twenty-one and needed no one's permission, but I dutifully called my parents to tell them. They didn't come to the ceremony and I didn't invite them. Bill's parents weren't there either, as they lived in Perth, Australia.

We had one funny escapade in the courthouse. Bill's best man was an Englishman who had overstayed his visa and, after getting into minor trouble, had been hauled into the same court. He had been told by the judge that he had to leave the United States. As we entered the courthouse for the marriage ceremony, the best man recognized that the presiding judge was the same one who had deported him. He sucked in his breath. You could see him grow about two inches as he stiffened. "Oh, my God. I can't do this. I can't go in there."

We tugged him in with us and though I believe that the judge recognized him, he overlooked the minor matter and performed the ceremony without batting an eye. Later, over champagne toasts on the beach, we laughed until we were sick.

"Here's to Patty and Bill. Cheers!"

"And here's to the judge, may his vision and memory never improve!"

A blending of two very different lives was in motion. We shared a little apartment overlooking Santa Barbara's beautiful harbor and I thought I could live there forever, until I started to learn about operating a boat, diving for abalone, and spending countless hours at sea. Bill's fiberglass craft was twenty-eight feet long. He said that I could be of some help as a crew member and checked me out at the helm so that I could drive whenever he needed me to take the controls. Fishing became our daily regimen.

We sailed twenty-seven miles from Santa Barbara to reach the Channel Islands, five uninhabited islands with additional small islets that were home to countless seabirds and mammals. The islands boasted hundreds of sea caves and millions of tidal pools in which fishermen and outdoorsmen searched for crabs, sea anemones, sea urchins, starfish, and abalone.

Bill taught me to gun it when we crossed a kelp bed in the Santa Barbara Channel, saying, "Don't let the propeller get caught in the seaweed. It will cause the engine to cavitate." He also taught me about the mollusks that were confined to the coasts of California and Japan. He said, "Abalone are prized for their broad, ear-shaped shells. They're lined with mother-of-pearl that become buttons, jewelry, and souvenirs. Abalone are also prized for their large, edible foot, which is served as a restaurant delicacy. They are worth their weight in money."

Bill showed me to recognize some of the varieties of abalone and how to avoid getting my fingers caught between the shells and the rocks. "Big Reds can get to be about a foot wide and have terrific suction," he warned. "Just slip the abalone knife under 'em while they're relaxed. That's the time to pry 'em off the rocks."

He showed me how tightly they could draw to the rocks, saying, "If you accidentally touch them first, they'll tense the muscle. You'd be amazed at how the foot can squeeze. It's near impossible to get a knife under 'em then. They're amazingly strong."

Bill, who was seven years older than I, had obviously amassed a good amount of experience before I came into the picture. It was his boat and he was the acknowledged leader. It was his fishing gig and I was the apprentice. We spent hours and sometimes days on his boat and, at first, it seemed like a blast, pure fun. I learned to dive, I learned to use Bill's "hookah." A hookah is an Eastern smoking pipe with a long, flexible tube that is used to draw the smoke through a jar of water by which it is cooled. Bill's device was a breathing tube connected to a compressor with a hose through which we could draw air. It enabled us to stay underwater for longer periods.

He'd say, "Take the hookah down with you, Patty, but watch yourself. The kelp can tangle badly."

Diving could be electrifying. It was challenging to find abalone or sea urchins, to judge the depth and swell of the water, and to pay attention to the drift of the tides. I loved hearing the gulls, watching storm petrels wheel overhead, and swimming not far from the seals, sea lions, and otters that lived on the islands. The crisp smell of salty spray at first was synonymous with pleasure.

I enjoyed turning nut brown in the sunshine, but I learned to associate the salty spray, the pounding of waves, and the flight of pelicans and cormorants with the more frightening aspects of the shore. Diving could be terrifying. Sometimes the pull of the tide was extremely strong and I got exhausted trying to buck it. Sometimes I held my breath as I dived, wondering what I was doing there and why. The hookah, our only source of air, could get caught on long strands of seaweed and whipped out of my hands. It was unnerving and dangerous.

The boat was well made, very strong and fairly fast, but life on the ocean became monotonous. The newness wore off quickly and work on and around the boat edged toward drudgery and sometimes fear. It was always edgy to me. I loved fast machinery, but I didn't love the water. I enjoyed the sun and the surf but watched days disappear into one another like swells rhythmically rolling toward the shore, each one indistinct from the next, the sameness interminable. I also learned that Bill, although a nice guy, was kind of a hustler, out to make a buck, legalities be damned.

Although they say that ignorance is no excuse, I didn't know the rules. It was quite a while before I realized that we were often doing the forbidden, going out at night to gather abalone wherever we could find it. I knew that restaurants paid good money for the meat and that tourist traps bought the shells for resale. I knew that a good haul could net us a lot of money. But I didn't know, at first, that "beach walking" was illegal as well as environmentally wrong. I began to see Bill's ability to skirt the law, but I rolled along for the ride.

I could have gotten into serious trouble and even gone to jail. I learned much later that abalone had to be taken out of so many feet of water. It was legal to fish the Channel Islands, but it wasn't to be done in the dark of night. It was defying those rules that brought some of my most terrifying memories.

We often snuck the boat quietly out of the harbor at night, crossing the shipping channel that was traversed regularly by large tankers and freighters that traveled along the coast. Much of the time, we operated in zero-zero visibility and in fog. With no radar of our own and in the middle of the channel, we were always in grave danger of collision. At times, our only recourse was to stop the boat to listen for fog horns. The sounds of the night and the slapping of the waves could have been pure joy. Instead there was the acute tension that came from never knowing whether we were being borne down upon by something huge and powerful. No ships ever closed in on us, but the threat was constant.

Sidling into the water at night, inky waves slapped against the hull, the swells heaved, and long fingers of kelp slithered across the ocean's surface. As we moored offshore of some of the islands, the water seemed sinister, dark, and deep. Miles of kelp beds churned in wait, ready to entangle legs, arms, the hoses. It felt slimy and creepy. No matter how logical I tried to be, my imagination ran amok. I could imagine creepy things, twisting eels or the tentacles of octopus, curling around my legs and tightening to draw me under.

Wearing wet suits and miner's helmets with lights, we left the anchored boat and swam, pushing our hard rubber dinghies toward the shore. Lights bobbing in reflection cast eerie gleaming streaks over the water and left long dark shadows. Kelp tangled in our ankles. We worked feverishly and carefully all night long and I found it much more frightening once I knew that we weren't supposed to be there. But I was along for the ride as usual, wanting to experience everything and still unconvinced of any real control over my own destiny.

After we gathered the abalone, we would swim with our gunnysacks filled. "Let me show you, Patty," Bill said the first time. "Swing the gunnysack into the rubber dinghy, and then lie down on top of the sack and paddle with your arms out to the boat. Watch me."

His arms were longer and much stronger than mine. He'd grown up around boats and felt at home in the water. My first realization that people are drawn to certain elements dawned on me while watching Bill Beck. He was inexorably drawn to water. That anyone else would feel anxiety in *his* element, that in which he felt so natural, was beyond him.

I hated every moment in that cold, dark, rolling water. Sometimes the waves threw me off the dinghy and I hated the feeling of helplessness. Even if logic told me that it was just seaweed stroking me, I shuddered with revulsion.

I had learned a method of detachment during my many tirades with my parents. Whenever I found myself in a repulsive situation, I disassociated my mind from my body, still able to function as if from a distance. Sometimes I felt as if I were astral traveling. It had saved me in some of my worst moments in the past and it was all that saved me in the inky, churning shallows of the Channel Islands.

Bill would harvest and load the dinghy. I would paddle it to the boat, and a hired hand swung the sacks onboard ship. I was tough enough to swim well enough to pull the dinghy, the full gunnysack, and my own weight through the waves, but it was simpler before sunrise. Waves would start to build about then. I struggled with every ounce of strength to keep the abalone from being washed overboard. A good load brought as much as $1,500 and I knew full well that was too much money to lose.

Besides, like any crew member, I knew that Bill was in charge. He was hard on himself and he could be hard on me. I had to perform.

Our worst night finally came. Just as we approached an island, turning into a sheltered cove, Bill yelled suddenly, "Jump, Patty! Get off the boat! Shit! *Jump!*"

The boat had caught fire. He'd barely yelled when he shoved me roughly into the water. The boat was flaming and I panicked. I was wearing boots and a coat, and, thinking I was drowning, I started hyperventilating because I was so terrified.

Bill jumped and swam over to rescue me, recognizing that I was going under. The clothes and the boots dragged me down, and, as I fought to keep my head above the surface, panic didn't help.

Moments later, it seemed ridiculous to discover that the water was only about four-feet deep. I hadn't realized that. All I knew was that although depression had not long before nearly driven me to suicide, this was the closest I had ever come to dying. I struggled to breathe. I didn't want to drown. I wanted to live!

Bill grabbed my arm and helped me. We kicked and dragged ourselves toward the shore, the boat fully engulfed in flames behind us. The cove was narrow, framed on either side by ragged, jutting rocks that formed a natural grotto. The flaming boat lurched directly toward us propelled by relentless waves, a terrifying fire-belching behemoth.

I screamed, "God! This is crazy! This is a wild and terrible dream!"

Once safely on the beach, we lay on the sand for what seemed to be hours, chilled and sodden. A coast guard rescue team eventually came by boat to take us from the island, but I could tell immediately that they didn't believe the fire was accidental. You could see the accusation in their eyes, hear it in the tone of their voices.

I was relieved to be alive, yet strangely dead inside. I couldn't think straight. I just wanted to be home in our beach apartment in Santa Barbara. I wanted to be on solid ground, out of the water and away from it. It was not my element and I was not about to give my life to it.

When insurance people started coming around, I asked Bill what was happening, what was really going on. But I never heard any answers. Did he set the fire himself? He had been talking about returning to Australia. I knew he'd been trying to sell the boat in order to go to Australia, but did he decide not to wait and set the boat on fire instead? Unbelievable! He never admitted it, but I grew suspicious. Suspicion ate away at my trust in him, a cancer to our relationship. Was this the beginning of the end of our marriage?

I recalled that my dad had seen some of the hustler in Bill that I had been too blind or too naive to see. He had come to visit us in Santa Barbara, trying to make some amends, trying to rebuild some fences, but I could tell that Dad didn't care for Bill. That memory cast further seeds of doubt.

I was beginning to discover, however, that steady work didn't appeal to Bill, and that he had a million and one ideas for making quick money. He wanted things to come to him quickly and easily. But some things came with explosive speed, things that weren't what he expected at all.

Bill repeatedly mentioned returning to Australia. "What do you say? There's nothing holding us here now that I can see. There are shipwrecks off the west coast of Australia, promises of treasures that I'd really like to dive for."

I've always been like a sponge, eager to absorb everything new and exciting, and, in those days, everyone I met was a trip. My travels were voyages of discovery and I stifled any artificial expectations and looked at life with fresh eyes. I was wide open to experience and the thought of Australia was provocative. Why not go to the land down under? Why not discover what it held in store?

What lay ahead? I remembered something that I had read in the *Haight-Ashbury Free Press*: "We owe to our first journeys the discovery that place is nothing."

SEVEN

The Land of Oz

I wasn't the least bit interested in diving for sunken treasure, but I liked the idea of gold. I told Bill, and meant it, "Australia would be a trip. There sure isn't much here for us anymore."

I wondered where we were headed. We had begun to lose much of the mutual respect and cohesion that would have helped our marriage to grow. My trust in him had been badly burned with the flaming fishing boat, and, without trust, our relationship was shaken.

Nonetheless, the thought of Australia was a great lure. I had begun to appreciate an outdoor lifestyle—getting tan and being in a less stressful environment than in the cities I'd grown up in. Australia, I'd heard, was a sun-filled and exotic paradise. I took advantage of my ability to deadhead to Sydney because my father still worked for Japan Airlines. I traveled there alone. I was leaving for another continent, another hemisphere, an unknown, a question mark. Part of me wanted to shed my relationship with Bill and continue on all alone, and part of me wanted to see Australia through Bill's eyes, with an Australian who knew and loved his own country.

I arrived a few days before Bill, and taking a taxi from the airport to a convenient hotel, I was entranced with the driver. He was a big, friendly ocker, the quintessential Australian bushman, and his accent was so strong that I could hardly understand a word. I happily anticipated learning more about my new land.

Bill met me in Sydney. "We're goin' to fly to Adelaide, and then we'll head for Perth to see my mother and stepfather," he explained.

Traveling from Sydney in New South Wales on the southeast coast to Perth in western Australia on the southwest was roughly the equivalent of traveling from Charleston, South Carolina, to Los Angeles.

"Please, instead of flying, can't we take the train? I want to see the wildlife. I want to see Australia up close."

The question was the request of an innocent. Little did I know that between Adelaide on the Tasman Sea and Perth on the Indian Ocean lay miles and miles of space, relatively few towns, and only the two large cities of Melbourne and Adelaide. The Australia National Railroad was happy to carry us the long distance, but most of that which we crossed was the Nullarbor Plain. Just as the Aborigines had recognized in naming the region, it was a flat, treeless region. *Nullarbor* means just what the name implies—no trees! And where there were no trees, there was *nothing*! It was a wasteland. We spent three days cooped up in a train eating food that tasted like cardboard and clicking past mile after mile of sand.

I had envisioned seeing cockatoos and kookaburras or huge ostrichlike emus. I'd seen Australian wildlife pictured so beautifully in magazines like *National Geographic* and I thought that we would see the kangaroos, wallabies, koalas, and wombats for which Australia was famed. Instead, we saw nothing. I did finally start to comprehend the accent and some of the Australian language and to see what their culture was all about, and when we finally pulled into Perth, I was overjoyed. It was in December, summer down under, and Perth buzzed with activity. Perth meant civilization.

Bill and I went straight to his mother's house in Naval Base, a small town south of Perth in which we rented a small cottage. A friendly woman, she and I liked each other immediately. Once we became acquainted, Bill's stepfather Fred was cordial to me, too.

Bill immediately set his mind to diving. For years, he had read about sunken treasure on the western shores of Australia. His heart was set on gold.

Bill had never known his biological father, a U.S. Navy pilot who was killed in Australia before Bill's birth. I thought later that had his father lived, Bill would have been a different person—less driven, competitive, and macho. Like a team of horses, Bill and I were well-matched—

restless, headstrong, and athletic. But there was divisiveness in our basic psyches. Despite our shared qualities, we were drawn to different elements and I found it increasingly difficult to immerse myself in his. Some of the qualities that I found intriguing when we first met turned out to be what drove me away. He had a sense of humor, but he tended to laugh at things that I found serious. I thought he was ambitious, but he wanted things to come easily. His was a buy-a-lotto-ticket-and-strike-it-rich mentality; mine was a more mellow, wait-and-see, less greedy approach. We both began to strain at the harness, pulling away from and not toward one another. But I said little, still going along for the ride.

My memories of Australia, however, are not limited to memories of Bill. They are vivid recollections of an intriguing time, a fascinating place, and an exciting experience. I loved just saying the names of some of the nearby villages. They almost rang with their own form of poetic music: Pinjarra, Wyalkatchem, Koolyanobbing, and Kojonup. Australia was unusual in many ways.

Gold had been a major inspiration to settlement and population growth in Australia at almost the same time that it drew the population westward in the United States. But Bill was not interested in the mining of the land. His imagination was captured by the many shipwrecks that had sent gold-laden ships to the bottom in the rough coastal waters of Australia's west. To an expert diver like Bill, the lure was magnetic.

"This is a big chance, Patty," Bill said. "I just know there's gold down there. Let's plan to sink everything we've got into one great boat. We'll head for the wreck of the *Trial* just off the Monte Bello Island off North West Cape."

"I'm not a skilled diver. I can't go into that water. . . ."

"This isn't abalone fishing. Anyway, I've a pal, Les, who'll go with us. We'll need three. We'll be diving in rough waters of the Indian Ocean. The stakes are pretty high."

I'd met Les and I liked him. Originally from England, he had lived in Australia for a long time. Les, Bill, and I dove into the boat-building mode. Bill estimated that we would be able to start diving within a year, or, at the outset, two. He said, "We're gonna outfit it right, too. We're gonna get a metal detector and we're going to build a pump that'll really suck sand."

Under the protected cover of a rented shed, we spent our days fiberglassing. Our cottage was nearby, perched on the beach between Freemantle and Rockingham and close enough to the water for us to feel the minutes and hours of each day tick by in sync with its steadily pounding rhythm.

We started a menagerie when we acquired a goat and then, as a Christmas gift, Bill gave me two Dobermans, Nina and Alexi. When I wasn't up to my elbows in slurry and fabric in the boathouse or making and serving avocado and mushroom sandwiches for the three of us, I worked at gardening, cooking, caring for the goat, and raising and training the dogs. A handful, they were like a pair of little kids.

Our cottage was hardly fancy, and rent amounted to about ten dollars a week. The sinks drained into the dirt outside, but at least we didn't have an outhouse. Located not far from Bill's mother and stepfather's home, our cottage was between the ocean and a vast tract of public land that was filled with black boy and gum trees and peopled, like a warren straight out of *Watership Down*, with millions of rabbits. We had plenty of room to call our own. The terrain was desert and brushland, and although it was initially a little awkward to think of December, January, and February as being the summer season, we spent Christmas on the beach. Summer days were hot and sunny and when I wasn't busy with helping to build the boat, I walked and ran with the dogs at the beach. Miles of glistening white sand dotted with pale pink shells and occasional water-softened bits of driftwood encouraged the artist in me.

To make ends meet, I took a part-time job at a local company, the Kwinana Nickel Refinery. I didn't enjoy secretarial school in Japan, but I liked and valued secretarial work for its own qualities and I was good at it. The job gave focus to each day and I liked the organization. It also gave me a great opportunity to get acquainted with Australia and to add new friends to my life. A job, the pay notwithstanding, gave form to an otherwise essentially formless series of days.

A third dog joined us: a six-pound ball of muscle and spunk, a silky terrier named Whiskey. Whiskey literally jumped into my pickup, taking charge of the troops. In no time, he established himself as the leader of the triumvirate, a tiny leader, the despot of the Dobermans. Whiskey came from a friend who spent a lot of time driving long distances, so he was a great little traveler, used to living in cars. A great swimmer, Whiskey took to our beach immediately.

Whiskey's owner was leaving Australia and couldn't take him along. When he asked if I would like to have him, I said, "You bet. He's a great little dog."

His leap into my car took him straight into my heart. I loved him almost immediately and it wasn't until later that I discovered his one bad habit. He liked to fight. At the slightest provocation, he attacked, sinking his teeth into any available part of another dog's anatomy, the lower the better. With little or no warning, he tore into dogs twice his size, especially big black ones. Whiskey protected me even when I didn't think I needed protection. He was a terrific guard dog, and, in turn, he kept me on guard as well.

As Bill had predicted, we moved onto our thirty-two-foot-long, fiberglass "stink," or power boat, the *White Ghost*, by 1975. We ridded ourselves of everything considered to be unnecessary baggage. We gave up our cottage, left the Dobermans with friends, gave the goat to a Yugoslavian family (who eventually ate it, I later found out), and with Whiskey for companionship, started out of Perth, heading north along the west coast of Australia.

Les, accompanied by Bill's stepfather, started north in a pickup truck. We intended to rendezvous with them eight hundred miles up country.

At first it was the ultimate in feeling untethered. We cruised into the water with Whiskey, a cassette player, and my tapes of Yes, Neil Young, and classical and John Lee Hooker collections. Surrounding us, except for the coast laced with rocky promontories and snow-white sands to our starboard, were heaving miles of turquoise and sea-green ocean for us to scope out. Whiskey put his nose into the wind and let his silken hair fly.

Boating along the west coast of Australia was not for the cowardly. We were navigating almost a thousand miles of rugged, windswept coastal waters, waters rife with riptides and huge breakers, frothed by storms and churning with eddies. The reef varied from hugging the shoreline, only a matter of feet offshore, to winding more than a mile or two away from the coast. Like an outlying border, it ran the entire length of our planned journey and formed a barrier between the Indian Ocean and waters of Australia's rivers, deep bays, and shoals. It is a rough, windswept, and relatively barren area influenced by the west Australian current and occasionally ferocious storms. There are a myriad of good reasons why so many shipwrecks lay beneath the waves of that coast.

Just as air is less turbulent above cloud layers, waters are usually smoother and deeper outside of a barrier reef. But it was more hazardous for us to ply those waters because of our equipment limitations—we had only one engine and no radio. In outfitting the boat, Bill had purchased the bare essentials, focusing on the equipment needed for retrieving gold. He insisted that we couldn't afford a replacement engine or a radio. When the going was impossibly rough or rock-strewn between the inner banks of the reef and the continent, we took to the ocean on the outer banks of the reef. It was a relief for both of us—a respite from the relentless pounding of the waves—but we had to ignore the fact that if the engine failed, we'd be at the mercy of the tides.

Had I been blessed with as much seafaring experience as Bill, who accepted responsibility for the trip, I probably would have wondered about the dangers inherent in plowing through hundreds of miles of open ocean. I accepted no responsibility for the voyage. As long as the ride was fun and exciting, I was along for it. Had I not been naive, trusting, and a bit intimidated, I might have insisted on a radio. (Haven't we learned an important lesson from Amelia Earhart's fateful 1937 flight in which a neglected radio antenna played a major role? Wasn't it that long, slim, and vital cable that was left behind against the recommendations of the revered and experienced stunt pilot Paul Mantz? Might that have been the magic umbilical cord that changed history, turned her mysterious disappearance into a triumphal success of a round-the-world flight?)

To Bill, a radio was a luxury, but with his basic skill and competence, we navigated outside of the reef during the days and headed to shore to inlets cut between the reef and into the rocky land mass at night. We were chasing after a shipwreck and trying to keep from being one ourselves. As so many other times in my life, I went with the flow, like a leaf in the wind. I put my fate into the hands of another and trusted the *White Ghost*. After the explosion in Santa Barbara, however, I never completely trusted Bill again.

By the time we'd left the States, I'd recognized that troubles brewed beneath our surface civility. Being alone together without respite was hard on our marriage—and our sanity. Bill could be charming when he wanted to be, as could I, but he could also be intense, critical, and demanding. In *his* boat on *his* water, he was the master, and I was the slave. Tension almost drove me crazy. He was the sailor, the boat builder, the Australian in his own land and in his own element. I tried to practice my talent of disassociation, functioning normally but with my mind somewhere else, where it couldn't be controlled by anyone else. I saw no other choice, and, eager to see more of Australia, I literally floated on the sea.

Having sunk most of what little money we had into the *White Ghost*, we existed with one of Bill's favorite vocations and avocations, fishing.

We fished every day. Bill had all sorts of exotic Penn reels and rods, and as we cruised along, his line cruised behind us making its own tiny wake within a wake. We trolled for Spanish mackerel, sailfish, swordfish, and tuna. Occasionally, when we pulled into sheltered bays or coves to anchor for the night, Bill jumped off the boat, disappearing underwater like a fish. He often surfaced with a giant rock lobster for our supper.

I caught many but never could bring myself to kill a fish. I learned how to do everything else that needs to be done to prepare them for cooking. I scaled and definned fish, gutted and filleted fish. I flaked, curried, fried, sautéed, and baked fish. I cleaned and steamed fish and I learned to stir up a dynamite fish chowder. I was a fishmonger, a modern Mollie Malone.

Life on the Indian Ocean filled me with awe. Huge turtles swam past our boat and flying fish and sailfish skipped over the water in turquoise rainbows. We once swam with manta rays when we were quite a ways north. Tidal pools held rare wonders—hermit crabs that were very vulnerable when they outgrew one shell and scurried for another, poisonous blue-ringed octopus, and sea snakes. On the top of the continent, where the influence of the Timor Sea affects the weather and creates a tropical climate, I learned to be careful walking along the shore. Stonefish, whose spikes could inject an excruciatingly painful poison, buried themselves in the sand and were difficult to avoid. I learned to watch for slight depressions and to take care where I stepped. In northern Queensland, the stonefish were joined by another danger, sea wasps. Those huge jellyfish dangled long poisonous tentacles, one spike of which could cause a painful, agonizing death.

The *Ghost* carried us up the coast past Yanchep, Dongara, and Geraldton during the days, and we continued to duck inside the reef each evening to anchor for the night. Getting inside of the reef wasn't a simple process; it took skill. That was one area in which Bill's experience stood him in good stead. He searched for inlets, some tiny and barely visible beyond huge breaking waves. A man in tune with the pulse of the ocean, he chose his spots for penetration and amazed me by finding the right channels for the size and weight of the boat. He held back, the power reduced, waiting for swells to subside, holding off for the perfect moment. Then he pushed the throttle, balls to the wall, and we dashed inside the reef. Nothing was guaranteed. There were times we were stuck in the shallows, missing a groove deep enough for our clearance. The object was to avoid bottoming out or hitting our propeller. Sometimes we were forced to wait for an incoming swell to loosen us from our perch, hoping that the wave wouldn't be strong enough to pound us to smithereens. Crossing the reef always made my heart pump faster.

Civilization as we know it ended after Geraldton, but we pressed on to Kalbari. Shark Bay lay ahead, and its name was no misnomer. I hadn't learned to love diving or snorkeling and the presence of sharks gave me one more reason to stay aboard the boat. We dealt with sharks in California, but they were primarily blue sharks, small and relatively harmless. In Australia, the sharks were for real. Bill had two old scars on his leg from a shark bite. In the waters through which we plowed were hammerheads, great whites, and tiger sharks—all unpredictable, all deadly, all huge aerodynamic creatures that constantly prowled for something to eat. I was convinced they would gobble a human in a minute if given the chance, and it was a common sight to see them gliding alongside the boat. I felt a tense fascination for the sea creatures from my vantage on thin layers of fiberglass that served as our separation and our protection. We saw huge whales and had heard of them tipping over small boats like ours. Little brought into perspective our rightful place in life's scheme better than viewing the grandeur of nature from the highest point on a towering mountain or from a solitary spot in the midst of one of the earth's oceans. I felt like a tiny star in an endless sky or a grain of sand on miles of shore.

From Kalbari to Denham and beyond was the most dangerous part of our trip. We cruised inside the reef in the deep and dark waters that crashed against the Zuytdorp Cliffs, the spray leaping high, then turning to mist and falling back with the flow for another run. Named after the Dutch East Indies ship that was wrecked against the cliffs, the sheer rock face rose majestically from deep under the water to over eight hundred feet in the air. An unforgiving combination of hammering ocean waves and unrelenting granite had crushed the big ship as if it had been a child's toy. We could only imagine what it could do to a small fiberglass boat were the fury of a storm to add to its ferocity. Even Bill was nervous about this stretch of water.

When we left the harbor at Kalbari, someone asked me, "What kind of radio do you have?"

"We have no radio."

"No radio? Are you crazy?"

"We couldn't afford one."

The man from Kalbari shook his head. He probably thought that we couldn't afford to be *without* one! He looked over at Bill and frowned.

"They think that I'm just a girl and that girls know nothing about machines," I thought, and they were right. I knew nothing about machines and I lacked confidence in myself.

The macho attitude wasn't his alone. Bill felt that way, too. That became more apparent every day. In a way, they were right. I had taken the helm and operated the boat, but I had also banged into the dock a couple of times when mooring. Bill made me feel inept. I felt the condescension and recognized that the longer we were in his Australia, the more macho Bill's attitude got. He figured that the galley was my domain.

I turned more and more to my dog, Whiskey, to my cassette player, and to my books for company. I flowed with the days and with the tides. Comfortable in cities of the world, I was learning the comforts of the wilderness.

To earn some money, make some minor repairs to the boat, and to take a break from the jarring, open sea, we anchored in a paradise, Coral Bay, and spent a few weeks. More beautiful than any photograph, Coral Bay's small but deep, turquoise natural harbor was ringed by white sandy dunes. Fishing daily, we sold yellowfin and mackerel to a local store and I made earrings out of beads, coral, and tiny shells, exchanging our earnings for gas and supplies. We met a couple from Queensland—Jill Bricknell and John Paterson, with and their son, Benji—who were camping on the beach. Jill and John became great friends and we stayed in touch.

We chartered our boat a couple of times for fishing trips. I was becoming competent enough to lead a charter when we gave up on putting the boat to that use. Both of us tired quickly of customers who, despite our warnings, paid no attention to us about either the fishing or the intensity of the sun. Northwest Australia has one of the hottest climates in the world—a hot, wet, monsoon-type climate in the summer that is influenced by the trade winds. It was frustrating that customers hired you to take them out fishing, refused to cover their heads or to protect their skin from vicious sunburn, and then complained about it.

Our idyll in Coral Bay ended abruptly the day we left. Stormy weather brought with it huge waves that pounded the reef. Instead of the usual eight-to-ten-foot swells, the surf rose to twenty- or thirty-foot monsters. Bill fired up the engine and pointed the prow toward a channel in the reef. We no sooner started through when he realized he'd made a gross error and miscalculation. An enormous wave came boring straight at us. We were committed to the reef and it was too late to turn back.

Bill screamed, "Hang on!"

We weren't wearing life vests and would undoubtedly have been swallowed by the Indian Ocean had we capsized.

I'll never forget the amazing sensation of feeling my heart stop. Completely.

The wave picked up our boat as if it were an annoying bit of flotsam and we were flung twenty feet into the air, the boat twisting crazily. Then, as if the bottom had dropped out beneath us, we crashed to the surface. Immediately we were sucked up to the crest of the wave, thrown a hundred feet forward, and slapped down onto the surface of the water behind the behemoth. We dropped with a thud on the other side of the reef. We had made it! My hands were raw and bruised, I'd hung on so tightly. Whiskey's tail was tightly between his legs, and his eyes were filled with terror. Ours was a solid little boat, but we were lucky that it landed right side up. If not, I have no doubt that we would have died. Maybe our numbers just weren't ready to be called.

We cruised into Exmouth, our next breather, on the Nor'Cape Peninsula, which is considered to be sacred by Australian Aborigines. The peninsula juts into the Indian Ocean just south of Onslow and creates Exmouth Bay. We put to shore for another extended stay and moved into the Nor'Cape Lodge while we readied the boat for its big journey, the cruise to Monte Bello Island, north and fifty miles offshore. It was there that the wreck of the *Trial* lay lodged in the sand under deep and treacherous water.

Les and Bill's stepfather joined us at Exmouth. Their task had been to bring the airlift, the device created with a Volkswagen engine and designed to suck sand off the ocean floor and uncover the buried wreck. Bill introduced me to another partner, a well-heeled physician or "quack," as they jokingly called them in Australia, who wanted to join the crew. He was excited to be part of the crew, and was able to add some necessary monetary support.

I got sick in Exmouth. The water tank in the *Ghost* held good water, but it was permeated by the taste of fiberglass. In avoiding it, I had consumed more than my share of soda pop during our voyage. My body had become dehydrated and I was suddenly flattened with an excruciating pain. I later learned that a kidney stone had formed, but at the time, I didn't know what had hit me.

Rushed to the hospital, I was treated by a *real* quack. It was a rural hospital and the chief doctor was obviously drunk. Slurring his words, he made off-color comments to me while I lay writhing on the table, begging for a shot to ease the pain.

I finally got my painkiller, and, because I remained in the hospital for a week, a few more as the days went on. Kool-Aid replaced liquid in my body while I endured a bed rest and slowly recuperated.

While I was in the hospital, I had a strange experience. I roomed with an Aborigine girl named Amy and we became friends. She was from far out in the bush and had been flown in to deliver her baby. We talked about ourselves and discussed possible names for the baby. The night that Amy started into labor and was taken to the delivery room, I went into sort of a trance. I'd been off the painkillers they had given me for several days, but I felt my spirit leave my body and I dreamt I was at the U.S. Naval Radar Facility on the cape. I went into the control deck and talked to the captain in charge. I asked him, "Why are you here on Aboriginal land? Don't you know it's sacred territory?"

I didn't wait for an answer, because I then flew into secret caves and was able to read the ancient hieroglyphics on the walls. I saw Amy's baby being born. He was a big fat boy and he was named Daniel, a name that we had not discussed. I awoke out of my trance when I heard the sound of Amy and her crying baby back in my room. She smiled at me, showed me her son, and said, "I have named him Daniel."

Aborigines have a long tradition of dreaming, or what we would call astral-traveling. I think Amy gave me the gift of a little voyage to her world.

I was sorry that we would probably never see each other again once we'd both left the hospital. But I was ready to leave hospitalization behind me. Although the rigorous boat trip had probably taken more out of me than I wanted to admit, I felt much stronger and looked forward to being back on the water.

When the boat was ready, Bill turned to me. "This is where you drop off, Patty."

"*Drop off?* What's that supposed to mean?"

"Three of us are heading for Monte Bello. There isn't room for you to go along."

"Fascinating. You needed me to help build the boat, fiberglass the boat, keep your bed warm, and cook your meals, but suddenly I'm excess baggage?"

"You go on back down to Perth with my dad. I'll catch up with you there."

We argued for a while, but finally I shrugged. My feelings were mixed, but I was admittedly ready for a change. I'd looked forward to the excitement of the adventure and it was enticing to think of actually finding and bringing up gold. Bill's enthusiasm had been contagious, and from all the reports of gold in the water off the coast, it sounded completely plausible. Part of me wanted to be in on the action. Another part recognized that our togetherness was stifling and that Bill had little faith in my competence. I was glad to be away from him.

Men and women, especially when the women are young, are often separated by their differing attitudes, but his condescension was frustrating. And his criticism didn't help my already-shaky self-confidence. He'd shown signs of a superiority complex in Santa Barbara, but the macho Crocodile Dundee attitude was prevalent in Australia and Bill tuned right into it.

I could hear my dad saying, "Patty, you should marry an American man. No one treats his wife better than an American man." It was a generalization, but the words rang in my head.

Sent back to Perth—the captain of the ship prevailed—I took Whiskey with me and we drove back down the long, rutted road with Bill's stepfather, who was a marvel in his calm acceptance of the long and arduous round-trip. One night, two kangaroos leaped into the road directly in front of us. There was nothing we could do; a swerve could have been disastrous. We stopped the car to check on them. We felt bad when we found them both dead. I always loved animals but felt lucky that neither the car, his stepdad, nor I were hurt.

The trek from Exmouth to Perth took several days. We bounced along more than eight hundred miles of corrugated dirt road that drew a crooked line through brush, sand, desert plants, and wide open country that was home to more wildlife than humans. What I had missed in the Nullarbor Plain, I saw in western Australia. In addition to the kangaroos, we watched emus and passed miles of fabulous white sand beaches that were tamed and shaped by a wild surf. While Bill and his two partners took the *Ghost* toward Monte Bello, his stepfather and I bounced along in the car. At the time, I was totally unaware that the opportunity to drive might have actually saved my life.

While I landed a job in Perth as a media assistant with Parkes Clemenger, an advertising agency, I assumed Bill was safely headed for treasure hunting. While I started to make a little money on my own and to develop my own social network, I wondered about how the diving was going. My boss, a woman named Gail, was in the process of divorcing her husband. She and I hit it off and discovered we had a lot in common.

Much later, I heard that Bill—miles away and in his own element—had pulled his boat up to a dock at Onslow, near Dampier, and started loading fuel from forty-four-gallon drums. A flame from a pilot light on the stove in the galley—*my* galley, the location where I would undoubtedly have been standing—ignited the raw fuel. The boat exploded! With a horrendous whooshing blast, air was sucked into the inferno and the *Ghost* erupted in a ball of fire! The three guys were blown in three directions, all of them landing in the water.

As the fire started to spread to the dock, Bill swam to cut the moorings and release the *Ghost*. It floated—still ablaze—to the far shore where, unfortunately, it started a forest fire that burned hundreds of acres of brush. The guys were extremely lucky. They survived with minor injuries but the boat was totally demolished. We lost everything that we owned, including my two precious cameras, a Pentax and a Nikonos, which were on board. It was déjà vu and I knew that it was Bill's debt from the Santa Barbara incident. The *Ghost* was gone.

My marriage, or what was left of it, spiraled up in smoke like that of the second burning boat. It was about time. Bill returned to Perth, but he couldn't get interested in anything. On top of that, he failed to understand that I had emotionally moved on and left him behind. What love we'd had was over.

Bill always wanted to hit big money some easy way, *any* easy way. I didn't like his modus operandi and I became increasingly dissatisfied with our relationship. It was tough to respect him when he floundered around trying to avoid work. I was beginning to gain some confidence in myself and in my ability to make decisions. I held a responsible and paying position and enjoyed my job.

I tried to break away and move out, but he followed me. Although he wasn't abusive, he did slap me once. That was the end.

In desperation, I called my parents, hoping to borrow enough money to make a change, to relocate in Australia. My parents had moved to Alaska, but they were living separately there. They had gotten a divorce and both of them were struggling to make changes in their own lives. My dad said that he would send money only if I returned to the United

States to be with them. That was an unappealing option, so I moved in with a girlfriend for a while.

I knew that Toni was nearing high school graduation and I wanted to see her, but I didn't want to return into the middle of my parents' troubles. That was no solution for any of us. I just wanted enough money to finance a move as far from Perth as possible, perhaps Queensland. I had heard that Queensland was a tropical paradise.

One of my oldest friends from Japan, now Carolyn Schweizer Benjamin, had moved to Australia from Japan and lived in Surfers Paradise on Queensland's Gold Coast. A nurse, Carolyn had married Ian Benjamin and they had a daughter, Tanya Joy. I thought of her as family, as a salvation of sorts, and kept thoughts of her in the back of my mind.

Bill showed up at my door with a really nice motor home, a caravan as it was called in Australia. I wondered where he'd gotten the money to pay for it but didn't ask, remembering that we had talked about getting such a rig and working our way around Australia, a trek made by many young Australians.

Maybe Bill thought we could mend our marriage, that we could actually work things out. As far as I was concerned, trust was gone and it was time for us both to move on. But I went with him. The caravan represented a way out of Perth to me. Although I figured that the two of us could exist together for a while longer, we skirted one another warily like combatants. I kept still, avoiding confrontations. I didn't provoke Bill, and, though we drew battle lines occasionally, we were civil to one another and got along reasonably well.

As we traveled, we found work to keep us in petrol and in food. I became a barmaid, pouring beer for the miners as I had poured Kirin beer in Japan at another time. I also fished and found work as a waitress, and Bill, too, cooked and made a little money as a fisherman. We slowly wound our way around the continent through the Northern Territory to Queensland.

Our life together had high spots between the depths like the swells and eddies of the Timor Sea. Being in such an awe-inspiring part of the world was so momentous to me that our personal problems were no match for it. We traveled thousands of miles in the outback, sometimes creeping slowly and sometimes moving very fast, skimming the ruts to keep our teeth and the caravan's suspension from rattling from their roots.

We ran short of funds in northwest Australia on the Ord River, south of Wyndham on the Timor Sea, in the city of Kununurra. Parking our small caravan to camp just upriver from the Ord River Dam, we landed exceptionally memorable jobs as cooks in Gulliver's Tavern. Our jobs allowed us to fish, primarily for a beautiful white fish called barramundi, then sell our catch to the tavern, and in turn prepare the fish for customers for the lunch and evening meal. The job seemed made for us. Bill loved to fish, I was pretty good at it, and we both did the cooking.

Camping above the Ord River Dam, we knew that we shared the river with the freshwater crocodiles—that it was more their river than ours. Sometimes in the heat of the night, curious crocs swam right up to within inches of me when I lay naked and still in the water for some length of time to cool off. I felt one with the rippling water, a river woman. Despite the terror I felt in the ocean when threatened with drowning, I could have had crocodiles and lizards crawling over me and I wouldn't have minded. The river and subtropical jungle brought out my earth and water elements.

Living and camping in the bush changed my life. I learned a lot about myself and began to learn who I was, where I wanted to be, and how my physical surroundings affect my psyche.

It was a time of soul-searching and I found that giving myself to nature put the rest of my worries into perspective. With larger and more ancient forces in existence, I let myself be guided by them. I tried to turn my life over to the force of magical energy found in life. Jackson Browne's music soothed me and I spent a good deal of time alone, sitting on top of the dam watching the water roll down the concrete slides into the river, wondering what it would be like to go with the flow, all the way to the sea, finally knowing that I wasn't only part of the current but that like the dam, I had some control over my direction.

Once the onset of the rainy season threatened, it became time to move on. Bill insisted that once the rains came, roads would become quagmires of mud and driving out would be impossible. We continued on through the Northern Territory to Katherine Gorge, Devil's Marbles, and across the outback of Queensland into the tropical paradise of the Queensland Coast. Closely resembling the Hawaiian Islands, the region had shores that skirted with cane fields and palm trees, extended long, white sandy fingers ahead of us for miles.

Most Queenslanders that I met were laid-back. Queensland headed the list of alternative lifestyle capitals of Australia. At first laissez-faire attitudes seemed charming and healing, but I had lived with those attitudes long enough. I found that I tired of them. I had had enough of the river woman existence and was looking for something bigger, something more substantial. I didn't want to live on a beach, fishing, cooking, and collecting shells for the rest of my life. I wanted to accomplish something. I wanted to be better educated, to have something about which I could feel pride. I thought of what I'd heard Woody Allen say, that he didn't want to get too mellow or he'd just ripen and rot. I didn't want to rot. I wanted to better myself and I wanted to do it on my own.

After some harsh words, Bill finally left me in Surfers Paradise with Carolyn and went on his own way. Despite everything, I appreciated the fact that had I not met Bill, I may not have discovered Australia. We called it quits in May of 1976 and I never saw him again. As if a weight had dropped from my shoulders, I was relieved to be on my own again, but I had to credit Bill with giving me a wealth of knowledge that I valued and probably had no other way of learning. Our boat building, the lore of the sea, and the exhaustive coverage of the continent was part of my store of knowledge now. Bill was talented and resourceful, clever with his hands. He taught me to respect and care for machinery and engines, to appreciate and react to the subtleties of weather, to follow a navigational chart, and to read the ebbs and flows of water. These were things comparable and opposite to the air that would make me feel alive.

I discovered that the University of Queensland in Brisbane offered something of value for me. I applied for and was hired as an office manager of the psychology department. Carolyn; my new job; a reacquaintance with Jill Bricknell, my old friend from Coral Bay; and making a brand-new start became my salvation. I threw my energies into enjoying Queensland, the university, the support and pleasure of a widening circle of friends, and my work in the psychology department. I learned a lot from the papers that crossed my desk, the words of the professors that I typed, and the students' submissions that I read and organized. As an employee, I was able to enroll in classes and I studied geography and Japanese.

With Whiskey, I was happily on my way. I had choices to make and I faced the world on my own. Jill was wonderful to me, welcoming me for a while into the home she shared with John Paterson and their son, Benji. Another friend, Murray Collins, generously lent me a hundred dollars to buy a bicycle so that I could get between work and home. After I had worked for a while and accumulated some savings, I turned that bicycle, plus a little money to sweeten the deal, into a Honda motorcycle. I rode it for six months before I could afford a car. For a while,

Whiskey and I rode from Brisbane to Surfers every weekend to see Carolyn and to go to the beach. Like a little biker dog, he perched on the fuel tank with his nose sniffing the air.

Eventually I was invited to share a big Queensland house, 44 Dudley Street, with three other people: Vicki, Lenny, and Doug. The house was on stilts and delightfully cool during the hot summer.

Two of my best friends, Americans Art Veno and Jim Gardner, were professors of psychology. I learned a lot from their cool wisdom as I typed papers and tests, prepared work for them, and attended classes. I absorbed information like rich, dry soil absorbs rainwater. As time went on, I toyed briefly with thoughts of medical school, but figured I wouldn't be able to stick with it even if I were accepted.

Our social scene usually gravitated around either Art's house or the house shared by the twins Greg and Donald Hall from Ipswich, Queensland. Another magnet was the country home in which Peter Pamment and his girlfriend, Rosie, lived. When we went out there, Rosie always obliged us and let us watch her churn butter.

One of our roommates, Lenny, was the stage manager for the Queensland Theatre Company, a great connection for free passes. Lenny saw to it that we attended the theater for opening night performances and the parties that followed the performances.

Between September and March—the summer—we found rivers in the mountains for swimming or we went to the beach. Sometimes we snuck into the university pool to skinny-dip to escape the heat of the hottest nights.

I was surrounded by university values and ideas and, predictably, I began to chafe at the rules, the regulations, and the politics of my adopted continent. As the 1960s had brought foment in America with a countercultural movement and times of activism and protest demonstrations, so, too, did the 1970s in Australia. Involvement with the psychology department and the liberal attitudes prevalent in the university encouraged my becoming an outspoken activist supporting the rights of Aborigines. The premier of Queensland was Jo Bjelke Petersen, a reactionary with a lot to lose. An established landowner, he seemed more interested in protecting his vested interests than in protecting the rights of the natives who owned it before him.

My disillusionment was sincere. Personally, I had seen the atrocities being perpetrated against the Aborigines in Australia. It was common knowledge that the Australian system had no respect for the indigenous people, that some people even hunted and shot them for sport. The Aborigines weren't generally allowed into bars or restaurants. Even at Gulliver's Tavern in Kununurra, they were limited to the outside beer garden. Once in a great while, an Abo would dress in his finest clothes, come into the bar, and sit at the counter for a drink, making a stand. When it happened, the mood was electric. I was touched beyond belief by the quiet dignity of such scenes.

I saw Abos beaten by policemen, seemingly without cause, and saw settlements designated for Aborigines that were located in the middle of the desert, far from their native lands. Most were nothing but roadside pit stops that centered around a bar and the town decoration of a pile of beer cans ten feet high.

It seemed to me that the treatment they received was nothing but genocide. It was based on policies that had been established by the Australian government with the first settlements of convicts to arrive from England and Ireland.

With a sincere desire to help the Abos reclaim their native lands and to be treated like human beings, I became part of my new country's protest movement.

My good friends Art; his wife, Liz; and Jim Gardner became increasingly concerned and involved with the social problems of Aborigine rights and the mistreatment of people in mental hospitals, and I sided with them. I wondered if our protests could instill in laid-back Australians some of the fervor with which we had protested perceived wrongs about the Vietnam War in San Francisco. Firmly convinced of the existing inequities, I joined a number of protest gatherings in Brisbane, not always with successful results. Jo Bjelke Petersen had decided that he would make it illegal to march or protest or even to gather in groups in public. Even peaceful demonstrations drew responses from the police. Sometimes they dragged large groups of us off in police wagons. (We usually gave them fake names when they booked us.) They jailed us long enough to cool us off so that we would disperse quietly.

When Art and Liz moved to Zambia and Jim left for South Africa, my peripatetic soul was chafing. I began to wonder where I was headed. I felt as if I had probably spent enough time and energy in rebellion, voicing concerns, and reacting against society. Though I had some really good American friends, I wasn't meeting men in general that I considered as partners. I began to think about leaving. It was not a conscious decision. I didn't say to myself, "I am going to go look for a man in

Australia, in Alaska, in America, in Africa, . . . wherever!" But relationships are important in life and I grew curious once more.

On Christmas Day 1977, my housemate Vicki and I decided to drive her car from Brisbane to the Rainbow Music Festival in Canberra. Having advertised on the university bulletin board for someone to share expenses and help with the driving, we got a reply from a girl who called herself, coincidentally, Rainbow. It never occurred to us to ask, but we later discovered that she had no driver's license and didn't know how to drive. With the bliss of the unknowing, the three of us headed for what we hoped would be a fun weekend. Rainbow was bizarre, even for us. With earrings piercing her nose, she dressed, as did the emperor in his new clothes, in transparent fabrics.

Somewhere on a country road in New South Wales, late at night, Rainbow was at the wheel and I was stretched out on the back seat, dozing and drifting to the sounds of Warren Zevon. Suddenly, Rainbow lost control of the car. The car spun off the road, tumbling end over end and flipping at least three times. It was jolted to a stop upright and pasted onto a huge boulder. We had been churned like some of Rosie's cream into butter.

Thrown around the car, I wondered when I would die and what death would feel like—astral travel of the day. It was almost a peaceful feeling, like I was floating, detached from reality, until I heard Vicki. She suffered from asthma and I could hear her gasping, trying to get some air. Rainbow couldn't talk and I couldn't walk. I crawled out of the back seat, struggling to find Vicki's inhaler for her.

Luckily, we weren't in the distant wilds of the outback. Someone saw our accident and sent for help. An ambulance eventually arrived to deliver us to a small clinic in a nearby town.

One glance at Rainbow threw the doctor and nurses for a loop. Though we hadn't been drinking, they recoiled from us in horror. They treated us as they had sworn to do to the ethical Hippocrates, but they acted as if we were freaks or worse—*hippies!*

Tortured with pain, I lay in bed for three days unable to walk, although they assured me, after seeing X rays, that my back was not broken. Vicki and I were released from the hospital together and our roommate, Lenny, drove up to take us home. It took a while before the pain in my back went away, and it was hard to sit for any length of time. Doing secretarial work was painful and my back gave me trouble for years.

I was beginning to become restless. Art and Liz had moved to Zambia, Jim to South Africa. Life was just going on but nothing new or momentous was happening. I became discontented. The accident was one of the catalysts that shaped my decision to leave Australia. Another was the death of Whiskey, my faithful, good little buddy, my companion on the entire long, strange Australian journey. If Whiskey had sensed me packing for a trip, he would sleep in my suitcase to make certain that he wouldn't be left behind. If I traveled on a bus on which no dogs were allowed, I put him in a basket, covered him, and told him to be quiet, and he never moved a muscle. Whiskey, who shared my cottage, the boat, the caravan, and a string of houses, was my little biker dog. He was the eager one who rode everywhere with me, all six pounds tensed for the joy of motion and the wind in his ears. He was an exceptional dog, but aggressiveness toward other dogs proved to be his downfall.

One evening, someone brought a big black Labrador retriever to our house, and, while we ate indoors, we placed dishes of food for the dogs outside on the back patio. Nearby, a row of bottles filled with brewing homemade beer fermented, more volatile than usual in the hot and sultry evening. Whiskey, who couldn't abide big black dogs anyway, took after the Lab when it stuck its muzzle into Whiskey's dish. With a snarl, Whiskey grabbed onto the big dog's ear.

The dogfight erupted into a dreadful turmoil of flailing legs, snapping, yipping, and a whirl of black and brown spun by rolling, tumbling animals. The angry dogs slammed into some beer bottles, causing one to ricochet into others. Like dominoes, the chain reaction became a litany of violent explosions. Beer splattered and, much worse, shards of glass exploded directly into Whiskey's face. Glass split one of his eyes. I ran outside and cradled Whiskey in my arms.

Sobbing, I dashed into my bedroom to call a good friend, Steve, a third-year veterinary student. He couldn't make much sense of my incoherent babble, but he came right over, concerned and willing to do what he could to help.

Steve was too late. Whiskey died and Steve helped me bury him under a jacaranda tree behind the house. For years afterward, I seemed to hear his little footsteps padding behind me.

Although I had toyed with leaving Australia, I never would have left Whiskey. Strict quarantine laws had kept me in the country; I knew that I couldn't return without Whiskey's having to be quarantined for six months. Now, I had no ties at all. I gave in to my restlessness.

Since having been estranged from my parents, I had seen neither of them nor Toni in the more-than-four years that I had been in Australia. I thought about Toni and worried about her. She was a senior in high school. She had started to learn to fly, so I knew she was doing pretty well by herself, but I also knew that she was living with our dad because of the divorce.

It was June 1978. I had spent far more time elsewhere than in my native land, so I decided that I would take a look and see what it had to offer. I'd saved enough from my salary to afford to leave and I was an independent agent now. I would go see Toni, see how she was getting along, see how my mother and father might have changed over the four years, see Alaska, and then make up my mind where to go and what to do.

My favorite philosopher, Krishnamurti, said that discontent could be suppressed by momentary satisfaction. He continued with the thought that discontent that flowered could destroy that which is not true.

I decided not to let discontent flower any more than it already had.

EIGHT

Fireweed

Old-timers in Alaska insist that they can accurately predict how cold a winter will be by the shape of a wildflower, the fireweed. If its blossom grows tall and thin at the top, winter will be long and hard. If the fireweed blooms with more fullness, winter promises to be warm and wet. It has to do with being in tune with greater forces.

I was a bit out of tune with those forces in 1978 and my discontent traveled with me from Australia to Alaska. I visited my family and redis-covered the conflict of opposites. Why do people stay together long after things are over? I wondered if my parents had been victims of Victorian concepts, shaped by their parents before them and held by the tenets of the church. My mother's mother had been divorced, but like my father's poor hearing, it was never mentioned, never discussed. It was the *D* word. It must have taken a great deal of soul-searching for my parents to resort to divorce.

Interpersonal relationships confounded me. But I think that few fami-lies truly live up to the Rockwellian images of perfection that saturated magazine ads and storybook covers. By contrasting our own lives with those of Rockwell's characters, haven't we often unfairly judged our-selves and those closest to us?

I was mortified to find my mother in the Salvation Army Detox Cen-ter, but at least she was well cared for. Hesitant about visiting either my mother or father after having almost completely severed our bonds, I was only anxious to see Toni, to help her find a place to stay. There had to be some respite for her from the tensions of divorce.

I admired Toni immensely. She had always known exactly who she was and what she wanted to do with her life. I knew that she was going to be simultaneously entering college and taking her flight training—no mean feat. She had been intent on an airline piloting career from a very early age and had been just fourteen years old when she started her pilot training. I admired her dedication and her tenacity, her willingness to work within the system to get what she wanted. She was a tough cookie, but, still, I worried about her.

Dad eventually married a lovely woman named Anna Lies. Toni went off to Anchorage Community College. Toni paid much of her own way and thrived on the flying that she was doing. She had solid goals. It was good to see her directed, headed toward becoming the successful person that she is.

I moved on, too, after my brief tumultuous visit in Anchorage. Through the Alaska Job Service, I found a job in the Alaskan bush, waitressing at the Kuskokwim Inn at Bethel. I had visions of working in a lodge and, when I took the job, imagined that I was headed toward a tiny alpine village, a charming mountain retreat.

The Australian bush was a wilderness, but little prepared me for Bethel. I was adaptable—to the streets or to luxury—but Bethel was a real trip to the wild side! Another Nullarbor, a flat, barren, treeless area, Bethel served about five thousand Yupik Eskimo people from around the large Kuskokwim region of southwest Alaska. Actually, the area wasn't completely barren. One single tree was planted on the road into town with a sign on it: *The Bethel National Forest.* At least the people of Bethel had a sense of humor.

Located about 450 air miles west of Anchorage, 75 air miles south of the Yukon River, and 500 air miles southeast of Russia, Bethel was one of the inland gateways to the Bering Sea. Flattened by the glaciers of earlier eras, Bethel could be navigated throughout the summer almost entirely via the rivers and sloughs—the moving highways—with skiffs and boats. In the winter, travel was by snowmobiles, or "sno gos," the machines that modernized the bush. Until they were introduced, airplanes and dog sleds were people's only means of moving from one village to another.

Waitressing and cooking, good jobs for the young and single, were plentiful during Alaska's summer. Large turnovers existed, so it was easy for me to get a job for a few weeks or months. There were few expectations of long-term commitment and that was fine, too. I had no long-term goals for Alaska. Since the minimum wage was the rule and there were no benefits, waiters and waitresses worked for tips, which were what you made them. Working for tips was the fun part of my job, one of the only things that made it interesting. It forced me to make contact with my customers and to play with the psychology of all kinds of people.

People flocked into Bethel from more than fifty outlying villages for business, for the hospital, to shop, or to kick up their heels and party. No roads ran into Bethel and it boasted only seven miles or so of paved road in town, a ribbon of asphalt that heaved with changes in the permafrost. Bethel was designated as a "dry" town, in which sales of alcohol and bars were illegal. The ban made drinking even more enticing, and, legal or not, Bethel bounced with booze.

The bootleg whiskey business, run primarily by Yugoslavian taxi drivers, kept anyone and everyone in anything they wanted. Alaska's Eskimos and Indians had been introduced to alcohol by white men early in this century. Like those who introduced it, some handled it without a problem and some hadn't developed a tolerance for it nor learned to drink in moderation. It was either "drink to get drunk or don't drink at all" for a lot of people.

It was in Bethel that I was surprised to see marijuana growing in full view in peoples' window gardens. It was explained to me that it was legal in Alaska to grow for your own possession.

Provided with a room in the annex of the Kuskokwim Inn, I started my job, working the two-in-the-afternoon-to-eleven-o'clock shift, which meant I could sleep in and wake up at any time. Whether it was morning or night was sometimes disorienting in the dusk of long Arctic nights.

On the job, it wasn't unusual to see someone enter the restaurant and fall flat on the floor, dead drunk. The first time that happened, I wasn't sure what to do. I learned to call for help from a "dry out," one of the detoxification centers—strange bedfellows to a "dry" town. Surprises gradually became the expected.

I discovered that Bethel was a one-tree, one-road, one-airport, and nothing-much-else-happening town. What little charm it had offered at first was lost pretty quickly. I often watched the single commercial airplane from the window of the Kusko Inn leaving once a day and thought, "*Oh, God, I could be on that!*" But I wasn't sure where I would go. I'd thought of Africa, where Art and Jim had moved, but I didn't know if that would be the answer and it seemed farther away than ever.

I decided to stick it out and save money for whatever my next adventure might be, and Bethel remained my home for the season. Situated at the foot of the Kuskokwim Mountains and at the fingertip of Kuskokwim Bay, Bethel nestled the bank of the Kuskokwim River in Alaska's southwestern corner. Bethel was *ruled* by the Kuskokwim River, which nibbled on the riparian areas, eroding them until buildings tipped and fell off the bank. In an effort to stem the erosion, trashed cars sandbagged the banks, ugly eyesores on the beach, a term that elsewhere would conjure up images of warmth, soft sands, and whispering palms.

Downtown Bethel was etched with a series of boardwalks that spanned nothing but mud. The boardwalks, a necessity because of oozing silt, wound around and across sloughs that emptied into the river.

Bethel was unique and especially appealing in that I survived it. The town never truly grew on me, although I liked the Old West feel of the place, and, as usual, *people* helped me to enjoy that summer. I met Yupik Eskimos and discovered how smart, witty, and resourceful they are. A good-looking people, they have more than a few fine pool players. I made friends with several locals including an Aleut named Joe from the Pribilof Islands. Joe drove a taxi and gave great back rubs to my friends and me.

Treated to my first helicopter ride in Bethel, I went up in a Bell Jet Ranger. When the pilot asked if I wanted to see the tundra, I nodded, "Yes!" He plunked the aircraft down, landing on what felt to be a weird grassy-covered ocean. The pilot explained that the permafrost layer never thawed, so the tundra in summer feels soft and mushy.

I climbed out and bent down to see a fascinating miniature world on the surface. The tundra resembled a little forest; lichens and mosses looked like tiny pine trees and bushes. I would have taken more time to study it, but the infamous and amazing Alaskan mosquitoes swarmed us. We swatted at hundreds of the pests, but it was impossible to swat hard and fast enough. They obviously could drive a person totally insane.

We ran back to the helicopter and the pilot started the rotor blades turning before we even got the doors shut. I learned in one vicious outing why the Alaska Federal Aviation Administration requires that pilots carry one mosquito headnet for each passenger as emergency survival gear during the summer months in Alaska.

My best friend in Bethel, Sandy, was a high-energy blonde who made friends with everyone very easily. She worked at the Kusko with me and helped my summer pass quickly. Sandy told me one day about a guy named Harry who owned an airplane, a Super Cub on floats. He'd invited us to take off a couple of days and go flying with him, upriver.

The escape sounded like fun. I put a few necessities in a backpack and off we went one early morning in August. Harry drove us to Hangar Lake, where his floatplane was anchored in the water, and directed me to the baggage compartment in the aft portion of the airplane. (The Super Cub was a two-seater!) He figured that since I was smaller than Sandy, I could sit on the floor of the airplane. I climbed in, and, when I was all scrunched up—no seat, no seat belt, my backpack wedged tightly behind me—he swung a big jug of wine into my lap.

Sandy scrambled into the rear seat, directly in front of me, and he strapped her in before taking the front seat, going through the start procedures, and getting underway. We headed upriver, flying low, at treetop level. I was all eyes. This was to be my first bird's eye view of my new home.

We cruised past Aniak, Tuluksak, and Kalskag—Yupik Eskimo names for small villages on the river, settlements in which most of the people spoke the native tongue exclusively. Our first stop was in a pond adjacent to a hunting camp owned by a friend of Harry's. We ate with him, then climbed back into the Cub to fly across the tundra. The land became more wooded and rolling, totally devoid of civilization. We started to see wildlife, large birds and shaggy moose. We were miles from *everywhere*, crossing over remote reaches of Alaska between Bethel and Fairbanks—no towns, no settlements, not even a hunter's cabin below.

I couldn't help but compare Alaska to Australia—the *bush* versus the *outback*. Alaska seemed younger, as if the land were renewed every year after the snow and ice melted. Did a brand-new Alaska come into being each and every summer? Did it take an entire summer for the flora to reproduce itself, for miniature trees in the tundra to grow an inch tall, the columbine to bud and flower, and the fireweed to turn various shades of purple and magenta?

From my nook in the rear end of the Cub, I watched the sun roll around the horizon like a ball bearing, knowing it would dip below the horizon for a little while during the night. Having that touch of dusk in the summer and light in the winter helped us to keep our bearings, delineate a twenty-four-hour day.

Harry explained that we were cutting across the tundra from Kalskag to the Yukon and that we would plan an overnight stop in Holy Cross, on the Yukon River. Yelling back over the roar of the engine, Harry told us that his wife was originally from Holy Cross and that he had a lot of friends there. He told us that we could stay at the inn. Once we secured the plane for the night, we had dinner and drinks with Harry's friends and a chance to look around. Like the rest of the villages along the Yukon, Holy Cross was inhabited by about one hundred people, primarily Yupik Eskimos.

The next morning, Harry went to make a telephone call, but he never got access to the village's one phone line. The village leader, who was hopelessly drunk, had locked himself in the village council office—the site of the only telephone—with the key, a bottle of gin, and a gun. We climbed back into the Cub and took off to cruise down the Yukon toward Russian Mission, then to cut across the tundra again to make our way back toward Bethel. By this time, Harry had proven to be an amazing drinker with an astounding tolerance for alcohol. Once airborne, he had turned and called for me to pass the jug of burgundy forward.

I hesitated, looking out of the windows at nothing but wilderness below, but Sandy urged, too. I didn't know all the rules of the air, but I knew it was wrong to mix alcohol and machinery. There were a few lives at stake and, apparently, I was the only one who took that seriously. It seemed like the more Harry drank, the lower he flew. Sandy giggled and Harry flew lower. I guess sometimes you just have to give up any thought of control and go with the flow, no matter how weird the going gets.

Harry saw a bear sow with her cubs and dipped to buzz the huge, muscled, blonde grizzly, scattering her two half-grown cubs. When the plane was near her eye level, she reared up on her hind legs—all nine feet of her—and swatted at us as if we were an annoying fly. Harry laughed. I felt bad, squirming as I watched her lumber off, gathering her cubs, and heading for the brush.

Near noon, we slipped to a landing on a slough next to an empty but stocked hunting cabin and lunched on dried salmon jerky, or "strips," and more wine. When we went to get back into the airplane, it had settled in its parking place and was mired in thick gooey mud. Harry tried to push it into the slough, but it wouldn't budge. I started to get paranoid. I didn't want to spend the night because my experience told me that men, alcohol, and young, single women were a risky mix. I didn't have much trust at that point. I had seen too much.

I pointed Harry toward a big chunk of wood and told Sandy to push on the strut when Harry had the wood wedged under the float. Harry used the wood as a lever and Sandy and I put our shoulders into it. We finally got the plane freed from the mud and into the water. I wanted *out!*

We made it and flew back to Bethel. Ironically, that trip made the summer for me. It demonstrated to me that much of Alaska is a mystery to those who don't fly. The airplane opened up Alaska's beauty to everyone who chose to venture into it. Most of Alaska was impenetrable other than by air. In a few flying hours, miles could be covered that would take weeks by some other transportation, if they could be crossed at all.

By early September, I was chomping at the bit. Alaska's winter was a world away from Australia's tropics. Though I'd never liked the town, I wondered about Anchorage and what opportunities it might hold. As I watched as the Wein Air Alaska aircraft (the *Weiny Bird*) took off each day for Anchor Town (as we called it), I grew more restless. Once again what was meant to be happened or maybe I willed it to be. Hilda, the big, tough German head waitress at the inn, fired me. It boiled down to insubordination. She insisted that I wear a hideous brown polyester uniform and I didn't want to be caught dead in it.

Hilda's decision was timely and just the push I needed toward the airport. After a night of saying good-bye to my favorite people—a few guys who were staying at the inn while they were in town working on construction crews, a pot-smoking state trooper, and a few local Eskimo and Aleut friends—I headed off for my own trip on the Weiny Bird to Anchor Town. As soon as I left, I was casting about for my next step.

I took a break and my father, perhaps trying to make amends, gave me an airline ticket to visit Grandma Antho, who had moved to Florida from New York. My grandma had always helped me put things in perspective and I loved visiting her.

Grandma was a storyteller and she fascinated me with her stories about her life, her travels, my grandfather, and my father when he was a kid. She had a way of focusing on others, making them feel good. She passed on the important gems of wisdom. She called it Grandma's Finishing School, and I was always better for having seen her.

For a while I thought about getting a job and living near her on the beach, but, after having spent a few years in the Australian outback and the wilds of Alaska, Florida was much too mainstream America for me. Before I entered society on a larger scale, I knew I needed time, several years actually, for my soul to heal and regroup.

So, like a yo-yo, back to Alaska I went. I found a tiny apartment in an area of Anchorage called Spenard, an eclectic and funky collection of apartment houses, bars, and massage parlors. Spenard was home, at one time or another, to every person new to Anchorage.

I spent a couple of months scoping out job opportunities, thinking briefly about returning to Australia. But I wanted to move on, to face a different future. Close to becoming one of the ranks of the thousands of young drifters who worked for a while, saved some money, traveled, then worked again, I was wary of repeating the cycle. I've always known that travel is a fantastic education and the best antidote to cultural ignorances because travelers learn wonderful and worthwhile things—geography, culture, differences, similarities. I think that people learn tolerance by getting into someone else's headspace and reality, by looking at life through some else's eyes or from another country. Yet I needed to find something that captured my imagination and gave me something to do and some money that covered expenses.

I was hired to work part-time at the Alaska Department of Fish and Game and thought about taking a seasonal job as a fish counter in Anvik, south of Grayling on the Yukon River. That job was limited to three months and didn't start until the following June, so I kept trolling. Two other job opportunities came along. One was in Barrow, the spot from which many polar flight attempts began, the northernmost town on Point Barrow in the Arctic Ocean.

The other job opportunity was in Dillingham, in the southwest on the Nushagak River. In the Alaska Native Claims Settlement Act (ANCSA) of December 8, 1971, native Alaskans were awarded a settlement of $962.5 million and forty million acres of land. In addition, Alaska was divided into thirteen regions. Each region had its own corporation to administer the money and the land received by the natives. In the Bristol Bay region, the Bristol Bay Native Association, or BBNA, was that nonprofit arm charged with administering state and federal grants and programs. I was offered a job with BBNA.

I accepted the job in Dillingham and landed in my new home, about three hundred miles southwest of Anchorage and only accessible by air in February's cold and icy darkness. The temperatures dropped to −20 degrees the day that I arrived. I wasn't prepared for the outdoors in which

I would be spending so much time. I could get away with lightweight outer clothes in Anchorage, but not out in the bush. My saving grace, the only thing that kept me warm during the winters, was a giant old-fashioned mink coat that wrapped around me almost twice. I thought it was beautiful, but I probably looked like Big Foot wandering around town.

Dillingham proved to be a great town—a vast improvement over Bethel. Located just west of the Aleutian Range and north of the Alaskan Peninsula, Dillingham enjoyed a protected location on a cove of Bristol Bay on the Nushagak River. The town proved to be the new adventure I was looking for. As a melting pot of three thousand very diverse people and a center of the salmon fishing industry during the summertime, it offered a different flavor than Bethel and greater opportunity—in more ways than one.

I met and became friendly with Sue Maddox Flensburg, even roomed with her in her tiny, remote cabin. Like many others in Alaska, Sue also had a sled and a team of dogs and I enjoyed caring for them whenever she was away or out fishing. The dogs stayed tied up most of the time during the summer and were fed slop mixed in huge vats that combined dog food with boiling water. In the winter when the dogs were working, burning more energy and surviving the cold, Sue increased the amount of food and enriched it with fish and whatever animals she trapped, primarily beaver.

When a twelve-by-sixteen-foot cabin became empty—a place that I could call my own—I moved into it in a hurry. Home was a small cottage in the woods with no running water, its bathroom an outhouse at the bottom of the hill, but it was cool. I loved my little place in the trees. There were even a couple of airplane fuselages that the owner had stored out front—harbingers of things to come. I had everything that I needed— a good job; some friends like Dave McClure, Fritz Johnson, Debbie Tennyson, Sue and Michael Allen; my books and music; notebooks; watercolors; and a good pair of boots. I drove a three-wheeler around town and lit my home with thick candles whose flames softened all the edges of the room and flickered with warmth. I became friends with Helen Chythlook, who taught me more of the culture of native Alaskans. I felt very fortunate and content, plus I was making good money and could save for my *next* adventure.

I didn't have a car, but the office of BBNA was only a half-mile walk. I showered there, which solved any minor inconvenience of having no running water. On days that blizzards were so bad that the path to the office was obscured, I happily holed up until the storm subsided. The weather was cold but not nearly as extreme or as dark as above the Arctic Circle. I had heat but no phone. Life was simple, giving me time to read, write, and paint a large mural on my cabin wall.

Having taken a course to become a certified emergency medical technician, I volunteered for the Dillingham Crash Rescue Squad. We wore radio beepers and responded to the firehouse whenever called. People were hurt when they crashed motorcycles and cars on the slippery loose gravel that coated most of the roads. People were often injured in production-line accidents in some of the canneries in town, some of them chopping off fingers during the processing of fish. Some fell off docks. The area was remote and people sometimes died before help could get to them. It was a serious, intense role. With other volunteers, our job was to get accident victims to the hospital, keeping them alive en route. If injuries warranted, an air ambulance flew in from Anchorage to medevac a patient to a larger hospital. Sometimes I drove the ambulance. Sometimes I sat in the back, holding victims' hands, reassuring them. I was good at that.

There was a high burnout rate for rescue squad volunteers and paramedics. The job wasn't easy, but it helped me to clarify the values of life. A few calls were memorable for their tragedy.

On the gentler side, I volunteered at the Dillingham Public Library. That gave me the chance to read to my heart's content about everything from physics to the history of religion. For the first time in my life, I began to feel a sense of community. In a short time, I was offered a promotion and the responsibility of working with the region's twenty-nine villages. This was an opportunity that probably wouldn't have been offered to someone without a college degree in the lower forty-eight. BBNA, as overseer for state and federally funded programs, was designed to offer assistance in remote villages, and, for my part, to direct and organize economic development.

I didn't have a boyfriend and hadn't a serious relationship in the three years since leaving Bill Beck, but I had a lot of friends. I wasn't really looking and the idea of a relationship seemed confining to me. I was taking care of other aspects of my life and happy with the status quo. I was meeting new people, seeing a new part of the world, enjoying my own work and company, and able to see Toni every once in a while on trips to Anchorage.

Then Bob Wagstaff came into my life and rocked my world. I think I fell in love with him before we even met. He had been described to me and I had a strong intuitive feeling that he was going to be important in my life. I took one look at him, and that was it. Fate had gotten us together.

Bob, with his long dark hair and beard and dark Scorpio eyes, seemed to look right into my soul. He was a good conversationalist and a snappy dresser, mixing lumberjack shirts with red suspenders, corduroy pants, and leather boots. He liked fine wine and good food and he piloted his own airplane. He had a love of the wilderness combined with sophistication. Perfect! Bob had moved to Alaska in 1967 directly after having graduated from law school at the University of Kansas. In addition to practicing criminal, divorce, and native law, he practiced Constitutional law, his real love, and argued two cases before the U.S. Supreme Court. In 1974, he argued a case in front of the Alaska Supreme Court that resulted in legalizing the personal use of marijuana in Alaska. A masterful litigator, he was considered to be one of the best lawyers in the state.

We met in J. P. Godfrey's apartment and one of our first conversations was about flying—about flying in Alaska with its moody, unpredictable, vacillating weather.

Bob, whose primary law office was in Anchorage, had a second law office in Dillingham. He flew to Dillingham for his monthly office visit and to spend time with his friend J.P. and our mutual friend, Sue.

Sue included me in the group, and, a month later, when Bob returned for another visit, dinner, and fishing trip with J.P., I invited them over to my cabin. Bob brought along some fish that he had caught, and I impressed them all with some fish recipes that had been my Australian specialties.

Talking with Bob outside on my porch that night, I felt sparks of magnetic energy jumping between us. I knew beyond a doubt that we were destined to be together for a long time.

One of the first times that Bob and I spent together, I flew to Anchorage for the weekend. He picked me up at Anchorage's airport and took me to the Lake Hood Seaplane Base, where we sat in his orange-and-white Cessna 185 on floats, N93033. Having spent so much time listening to my father and flying with him occasionally, even taking the controls, I was able to surprise Bob with some of the things that I knew about airplanes. He accused me of not telling him that I already knew how to fly.

I told him that I'd never learned and explained about my father's and my sister's careers. I said, "Maybe it's my turn."

"What's the matter with right now?" he asked. "I'll get you started."

Bob held his instructor's rating. He smiled at me, and leaned across me to secure my safety belt. Like most single-engined airplanes, his Cessna was equipped with dual controls, so he was able to get me started. "Let's fly," he said, climbing out temporarily to untie the airplane. "Are you comfortable? Can you reach the rudder pedals?"

I nodded and felt in a daze. He hopped into the left seat and fired up the engine.

A shiver played down the middle of my back as he taxied the big airplane out away from the dock, advanced the throttle, and headed across the water like a sleek waterfowl unleashing a spray. We felt the rhythmic slapping of waves that tapped a staccato beat, faster and faster until, suddenly free of the water, we launched into the air and pulled upward. It was joyous, a thrill, and for an instant all of the clutter of my mind was stilled. As fast as the droplets formed on the windshield, they were streaked back by the air that cradled us and lifted us high over the water and trees. Within moments the windshield was dried. Evergreens that had loomed as monstrous giants shrunk in size as the perspective changed from that of a groundling looking up to that of a soaring eagle high above all that he surveyed.

When Bob let me handle the controls, all the searching to that point synthesized in my fingertips. Almost effortlessly, I turned the airplane from the left to the right, banking over the lush valley below and climbing to feel on a par with the height of the distant mountains. I no longer doubted what I wanted to do with my life. In that instant it was revealed. I wanted to fly.

We flew together a lot after that—he, the mentor, and I, the protégée. And what a student I was! I was ecstatic to be turned onto something that gave me a unique perspective, a feeling of accomplishment. I absorbed everything that Bob said and mimicked everything that he did at the controls. I was eager to learn to handle the airplane with the confidence that exuded from him. I enjoyed fishing, sightseeing, and walking on the beach with him after landing on quiet portions of rivers or tiny jewels of mountain lakes. I had a lot of faith in Bob's flying, and when my job sent me to visit distant villages, we both enjoyed the pleasure of navigating to the diverse sites in his seaplane.

Bristol Bay was one of the most culturally diverse regions in Alaska. Villages around Iliamna and Lake Clark were primarily home to Athabascan Indians. In the center of the region, villages were inhabited by Yupik Eskimos. Inupiat Eskimos lived in the northern part of the state and in the Arctic, and, in the southern part, where the Alaskan Peninsula became the Aleutian Chain, villages consisted mainly of people of Aleut descent.

There were few, if any, roads that linked villages, so I had to charter an airplane, or, whenever Bob was available, I chartered him. My job was to meet with members of the village councils and village council leaders. We discussed economic needs, how they'd been met in the past, what was currently required, and what was expected or desired in the future. High on the lists were necessities like boat docks, sewage treatment facilities, and community centers.

Because I had been promoted to economic development planner with BBNA, part of my job was to update a booklet called *The Bristol Bay Region and Its Economic Development*, initially written by Andy Golia, who later became my boss at BBNA. The program intended to correctly assess the necessary economic development of each of the Eskimo, Indian, and Aleut villages and to help them identify and prioritize projects that could later be funded by state or federal funds. In compiling the booklet, I asked, in addition to priorities, that a representative of each village write a poem. This personalized the booklet and added the distinct flavor of the people in addition to the statistics that were required.

My life had taken a dramatic and wonderful turn. I could hardly believe that I was in western Alaska running a program funded by the federal government and charged with the study of dire needs of fascinating groups of people. Mine was the unique chance to delve into the culture of peoples I'd known nothing about but had grown to respect and love, an unparalleled opportunity to get to know Alaska in some depth. I took full advantage of the chance and looked forward to each and every day.

Part of my trust in Bob's flying, too, stemmed from my first trip into the bush for BBNA. Only having been in Dillingham a short time, I was asked to charter a flight to King Salmon, on the Naknek River, as BBNA's representative on a Department of Fish and Wildlife survey trip around the Alaska Peninsula. I booked a flight with one of the local air taxi services, and, strapped into a Cessna 206 with a full load of mail, we took off from Dillingham's hard gravel runway. The pilot, a young guy, headed for King Salmon with an intermediary stop at the village of Portage Creek.

This was in March, breakup season in southwestern Alaska. Days were getting longer and deep accumulations of snow and ice began to melt, a slow, messy melting process; I could see the sogginess of the ground. Dirt creamed into mud and grasses of the tundra poked inquisitive fingers through cracks in its icy white blanket. I didn't yet know how challenging landing on this became for pilots accustomed to short dirt landing strips. This mud had the same pervasive way of clinging to aircraft tires as it did to boots and shoes. Tires coated with congealed mud bogged airplanes down and added drag that was almost impossible to overcome.

Already heavily loaded, we landed at Portage Creek's 1,800-foot dirt strip and picked up a guy, increasing the load some more. Rolling for a second takeoff, it was obvious even to me that we were not going to make it. I braced myself as the pilot slammed on the brakes at the end of the runway and yanked off the throttle. Like a dog that has romped from firm footing onto a sheet of ice, the airplane slewed through the mud. It skidded as if scrambling to keep a precarious balance, sailed off an embankment, and rose up onto its nose. Momentum carried it almost upside down, and there it stopped, poised in an inverted position over the ground.

Like the others, I braced myself, unbelted, and crawled out of the plane. All three of us stood there in disbelief for a moment, then our knees started rattling like old bones. The pilot slithered away like a lizard and disappeared.

In stark contrast, Bob, who loved flying, was a careful pilot and very competent. He seemed to fully enjoy his every moment in the air. Though his ex-wives didn't enjoy flying, I was eager to share this love.

When his schedule permitted, we flew between Dillingham and my outlying villages. We wanted to be together and he also saw this as a great chance to do more bush flying. Without a doubt, flying with Bob was far safer than flying with chartered pilots I didn't know and about whose flight capabilities I had no idea.

One of the first villages to which we flew was the Eskimo village of Ekwok, on the Nushagak River. It was springtime; the tundra was changing from white to green, and villagers were preparing their fish racks for the summer fishing season. Bob and I combined business and pleasure, learning to fly and getting to know each other. I felt more alive than I had ever felt in my life. Things were coming together for me. For a change, I had a clear vision of who I was and where I wanted to be, even though I didn't know or care where it would lead.

On each of our flights, Bob taught me important lessons—everything that would help me to stay alive. He gave me Wolfgang Langewiesche's *Stick and Rudder*, a book that was written in the 1940s, has educated thousands of pilots, and will last into the future as a classic.

I looked upon my opportunity as a most generous gift. I deeply appreciated the incredible chance and took to it as a duck to water. Like the view through a camera lens, my life started to come into focus. I was taken into the air and I was taken by the air. Flying opened a door into a whole new world. It made incredible sense.

Writer Diane Ackerman learned to fly, and, in her book *On Extended Wings*, she wrote eloquently of flying as a cure for the fidgeting of the will. In flying she found release from the human condition and a temporary and valuable removal from small things to put them into perspective.

I took to the air and temporarily could not differentiate between lupine and fireweed, yet could bring closer an entire scene of tundra, rivers, mountains, and moose. I wished everyone could fly. I wished everyone could fly in Alaska. Fully alive with my opportunities, I soared into the sea above me. With fire as my power, I journeyed into my element, the air.

Krishnamurti was so right when he suggested that our own selves embody the world. He urged listeners to discover the key to those inner selves and to understand that the key is within our own grasp, and ours alone.

NINE

Alyeska

Alyeska, the native name for Alaska, became increasingly more a part of me, inexorably tied in my mind to flying. Aviation, Bob's pleasure for a quarter of a century, my sister's and my father's chosen career field, and the source of my Uncle Jack Combs's success in wartime, transformed my life and became my own magic carpet. Flying is a turn-on. It's a matter of dynamics—the mastery of a machine and of three-dimensional elements in which not everyone feels comfortable at first. But when it has been mastered, *that* is the thrill!

I'd been surrounded with the sights and sounds of airplanes since infancy. When Bob and I first climbed into his seaplane, I felt at home. Flying was what I had wished for, what made sense to me. The cockpit was a comfortable place to be and it was intoxicating, better than anything else I had ever tried—*anything!* It demanded focus and intensity. When I was in the air, everything else paled in comparison.

I could sense a bit of tension in Bob the first few times that he let me take the controls for takeoff and landing. The Cessna 185 floatplane, powerful with its 300-horsepower Continental engine, was tricky for a new flight student; but he was a good instructor. He knew that I would never learn if I weren't given a chance to use all of my senses—to have hands-on training, to use my feet in sync with my hands and to be able to feel the controls, to hear the engine sounds, and to see the visual cues internal to the cockpit and in the glorious realm of the sky. As I gained a little proficiency, I increasingly developed more of a spatial awareness. Out of the corner of my eye, I saw Bob and sensed some of his feelings. I could tell that he was attuned to the airplane during a takeoff roll, his every sense alert. I saw the beginnings of a smile, a twinkle in his eyes, each time he firewalled the throttle, thrusting it forward to demand all of the power the engine could produce.

I loved speed and I loved the thrill of sailing across the water, picking up momentum, and feeling the chop of the waves relayed to my fingers through the control yoke. I loved feeling the last clutching moment as the pontoons shook free from the grip of the water, the tension of the surface, and then the dramatic smoothness as we climbed into the air. We streaked into the sky, water droplets slicing back on the engine cowl, their tracks parallel to the flight path we swathed in the air. It was all I could do not to laugh out loud. Never had I known such a clear feeling of excitement.

"I love this!" I said to Bob, delighting in the mastery of the machine. "And I love Alaska! Look out there! The glacier is almost turquoise. God, this scenery is fantastic—in every direction! It's—*uh oh*."

The engine's drone dropped to a whisper. The big airplane seemed to claw for its place in the sky. Its nose dropped and I fought the weight of the yoke. Bob had pulled the throttle to idle. He said, his voice terse, steady, and instructive, "Check your airspeed. Fly the airplane. Get the nose down and level your wings."

"What's happening?"

"We're simulating an emergency. You were getting too carried away and were forgetting something."

"What was I forgetting?"

"To pay attention. You weren't concentrating. When you fly an airplane, you have to be able to divide your attention. Enjoy that scenery all you want, but don't get so wrapped up in it that you forget you are piloting an airplane. Distraction has killed too many, and you're not going to be one of them if I have anything to say about it. Remember, you could lose the engine at any time or have a hundred other incidents crop up. You have to respect that. You have to be aware."

I took to the opportunity to fly with a passion. Like inscrutable pieces of a jigsaw puzzle coming together into a whole beautiful scene, pieces of my life's experience were blending. For one long instant, I suddenly sensed direction, although I wasn't sure yet where the direction would lead.

Bob must have known that he was giving me a precious gift. I wonder if he knew he was giving me much more. In teaching me to fly, Bob gave me the chance to develop a talent and he gave me an opportunity to focus my life, a chance to corral and direct my wild and free-floating energies, and the chance to gain self-confidence in my competence and abilities. I could see from the first flight that flying added true meaning to my life. It was something at which I could be myself and at which I could excel. This was key.

Ever since I was a kid, I always had the feeling that I had to hide some essential part of myself, that I could never truly show the real me. I was either too rambunctious or too shy, or was (shame on me) just having too much fun. The magic of flying was that I could be good and I didn't have to maintain an exterior to please others around me. I could be wholly myself. Simply a pilot, I had no reason to make excuses to anyone for anything. I could be good at it and still be myself and was due respect simply for my abilities. It was a good fit. I had a new passion . . . or two.

Flying gave me a new attitude. My basic strength of character had seen me through rough times, but my self-confidence and self-esteem had been on shaky ground. In confrontations, I tended to agree with people rather than argue and tended to run away from an unpleasant situation—to become the escape artist. I had no good sense of worth, until I flew.

There was a lot to learn, but that was part of aviation's mystique and part of its joy. I knew next to nothing about engines, not even what a cylinder was. I discovered that every flight varied from the last, and, if I was smart, I learned something new upon which to build. There was no room for complacency, no room for dreaming. Aviation was the great equalizer. It mattered not who I was, rich or poor, male or female; there was equality at the yoke in the cockpit.

Bob was patient. He searched for repeated opportunities to help me achieve self-esteem and a sense of accomplishment. Instead of being restless and rudderless, I conformed to being harnessed in seat belts and shoulder straps that connected me to the big seaplane. It was thrilling and I felt excitingly alive.

My first logbook entry, "June 29, 1979, Cessna 185/A, Registration Number 93033, Introductory Flight," was signed "Robert Wagstaff, Certificated Flight Instructor, Instrument Rated (CFII) #1691209."

Bob's instructor certificate, issued for two-year periods, was due to expire in December 1980. We had a year and a half before he had to renew. I hoped that maybe by then, I would be a licensed pilot, too.

I could hardly wait for each new lesson, each new flight, each chance to be with Bob. He made it challenging. He made it fun and we had a ball. He taught me straight and level flight, to turn, climb, descend, properly trim the controls, and preflight the seaplane. He taught me to navigate, to take off and land on the water, and to plan and execute cross-country flights. He challenged me and he praised me when I did well. It was great!

Bob was anxious for me to share his love for Alaska and his enthusiasm was contagious. From him I learned that flying was the only way to truly *see* the majestic peaks and valleys, the rivers and beaches, the woods, the wildlife, and to take in Alaska's fresh and awesome scenery.

Every chance we got, we explored Alaska from the air. We flew over Cook Inlet, formed by the ocean and the Matanuska River. We flew to the Arctic, Bettles, Kotzebue, and the Brooks Range, where we checked out the oil pipeline and glacier lakes. In the course of learning to fly in the Alaskan bush, we navigated, landed, camped, fished for salmon and arctic char, and watched big fish return up the rivers during their spawning runs.

As our relationship deepened and we recognized the direction it was going, Bob helped take care of one legal step facing me—a bit of unfinished business. I had married Bill Beck on June 16, 1973. I had left him in 1976 and left Australia in 1978. But our marriage bonds had never been severed officially. The divorce decree was issued in Anchorage on October 17, 1979. It was, if only technically, another of my life chapters coming to a complete close.

As that door shut, another opened. Aviation, with all of its various challenges and joys, pointed my life in new and positive directions. Bob and I took to the Alaskan skies and together we explored my new home. There aren't too many places on earth where pilots can soar amidst majestic scenery, be awestruck at the grandeur. Surely no other place treats one's senses to overwhelming beauty while on chart after chart of landing sites, lists such warnings as "Runway condition not monitored," "No snow removal on runway," "Ski-equipped aircraft only," or "Moose activity."

I never saw a sign that warned, "Bears." Those demanded constant vigilance.

Bob taught me a lot about the art of living in the wilderness in and around the airplane. Although I had some experience with bears during my stays in Bethel and Dillingham, I wasn't fully aware of how seriously bears had to be taken.

One warm summer afternoon, we had flown to one of our favorite river haunts, tied down the seaplane, and gone for a walk. "Bears can be very unpredictable," Bob said abruptly and in a firm but quiet voice. He had broken a companionable silence.

"Bears? What made you say that?"

Bob pointed to the long trail ahead of us, tracks in the sand that led parallel to the water and stretched all the way toward the airplane up ahead. A bear, not in any particular hurry, had lumbered along the beach. I knew enough not to regard bears as cute, little, furry, fun creatures. I also knew better than to panic. The bear tracks went straight past the airplane as if the animal had ambled by without stopping to sniff it. We had heard of airplanes being ripped open by hungry bears that had gotten the whiff of picnic food in the baggage compartment.

"I think he's gone," Bob said, lowering his voice. "Let's keep going. Get into the plane and fire up."

We stepped up the pace and I followed his directions. I climbed into the pilot's seat to get the airplane started as he pushed it off the bar. Once in the plane, I realized that I had been staring at the brush, expecting a bear to come crashing out toward us, ready to rip us to shreds. I felt curious as much as I felt the rush of adrenaline. I pushed, pulled, and twisted through the engine start procedures while Bob shoved us off the soft sand and out into the deeper water. He vaulted onto the right pontoon and climbed into the seat beside me. "Let's go," he said.

So many articles and media pieces tend to portray bears as adorable little "teddies." In Alaska, no one appreciated the television show *Grizzly Adams* and the relationship between a man and his gentle "pet" bear. It set a dangerous precedent among non-Alaskans for a state that thrived on the tourist trade. I watched people make a fuss over wild baby animals and wanted to say, "If you're traveling in Alaska, you'd better learn right out that these guys aren't cute. If a bear gets as close as the deck of your home, you will be lucky to live to tell about it. Summer cabins on the north slope have huge spikes protruding through the walls from inside. Hungry bears have been known to rip the cabins apart. You don't fool with them."

Every year people were mauled and killed by bears. The guy who replaced me in my job in Dillingham was eaten by a bear on a river trip near Katmai National Monument. It was never determined whether he was eaten by the bear before or after he died, but they found his remains amid his raked and scattered belongings.

Bears are *very* unpredictable and we saw them *everywhere*. A shotgun had to be kept handy and even that wouldn't always stop them. When camping, we resorted to tricks. Our biggest "trick" was an automatic weapon—a Heckler & Koch 91—that we erected on a tripod near our campsites. I also learned from my Eskimo friend, Andy Golia, that guys sometimes walked the perimeter of the campsite peeing to establish the human scent as a warning, a device to keep bears from coming too close. That was less easily accomplished by women but could be done.

Camped on an island in a lake on the south slope of the Brooks Range, we had chosen the location in hopes that it would be as bear proof as possible. Just before dawn, we heard a noise. We were groggy with sleep and fuzzy from the 151-proof rum we'd consumed the night before, and, instead of grabbing the gun close by, we leaped to our feet, jumping out of the tent. An *enormous* blonde grizzly bear, nine or ten feet tall, stood a few feet from us, staring at us with huge round eyes. His size was magnificent and his power was awesome, *fantastic*. For what seemed like an eternity, he tensed. We stood rooted to our places, staring, not feeling fear but stiffened with the same raw reaction of the bear. For seemingly no reason, he whirled and jumped into the lake. A beautiful swimmer, he sliced away from us, leaving ripples in his wake. We both trembled with the realization that we were extremely lucky. It could easily have ended another way.

Alaska was a tough place to work and play and it attracted tough and earthy people. In Alaska's frontier melting pot, you'd find a Texas redneck oil worker sitting at the bar next to a long-haired musician, and Eskimos mixing with yuppies. A solidarity in people was brought on by the harsh climate and the demands on existence. Alaskans pride themselves in thinking that the weenies don't make it, and they don't.

If you flew, you had to be prepared to survive. Anyone who crash-landed in a small plane in Alaska and survived had to be prepared to walk out of the bush, even when flying close to Anchorage. From the city it was only a matter of minutes after takeoff until you'd be in the wilderness of the Chugach Mountains or over the tidal Cook Inlet. If the airplane was not float-equipped, chance of survival in the frigid water of the inlet was nil.

My logbook became my diary and I started to fill its spaces with magical flights to places with lyrical names—Iliamna Lake, Kodiak, Aleknagik, Kenai, Whitehorse, Susitna Valley, Denali and Katmai National Parks, and Talkeetna. Names themselves evoked images but better still were the incredible views of an unforgettable wilderness that blended the browns, greens, and blues of land, vegetation, and water. Although we flew from still, reflective waters, we cruised by cascading, frothing, churning, flowing water; we saw creeks embroidered with ice, whitecaps lapping at blue-green glaciers, and towering icebergs. We flew below the crest of the terminal of glaciers, looking up the icefall in Prince William Sound. We saw seals and sea otters playing on drifting floes. Odors of fish and seaweed seeped into the enclosed airplane cockpit, and the smell of alder and the screeching sounds of terns and seagulls pierced the silence after we had splashed to a landing and shut down. In their own element were moose, elk, and bear, white-crested bald eagles, brown golden eagles, and fields of wildflowers with shaggy white bear grass, red-hot pokers of Indian paintbrush, fireweed, and purple mountain lupine. From the Klondike to the Yukon, Bob's airplane gave us wings and bird's-eye views of picturesque nature and of life at its wildest.

I started living in tune to weather systems for the first time in my life. Bob taught me that the first thing a pilot does upon waking in the morning is to check the sky—for wind direction and speed and for the shape, color, and height of clouds and the stories they forecasted and told. I watched, especially, for changes from the previous day's weather. Wherever we went, he reinforced my weather knowledge with explanations, pointing out, for example, lens-shaped lenticular clouds and describing what they meant in the way of strong, high-altitude winds and possible roll clouds and turbulence on the lee sides of the mountains that they capped.

He insisted, "In Alaska, changes come quickly and often."

I learned to respect the airplane and its limits and learned a lot about mine.

During the winter, an hour's worth of sightseeing was generally an all-day proposition. There were virtually no hangars for airplanes; most were tied down outside all year long. To fly, we went to the airport early in the morning to preheat the engine using a Red Devil heater. While that thawed the power plant, we tackled the deicing of the airplane. Bob and I shared the job of pulling off the bright red wing and windshield covers, shaking the snow and ice from them. Then, with big brooms, we brushed snow and ice from the control surfaces and the fuselage, the body of the airplane. With sharp plastic credit cards we scraped any exposed window surfaces that were covered in ice. Only after approximately two hours, with the engine preheated and the oil warmed, did we remove the engine cover and check the quantity of the oil. Then the plane was ready to be untied from its tie-downs. Bob said, "You don't fly in the winter if you are in any kind of hurry."

Sometimes it was glare ice on the taxiways that made taxiing to the runway tricky, especially if the wind was blowing. Other times, it happened that after spending two hours getting the plane ready for flight, an ice fog rolled in and canceled flying for the day. You learned patience and acceptance, or drove yourself crazy.

As I learned to respect other people, I gained respect for myself. Flying in Alaska taught me more about man and his machines as well as the grandeur and the potential fury of nature than any textbook. Confidence came concomitantly with mastering the challenges. Those were some of the gifts I received, and, through new application of perseverance and determination, some of the responsibilities I began to accept.

Bob guided me. We talked about flying and he referred me to his library of books, which he encouraged me to read. A conscientious pilot, he gave me a good start with solid fundamentals and good judgment upon which to build. But the time came when Bob suggested that I switch to flying a small land plane to continue my flight training. I decided to find an instructor in Dillingham.

Bob offered me the gift of a private license. He said, "I really want to give you something. It's obvious that you really like flying. You have a talent for it and I think you're serious about it. It's my turn to give a return on my investment in aviation."

Generosity has always been a trait I admire. Bob lived this philosophy and I was the lucky recipient of his creed. He said, "I really believe that aviation is something to which you have to give back because aviation gives you so much." I've never forgotten that.

To switch to land planes, I looked for teachers in Dillingham, bush pilots who had flight experiences that honed their talents and reputations with proven safety records. They offered unorthodox training sessions, equally as intent in teaching me to survive in Alaska as to teaching me to master the intricacies of flying. I took lessons and accrued flight hours with instructors like Phil Bingham, an experienced bush pilot who owned an air taxi service. Instead of S turns along a road, a classic student pilot exercise in wind drift control and control coordination, he taught me by flying low, right down on the deck, turning to stay directly above narrow, winding rivers and creeks. Instead of weaving back and forth in sharp turns over a straight road, I wove a snaky, sinewy trail over the circuitous waters below. Instead of Chandelles and Lazy Eights, classic commercial coordination exercises, [1] we flew into the foothills of the mountains and closely followed the contours of the terrain, dramatically climbing, diving, and turning while also keeping a lookout for wolves. I had more than my share of luck, but I also always sought out the best teachers.

I kept my job with BBNA for a while, but my priorities changed dramatically. Instead of commuting to and from Anchorage to see Bob and to fly at Merrill Field, I finally quit and moved into Bob's house. He and his son Ian lived deep in the woods in the beautiful mountain valley of Indian, twenty miles east of Anchorage on the upslope of the Chugach Mountains. Bob's land was on five acres of prime Alaskan real estate and dotted with a variety of evergreens and wildflowers, devil's claw, and columbine. A glance out of the window treated us to a rare view of the waters of Turnagain Arm and the Kenai Mountains, of ever changing weather and cloud formations, breezes that caused the tallest of trees to bend gracefully, and eagles and owls perched high in their branches. It was a fairy tale, an enchanted valley.

Alaska's highways in the sky took the place of a network of roads and was essential to delivering mail and supplies to most of the villages for services, emergencies, search and rescue missions, routine surveillance—the list went on. Aviation was the lifeline between villages and between Alaska and Canada and the lower forty-eight states.

Alaska allowed pilots who had already obtained their private pilot certificates to take advantage of a student loan program to pursue commercial ratings and beyond as graduate students. That policy made all the difference to me. I discovered that, just as I could have accessed the federal Veterans Administration program that contributed to flight

---

[1] Please see Appendix 1 for descriptions of all aerobatic maneuvers.

training and careers in aviation had I served with the military, I could arrange financial assistance toward advanced piloting ratings.

Bob and I talked it over. I determined that I could borrow up to seven thousand dollars a year to pay for any training that followed the private license. At forty-five dollars per hour and a requirement for more than two hundred hours to obtain the commercial license, the loan wouldn't cover the cost but would certainly offset the total. I assumed that I would amass about four hundred flight hours before I had earned all of my licenses and ratings. That would escalate my costs to between seventeen and twenty thousand dollars. But that amount would be offset by my acting as a flight instructor and being hired—and paid—for as many of those hours as I could arrange.

It was ironic that I was applying for a student loan. For someone who had found little pleasure in being a student, I almost felt like a fraud. On the other hand, I loved to learn and was now hungry for knowledge that would give direction to my life. I dove eagerly into the opportunities that were available. As I accrued licenses and ratings, I could become a flight instructor and start being paid to fly, an enticing idea. The rules were such that once the loans were repaid, 10 percent of the total amount was reduced for every year that I remained in Alaska, up to a total of 50 percent. Designed to encourage pilots and piloting in a state that required aerial transportation, the policy ensured a cadre of skilled pilots for the aviation industry. From a personal standpoint, it seemed too good a deal to pass up.

Bob agreed. He said, "Take advantage of opportunities when they are available."

I started, slowing only for Alaska's winter weather. With the coming of the time of short days and long, cold nights—an uncommonly beautiful time in Alaska—flying sessions dropped to few and far between. I remained at home with Ian, who was less than delighted with my presence, almost every day. His mother, Nikki, and two brothers were out of the state, so he undoubtedly felt challenged by my arrival in his and his dad's home. We stayed out of each other's way, warily seeking a sort of truce. Generally, I escaped into aviation books.

When I had arrived in Alaska two years earlier, I had no plans to stay. I saw it as a temporary stop on my way to new adventures, but as the winter of 1980 thawed into spring, I logged my flight time and kept close track of the data that marked my path toward licensed pilot. I flew a Cherokee 180, a Cessna 150, a Cessna 152, and then a Beech B-19

Sundowner—all land planes. My instructor, Brian Aklin, signed me off and I took off to fly an airplane all by myself for the first time. I soloed the Sundowner on March 27, 1980.

I exulted, as everyone has who has piloted an airplane alone since Orville and Wilbur. I remember thinking, "Wow! I can't believe they let me do this! I can't believe I'm up here by myself!"

I knew that I still had a great deal to learn, but I handled that airplane all by myself. I judged when I had reached the proper altitude and when I was the proper distance from the airport—not too close, not too far— and it was up to me to put the wheels gently onto the tarmac, keeping the airplane aligned with the centerline. It was as if I were placing twelve or fifteen hundred pounds down on a runway made up entirely of eggs. I flared, held the nose up, and said aloud, "Hold it off. Don't let it touch. Hold it off," until the wings gradually released their lift and let the aircraft transform from a flying machine to a ground vehicle. It was magical. I was euphoric.

I took off and landed three times—a good landing on the first touchdown might have been considered a fluke! After having made three good landings, I knew it was no fluke. I felt a sense of accomplishment that had never been mine before. There were many other pilots before me, but not everyone in the world can handle an aircraft well. Not everyone in the world had done what I had just accomplished. It felt unique and it felt great!

Everyone who flies recalls their first solo and now I was one with them. It was a thrill to take the bird around alone and then to start logging the time in my own hand as Patty Beck, Patty R. Beck, Rosalie Beck. As I logged my name in various ways in my book, I was experimenting with who I was and who I wanted to be. In order to be licensed as a pilot, my first solo led directly toward the private license, and that was but a building block to adding an instrument rating and then reaching for the commercial ticket and on to flight instructor.

There were several reasons for throwing my energies into flying. Indian was a spectacularly beautiful place, but I never felt completely at home there. I had moved into the house that Bob and Nikki had built and, even though she'd chosen to leave and move to Hawaii, it was hard to adjust to what had been her home. I suppose the fact that I had shown up in what had been Ian's domain instantly made me the ogre; it was a challenge to live with Ian, a 5½-year-old at the time. Bob's and my ideas of discipline toward Ian differed, and since Bob worked outside of the home, we spent disparate lengths of time with him. I had little experience with kids, and though I tried to fill in as best I could for his mother, that was an impossible mission. When Bob failed to make Ian behave, I found the situation impossibly frustrating. It put knots in my stomach. I didn't feel it was my place to be the bad guy.

There weren't many neighbors, but I got to be friends with Doug Drum, who owned Indian Valley Meats and specialized in canned and preserved reindeer meat. I joined Ted Wall, a professional florist who lived down the road with his wife Sue, in a gardening project for a while. Other neighbors were Alice and Dennis Stacey and their son, Thor. The Staceys built and lived in a cabin on a mining claim that Bob leased on Indian Creek. Dennis paid annual rent to Bob in gold dust.

It wasn't all perfume and roses. Some weren't overly thrilled to see me show up on the scene. A lot of Nikki's friends remained in the area, especially in Bird Creek, the next valley, where she had run a small co-op health food store with several others. I felt as if they considered me a bit of an interloper. Because of the flying, I generally had more in common with men than with women and sometimes that was perceived as a problem.

When Bob was enmeshed in a trial, I spent my time at Merrill Field, the general aviation field in downtown Anchorage, pursuing my advanced ratings. I found a home away from home. I also found a good flight instructor, a previous client of Bob's, Dean Kurtz, at Wilbur's Flight Operations on the east ramp. Dean and I flew in a Piper Cherokee, practicing maneuvers and emergency landings.

One day I called to schedule a flight with him, and there was silence on the telephone. Ann Wilbur came to the phone and told me gently, "Dean was killed. He was flying around Denali. It was a honeymoon flight for two Japanese couples that wanted to see Mount McKinley."

I could barely think straight.

It had evidently been a clear day and he was circling just below the rim of a box canyon. It must have been clear air turbulence that smashed his Cessna 206 against the wall. McKinley makes its own weather.

Bob and Dean were buddies, two who shared a love for aviation, dark rum, and dark-haired women. Bob had purchased a Cessna 180 from Dean and had kept three instruments from Dean's plane to put into the 185 floatplane. They included a radar altimeter, a sensitive device used to measure height above the ground. On the day Dean was killed, Bob was flying locally in his 185 when, inexplicably, all three of Dean's old instruments quit. They just stopped working. Bob tried to troubleshoot the problem but found nothing wrong with the electrical system.

After landing, Bob had the instruments checked out by an expert at a local avionics shop, but they couldn't find any problems, either. Then he heard about Dean. He needed no explanation. Dean was the first of a long list of friends I've lost in aviation. I cried when he died.

When I wasn't flying, I got into the earth-mother mode in Indian—my fantasy. I tended the garden, fixed elaborate meals with homemade breads and soups, wrote poetry, and read books. I raised birds, geese, chickens, ducks, and the occasional turkey and guinea fowl. I studied herbs and made herbal potions and remedies as gifts for friends. I ordered fowl from Stromberg's Mail Order in Iowa, and it was always exciting to see what arrived in the mail, like the geese that became our guard dogs, especially valuable for chasing strangers from the bridge that crossed the creek and linked with the path to the house. Chickens kept us in fresh eggs. In the winter, infrared lights warmed them in their coop and I fed them dried stinging nettle to encourage my hens to lay. Sometimes hawks, wolverines, or stray dogs threatened to massacre my birds, but I would call Doug who raised birds himself and whose crack shot helped us take care of the renegade of the moment.

A rural existence sounds idyllic and looks pastoral, but looks can be deceiving. A ton of work was always required, and as much as I enjoyed my own company, I also enjoyed being around friends; I grew lonely in Indian. Bob rarely took a day off and when he did we spent it flying. When I was home, I was either alone or with Ian, who wasn't interested in talking to me. Once I spent a week alone while Bob was away on a business trip and Ian was in Hawaii with his mother. As a test, I challenged myself to not speak to a single soul. What started out as peaceful ended with me talking aloud, almost desperate for some sound of humanity. By then I realized that I had organized the bookshelf for the umpteenth time and a loneliness-inspired lethargy began.

As my love of flying increased, household chores became more mundane and less appealing. I began to tire of domesticity. It had held my fancy for a while, but now that I'd experienced it, I knew that it was not going to satisfy me for a lifetime.

Flying, on the other hand, was scintillating enough for two lifetimes. I finished my flight lessons in Anchorage, passing my private pilot written and flight tests. Officially I became a pilot on September 10, 1980, the day before my birthday. Bob and I celebrated.

I obtained my seaplane rating and added it to the private ticket in August, 1981. Then I studied, tested for, and added the instrument rating in November 1982, although, right from the start, I knew that flying in instrument weather conditions—a steady, droning, constant, wings-level chore—was not going to be the ultimate for me.

For the first time in my life, I didn't look for an escape whenever training went a bit sour. I didn't run away when things didn't go as planned. I was hooked into a program, committed to flying, and cognizant of the organized schedule that was before me. I found something worthwhile, a place I belonged. I became increasingly determined to not only succeed but excel. Besides, flying in Alaska without an instrument rating, which gives you the ability to maintain control of an airplane when you cannot see the ground, was almost like skydiving without a parachute. When the weather deteriorated, as it often did, a pilot without the capability of flying solely by reference to the instruments had to land or press on into a situation that might quickly become more than a person could handle.

I became an airport regular, flying constantly and finally finding something that was worth the discipline I had never before required of myself. If I hadn't the future envisioned before me, I knew where it took me every day. I was comfortable at Merrill Field, where most of the non-commercial general aviation operations took place. I liked the energy level of the other pilots and I liked hanging out there. I literally flew through the years, not sure of my goals, but that seemed unimportant.

I found the right flight instructor to help me finish my ratings—Tom Robinson, a nice, friendly, laid-back guy who didn't believe in the old-fashioned military approach of yelling at me in the cockpit, like some of my other instructors. Tom and I got along just fine.

By the spring of 1984, Bob was sufficiently comfortable with the way I flew the big Cessna floatplane to give me a set of keys. Before we put it on floats for the summer, I took off toward the west to pick up my old friend Sue Maddox Flensburg in Dillingham. We intended to fly around southwest Alaska, and, once airborne and out in some of the more remote areas, we caused a fuss everywhere we went. Even in Alaska, where almost everyone is involved with flying and piloting, we discovered that the sight of two women in a big Cessna tail dragger was a big deal.

We'd hear, "I've seen one woman in a 185, but never two."

"It's tricky flying out there. Sure you can handle it?"

"Are you sure you know what you are doing?"

Those making comments weren't being snide. They were right. It *was* tricky. There weren't many airports. Fuel had to be properly planned. And the weather could be as unpredictable as a bear. Cold fronts moved rapidly, ceilings dropped, or winds picked up in no time at all.

On the very first day, I was trying to get the two of us from Dillingham over to Bethel. It wasn't as simple as it sounded. Instead of following the Nushagak River down to the coast and over to the Kuskokwim River to Bethel, I decided to fly directly in order to arrive by evening. But our flight was hampered by inclement weather. Cloud ceilings hung over our heads like huge drapes curtaining the stage. We couldn't pick up navigational radio aids, and, as the weather deteriorated, I managed to get completely lost in a series of canyons and valleys west of the Wood River–Tikchik Lake system, north of Togiak.

I flew into what I thought was a valley that would lead me out of the lake system and into the flatness of the tundra, but it turned into one of the great challenges of mountain flying—a box canyon! With deteriorating visibility, low ceilings, and a psychological desire of not admitting I was lost, I was lucky that I was familiar with the airplane. As the ground around us pressed in on us, I reacted almost instinctively and executed a turnaround maneuver that was a bit wild but flipped us up, over, and turned us around. Whatever it was, the maneuver saved our skins.

It was lucky I could even see the opening of the canyon when I turned around, the visibility was getting so bad. I thought, "Hell, I still don't know where I am. I can't even breathe a sigh of relief!" But I said nothing. I didn't want to worry Sue.

The weather had deteriorated and the ceilings had lowered so much that when I flew out of the canyon and saw a long valley stretched ahead of me running north to south, I figured I had two options. I could either land in the tundra like an idiot, embarrass myself and become a traitor to my gender, or I could climb out of it on instruments. I thought, "This is nuts. People get killed doing stupid things like this. Oh, God!"

Sue sat there, her trust in me implicit in her face. I looked over at her every once in a while and smiled. But inwardly I was making promises to God that I didn't know if I could keep.

Even though I had my instrument rating, I had little actual experience flying solo and relying only on the instruments. Bob was always such a fabulous instrument pilot that he generally did the flying when we were in instrument conditions. During my instrument training, I used to fall asleep under the hood, the eyeshades used as instructional devices and designed to keep eyes in the cockpit scanning the dials. More than once my instrument instructor had to wake me up. I even drifted off to sleep with the drone of the engine when Bob asked me to fly as safety pilot for him while he was practicing instrument approaches to stay current. I loved being in the air, but I preferred to skim the trees or a river. I liked the blurring speed, the wild mixes of colors, odors, and sounds, the sensory input that gives me such a charge.

I glanced at Sue and felt a rush of heat course through my body. I knew I was responsible for her and wished that I knew where we were. How high are the mountains? How far away are we from them? My mind raced with such questions.

I clawed for altitude like a swimmer claws for the surface, almost instinctively holding my breath. For an instant I was back in inky waters and Bill Beck's boat was about to explode. I didn't think we were going to run into a mountain, but I could *not* exactly pinpoint our position. I just knew we had to keep climbing to get above the highest peaks, and I hoped we were still in that long valley somewhere north of Togiak.

Roughly one hundred miles out of Dillingham, we had climbed to about 11,000 feet, which was, according to my chart, plenty of altitude to get us over the tops of the highest mountains, and I headed east, the general direction of Dillingham. I glanced outside of the cockpit.

"Ice!" I couldn't help myself. I said it out loud. Crystals of ice were building on the leading edges of the airplane and were very visible on the left tire. Fear clutched my abdomen and I could feel the tension creep along my shoulders and up into the nape of my neck.

The part of me that had been well trained came through. I could almost feel myself steel and do what I had to do. No other pilot was in the airplane with me. Like it or not, I was pilot in command and whether we lived or died was totally up to me.

I kept talking to myself in my head, not wanting to give off any bad vibes to Sue. "No, just keep on climbing. You'll be fine. You'll break out any minute now. Turn on the pilot heat so that you don't lose your airspeed indicator. Keep your speed up, the wings level." I glanced over and Sue was as calm as she could be. That's when I knew I could do it because I had her trust. She had faith in me. Sometimes that's all it takes in life to survive, one person who believes in you. Sue and I weren't going to be statistics if I could help it!

A glance outside told me that the ice situation had stabilized. That is, it didn't get much worse, but it didn't get a lot better either. I tried a couple of different altitudes, but we were still in the clouds up to 11,500 and 12,000 feet, and, because of the proximity and height of the tops of the mountains, I didn't dare descend to get into warmer conditions where the ice might melt. I just kept flying the airplane.

Every now and then, we had a break in the clouds and I caught a short glimpse of a jagged mountain peak. I sweated.

Headed in the general direction of Dillingham, I finally got close enough to pick up the signal from a radio navigational aid. Although she said nothing, I am sure that my feeling of relief was palpable to Sue. Tuning the navaid, I finally got my bearings and turned to fly directly to Dillingham. I discovered that we were about sixty miles west-north-west—and headed home!

Like a miracle, Dillingham was the only place around that wasn't socked in with fog and low clouds. I felt my guardian angels working that day. We landed without incident and tied down the airplane. I saw a couple of guys I knew on the ramp, Dave Bogart and Phil Bingham, and Dave asked why we weren't in Bethel.

I answered as nonchalantly as I could that the weather had come down and we came back on instruments. Then I turned to Sue. "Let's go get a drink!" It was the first time, I think, that I ever felt like I *needed* a drink. We tossed down two drinks at the Sea Inn bar and made up our minds to depart again the next day, taking the longer way around the coast.

I also needed to sort a few things out. I was beginning a phase in my life in which there were no outer limits, nothing to stop me from accomplishing something. But what!? I loved flying, but I couldn't help thinking, "What now?"

Bob wanted to buy a small Cessna, a tail dragger, for us. He said, "Well, you can work on your commercial license. You could fly around Alaska. There's plenty to see that we haven't explored."

"Build time?" I asked. "For what? I can't really afford to fly around all the time, and how many times can I fly to Wasilla for lunch?"

He added, "I told you before. You don't know where these things are going to lead. If you have an opportunity, go with it."

That was a great lesson. I took his words to heart.

Amelia Earhart once stated that women are challenged to try things just as men have. She acknowledged, too, that if there is failure, it should be taken as a challenge to others. I had no intention of failing. Besides, women in aviation can't afford to fail like men can. There are fewer and they are under so much more professional scrutiny.

Had I not been in Alaska, my life would have been very different. It's an interesting mind game to play. Alaska is a rugged, diverse, and widespread country and population. And its waterways and airways are not only helpful lifelines for the people of the state but requisites for life. Who could deny the value of rivers and the boats that plied them? Who could have a taste of visiting the remote reaches of Alaska, as I did with my job with the Bristol Bay Native Association, without appreciating the value of aviation? Certainly the officials of the state government valued its importance. I've often heard that one out of every five people in Alaska has a pilot's license. Flying is not considered as frivolous as it tends to be considered by officials in the lower forty-eight. Airplane noise is welcome in Alaska, its importance recognized by all who stand to profit from it—those rushed to hospitals, those found lost and disoriented, or those who need speed for their travel, their cargo, or their mail.

There were innumerable role models in the Alaskan sky before me. Now that I had joined them, what was I going to do with my newfound passion?

TEN

Axes

I have always loved speed—fast cars, running horses, and spinning around crazily on carnival rides, as fast as a machine could go, as blurring a sensation as possible. I remember the ninth birthday party of a friend with whom I'd grown up in Japan, Debbie Corroone. Her mom took a group of us to an amusement park in Tokyo. Debbie said later, "There were no regulations, and the amusement park go-carts could be revved up to really fast speeds. My mom got us all squared away with go-carts, and the next thing she knew, Patty was speeding around the track, going way too fast and zooming past everybody. My mom almost had a heart attack."[1]

For someone so enthralled with the fast lane, thoughts of buying a tail dragger or any other small, single-engined plane for flying from point A to point B failed to inspire. I told Bob, "I think what I really want to do is to fly aerobatics. I pestered my dad when I was little with, 'Tell me what it's like to do a loop' and he shrugged it off as 'No big deal.'" Bob smiled. "More than anything, I've wanted to try it for myself. I think that I might love doing aerobatics."

It was 1982. I was as current as a pilot could be, flying several times a week and accruing precious hours of experience, but I had no sure goals.

---

[1] Corroone, Debra, personal letter, 1996.

I had no ambition to be an airline pilot, my father's and sister's domain, and I couldn't picture being a flight instructor forever.

I'd never been to an air show or even seen aerobatics flown, but one day I purchased a copy of the International Aerobatic Club's (IAC) magazine *Sport Aerobatics*. It wasn't long before I began to subscribe to it.

Bob told me that he'd heard about a flight instructor in Anchorage named Darlene Dubay, who offered instruction in aerobatics in a 150-horsepower Bellanca Decathlon. He suggested that I take the introductory course in aerobatics and see how I liked it. He generously offered to make a gift of the ten-hour course with Darlene.

Outwardly, I was confident and eager. Inwardly, I had some doubts. I wondered about my aptitude for aerobatics. I looked forward to it so eagerly that I knew it would be a big disappointment to find that I couldn't take it physically or that I didn't have a talent for it. I didn't want it to be anything less than perfect.

It isn't unusual for pilots facing their first flight in aerobatic training to hope that the flight instructor will be impressed. A first-timer is generally a bit uptight—*not* over the idea of pushing the airplane through all three axes of movement, but because most pilots want to hear, at the completion of an instructed flight, flattering approval or something like, "Wow, you're a natural."

That rarely happens.

Some aerobatic instructors, too, are guilty of wanting to impress students with their own talents. Some, accustomed to tumbling through the air in every conceivable attitude relative to the horizon, take fiendish delight in showing off and frightening the wits out of students who would, if treated a bit more gently, learn to become avid aerobatics enthusiasts.

I couldn't wait to start boring holes in the skies over the green-sloped hills of the Chugach. Darlene Dubay was a patient and competent instructor, low-key and easy to get along with. Throughout my training, she saw to it that I knew where we were going and what we were going to do. She instilled an easy confidence. At each lesson, as we walked around her red Decathlon, preflighting it, she explained some of the things we would be doing.

My logbook showed that Darlene and I first flew together on June 14, 1982, in her 150-horsepower, red Decathlon registered as 8592. This first lesson was a revelation. It was delicious, better than I hoped it would be. I was ecstatic! We did loops, rolls, spins, and, though I was disoriented and spending most of my time trying to relocate my position relative to the horizon, I loved my first real taste of aerobatics.

"I don't need to tell you that's a loop, do I?" Darlene asked at one point, with a smile. "You try it. Remember what we talked about on the ground. Keep your wings level on the climb. Don't be hesitant in initiating the climb or you'll lose speed on the top."

After about forty minutes Darlene said that our time was up and that we should return to the field. I felt great—a little lightheaded, perhaps—but I didn't want to come in for a landing at all.

I loved my lessons with Darlene. Words can't describe the aerial arcs we painted in the sky. Nothing prepared me for the joy. The actuality of soaring high above Anchorage, tumbling, twirling, and spinning was like the most lighthearted of dances. As I heard the engine build up to a lion's roar in the dive, then soften to a purr as the nose of the airplane was pulled up toward the vertical and over the top, the earth below rolling back to a level position from behind, I laughed out loud. I felt completely happy.

For ten hours we dove eagerly into wingovers, aileron rolls, two-point rolls, spins, slow rolls, Hammerhead turns, and the turn-around maneuvers—Cuban Eights, Chandelles, and Immelmanns. The slow roll was the hardest maneuver for me to master because it required the most coordination. As I rolled the wings to knife edge, to inverted, then back to knife edge before getting back upright, I had to hold the nose on the same point of the horizon all the way around. There was a lot of stick and rudder work necessary to make that happen, especially in a Decathlon, which rolled rather slowly.

I learned there was more to aerobatics than just knowing how to do a loop and a roll. Since the earliest days of aerobatics, pilots have sought to be precise in executing every aerobatic maneuver, how to perfect it and where to look on the horizon to make perfection possible. To do a loop, for example, I would start the pull, making sure not to pull too hard, or a stalled wing might dissipate speed and energy for the arc that needed to be drawn. Nor could I pull too gently, or energy would be inadequate to crest the top of the loop, again possibly resulting in stalled wings and an inadvertent spin.

Was it simple? No! My keeping reference to the ground *and* monitoring the airspeed was complicated in turn by my taking care not to pull too many Gs, forces equal to the acceleration of gravity, in order to avoid overstressing the airframe. It was essential, too, to keep speed from developing on the backside of the loop so as not to go over redline in order to avoid exceeding the speed capabilities of the airplane.

The first time I did a loop, I took the controls, glancing outside and clearing the area for traffic. My senses were in harmony with the environment, my heart pounding in rhythm with the engine. I loved it! Up and over we went. It wasn't perfect, but it wasn't a disaster. I mean, I didn't stall out on the top, or dish out, or fail to complete a loop of sorts. We did a second loop for the fun of it.

"Let's do a spin to the right," Darlene said, after we had climbed back to altitude again. The buildings of Anchorage sprawled toward the lower hills and I could see the cerulean blue of Lake Hood with floatplanes circling to splash down at the seaplane base. Some of the distant mountains, their peaks crested with snow and softened by clouds, were forested with a hazy green and tinged with smoky blue, blending with the water and with the sky.

"We'll lose between 600 and 1,000 feet of altitude in a spin," Darlene said. "Let me demonstrate one, then it will be your airplane." She was cool. I could feel her confidence flow my way. "This time we're looking for a full stall."

She eased the airplane away from the ground, following the curved upward line of the distant mountain. With the control yoke fully back, she pulled the power to idle, waited momentarily for the airplane wings to stall, then applied hard, full right rudder. She grinned at me as the ground, the water, the hills, the trees, and the houses twirled into a corkscrew in the windshield. We spun until she briskly stopped the turn, broke the stall with forward elevator, and brought the nose to level flight again.

"Like that?" she asked.

"It's great!"

"Now you try it."

Although fun was a large part of my quest, confidence, consistency, and capability in *any* airplane were my goals. Darlene wanted me to feel comfortable through every axis of the airplane's movement and about my ability to control it. Not only did I gain reassurance in my own abilities to master something so challenging, but I gained overall confidence in my abilities as a pilot. I knew I would be much more in tune with *any* airplane I flew from then on.

During my lessons with Darlene, I realized more acutely than I had before that the air is my element. Immersed in dizzying spins, rolls, loops, stalls—every conceivable realm of rotating, revolving, turning, rushing flight—I felt as if I had found something for which I had long been searching. I found myself strengthened in the process.

Darlene concentrated on the essence of each maneuver without delving too deeply into the technicalities of aerodynamics. We started out mildly and quickly moved to the extreme, one maneuver built upon the previous, and she gradually allowed me to become master of the airplane. She would demonstrate a maneuver, then I would try it. After a few hours of lessons we started putting series of maneuvers together. Darlene was interested in and taught competition, precision aerobatics, as opposed to just flopping around, and she knew the size of an aerobatic box, a specifically sized bit of airspace in the sky. When she flew me through the actual size of a box, I laughed. "That postage stamp? What a joke! You expect me to do a series of maneuvers within that?!"

Darlene and I had fun together. With her guidance I explored the Decathlon's envelope and put the little airplane through all of the maneuvers for which it was certificated and an unauthorized Tail Slide to boot. Although aerobatics had an "out-of-control" uncertainty to it, it *could* be controlled. Being able to fly an airplane in *any* attitude added a whole new dimension to flying.

One day, out flying aerobatics near the Chugach, we pulled up into a Hammerhead—a vertical stalling turn. The plane stopped. I pushed right rudder, shoving the stick to the left. At the same time, Darlene pushed left rudder and the stick to the right. In the blink of an eye, we had canceled each other's efforts and the plane parked itself in the air vertically and shuddered before sliding a long way backwards. Then it flipped over.

When I asked Darlene what maneuver we had just flown, she answered, "I think we just did a Tail Slide, Patty."

Tail Slides are not one of the approved maneuvers in a Decathlon. The tail surfaces are not guaranteed to be strong enough to withstand forces that might occur. We laughed aloud. We wouldn't do it again purposely, but we were both glad to have inadvertently been through it.

After my course was over, I returned to fly with Darlene occasionally during the rest of the summer. Her critiques were valuable and further instruction helped to hone my precision. We added Reverse Cuban Eights, inverted turns, and worked on my favorites, the snap rolls—the quickest, wildest of the maneuvers.

I continued to fly with Tom Robinson, took flight tests with examiner Al Mowry, and focused on my advanced certificates and ratings. Tom and I practiced all the maneuvers that a plain vanilla Cessna 172 could handle: Chandelles, Lazy Eights, stalls, and spins.

Bush flying—a way of life in Alaska—was my introduction and, to teach well, I wanted to become better at it. I asked one of Bob's favorite people and flight instructors, Alden Williams, to work with me on bush flying techniques. Alden, a legend in Alaska and the consummate bush pilot, flew DeHavilland Otters all over the state when they were one of the few planes that Wein Air Alaska operated. Alden personifies the famous statement: "There are old pilots and there are bold pilots, but there are no old, bold pilots!"

I loved flying with Alden. He taught me how to slip the airplane, a glorious cross-controlled maneuver that is almost like skimming sideways down a kid's slide, to a spot landing. Slipping the airplane is a great technique for cross-wind landing conditions; I found that for visibility purposes, I almost always slipped to land.

Alden even taught me a few things when we weren't flying together. Once, when I was flying with a student at Anchorage International Airport in a training plane, a Cessna 150, the tower controller cleared us for an immediate takeoff. I taxied onto the runway and pushed the throttle in. Just as the plane departed the runway, I saw a pair of tires and a full set of rivets! Another small plane was descending right on top of us! It took a second or two to register exactly what was happening, but when I did, I slid the airplane off to the right and continued on.

I radioed the tower and said, "Did you see what just happened?"

My question was met with silence from the controller until he said something like, "Cleared to the west."

A few days later I saw Alden at Merrill Field. I told him how indignant I was about the incident. "The tower obviously made a huge mistake by clearing me onto the runway as another plane was cleared to land!"

Alden said, "Well, I guess you both made a mistake."

"What do you mean? They cleared us both."

He said, "But *you* didn't look."

From then on, I learned to keep my eyes open and, when I do, I think of Alden.

During the midwinter cold and long hours of darkness with much of the flying slowed, I studied and passed my written aviation tests, a requirement for taking a flight test for each certificate or rating. During midwinter, Bob and I headed south so that he, too, could take advantage of Alaska's student loan program. Bob decided to add both a DC-3 type rating and a Citation jet rating to his certificates. In 1983, we flew to Dallas, Texas, and he enrolled in a Citation jet type rating course. As an aviation lawyer—one of the aspects of his law career—he felt that added type ratings would provide additional knowledge.

While Bob mastered the Cessna business jet, I commuted between Dallas and Fort Worth to take aerobatic flight training with one of the masters of aerobatics, Duane Cole.

Duane had been an exhibition pilot and instructor since 1939, the founder of the famous Cole Brothers Air Show, and twice National Aerobatic Champion. Duane possessed such a wealth of knowledge that he forgot more about flying than most people will ever learn in a lifetime. Long a familiar face in both competition and air show aerobatics, Duane amassed an incredible list of pilots that he had introduced to aerobatic flight and others that he coached.

Duane worked with me on spins, Immelmanns, Hammerheads, Cuban Eights, knife-edge flight, and Reverse Cuban Eights. He put me through all of the rolls a body could stand. I was being taught by one of the best.

Duane said about me, "I knew right away that she was one of those naturals."

I loved hearing it, but I never believed it was true. I was just up there flailing around like everyone else.

But I had the chance of a lifetime. I listened to Duane carefully, watching how he handled the controls so confidently and, when he talked to me after flying, I hung on every word. I was in awe. Duane flew with me in Bellanca Decathlon 5066 Uniform. He was a patient, seasoned master of aerobatic instruction. I had to pinch myself to believe how lucky I was to fly with him. I appreciated all the help that he gave me.

Throughout the year, I flew as a safety pilot for Bob for hours and miles of instrument flight. I earned my commercial license and my multiengine rating and topped it off by becoming a Certificated Flight

Instructor (CFI). This legitimized everything that I had been doing—all the hours I was flying and all the experience I was amassing. I immediately ordered business cards, my first. I was a professional pilot and I was truly proud.

I spent the late winter and early spring of 1983 teaching student pilots and learning from the experience at the same time. My flying improved as well, as Duane had predicted. Duane believed that any flight instructor truly begins to learn to fly after he or she starts to teach others. By analyzing the errors of students and demonstrating correct procedures, a flight instructor's own talents are challenged and honed.

Jack Nielsen, or "Smilin' Jack" as my dad called him, a longtime Alaska fixture and quite a colorful character, gave me my first flying job as a CFI. Captain Jack, a JAL pilot I had known since I was a kid, had operated a couple of aerobatic flight schools in Alaska before I moved there. Later, after 1984, when I owned my first aerobatic airplane, he flew with me and was the first person to show me rolling 360-degree turns and outside maneuvers.

At Jack's flight school at Merrill Field, he utilized the Piper Tomahawk trainer. It wasn't my training mount of choice, but it did the job. Jack turned me loose with students.

Jack leased planes from a nearby school, one infamous for its relaxed attitudes toward proper maintenance. As we were landing in one of the little Pipers with a student one day, our wheels no sooner touched the tarmac when the right gear collapsed, skewing the airplane sideways and dipping the right wing dangerously close to the ground.

We didn't do a ground loop, a crazy circling, wing-dipping action of turning end for end during a landing roll and for which tail draggers seem to show a propensity when mishandled by the nut at the wheel. We also didn't wreck, so I took over for the student and taxied gingerly to the hangar. A bolt that should have been changed had sheared in the landing gear, and it was a miracle that we weren't in a tangled heap of metal at the edge of the runway.

My second instructing job was at Bob Blake's Alaska Air Academy, also at Merrill Field. Bob's school took full advantage of the Alaska Student Loan Program and invited students to deposit their entire checks into the school bank account in return for deeply discounted flying hours. Everyone wondered how they could operate so cheaply. The answer became apparent. I showed up early one morning to fly with a student and the doors to the school were boarded up and plastered with signs. Apparently the smooth-talking Mr. Blake disappeared with the entire bank account, with not so much as a thought of the poor suckers who had given him their money.

After that, I freelanced for a while, getting my own little contingent of students. I specialized in bush techniques and tail dragger checkouts in planes like student-owned Cubs and Piper Pacers. I flew in airplanes that were unfamiliar to me in situations that were not of my choosing and discovered that when thrown into a situation where I *had* to perform, I could rise to the occasion.

I entered a Carl Ben Eielson Air Race, named for the famed pilot from Hatton, North Dakota, who pioneered bush flight in Alaska. An efficiency race with first prize going to the pilots who had the best time and most accurate fuel-burn estimate, I flew with an old friend of Bob's, a lawyer from California named Bill Pinkus, in his Cessna 170. By the time I flew to Fairbanks, raced from Fairbanks to McGrath, and returned to Fairbanks, I had topped 375 flight hours in my log and truly recognized the self-confidence that flying made possible. I discovered that I was good at navigating and estimating our fuel burn—with little help from instrumentation. We came in third, feeling a bit cheated by the bells and whistles of the higher-tech planes flown by some competitors.

With each passing day, I was accomplishing something, learning something new. My flying, competing in air races, and giving instruction to others formed a strong basis for my overcoming most of my "Shit! Don't they know I'm just a hippie?" fears. I took aerobatic lessons, flew aerobatics solo, bored holes in the sky with Bob, and flew with student after student. With each of them, I urged that they consider taking the ten-hour aerobatic course, convinced that it would make them better pilots.

My father and his wife, Anna Lies, invited us over to dinner a few times and I discovered the fun of occasionally flying with my dad in light planes, a novelty to a 747 driver. Our relationship was on the mend.

By 1983, the student loan program helped me to acquire all of the important licenses and ratings: commercial, instrument, multiengine, seaplane, and Certificated Flight and Instrument Instructor (CFII). One more that I wanted—the helicopter rating—eluded me. My one helicopter flight in Bethel had stayed with me; I had been intrigued with helicopters ever since. Bob, who had already been working on his helicopter rating in an older Bell 47-G at Wilbur's Flight Operations, had raved about a gifted and fabulous instructor, Joe Wilbur. I asked Joe to teach me to fly helicopters. The day that I was to solo on the helicopter, snow covered the ground and the air was shivery, wintry cold. Before he turned me loose, Joe got out of the helicopter and brought over a case of oil, which he strapped into the seat he vacated to compensate for lateral weight and balance. He said, his words punctuated by his breaths of air that streamed from his mouth, "Just take it around the patch a couple of times, then land."

I'll never forget soloing in the Bell 47, its rotors beating the still air in a staccato rhythm, twirling snow into a delicate white storm around us as if we were inside a glass ornamental ball and we'd just been shaken. In awe, I felt as I had with my first airplane solo—"Wow, I can't believe someone would trust me enough to let me do this!"

Once having soloed, I flew the Bell alone out of Anchorage or to the mud flats by Cook Inlet. I wrote my initials in the snow with the helicopter skids, kicking the snow up above the rotor blades. Sometimes I landed in a confined area in a stand of tall pines only to see a big bull moose staring straight back at me, his head high as his nostrils flared. Unfortunately, the student loan money ran out before I completed the training and my helicopter rating was put on hold.

In the summer of 1983, in a momentous, life-altering event, Bob took me to my first air show, the Abbotsford air show in British Columbia. I looked forward eagerly to seeing my first air show, but, as usual, I carried no expectations with me and I wasn't disappointed. I was blown away! It was huge! Abbotsford, one of the hottest air shows in North America, featured some of the best air show pilots in the world. Bobby Bishop flying his Coors Light Silver Bullet BD-5 Jet, Jimmy Franklin flying his Waco Mystery Ship with Johnny Kazian walking his wing, and Bud Granley flying the famous P-51 *Miss America* were just some of the outstanding acts. A J-3 Cub comedy act—the pilot pretending to be a drunk farmer—had me fooled for a while. Military demonstrations and war bird flybys thundered past and, even when parked as so-called static displays, the airplanes perched on the ground like creatures of the endless sky that were temporarily chained to the turf and chafed to be released.

From behind the spectator barricade, I carefully watched performers preparing their planes and instantly knew that I was on the wrong side of the fence. Just as I had felt as a kid at the circus, when I'd wanted to jump into the ring with the horses and be a bareback rider, I felt an incredible sense of frustration not to be in there with them. I didn't want to be a spectator; I wanted to be a part of their lifestyle, their scene.

As if my first air show wasn't enough, we flew to see our first aerobatic competition—the IAC Championships in Fond du Lac, Wisconsin. I knew a little, having only read about contests in the club magazine. Again, I had no preconceived ideas about what should be flown or how it should look, but as I watched I knew I was seeing true skill and artistry in the sky. Contest flying thrilled me. It was beautiful to watch and I instantly knew that I, too, could compete.

As winter weather thawed into the spring of 1984, Bob and I bought my first aerobatic airplane, a new (to us) Champion Bellanca Decathlon, 1118 Echo. With a 180-horsepower engine, my beautiful Decathlon was painted a patriotic red, white, and blue. More than just a transportation vehicle, it was designed for aerobatics, built with great strength to withstand the loads that are imposed in higher G flight. The day it was delivered to Merrill Field in Anchorage, I drove out to see it and felt tears of joy burn my eyes to see it perched on the ramp waiting just for me. I could scarcely believe it. I was amazed that Bob had faith in me that justified giving me such a glorious gift.

My first flight in 1118E was logged on March 3, 1984.

Flying aerobatics in my own airplane, I spent the spring of 1984 with a narrowed focus, something new and exciting for me. I also saw more of my father. Dad had built a house in Rabbit Creek, just outside of Anchorage, and moved into it with Anna Lies. Anna, an intelligent and understanding woman, had become a great influence on my father and a good friend to my sister and to me. Dad's temper had lost some of its rage and his drinking became more social and less self-destructive. He had retired from Japan Airlines in 1983 and on his last flight, Bob, our friend Steve Conn, and I flew our Baron outside of Anchorage to meet him. We followed Dad in, videotaping his last landing at Anchorage International Airport in a Boeing 747.

Dad asked me to fly with him a few times as he made the transition to light planes. We flew in a Tomahawk, a Seminole, and a Cessna twin. His first—but *only* his first—landing was funny. He tried to flare a two-place Piper for a landing when we were still about 50 feet off the ground. In flying the big stuff for so many years, the habit was with him. Despite never having flown anything that small, after the one mistake, he had it down.

I decided he'd had enough "recurrency" training when I had to wrestle the stick from him in order to fly the plane myself. "Okay, Dad, I got it. It's my airplane!"

I took him up in the Decathlon a couple of times and we did some rolls and loops, but I think he always felt more comfortable as PIC— pilot-in-command.

I also flew with my sister, Toni, as often as we could arrange it before she took a flying job in California. When I completed my instrument instructor rating, Toni wrote in my log: "To a super pilot and fellow av-8-trix. Love, your CFI sister, Antonia Combs."

Life was falling into place for all of us.

It was obvious that I was hooked, but after having bought the Decathlon, I asked Bob, "Now that we have this airplane, what do you expect of me? What would you like to see happen?" Bob was supportive, knowing full well that I was finding my niche. He seemed to enjoy it as much as I did and recognized that I was coming into my own. Bob said he thought I should compete in one contest and perform in one air show and see how each went. Part of me knew that I could do it and part of me was overwhelmed with his challenge and his generosity and with this fantastic opportunity.

I received an invitation to fly in the biggest air show in Alaska, at Gulkana, in May of 1984. I accepted and felt great about it. I was kind of amazed that anyone would want to see me fly, but I jumped at the chance.

I had to demonstrate my capability with our local good-guy fed, or FAA man, Sid Stone, who watched me fly my routine from the ground. I dove and climbed, looped and rolled beside a mountain in Birchwood outside of Anchorage. Sid gave me a 1,000-foot waiver which meant I could descend no lower than 1,000 feet above the ground.

My first appearance as an air show performer went over the public address system by the famous air show announcer and "voice of the National Championship Reno Air Races," Sandy Sanders. All Alaskan locals who had aerobatic airplanes were invited, including all members of the local International Aerobatic Club (IAC) chapter to which I belonged. Doug Geeting, the famous Alaskan mountain and glacier pilot; my instructor, Darlene Dubay; Lee Watne, who owned a fixed-pitch Pitts S-C; Rick MacAdoo, who flew a single-seat Starduster One; and Mike and Deana Barbarick, with their Pitts and Decathlon, respectively, were included. I felt ready, but to actually take off in front of a crowd and perform was another story.

Gulkana was always a nice show. They *paid* me for performing, a nice $300 that I used to buy an eighteen-speed mountain bike. Later, it would become my mount for exploring, escaping the tensions of air show scenes at an airport, or simply transportation. All I had to do was put triple-one eight Echo through its paces. With Duane Cole's help, I designed a routine with Cuban Eights, Reverse half Cuban Eights, a triple loop (my big maneuver), rolls, and point rolls. Sandy announced each step, his voice reverberating over the public address system. I turned and twisted my pretty little red, white, and blue airplane and sailed in for a glorious landing. As I taxied in, my window was open and I could hear very plainly that Sandy called over the loudspeakers: "Here she is! Patty Beck! Give her a big round of applause!"

He said something like: "This little gal flew her heart out! Let her hear you!" I could hear and see all of the people clapping. It wasn't a huge crowd, but it was big enough for me. I thought, "Oh, my God. I am *not* going to get out of this airplane. All of that attention is focused on me. I could die."

I just kept taxiing. I rolled on, glancing at the crowd and then staring straight ahead. I taxied past everyone and all the way to the back of the airport to the hangar. I put the airplane away and started wiping it down.

Later on, people asked, "Where'd you go?"

"Oh, wasn't I supposed to just bring the plane back here?" I said.

Like anything else, once the newness had evaporated, I started getting used to facing a crowd after a performance, but like the child that hated shaking the hand of the newly introduced adult, I wanted to hide, to fly away. If Bob hadn't been there, I might have.

In addition to learning all that I had to know about flying, I had to become a showperson, an entertainer. I knew that if I could successfully arrange the steps and have the intricate aerial dance flow smoothly, then I could fly it.

Bob and I incorporated and Patty Beck Air Shows, Incorporated, was formed on July 9, 1984. I flew in a couple more shows that summer in Soldotna, Anchorage, and Fairbanks. In the latter, I saw a friend from Fairbanks, Bob Veazie, who was one of the first I'd met who had actually competed in an aerobatic contest. With such lofty credentials—he was a *competition pilot*—Bob Veazie rose in my esteem from mere mortal. He had purchased a powerful two-seat S-2B Pitts, a craft that was light-years away in performance from the Decathlon. He offered me a ride in it and I jumped at the opportunity.

I thought I had died and gone to heaven in more ways than one. That it was the most powerful, fantastic, certificated aerobatic airplane available to date was important, but I also appreciated that Veazie, a dentist, did far more for my well-being than any chiropractor or back surgeon that I had ever seen. I'd been troubled with back pain for years, tedious reminders of past car accidents.

I flew with Veazie, an aggressive pilot and, during a speedy descent, he tossed in a violent outside snap roll. All I could hear and feel was a big "crrraaacck" as all the vertebrae in my back straightened out. I felt dizzy and light-headed and thought, "I've broken my back! Something horrible has happened!" Yet after we landed I realized that my back felt good. From that day on, most of my aching back problems were over.

Veazie was like many of the people I have met in aerobatics—helpful, friendly, and willing to share routines and flying secrets, willing to discuss technique and new maneuvers . . . at least until you become a real competitive threat! (Like in *any* competitive sport, I believed the *only* way to improve was to have real competition and something against which to judge yourself. The more our competitors improved, the better we became ourselves. It was academic, but, unfortunately, it was not an idea shared by some of my competitors.)

I bought a book that described the shorthand of aerobatics, the Aresti Key. That was one more aspect of aerobatics that fell into place for me. Always a lover of handwriting, learning foreign alphabets and symbols, I once drew up an entire alphabet of symbols that I used as a code when I wrote to my friends. One of my dreams as a kid was to be a spy, a code breaker. Aresti symbols were just that, a code. I had no trouble learning the symbols while mastering the new airplane.

Count José L. Aresti, a Spaniard, spent years developing his fabulous system of aerocryptographics. The original Aresti book, an eight-by-ten-inch paperback, boasted list upon list of aerobatic maneuvers, all valued and ranked according to difficulty—a K factor. If an aerobatic pilot flew a maneuver that is valued at 10 K—a simple roll, for example—and scored 10, he or she was awarded 100 points for that particular maneuver. A 25 K maneuver—perhaps a loop with a roll at the top—flown well enough to earn a 10 scored 250 points. Designed for a specific airplane, a Bücker Jüngmeister aerobatic plane, the list included several maneuvers that a Bücker could do, like four rolls on the vertical—going straight up! As airplanes became more powerful and aerobatic styles changed, competition rules caused a much-needed revision of scoring. Eric Mueller of Switzerland contributed a great deal to revise the original Aresti system, but it retained its place as a base upon which to build.

It was during that air show in Soldotna that I took one of my friends flying, Jim Eshenhower. It was in late July, the same day I left for the states to fly in the contest in Fond du Lac, Wisconsin, where I would compete. That's when Jim lost his big wad of keys—the keys that, combined with my inexperience, nearly killed me in Hibbing, Minnesota.

It was intriguing to have an eye to the past and a foot into the future and see the next step ahead, something to look forward to. I was in the midst of some of the most exciting days of my life.

I knew that Buddha taught of the road to enlightenment. Blyth, who authored *Zen and Zen Classics*, explained that enlightenment was the ongoing travel, the destination never reached. I was in the midst of mind-boggling, fabulous activity and, at this point, my destination was nowhere in sight.

ELEVEN

Horizons

After the air show in Soldotna, I climbed into my little airplane for a real adventure. Flying the Decathlon from Alaska by myself—my longest solo flight—carried me to momentous changes in my life. I planned to compete at the intermediate level in my first contest at the 1984 International Aerobatic Club contest, Fond du Lac, Wisconsin.

Flying thousands of miles across Canada and the western states was not a common trek for anyone and, although I relished the challenge, I also came close to missing the contest! Not only did I have to survive the control failure due to the wad of keys, but deteriorating weather forced me to the ground and almost stopped me as well.

Bob flew his Baron—twin-engined, fast, and designed for flight in instrument weather conditions—from Anchorage to meet me in Hibbing. We took off on Sunday, the day of the contest registration, and played follow-the-leader toward Fond du Lac, Bob departing into some dicey weather ahead of me. We hoped to land in plenty of time to enroll.

Bob made it to Fond du Lac, but my airplane was slower and that gave the weather more time to deteriorate. I was enveloped by a solid wall of water halfway between Hibbing and Fond du Lac, as an ominous mass of clouds lowered the ceiling and rain pounded relentlessly on my airplane. I was forced to descend, feeling as if a great thumb was pressing on the top of my airplane and pushing me down out of the sky. As much as I wanted to compete, I wasn't about to kill myself getting there. I put down on a grass strip, disappointed that it offered no fuel, no office, and no attendant. I waited for several hours—until after dark—hoping the weather would improve, but that wasn't to be.

Feeling really bummed, I finally used the available pay phone and called a cab for a ride to a local motel. I kept calling until I reached Bob, who told me that I had to arrive by early the next morning to make it onto the schedule of competitors.

I willed Monday's weather to be good and took off as soon as the heavens responded. When I finally arrived in Fond du Lac, Mike Heuer, then-president of the IAC, told me that I wasn't too late, that I could compete. My relief was audible.

The competition and the people who had gathered were all that I had hoped for and more. I was in awe of the heavy hitters. Clint McHenry and Tom Jones were there with their Pitts S-1T and S-2S, respectively. Amos Buetell was flying his Pitts S-1T *Tiger Lady*, Harold Neumann had his Monocoupe *Little Mulligan*, and Sam Burgess flew his Bücker Jüngmeister. Giles Henderson, who generally won the sportsman category, was ready with his beautiful clipped-wing Cub; and Bob Davis brought his homebuilt and modified Laser.

I could scarcely believe that I was among such outstanding pilots and that they were so approachable. When asked, Bob Davis and Clint McHenry gave me more than my share of help and advice, and they had my deepest gratitude. I learned right away that true champions will always give of themselves, if they are asked.

I decided that as a beginner, I would ask for advice from those I respected. I hoped, too, that if I ever reached their levels, I would pass on their kindnesses to others. It was great that they were so approachable and friendly. I paid attention and listened to those who knew much more than me.

I had my first opportunity to watch aerobatic judges and, in the relentlessly hot, sunny summer in Wisconsin, with competitor after competitor to evaluate, I appreciated that theirs could be a difficult and somewhat thankless task. [1]

---

[1] I talked with some of the judges to find out where they placed their emphasis. They told me that they looked for precision—straight vertical lines, 90-degree angles, 45-degree lines, and precise, correct execution of maneuvers. Position-

I also had a chance to look at the latest in aerobatic competition air-planes and to see how my little factory-built Decathlon, a high-winged monoplane, compared to the gaggle of wings on the grass. The very few single-winged monoplanes on display were much more sleek and clean than the double-winged biplanes—and each was a homebuilt. Most of the designs were based originally on the Stephens Akro, which was then highly modified, redesigned, and developed into the Laser by Leo Loudenslager. Leo, who holds a position of utmost respect and to this day remains unbeaten in his long tenure at the top, is an airline pilot, air show pilot, World Aerobatic Champion, and an unprecedented seven-time U.S. Aerobatic Champion. Walter Extra, in turn, when designing his first monoplane, the Extra 230, leaned heavily on Leo's design.

Entering the contest took all of the concentration and confidence that I could summon. It was scary to think of actually flying before people who were judging me, grading me, and evaluating my flying. With ragged nerves and butterflies in my stomach, I took off when my time came. Once in the air and ready to enter the aerobatic box, I wondered, "What the hell am I doing here? Why am I doing this?" I *knew* that I had to justify all of the time and the expense in order to keep flying, but I felt sick. The flying part was a pleasure, but it was a nightmare to think that I was being scrutinized, that my flying, my maneuvers, and the control of my airplane were as much under microscopic investigation as any sci-entific specimen. I had to shake off the nerves, telling myself, "I don't care what they think. I just want to fly. This is simply one of the prices that I have to pay."

Flying in the intermediate category, I ended the contest in twenty-third place, relieved to have finished. But when they asked for volunteers to fly an air show, my hand went up. I was gung ho for air show experi-ence and, if one were to rank my enthusiasm, instead of twenty-third, I would have vied for number one. There was no judging in air show per-formance and, contest over, the heat was off.

---

ing and balance of the flight were judging criteria, but the dynamics of style also entered into the competition. A pilot could wow the judges or could put them to sleep. In addition, boundary judges with special sight devices measured any penetration of the boundaries of the box. Each "out" carried with it a thirty-point penalty. Using the Aresti system, aerobatic judges were guided by a rules manual and trained by leaders in the International Aerobatic Club of the Ex-perimental Aircraft Association. I knew that objectivity was the aim, but suspected that subjectivity was hard to suppress.

To perform in the show, I had to maintain at least 1,000 feet above the runway. I was sure that I looked like a housefly to the crowd below—and about as exciting as one, too—but I performed and gained one more chunk of valuable experience. In air shows, as in any career field, apprenticeship precedes achievement.

Except for a gusty wind, the weather smiled on us at Fond du Lac, but air show pilots must adapt to flying in conditions they would never necessarily choose, occasionally in weather in which they wouldn't dare *practice*. I have flown in 50-knot howling winds, on the ragged edges of thunderstorms, in horrible rain showers, in ferocious turbulence, and in all sorts of beastly weather. I've seen funnel clouds touch down not far away. Fans may be huddled under umbrellas or streaking for the safety of their cars, yet a show-must-go-on attitude prevails. Some shows are canceled, some are interrupted, but most of the time, you fly!

On air-show day in Fond du Lac, I landed after performing and taxied with a quartering tailwind filling the wind sock and turning it from a drooping rag into a stiff-armed gesture like a military salute. The wind shoved at the tail of my Decathlon as I turned into the ramp area. My smoke oil, normally held in a tank located in the rear of the craft and adding weight to the tail, was depleted. Between that and a low quantity of fuel, the airplane was pretty light all the way around. A gust of wind pushed the tail up and bang! The propeller slammed into the ground! Given an unexpected shove by the wind, the airplane had nosed over and the propeller had whacked to a stop!

Seeing the bent propeller staring me in the face, I glanced at Bob, who was standing nearby, his mouth open in surprise. I put my head down on my arms on the panel. I wanted to die!

A damaged prop meant the possibility of a damaged crankshaft, a damaged camshaft, the need for an engine overhaul and a propeller repair or replacement. I was mortified.

Herb Cox, an IAC volunteer, came over and, in his gentle, comforting way, told me that I was going to have to get out of the airplane, but I felt as if I were anchored to the seat. I wanted to wait until all the people had left the airport.

Herb pointed out that it would be a lot worse for me to stay in the airplane. He said, "The crowd thinks it's just part of the show."

A small red convertible from the previous week's convention and fly-in at Oshkosh stood, its engine running, poised to parade performers back and forth. I was expected to do the parade lap, wave, smile, greet the crowd, sign autographs, shake hands—be a regular politician. As difficult as that was for me, it was part of the job, another price that I simply *had* to pay to fly. Herb helped me out, put me in the parade car to drive up and down in front of the line of spectators. I put on my biggest smile, even burst out laughing. I held my head up as high as I could. There was no way I was going to give anyone the satisfaction of knowing how stupid I really felt.

Bob was as ready to take off in the twin-engined Baron as I was. I left the Decathlon with the manager of the fixed base operation on the field, asking him to please make the necessary repairs, and told him we would contact him later. Bob and I hustled into the Baron and took off.

For years "my" dent in the cement by the fuel tanks at the Fond du Lac Airport remained. I was sorry when they repaved the area because it was always a good reminder to me that I had forgotten one of the basic rules of tail dragger flying. A tail dragger has its third wheel at the tail of the craft, with the main gear at or near the cockpit. A tricycle-gear airplane has its third wheel under the engine cowling or at the nose of the airplane, and its center of gravity location generally results in more stability in landing and taxi situations. As I well knew, because of the added attention required in the ground handling of a tail dragger, one of the cardinal rules is that you *never* quit flying them until they are in the hangar or at their tie-down spot on the ramp.

Life is a series of firsts—first contest, first air show, first time I really dinged a plane. I had run into some runway lights in Anchorage, practicing doing short—too short—field landings. That wasn't much of a headache. *This* was for real.

When a pilot has an incident, it brings out the hangar stories. Most pilots have had incidents, and tales become a form of therapy for the one with a current problem. I didn't hang around to commiserate. I had other plans.

The week had held just the right amount of intensity for me. It had been great. Not only had I flown three thousand–plus miles, survived the jammed control stick, and managed to get past nasty weather, but I also competed. I'd learned a lot in my first attempt to perform aerobatics within the confines of the box of imaginary airspace and I had performed in my fourth air show.

To put the frosting on the cake, Bob and I were quietly married. My father's words —"When's that guy gonna put a ring on your finger?"— were typical of the comments we were getting from family and friends.

For our own part, after four years together, we had decided that it was time to be married. Going off by ourselves during the course of the aerobatic contest, we had a small ceremony at the courthouse of Oshkosh, Wisconsin. I wore a skirt. We drank champagne and, although I didn't change my name at the time, Patty Beck became Mrs. Robert Wagstaff on August 10, 1984. The sky held *no* limits for us. While the airplane was repaired, Bob and I returned to Anchorage via Jackson Hole, Wyoming, to visit his family at their ranch, before taking some time for ourselves.

Having enjoyed the competition in Fond du Lac so much, I set my sights on the U.S. National Aerobatic Championship in Sherman-Denison, Texas, in September. I had one month to profit from some of the help that I'd gained in Wisconsin—one month to practice and to try to improve. Although Bob was an excellent instrument pilot and professional about his flying in every way, he wasn't as interested in aerobatics as I. He was very supportive of my interest and got as excited as I did about my competing. It was something that brought us closer together. We ignored the possibility that it might push us apart.

The national championship, which was held every year, was the trial for the Olympics of aerobatics, the competition that determined the best of all categories. On a biennial basis and for competitors only in the unlimited category, the nationals led to the formation of a national team that would compete on a global scale.

Like Olympic figure skaters, pilots in each category competed in three flights—the compulsory, the freestyle, and the unknown. The compulsory tested specific skill levels, theoretically making the playing field equal for all contestants. The freestyle, choreographed by the pilot, had to include certain maneuvers that were drawn from families of maneuvers predetermined for the category. It allowed individuality and a showcasing of the capabilities of the aircraft and the pilot. For the unknown, a list of maneuvers was published, but the sequence in which those maneuvers were to be executed wasn't known to a competitor until twenty-four hours before flight. A mental exercise, the routine could not be flown until actual competition. Contestants practiced the unknown on the ground, walking through the sequence with sweeping motions of their hands and pirouettes of their bodies, concentrating to commit the choreography to memory.

At Fond du Lac, I watched and listened to aerobatic masters. I knew from the first time I saw aerobatics performed that it would take a lot of practice, but it was a mountain that I'd wanted to climb, a challenge that loomed larger than life. This was what I had been waiting for—something big to commit to, something exciting into which to throw my energies. I became consumed. It had been my first contest and my eyes were opened wide.

Inspired by Clint McHenry and with practice and experience, I eventually learned to memorize an unknown sequence quickly. I made a lot of notes and developed a flow. Color codes helped me key particular directions like upwind, downwind, and cross-box maneuvers. I used the T and A, to and away, system of designating direction so that every maneuver ended up headed in the proper direction.

I returned to Fond du Lac to retrieve the repaired bird in early September. It was snowing when I test-flew the airplane, a cleansing white that painted the earth and corresponded with a newness that I felt within. I became comfortable with my airplane and, from Wisconsin, headed for Luck Field, south of Fort Worth, Texas, to train with Duane Cole. [2]

Readying to compete at the 1984 National Aerobatic Competitions, I wanted Duane's expertise. I stayed with the Coles for about a week and felt comfortable, as if I were part of their family. I appreciated Duane's fabulous help. He and I spent all day at the airport and, at night, we went back to his home, ate dinner with Judy, and then went for a walk on Luck Field's runway for exercise. He was a master and part of aerobatic history, a great teacher. When Duane insisted that a pilot should be able to fly through all three axes of an airplane's movement, he was right. The first, a straight line running lengthwise through the center of the airplane, is the longitudinal axis, around which an airplane rolls. The second, a straight line at right angles to this, is the lateral axis, around which an airplane pitches. And the third, a straight line perpendicular to the first two at their point of intersection, is the vertical axis, around which an airplane yaws. A pilot controls the axes with ailerons, elevators, and rudders, respectively. "Or," Duane insisted, "a pilot *should*!"

---

[2] Duane, a member of the aerobatic team that competed in Budapest, Hungary, in 1962, did a lot toward saving air shows for the rest of us. After several serious airplane accidents in the 1950s, the government threatened to end aerial demonstrations as they had done in 1938, prior to World War II. A debt of gratitude is owed to Duane for challenging the bureaucracy. He literally wrote the regulations that covered them.

After he was through critiquing my flying and making suggestions, Duane took off to practice his own air show routine. What an honor it was to watch him, to learn from him. I watched from the ground, in awe.

But not one of the contestants got to compete. The 1984 National Aerobatic Contest was rained out! The only thing undampened by the weather was the opening night "smoke oil" hangar party at Grayson County Airport hosted by Jimmy and Ava Ray and turned into an annual bash. It started a festive mood for everyone, and Bob and I had a great opportunity to meet the country's best aerobatic pilots.

Introduced to Bob Bloodwell, a cardiologist from Florida who flew a Pitts S-2, I was surprised by an amazing statement. Bloodwell leaned across the hors d'oeuvres table, pointed his finger at me, and said, "You are going to *be* someone in this sport."

I could never predict where inspiration might come from. Bloodwell had no idea who I was or how well I flew. Often people who cause me to believe in myself are relative strangers.

Bob and I strolled among the aerobatic airplanes at Grayson Airport sharing ideas about their relative merits. I suggested that the Decathlon might be less of a competitive airplane than I truly wanted and needed. I felt as if I had done about everything that I could do with it. Bob brought up the idea of moving up to a Pitts biplane. I knew I was ready for more performance and so did he.

During a conversation with Ron Fagen, a Pitts driver we had met in Fond du Lac who was at the nationals, we were surprised to hear him generously offer a half interest in his Pitts. He explained that we could continue to base the airplane at his airstrip in Granite Falls, Minnesota, and that we could work it out between ourselves as to which pilot would fly it and when.

I was elated. I didn't care if I had to be based in Timbuktu. We became part owners in Ron's biplane. I was headed for a goal and would do whatever I needed to get there. Bob was getting as caught up in the whole scene as I. We both liked the other pilots and being with others who enjoyed the incessant talk of aviation.

It was late September and the aerobatic season was nearing its end. Ron told me to feel free to take the Pitts out west for the few contests that remained scheduled, and Bob suggested that I fly in as many as possible to gain experience. All of us knew that Pitts biplanes were small, short-coupled, nimble, unstable little airplanes—a distinct advantage for aerobatics. We also knew they were easily maneuvered into inadvertent spins.

"In a blink, they can get into a spin out of almost any maneuver that decelerates in speed," most pilots familiar with the Pitts would say. It is really important to have proper aerobatic and spin training before flying one of these little airplanes.

Bob suggested that I take Gene Beggs' spin training course. Gene, who handled an airplane with finesse, was an aerobatic master from Midland, Texas. He, along with Eric Mueller, the Swiss aerobatic champion, and NASA's Jim Patton, had studied the aerodynamics of the spin. From their research, Gene and Eric had devised an emergency maneuver course that was a quick and efficient method of recovering from an unexpected or unplanned spin as long as you were at an altitude high enough to allow the aircraft space in which to be righted. The greatest danger in the spin is running out of altitude prior to recovery. In addition, the proper recovery techniques are imperative.

Gene, one of the nicest guys in the world, was a Texan, complete with his big cowboy hat and gentle drawl. When I saw him at the nationals, I told him that I was about to buy a half interest in a Pitts and that I would truly like to take his spin course. I asked about coming to Midland after the nationals. Gene politely told me that he was booked and that Diane Hakala, an aerobatic pilot from the East Coast, planned to take his series of lessons.

He must have seen the disappointment on my face. He told me to call early in the week on the off chance that he had a cancellation.

Bob left to return to Alaska and I decided that rather than waiting around to call, I would fly to Midland and *be* there. That way I would be ready in case of a cancellation, and that was the happy way that it turned out. When I showed up, Gene smiled and told me that Diane's cancellation had freed him to work with me. I was lucky.

There is far more to aerobatic training than having an instructor help you into a seat in an approved airplane, take off into the wild blue to demonstrate, and say, "You've got it," encouraging you to follow through. With such a superb instructor, I got a great introduction to the Pitts S-2A. He put me through the paces of his spin course, first fully explaining everything on the ground. We talked and I took notes. Then we flew. Much of his training was focused on aerodynamics—the physics of flight and why the airplane does what it does. Then, and only then, was it up to the student to put in the hours of practice necessary to perfect aerobatic maneuvers.

Spin training starts with an understanding of airfoils, or the shape of a wing; lift; the angle of attack; and the stall. Mueller wrote about the stall in his book, *Flight Unlimited*, and described it by using the French word *decrochage*. A more accurate description is possible with that word, which means "becoming detached." The stall is actually a breaking away of the airflow over the surface of the airfoil, or the wing, and results in a loss of lift.

Aerobatic pilots often use the term "breaking loose," or just, "breaking." That describes a reaction to the loss of lift. Stalls happen at any speed, and at any attitude (the position of the airplane in relation to the horizon): vertical, in a 45-degree angle, and going straight down. Some airplanes "break loose" at higher speeds than others. Some give you a lot of warning, as in the shuddering of a Cessna 172 or Piper Cherokee, and some give you almost none, like a North American T-6 or P-51 Mustang. Most aerobatic airplanes fall somewhere in between.

A stall depends upon the G loading of the wing, which, in turn, is affected by gross weight and atmospheric conditions, the tightness of the turn, and how abruptly a pilot pulls back on the stick.

Stalls or spins above a large cushion of air are no biggies. Pilots spin regularly in aerobatic airplanes. Inadvertent stalls and spins need that safe amount of airspace beneath the craft for prompt and proper recovery. The stall speed and feel of the airplane varies just as conditions vary from day to day and location to location and depend on things like altitude, temperature, and humidity.

For an aerobatic pilot to be considered proficient, it isn't enough to have an idea of when a stall might occur while flying low or close to the ground. An air show pilot must be experienced, current, and responsive enough to recognize and react rapidly and correctly. A good aerobatic pilot feels the airplane and wears it like a glove.

Spins are autorotations, not inherently dangerous in a proven and tested airplane that is properly loaded within its center of gravity range. But the loss of altitude during a spin can be greater than in any other basic aerobatic maneuver. Another problem is a loss of reference and use of the wrong recovery techniques. Gene taught that a Pitts can transition from an upright spin to an inverted spin just by recovering with too much of the proper control input. The airplane is so inherently unstable and snappy.

In an upright spin in a Pitts, the airplane loses between 700 and 1,000 feet of altitude in just one turn. The standard recovery technique? Break the stall with the elevator and push opposite rudder to the direction of the spin, stopping the yaw.

Aerobatic pilots have experimented with different types of spins—regular spins, accelerated spins, and flat spins. Pilots may enter and fly all three spins either from upright or inverted positions. Once a spin is developed, it is nearly impossible for a pilot to differentiate between whether the start was in the upright (or an inside spin) or the inverted (an outside spin) position. Spins can be fun and they can bite.

Aerobatic pilots have had problems with flat spins, especially when they enter the flat spin inadvertently. A pilot who lacks proper training and experience might use incorrect recovery techniques and run out of precious altitude too soon. Or a pilot might put in the correct control inputs but perhaps neglect to reduce power. Leaving a touch of power helps an airplane remain in the spin.

A good aerobatic airplane is inherently unstable and, unlike a docile training plane, it does not want to right itself and fly straight and level when the pilot releases the stick or the yoke. The quicker and more unstable the airplane, the faster it will spin. An aerobatic airplane that is properly loaded will respond quickly and positively to control input, making spin recoveries rapid and painless.

Gene, Eric, and Jim Patton made contributions for all of us when they investigated the world of spins and spin recovery. More than a few pilots have gotten into flat spins from which they seemed unable to recover. Yet, when there is enough altitude, the airplanes "miraculously" recover as soon as the pilot lets go of the controls in preparation to bail out of the airplane!

Gene's recovery method was (1) power off, (2) let go of the stick, and (3) push full opposite rudder. In his Texas drawl, Gene told me that better flight training is key and was why I was there. His ground training was thorough and his method was to be engraved in my mind for aerobatics and in case of an emergency: Close the throttle. Take the hand off of the stick. Apply full opposite rudder until the spin stops. When rotation stops, take the stick again, neutralize the rudder, and pull (gently) out of the resultant dive. "Power off! Hands off! Full opposite rudder!" I repeated it over and over like a mantra.

I needed to feel comfortable before flying the Pitts in competition. I also wanted to be coached in advanced maneuvers.

I packed a week's worth of training into the few days available, then returned to Sherman. With my newfound confidence, I soloed in my newly shared Pitts S-1S, N8078, privately thankful for the opportunity. Don Ort, everyone's favorite old-timer in the Sherman-Denison area, ran a large maintenance shop and hangar at Grayson County Airport. Always ready to help out with a wrench or a beer, Don witnessed my first Pitts solo flight. He parked next to the runway in his VW Bug and made a difference by simply being there. I flipped around in the sky a little bit. After I'd landed, I said to him, "That's a squirrelly little airplane."

I heard Curtis Pitts, the famed designer of the airplanes that bear his name, speak at a forum at the huge annual EAA convention and fly-in in Oshkosh, Wisconsin. He said, in response to a question about his airplanes, "There ain't no such thing as a squirrelly airplane, but there sure are a lot of squirrelly pilots."

I decided that wasn't going to be me if I could help it.

In October 1984, I flew the Pitts to my second two competitions: the Tequila Cup in Arizona and a contest in Borrego Springs, California. It was a blast to fly. With no radio and no working compass, I dead reckoned and pilotaged the hell out of the western states. I learned to do a credible job of reading sectional charts and, whenever I wondered where I was, I ducked down to Interstate 10 and read a road sign. I followed the highway and each mile notched another section of experience, another step toward not having to make excuses for myself, of gaining self-confidence in my abilities.

I loved watching towns and farms slide by. I checked wind direction and speed by the puffs or streams of dirt raised by tractors or the flapping of drying clothes pinned to lines. I chased clouds that tempted me into rolling up around them and twisting them into smoke rings. I skimmed over the country, my eyes on the roads, the rivers, the outlines of the states etched in fields plowed too often by generations of hardworking souls. I was alone in the sky, free to make decisions for myself, to land where I needed to land, or take off when I needed to depart. I could turn the airplane upside down and look at the ground with a different view, a different perspective. I could perform and I could compete.

Before I was born, philosopher Jean-Paul Sartre wrote that man must understand that he can count on himself alone, that he has his own infinite responsibility to create his own destiny. I accepted that responsibility and, with apology to Sartre, I discovered that infinite *possibilities* were within my grasp!

While I flew through West Texas skies, I sometimes rolled inverted for the fun of it and other times I flew upside down over the main street of a dusty, quiet, remote little town, just for a friendly hello. By the time I arrived at Avra Valley, Arizona, I was ready to compete. Wayne Handley, a famous air show pilot, won first and I won the second-place intermediate trophy at the Tequila Cup, sponsored by the Tucson IAC chapter. (Later we both had fun reminiscing, laughing as we admitted that Wayne and I were the only intermediate competitors!)

The stop at Avra Valley reacquainted me with friends. One, Amos Buetell—a legend in aerobatic circles—owned a hangar at Avra Valley. Little did I know at the time that I would someday be calling that very hangar my own.

After competing in Avra Valley, the Pitts and I headed for another competition in Borrego Springs, California, landing at Blythe, an old desert town on the Colorado River. Windy conditions in Blythe stretched all the way to Borrego, with wind speeds of 40 knots or more. After only two weeks of being at the controls of the Pitts, I didn't know if I had the skill for those conditions and didn't want to find out the hard way. Once on the ground, the Pitts safe in a hangar, I hung out in Blythe for a couple of days.

In Borrego Springs, my sister, Toni, and John and Martha King met me and cheered me on. John and Martha filled in for Bob, knowing that he couldn't make the contest. (John and Martha have been good friends and a great inspiration to me. When I met them in 1980, they were flying their twin-engine Cessna 340 around the country, including to and from Alaska, to give weekend ground school training for pilots, courses that have become phenomenally successful as video training tapes.)

After practicing alone in sunny skies over the sands of the desert for two days, I competed in the advanced category, which is one higher than the intermediate, in the Borrego Springs contest. I wasn't going to go home with any prizes, but I wasn't dangerous or anything and I struggled through, hanging on with more grit than polish. Then I had to fly the unknown. That was tough! I could barely get through it, breaking off once because I had screwed up a maneuver. I came back, screwed it up the second time, and broke off again. Rather than start back into the box for a third time, I said out loud, "The hell with it!"

I landed and, laughingly, I said to Toni, "Aw, I can't believe I did that." After the contest, Toni, the Kings, and I went hiking in Palm Canyon. Two experienced pilots from the Spanish Aerobatic Team had driven to the contest and watched. They gave me some pointers and advice. When I landed after the unknown, they shook their heads, grinning widely. That night they ate dinner with us and we laughed all the way through dinner.

I flew the "squirrelly little bird" back to Granite Falls in western Minnesota and left it with Ron Fagen for the winter. The temperatures may have been pushing the mercury up toward 90 degrees in the desert in Borrego, but by the time I got to Iowa the ground was covered with snow. The wind was howling out of the north-northwest and it was *cold*. My hands and feet were so cold I began to wonder if I could make such frozen blocks of ice work the controls for landing. To shift hands and be prepared for landing, I timed the last leg of my flight. Every five minutes I put one of my hands in a pocket, working it and pumping it to warm and loosen it up. I clocked the shift of hands so that during the last five or ten minutes of the flight, the right hand would be warm enough to handle landing.

Ron Fagen and I worked it out that we would share the Pitts for the entire 1985 air show and competition season. I left the little airplane and retreated to spend another winter in Alaska.

Getting to be a veteran of Alaskan winters, I had learned how to dress and had plenty to keep me busy, including a Nintendo game that consumed a lot of my time. I doubt that it helped me keep my hand-eye coordination sharp for flying aerobatics in the spring, but, at the very least, it kept my mind more nimble. The long, dark, and cold winter moved in and I sometimes had to force myself to realize that I wasn't living in a tunnel or in a vacuum. My life began to divide into two separate journeys, two separate parts. One side of me was a wife and stepmother, a homemaker, and the alter ego was a competition aerobatic pilot, a career woman on a course toward possible international competition and the equivalent of the Olympic games. Bob and I discussed where my aerobatics were headed. We both knew that there was a spot for a woman on the team—five women are selected and we only knew of four who would be competing that year. We decided that we would do whatever it took. Since teams are chosen among competitors at the unlimited level (the highest level of competition), I would have to practice to fly at that level. My goals firmed up.

In Anchorage, I began to see my father and Anna Lies more often. My mom had moved to southern California, so I rarely saw her; but Dad, happier than I had ever seen him, was starting to mellow out. He seemed less uptight, less strained, and was learning to be more content. Dad had always been a nice guy, but alcohol had exacerbated his inner stress. It was good to see the changes and to see him more relaxed.

I studied ballet, combining focus with concentration and forcing my body to move and to reach. I flew the Cessna 185, when the weather was cooperative. But after I'd done my last plié of the winter, straightened out the closets for the last time, and finished my last 2,500-piece jigsaw puzzle, I realized that I could identify with the pacing of the caged tiger. Being surrounded by solid walls is sometimes equated to being incarcerated in a steel-barred cage. I was edgy. I could hardly wait to get back into the Pitts, into the air.

I grew anxious to leave Alaska. Bob and I continued to struggle with my relationship with his son and I found it increasingly difficult to deal with the problems caused by children, separation, remarriage, and divorce. I resented that discipline fell to me. I did not want to play the role of a stepparent when I felt I always had to be the bad guy. I was drained by heavy winter snow, long hours of darkness, and family tensions. I wanted, like a snowbird, to head south.

TWELVE

Zen

If there ever were a time that I needed to concentrate and to focus, it was in 1985. In February I came out of Alaska like a hibernating bear, hungry to learn, eager to master what I'd been taught, raring to go. I was excited by the Pitts biplane waiting for me in Minnesota and determined to compete at the unlimited level and grab a spot on the U.S. Aerobatics Team—the Olympics of aerobatics, a direct descendent of the Air Display at the 1936 Olympic Games in Germany in which Czech, French, German, Swiss, Italian, and Romanian pilots competed. It would take more than flying and practicing. I had to get control of my head. I had to develop my own philosophy to be the best pilot I could possibly be.

Each of us has myriad sources for our beliefs and our values. My philosophy has been molded by my reactions to inequities and injustices that I've seen in the cultures of the places I've lived, the countries I've visited. My beliefs have sprung from agnosticism, fostered by the rigidity in my Catholic schools and the dark views held by the nuns who were charged with my formal education. I have been influenced by the people who shaped my life in Japan, by the ideas of the freethinkers by whom I'd been surrounded in San Francisco, and by the intellectuals I'd met at the University of Queensland in Australia.

I read voraciously, absorbing what I could of the metaphysical and the literature of Zen masters. Theirs was a message that I liked, an attitude that I needed to absorb if I were to move from being the free spirit that I had been to being the master of the goals that I was shaping. It was important to find that through a deep and concentrated combination of understanding and meditation, I could find ways to be more efficient, more focused, and more able to achieve what one author referred to as poetry, valuing each moment.

My challenge was to become centered and mindless, to shut out noise, and to ignore any distractions. Never able to concentrate easily, I was generally restless and found it hard to sit still, some of the classic symptoms of attention deficit disorder, or ADD. My friend, BD-5 Jet air show pilot Bob Bishop, later said that he believes that *all* aerobatic pilots tend toward ADD. He suggested that while people with this disorder have a difficult time focusing on several tasks, they are able to turn their high energy and intelligence into a *hyper*focus situation. Because an aerobatic routine averages anywhere from seven to fifteen minutes, it is a perfect situation for hyperfocus—short, intense periods of exceptional and extreme concentration for an immediate task, while the big picture is kept in mind. That is exactly what is necessary to excel in any extreme sport.

Departing Anchorage in early February, I flew in a commercial jet 30,000 feet above snow blankets of Alaska and Canada that carpeted the valleys and draped the trees all the way to Minneapolis. Frosty white continued to decorate my two-hour drive west to Granite Falls, and, before heading out to revisit the Pitts, I settled into a little log cabin in Jensen's Motor Court.

At Ron Fagen's hangar, I checked out the Pitts as if to reacquaint myself with an old friend and soloed again, but before I got my sea legs, everything came to a screeching halt. Granite Falls was a country strip with a runway that followed the contours of the land. The tarmac dipped at the end of the runway and a big sign warned *Caution! Taxi to the end of the runway to check for traffic.* I knew of the sign but, nonetheless, I slammed right into it. The impact jolted me forward against my harness, snagged the airplane to a stop, and tore the propeller into pieces.

The aircraft had to be repaired—an expensive overhaul—however, the mishap was a blessing in disguise. Having the cylinders bored, the valves reseated, the crankshaft magnafluxed, and the propeller repitched meant more horsepower would be tweaked out of the engine and would result in an aircraft that was more powerful and more responsive and hence, more competitive.

Forced to cool my heels, I exercised to stay physically fit: rode my bike and started going to the gym.

To be coached by one of my country's aerobatic masters, I went to Pompano, Florida, to train with our three-time national champion Clint McHenry, one of my favorite people. His coaching and advice was invaluable and I learned more than I would have dreamed possible. We flew for five hours together over the southern Florida skies as he demonstrated all the unlimited maneuvers possible in a 180-horsepower, two-seat Pitts. In the air, his demonstrations were crisp and precise. In postflight sessions, demonstrating with his graceful and articulate hands, he taught me something of the art of designing freestyle routines: creation of routines for varying wind conditions, energy management of the airplane, and presentation for judges.

I hung on every word of those that were willing to help me improve, to push me beyond my own limits. I had read that Leo Loudenslager always kept a training journal, so I started doing the same. I noted specifics of particular maneuvers and practice sessions and used the notebook for reference at important contests. As reminders, my notes reduced, if not removed, any guesswork.

Flying at the unlimited level of competition is radically different than at the intermediate level. At that highest level of competition, the learning curve skyrockets. Unlimited maneuvers are complex and rapid combinations of loops, rolls, and Hammerheads. The Gs are more pronounced than in any other category and the unlimited pilot has to be willing to pull a lot of positive Gs and to push a lot of negative Gs, both of which are physically exhausting. Unlimited maneuvers are flown at a faster pace and require a more dramatic use of energy and power. Routines are flown with more intricacy and at lower altitudes, not far above the unyielding, unforgiving ground.

Some pilots capable of flying in the unlimited category prefer to stay with advanced because it is not as demanding competitively. A successful unlimited pilot is totally committed and finds little time for any other hobby. It is so totally demanding that many make it their lives. This was perfect for me—something all-consuming, a challenge and a passion in which I could immerse myself. I was uniquely suited to the unusual demands and rigors of this sport, as it combined everything I liked to do.

Once the Pitts was up and running again, I flew south to reach a designated aerobatic box in Springfield, Tennessee, that Clint had suggested, a field where other aerobatic pilots met to practice. Waivered aerobatic boxes in the United States were few and far between and I was just one of many aerobatic pilots who had to fly hundreds of miles to find an ideal and legal practice site. (According to the federal regulations, elsewhere we were to maintain a minimum of 1,500 feet above the ground.) In unlimited competition, pilots were expected to descend as low as 300 feet, a proximity to the ground that had to be practiced for proficiency and was best practiced in a safe location, one protected for aerobatic flight.

Frozen February had a grip on the Midwestern states. Icy cold reached upward, cooling at 3½ degrees per 1,000 feet, until it blew like a great northern into the cockpit of my little airplane. I shivered my way to Terre Haute, Indiana, where I landed for fuel and a few moments of warmth and called Bob to check in. He chilled me further with some bad news.

"I know you won't want to hear this," he said, "but Amos Buetell was killed in an accident at Avra Valley."

"No! Not Amos!" Memories rushed back of my having kept my airplane in his hangar north of Tucson. Evidently his propeller had shed a counterweight and the resulting vibration shook the fuel tank loose and washed him in gasoline. Avra Valley's aerobatic box was two miles from the Avra Valley Airport and Amos, facing a massive fuel leak in the cockpit, gunned for the runway. In trying to drop quickly out of the sky, he landed with a strong tailwind. Wind picked up the tail and flipped the aircraft over, and it burst into flames. Amos died two or three days later.

He and I might have been on the 1986 Aerobatic Team together. I had lost a friend and aviation had lost a good pilot. I spent a little time on the ground at Terre Haute, trying to come to grips with some of the reality, acknowledging inherent danger.

I remembered that in Buddhism, the student must not allow any hesitation or indecision to enter her mind. I kept flying. Quitting wasn't an option, but thoughts of Amos's fiery death lingered in my mind for a long time.

When I landed in Springfield, twenty-five miles north of Nashville, Ray and Charlene Williams, who operated the field and were longtime supporters of aerobatics, questioned why I was there. I explained that I thought aerobatic boxes were just blocks of airspace, open to the public. They told me that I should have called to prearrange my arrival, schedule a time, and sign the waiver.

I apologized but made certain that it was all right to be there. I was starting to assert myself, to do anything in order to fly. They relaxed and treated me very well. I was made to feel welcome and fit in with the others who were there for the same reason as I.

Jimmy Goggin and his girlfriend, Peggy, offered me a place to stay in their house. In a phone call, I told Bob how much I liked the people I was meeting. I told him that they were cool, friendly, down-to-earth, and always ready to lend a hand or a word of advice. Determined to master the Pitts and to fly unlimited maneuvers at the same time, I flew three times each day. Jimmy and others offered to critique as often as possible and I gratefully took them up on it, concentrating on polishing the familiar maneuvers and mastering the new.

I spent an inordinate amount of time mastering flat spins, the autorotation of the aircraft in which the airplane flattens toward the horizontal. After having trained with Gene Beggs, my confidence level was high and I decided to practice them. I liked flat spins and I wanted to add them to my air show and to my four-minute freestyle competition routine. But I also knew that flat spins can strike and their venom can be deadly.

Airborne a short time later and having started at an adequately high altitude, I was in a well-developed flat spin. I initiated the recovery, but nothing happened! Like a top, the Pitts just kept spinning around and around, going and going and going. I was getting lower and lower.

It was bizarre. I started at 5,000 feet and, by the time I got to 2,000, the ground spun up at me at a frightening speed. Upper branches of trees seemed to be *right there*! In a mystical way, I stopped moving and the trees spun closer and closer toward *me*. I'd passed through 1,500 feet when I heard Gene's drawl in my head. He was on my shoulder like a guardian angel. I heard him say "Pow'r off!"

The trees reached for me like a mesmerizing, green whirlpool and I yanked at the throttle. The little bit of power that remained was just enough to keep airflow passing the wings, to maintain the spin. I imagined Gene's voice again, "Hands off. Full opposite rudder." I let go and kicked the rudder, hard! The spin stopped! I was able to level the airplane. I was *very* low, and I was shaking like the leaves I'd just *barely* avoided. Gulping in deep breaths of air, I aimed for a landing. I thought, "Get me out of this little death trap!"

I was trembling so badly that I couldn't properly set up for a straight-in landing. I dipped one wing and scraped the bottom of the aileron without even knowing it. I parked the airplane for the rest of the day and, without saying a word to anyone, lost myself in a mall in Nashville.

The next morning, at the hangar, Jimmy said, "I see you got your wingtip yesterday." My mouth dropped open. He said, "C'mere," and showed me. My smile was more a grimace. I shook my head and said, "That's minor compared to what *almost* happened. I was the closest I've ever come to dying in an airplane, Jimmy. I hated it. I hated being out of control. I hated scaring myself!"

I had to climb back onto the horse that had thrown me. I read Krishnamurti, who said, if I understood him well, that a mark is left by every experience, whether it be of pain or of pleasure, and that experience meant going through something. He urged that after an experience, to go completely through it and free yourself. That was what I had to do.

I took pleasure in mastering the Pitts, the single-seat craft that had been the single most challenging airplane for all pilots to land well. It takes seventy or eighty hours to truly master its intricacies and, even then, every landing was an event. And I came to believe that a person who could land a Pitts consistently well could fly anything!

After the session in Tennessee, I returned to Granite Falls and maintained my practice regimen. I flew three times every day, then went to my cabin-home-away-from-home, ate a sandwich, thought about flying, called Bob in Alaska, and crashed into my bed, exhausted. Flying unlimited aerobatics was exhilarating and intensely physical.

Pushing to compete at the unlimited level, I had maneuvers to conquer—vertical snap rolls, three-quarter snap rolls, and inside and outside one-half snaps as well as sequences to create. My regimen was relentless, my study schedule just as avid. And, again, I asked for help from the best aerobatic pilots in our country.

In mid-June, Gene Beggs came to Granite Falls to coach me just prior to my first unlimited contest. Frustrated with vertical snap rolls and tired of my little Pitts flipping suddenly into flat spins out of what should have been a good maneuver, I asked, "What am I doing wrong?"

Gene told me that it was timing. He told me to give myself thirty-five hours of doing nothing but vertical snap rolls and then I would develop a sense of the timing involved.

I gave myself the full thirty-five hours and more. With unswerving determination, I practiced.

I competed in about ten contests, flying all over the Midwest, and volunteered to perform in as many air shows as time and distance allowed. At 140 miles per hour, I flew from competition to competition in Minnesota, Ohio, Iowa, and Illinois and encountered all sorts of weather situations imaginable. Experience was the teacher.

I spent a lot of evenings alone in my log cabin studying and reading. I devoured one two-part article about Leo Loudenslager written by Dave Gustafson for *Sport Aviation*, the EAA magazine. I appreciated that it took an enormous amount of talent, perseverance, and some luck to come out on top as the winner of the U.S. National Aerobatic Championship and found it astounding that Leo won it an amazing seven times! No one before or since has come close to repeating that record. Leo, exceptional not only in his drive and in his motivation to win, built his own airplane, a highly modified craft that he named the Laser. He was the first person to fly a monoplane successfully in aerobatic competition and, in so doing, set new standards for subsequent generations of pilots. Imitation is the highest form of flattery and everyone started copying Leo. His competition aerobatics displayed amazing intensity, a tough act to follow.

Searching for inspiration, I read and reread the article about Leo until my copies were dog-eared. Leo set goals, stuck with them, and never gave up! As a competitor, he was phenomenal. I admired his dedication.

Motivation came from such reports, it came from within, and, as I traveled to air shows and competitions and widened my circle of acquaintances, it came from others, too.

My preparation for being good enough to make the team and to perform as an air show pilot took more than practice in the airplane, more than motivation and desire. There were no shortcuts, no quick, easy methods of getting to be a top competitor or a top performer and in demand at premiere shows. It took incessant work and complete dedication.

During practice flights, I gradually learned to weave together various maneuvers so that they flowed in an aerial ballet. Aerial choreography was not unlike synchronizing classical steps into a dance, and I was finding that spotting, a control for spinning turns, formed a basis for both. Aerobatics and ballet combine balance and strength with the focus, discipline, and mind control necessary to excel. Both are lyrical, both demand aesthetics, grace, rhythm, drama, consistency, and spectacle, the flair that delights an audience. Ballet even works some of the same muscles—primarily in the legs—that are needed for flying the Pitts. In the interest of doing strengthening exercise, I also rode a bicycle three miles to and from the airport every day. I did everything I could to ensure that I would make the U.S. Aerobatic Team at the U. S. nationals in September 1985.

In 1985 I asked for coaching from Betty Stewart, former national champion and twice women's world champion. In 1980, Betty's overall point score in the World Aerobatic Championship had been higher than the scores of two-thirds of the forty-two male competitors. In less than four years of flying at the unlimited level, she had gone on to win three gold medals, a silver, and the women's world crown. In 1982 she had been the first pilot, male or female, to win a second World Aerobatic Championship. After she had worked with me, I flew the Canadian National Aerobatic Championships at Gimli and won first-place foreign pilot. I went on to compete in a total of ten contests, each one giving me a chance to learn something about flying and something about myself, my own determination and goals.

I worked and reworked maneuvers; that was the fun part. But having concentrated on spatial awareness, to know where I was in relation to the ground and to the lines that were marked with particular spots on that ground; timing; repetition; correct control inputs; and precision, I found that one of the most difficult tasks was to remain inside the box of airspace. Fortunately, the more I practiced, the more the competition box seemed to enlarge. Confined to a cube of airspace 3,280 feet by 3,280 feet (or 1,000 meters) extending from a minimum of 328 feet above the ground for the unlimited category, I worked to develop a sixth sense about its boundaries. They were marked on the ground by white panels so the physical dimensions could be visible, but orientation was still a challenge when I was sighting from a rolling, twisting, spinning, turning vantage point. Also, the wings of the airplane often blocked the view of the panel markers. I was one of many who looked forward to inserting Lexan panels in the floor to improve my view.

It was hard for me to stay in the aerobatics box. Penalties were assessed for every venture outside of the box and, because they resulted in a loss of points and lower scores, they were to be avoided like the plague. In the worst scenario, flying too low could result in the ultimate—death. I'd flirted with that in the flat spin, an incident that I never wanted to repeat.

The flying part was easy. The tough part was to keep steady nerves while flying for the evaluations of judges and in full view of my competitors, my peers. Obviously, I had a lot to learn about stress management, mindlessness, detachment, and being egoless.

I read and reread the precepts of Zen. Eugen Herrigel, a German philosopher and one of the few Westerners who could articulate the distinctly Eastern Zen, wrote of the necessity of detachment, of disregarding an opponent or those watching with a critical, judgmental eye. His words taught me to clear my mind of all of my opponents, for the more I worked at trying to dismiss them, the more importantly they loomed in my mind.

Herrigel carried that further, suggesting that one learn to disregard oneself at the same time as one disregards an opponent. The state of "purposeless detachment" would lead to perfection, when there was no concern with self, no concern with competitors, and no concern with life or death, just the action itself. That was the challenge I sought to command. Proficiency would become spiritual, explained Herrigel.

I wanted to more than fly zero seven eight. I wanted to *wear* it. I loved the power of the agile, sensational machine. A passenger in a jetliner, streaking along at speeds in excess of 600 miles per hour and cruising at 35,000 or 40,000 feet above the earth, has little reference for motion and only a vague sense of any forward speed. Speed and power are heightened, however, when you're close to the ground and treated to a visual rush—streaks of blended color, a blur of trees, vehicles, and buildings.

I feel the most alive at the controls of a highly volatile, powerful mechanical marvel that is flown close to the ground. I *feel* positive forces sucking me downward toward the center of the earth, turning forces in every banking of the craft, and negative forces that threaten to catapult me and everything else in the airplane out through the canopy. I feel electrically alive from the top of my head to the balls of my feet when I am close to the earth, surrounded by ground rush and when I am tumbling, gyrating, rotating, dancing in space, and yanked or pushed by positive and negative Gs. [1]

---

[1] In physics, a G is more than just the pull of gravity, it is a unit equal to the acceleration of gravity. One *G* is referred to as a measure of the force on a body

After a summer filled with contests and air shows, I realized that I had met a lot of new people. More than once, some guys were surprised to see me get out of the airplane. I didn't fit their image of an aerobatic pilot. When I told of my desire to get onto the team, most were encouraging, but some scoffed, some laughed, and some even tried to discourage me.

---

undergoing acceleration and is expressed as a multiple of the body's weight. Aviators discuss Gs in relation to a concept called "load factor," the ratio of the total weight (load) supported by the airplane's wings to the actual weight of the aircraft and its human and inanimate contents. One G, then, equals the weight of that aircraft plus fuel, all baggage, and the weight of the humans aboard. The wings, in one G, are supporting one times the total weight. Turning flight brings centrifugal and centripetal forces into the equation. In order to turn an aircraft, the pilot must bank it. Once banked, the wings support additional turning forces, although the actual weight of the craft and contents haven't changed.

G forces increase weight incrementally. In a 60-degree banked turn, weight is twice what it is on the ground. The wings must sustain loads equal to twice the total weight. In a maneuver that cranks the needle on the accelerometer to six Gs, you weigh six times your normal body weight. As a 110-pound woman, I become a 660-pound behemoth. At six Gs, a 200-pound man weighs more than half a ton!

When you push an outside maneuver early in the season *before* you've developed your tolerance to G forces, your blood is forced up into your head and makes your eyeballs feel like they're going to pop out of their sockets. Tolerance must to be developed over time, through practice. When I push a negative G outside maneuver, my hair streams over my head like the writhing snakes of Medusa. My feet float away from the rudder pedals (so I have straps on them) and my body strains against the harness and away from the seat. Negative Gs are primarily found only in the realm of civilian aerobatic flight. Military combat pilots are more apt to pull positive Gs. Military scientists have explored high-G tolerances and have developed clothing—G suits—to counteract the pooling of the bodily fluids in the extremities, and military pilots go through centrifuge training. In a positive-G maneuver, the seat tries to swallow you. Your face takes on a grotesque grimace, the world grays, and unless you have physically exercised in preparation, you can black out.

There is a lot of research on the body's reaction to positive Gs but very little, if any, on negative Gs. Civilian aerobatic pilots are the guinea pigs. Many aerobatic pilots experience induced vertigo (a dizziness) as a result of their pulling negative Gs. This vertigo is more of a problem in the high-powered fast monoplanes, and these pilots have to be aware and work to develop the necessary tolerance before performing or competing.

Just prior to heading toward Sherman-Denison, Texas, for the nationals, Bob and I bought Ron Fagen's half interest in the Pitts. The September day that I left for Texas in *my own* Pitts was cool with overcast skies and a low cloud deck and, like pure freedom, it felt like getting out of school or a great Saturday morning. I was on the road again, ready and eager to go. Even the weather picked up on my mood and improved as I headed south. I flew with the wind. If I'd then known Bruce Cockburn's song "Child of the Wind," I would have added, "There are roads of the air and the wind."[2]

My route led to Duane and Judy Cole's for a week of prerequisite coaching and then to Grayson County Airport, the site of the former Perrin Air Force Base. There, I joined the nation's top aerobatic pilots for the competition that we call, simply, "the nationals." I expected no end to the encouragement I'd received to this point. I looked to each new acquaintance and the machine he or she loved to fly as a new thread in the network, another person to know, more lessons to learn. Practicing for the nationals, I met Tom Jones, Mike Stauter, Pete Anderson, Bob Davis, and Ken Larson, who piloted a Bücker Jüngmeister.

My goals—to fly unlimited well and to make the U.S. team—were hanging on the highest star, although a few of my doubts lingered. I still had trouble staying in the box that was only seconds across. Competition itself fires the adrenalin and concentration is as difficult for the pilot as it is for the Western Reining Pattern rider, the air racer, or the football player. Reining riders have been disqualified for having spun their horses five times instead of the required four; air racers have lost the race because they failed to keep track of the number of times they circled the pylons, and football players have lost games by making touchdown runs toward the wrong goalposts.

In *Sport Aerobatics,* editor Jean Sorg noted that I made up for a lack of experience with determination and enthusiasm. She added that I had leapfrogged rapidly to the highest level of competition.

At the U.S. Aerobatic National Championship a competing pilot must fly 70 percent of the required maneuvers for the category entered. I had to successfully complete 70 percent of the unlimited maneuvers. Most pilots choose a category based on the limitations of their ability and those of their airplane. The competition is keen and the competitors are

---

[2] Bruce Cockburn. "Child in the Wind," *Nothing But a Burning Light.* Sony Music Entertainment, Columbia Records. Compact disc. 1991.

all capable, but I was there to prove that I belonged among the unlimited pilots.

The nationals are held annually and, biennially, only the top unlimited pilots at the previous national competition are selected to represent the United States in the World Aerobatic Championship. In the United States, women and men have competed equally without segregation of scores since 1972,[3] in contrast to competing separately as they do in the world contests. Before 1972 a national champion (always male) and a "feminine" or women's national champion were selected, and that policy continues internationally. Although men and women fly the same programs in the same types of airplanes, there are separate sets of flight medals and trophies for men and women. Since men and women compete separately internationally, a biennial selection of a men's team and a women's team is a necessity.

Having been rained out the year before, all of us were eager to fly in 1985. The competition was acute and the tension palpable. I was especially tense. There were five women competing for the team. Bob was with me and was every bit as nervous as I. There were times that he couldn't even watch, the stress level was so high. I knew that I had to get scores that would result in a minimum of 75 percent to represent the U.S. in the world competition. The pressure was fantastic.

I watched the scores posted each day and, after all the competitors had flown and all the scores had been compiled, I was lucky (and delighted!) to take the fifth slot. I flew my best, got a few penalties, but got through it. I made the team! I was going to represent the United States in South Cerney, England at the World Aerobatic Championship 1986!

I *made* the team—my first year in competition! What a trip. My first aerobatic flight with Darlene had been in June 1982. Here, three short years later, I was on the U.S. Aerobatic Team!

The U.S. National Aerobatic Champion that year was Kermit Weeks, who led the team that included Clint McHenry, Henry Haigh, Gene Beggs, and Harold Chappell with Pete Anderson grabbing the alternate spot after narrowly defeating Tom Jones. The women's team consisted of Debby Rihn, Linda Meyers, Julie Pfile, Brigitte de Saint Phalle, and me.

---

[3] In 1972, America's Mary Gaffaney was the first American to win the title of Women's World Aerobatic Champion, and Betty Stewart won the gender title twice.

If anyone were to ask me how, I would tell him or her, "Listen! Learn as much as you can. Listen to everybody, even those from whom you wouldn't necessarily seek advice. Put all that you learn together and develop your own style. Take what you like and leave the rest. A lot of people never learn to listen, or their egos don't allow them to, and virtually nothing is more important."

As I headed home from the nationals, I made a fuel stop at the home of the Women Airforce Service Pilots (WASP) at Sweetwater, Texas, at an airport run by Bob Sears who just recently died of cancer. Sears organized an annual air show there, named in honor of the town.

I flew in, knowing about the air show and thinking, "I hope they ask me to fly the show."

Bob Sears came over when I landed and greeted me. He asked if I needed fuel. As he pumped gas, he suggested that I stay and fly.

I kept my voice calm, saying, "Oh, what a good idea. I'd love to stay and do a routine. Thanks for thinking of it."

I was bursting to tell him that I had made the U.S. team! I wanted to shout, "All right!"

I had grown freer, more confident, and even transformed by my new success.

...ee months, Patty took her first road trip from ...nia to New York with her parents.

Bob Combs, then a pilot with Japan Air Lines, takes Patty for a trip between Tokyo and Osaka, 1961.

...m 1958, Patty at the beach with her ...ther, Rosalie Patty Dorey Combs.

Signature de l'élève :

Padrisia Rosalie Combs

Patty was a student at *la Chatelainie*, a girl's boarding school, in Switzerland, 1968–69.

This 1951 photograph shows Patty at seven weeks with her mother. Her mother wrote, "Isn't this a riot of a baby raising hell? See her clenched fists? This is my favorite."

All photographs courtesy of Patty Wagstaff except where noted.

Patty married Bill Beck. They dove for abalon the coast of Santa Barbara, California in 1973 before moving to Australia.

In Australia, Patty and Bill Beck built a thirty-two-foot-long fiberglass "stink" or power boat, the *White Ghost*, and moved into it in 1975 with their silky terrier Whiskey, a six-pound ball of muscle and spunk.

working in Dillingham with the Bureau of Native
Patty helped with her friend Sue Flensburg's
team at the Beaver Roundup, 1979.

Preparing for a camping trip in Alaska in the early 1980s
with Bob's son Ian.

This cabin in Dillingham, Alaska was Patty's
home in 1979–80. It had no running water
and an outhouse down the hill.

nd Patty Wagstaff
married in 1984.

Clint McHenry and Patty airborne in their matching Extra 230 aircraft.

In 1993 with the late Bob He
former National Aerobatic C
Bob coached Patty in 1987–8
her Pitts S-2S.

Darlene Dubay, Patty's first aerobatic
instructor in Anchorage, Alaska,
in Patty's aircraft in 1991.

With seven-time U.S. National Aerobatic Champion and
World Aerobatic Champion Leo Loudenslager, 1995.

the middle of the duel of champions air show routine with Sean D. Tucker. *Bob Judson, BFGoodrich Aerospace*

Patty performing the Inverted Ribbon Cut in her Extra 230.

y pulling some negative Gs over the Midwest countryside in her Extra 260.

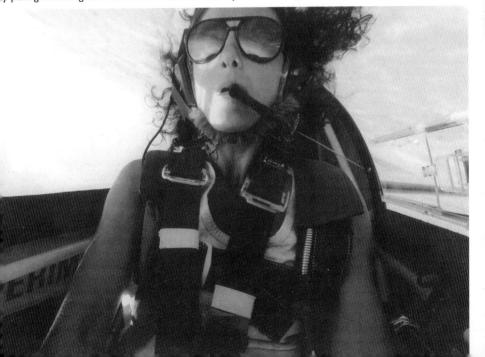

Patty's Extra 260, a one-of-a-kind aircraft, ca[n]
on display in the Pioneer Gallery of the Nat[ional]
and Space Museum, Smithsonian Institution.

Duane Cole presents the second Rolly [...]
Memorial Award for Excellence in Aero[...]
to Patty Wagstaff in 1992. This was the [...]
time she received this award.

Patty helped the U.S. women's team
take first place at the World Aerobatic
Championship in Red Deer, Manitoba,
Canada, 1988.

Patty and Bob Wagstaff in front of her display in
the Pioneer Gallery at the opening reception in 1994.
Patty's plane was donated by Kitty Wagstaff in memory
of Robert Wagstaff, Bob's father.

The International Council of Airshows (ICA[S])
awarded Patty the Sword of Excellence—th[e]
industry's top honor—in 1995.

...kosh in 1995 with world-famous test pilot
...Yeager and air show favorite Bob Hoover.

Patty signs autographs for young fans in Mar del Plata,
Argentina.

Patty with the late Rick Massegee in Austria during
the World Aerobatic Championship, 1994.

...lped initiate what became a worldwide effort to
...ecially equipped Ercoupe plane to Vitas Lapenas,
...nian pilot who survived a near-fatal crash.
...G. Thomas

...l air show crowd, this one at Muskegon,
..., 1993.

In the cockpit with Continental pilot Toni Combs, Patty's sister.

Patty, at the controls of a Pilatus Porter, in costume for her stunt flying in the movie *Drop Zone*, 1994.

Bob Combs with his second wife, Anna Lies, 1993.

Patty with her father Bob Combs, 1990.

Patty relaxes at the World Aerobatic Championship Oklahoma City, 1996. Patty was the top-scoring U.S. pilot at this, her last international competition.

THIRTEEN

Fission

After making the 1985 U.S. Aerobatic Team, in late September I returned to Alaska to spend the winter, and looked for a ferry pilot who would transport the Pitts to Anchorage for me. I wanted the airplane nearby so that weather permitting, I could fly, practice, and keep my cutting edge. I knew that the Pitts was built for aerobatics, not for a long cross-country trip, and I sought someone who was fully qualified in the airplane who could tackle the long flight in my place.

Gene Beggs agreed to ferry the S-1S from Texas to Anchorage, never having flown between the lower forty-eight and Alaska. He started out with my Pitts and a pioneering spirit, initially looking forward to what he hoped would be an adventure, but his anticipation literally cooled when he landed to take on fuel in Shelby, Montana. Temperatures had dropped and, to a Texan, it probably felt as if the Arctic Circle had moved south. Gene called me in Anchorage. "It's getting cold down here," he said.

"Well, yeah," I agreed. "This is the winter, Gene. You're headed for Alaskan weather. We told you to dress warmly and to bring along a gun. You expected it'd be cold, didn't you?"

Gene called again the next day and, in his inimitable style, drawled, "There's an inch of snow on the ground around heah. I'm gonna call

Delmar Benjamin. Is that OK with you? He's a Montanan. At least he's used to these *frigid* conditions."

Delmar, a talented pilot who flies the replica Granville Brothers Gee Bee built by Steve Wolf on the air show circuit, was a great choice. I knew the Pitts would be in good hands and could hardly blame Gene for returning to the warmth of Texas.

The Pitts sliced gamely through icy skies along the Alaska Highway to Anchorage and Delmar landed in temperatures that registered −40 degrees. It was so cold that despite a small heater in the airplane, the canopy had to be cracked to keep the windshield from fogging up inside. His down-filled gear failed to prevent shivering that started during his flight and continued for two days after his arrival. Montana probably felt like a tropical island when he returned—by a plain vanilla, pressurized, and warmed commercial jet.

An Alaskan winter had been a time to hunker down and respect the cold, enjoy the silence, to take dance classes, play video games, and cook. But this winter, with my own airplane nearby, I squeezed in some aerobatics when the skies cooperated. I couldn't let my skill level and G tolerance drop because of a lack of practice. I eagerly anticipated my first chance to fly as a member of the U.S. Aerobatic Team and in international competition in England in the coming summer. I had no idea what to expect, but I could hardly wait.

I believe we had one of the most fully winterized Pittses in history. Bob and I both flew our S-1S, named *Minnesota Fats*, during the winter and kept it at Joe and Ann Wilbur's Flight Operations. There it was kept in good condition under the watchful eyes of Brian Cox, the head mechanic, and Bruce Wilbur, Joe and Ann's son, who was later tragically killed in a plane crash into a mountaintop outside of Anchorage.

Hangars were rare commodities in Alaska, but we were invited to share a T-hangar at Merrill Field with an owner of an orange-and-black Pitts S-2B. We set up an ingenious remote phone system that allowed each of us, prior to leaving for the airport, to call from home to activate a kerosene heater so that by the time we arrived, the hangar and the airplanes were warmed. In addition, my Pitts had a battery heater and a Tanis engine heater that heated the oil in the sump to an acceptable temperature for flight. To fly, I'd push the airplane out onto the icy taxiway, bring an auxiliary power unit plug and the heated battery outside, and start the engine. The airplane had a cabin heater and I dressed in bunny boots, a snow suit, and a parka. Because Anchorage winter weather often includes a temperature inversion—that is, the air warms with altitude instead of the reverse—by the time I climbed to 2,000 or 3,000 feet above the ground, I was generally comfortable enough to turn off the cabin heat. We made it a point not to fly below zero degrees Fahrenheit lest there be a forced landing and subsequent "walkout." That intense cold would barely be survivable.

As a tail dragger pilot, I was used to no forward vision over the nose of the aircraft. I'd learned to rely on peripheral vision right from the start, but I discovered that winter flying had more to teach. Flying off ice and snow wasn't novel, but mastery of the little Pitts in snowy and icy conditions, with its extreme lack of forward vision and significantly higher touchdown speeds, was a real challenge. It was very difficult to maintain visual reference on runways, especially when minor mountains of plowed snow that rose eight to twelve feet or more on each side. The first time I landed on Merrill Field's short and narrow runway, I knew it could be a major mistake. Snow obliterated any references on either side and the nose of the aircraft covered the end of the runway. I had no concept of where I was on the ground. All I could see was white! Little warned me whether I'd touched down in the first third of the runway or was about to plunge into the snowbank at the end.

I was afraid to apply much brake and sent the little airplane sliding into a snowbank. When I successfully brought it to a stop without plowing any snow, I parked it in the hangar, breathed a sigh of relief, and went up to the control tower to speak with the air traffic controllers. I told them about my airplane, its capabilities and its limitations, and that Bob and I planned to fly all winter. From then on, they gave us the longer, wider runway and I discovered a mutual respect that could be fostered if pilots and controllers actually communicated.

Some days it was so icy that my little Pitts literally skated. On those days, I was more like a passenger than pilot-in-command as I taxied out, skittering and sliding sideways like a Sally Lightfoot crab. A wind, added to the equation, made me shut the engine down and I struggled to tow or push the Pitts back to the hangar, finding it tough to get a toehold on the ice for leverage.

Our T-hangar had been built on a recently completed landfill on the east side of Merrill Field. Decomposition was retarded in Anchorage in comparison to warmer climates, and our landfill had been covered too rapidly. We discovered later that serious methane leaks seeped into our hangars and into those near us. We heard that after we had moved out, those in neighboring hangars kept an eternal flame to burn off any leaking methane and thereby prevented an explosion. It was a wonder that when I dialed from the house and punched in the code that lit the kerosene burner, both airplanes and the hangar never exploded into a million pieces.

When Bob and I began, flying was a lark. We had no way of knowing the future, but after the purchase of several airplanes, we had a much better idea of the costs involved and the time that they would demand, time that we would spend apart. I had to ask, "Is it worth it? I'm on the verge of something. Aerobatics is liable to be totally consuming. Shall we continue to pursue this?"

Even though I think Bob knew in his heart how dangerous to our relationship this new passion could be, we were both aboard a freight train that was moving down a track. I don't think either of us knew enough about national and international competition and about the intricacies of committing to an air show career to intelligently analyze all potential consequences. We couldn't truly assess how much competition would cost and how much air show flying might earn, nor did we know the extent to which we both would become involved. We had signed on for a ride, individually and as a pair, and we were both intrigued and extremely curious. In this field we both loved, we were in the midst of an exciting aviation adventure, but we had no clear view to the future. We both realized that it was bound to be difficult to maintain a close relationship if we were to spend many hours, hundreds of miles, and a great deal of time away from each other as well as thousands of dollars in the process.

One evening before the holidays, I propped myself against a pile of my favorite stuffed bed pillows and told Bob that I saw a turning point ahead. Each time I had moved from one airplane to another—from the Beech, to the Decathlon, to the Pitts—I had honed my own talents and had pushed the limits of each airplane. We talked about purchasing another Pitts—a more powerful aircraft with potential for a more varied routine. If we were to buy another, I needed time to master it prior to the world competition.

I said, "Before we move toward an S-1T, we both know it's a more serious aerobatic airplane than *Minnesota Fats*. I think we'd better discuss just where I'm headed and what I'm going to do. If I am to compete on the U.S. team, I will have to hit as many competitions as possible once the season starts. We both know that I'm going to have to prepare for the toughest competition of my life. It's going to cost money and it's going to take a lot of time—more time apart and a lot of traveling."

Bob understood. He knew that I couldn't expect to compete at a global level if I wasn't working as hard as possible to sharpen a competitive edge, to be as precise and as practiced as possible, and to exercise as much control over my head as I needed. He also knew that the aerobatic contests were held primarily in the lower forty-eight, from one end of them to the other.

Each and every day, we both knew that I was getting more deeply involved in aerobatic competition and in all that it entailed. I said, "I'll be on the road and away from Alaska for the entire summer. *Before* we buy a new and more powerful airplane is the time for you to speak up. Do you realize how all-consuming this can be?" Bob assured me that he did. And with that, the decision was made.

Just after the holidays in early 1986, we negotiated the purchase of another plane, a Pitts S-1T.

The S-1T had more power than the S-1S, 200 horses this time, and its constant-speed propeller offered greater efficiency than a fixed-pitch prop.[1] Early in February of 1986, again leaving Anchorage for the great unknown, I flew to Tennessee to pick up the S-1T in Springfield, where Ray Williams prepared it for my arrival. I soloed the new plane, smiled, thanked Ray, and took off for the West.

I had decided to make Avra Valley, Arizona, my base of operations. This was a great location to fly; it had good weather, was quiet, and had an established aerobatics box thanks to the late Amos Buetell.

Between Tennessee and Arizona, I caught up with my sister, Toni, for a get-together. She was interviewing with an airline in Dallas and we took advantage of a good opportunity to spend some time together.

---

[1] When an aircraft has a fixed-pitch prop, the blades are attached to the aircraft in such a way that the pilot can do nothing to change the way the propeller chews into the air. Set at an angle that would bring the best performance in a climb, the propeller blades lost something in cruise configuration. With the constant-speed propeller, a pilot can change the pitch during flight. In the S-1T, I could select the pitch that resulted in peak performance and efficiency in cruise or in a climb.

Afterward, Toni headed for the Caribbean to continue to fly Twin Otters for Crown Air and I winged my way to the Sonoran Desert north of Tucson.

As if by karmic destiny, the Red Baron Squadron, the group of the first air show pilots I had gotten to know, was also practicing at Avra Valley. Keoki Gray had been the first to arrive and he was soon followed by the others, John Bowman, Steve Thompson, and Randy Brooks. We had a lot of fun practicing together and critiquing one another and I logged some time in their Stearman airplanes. Keoki and I tried dogfighting, pitting my feisty bumblebee of a Pitts against his big dragonfly of a Stearman.

One day, Steve Thompson suggested that since I had made the U.S. team, I was going to need to demonstrate my capability at formation flying. I had never flown in close formation with another pilot and Steve was about to show me how.

I was amazed to discover how hard it is to tuck your own airplane close to someone else's, wingtip to wingtip. Least complicated in clear, smooth weather, it took a lot of practice to be a passable formation pilot, not to mention a good one. It proved to be a workout when the heat of the Arizona desert steamed the air and mountain winds churned into turbulence. Just one such bouncy flight was a marvel of perpetual motion and concentration.

Each flight in the S-1T required of me new levels of competence and instilled in me some welcomed self-confidence. It didn't take long to discover how much I loved owning my own airplane and boring holes in the skies over the desert, skies tinged with blue lavender during the day that deepened into aubergine with the dark of night. My practice flights twirled me over a landscape reminiscent of a Navajo sand painting and spiraled the sand and the sky into blues, dusty beiges, reddish cinnamons, and purple.

The more I flew, the more I loved the open sky of Arizona. The more I flew, too, the more I wanted to wear the airplane.

To do well in aerobatics, everything must fit—the seat, seat belts, shoulder harnesses, rudder pedals, and parachute. Ron Fagen and I had shared the Pitts S-1S, and my 110 pounds and five feet four inches contrasted sharply with Fagen's stature; he substantially outweighed me and towered over me at over six feet in height. In our shared airplane, everything had to be rearranged each time one of us flew.

I didn't share the S-1T. That gave me an ultimate feeling of freedom. I hangared it in my own hangar, could push it out to fly anytime that I felt like it, and could return it to the hangar and wipe it down after every flight. I planned three practice flights a day and diligently worked toward having the airplane become an extension of me, as if I were wearing wings.

As much as I loved my Pitts biplanes, I couldn't forget Clint McHenry's Extra 230, which Bob and I had seen at the North Benton, Ohio, contest in 1985. It stood out in my mind's eye as so slick and beautiful. I had been in awe. Logic—and the pocketbook—had told me that it was out of our reach and beyond my needs at that time. Clint's had been the first to arrive from Walter Extra's painstaking labors in Germany and everybody had their eyes on it, curious to see how it performed. I wanted to see its design proven for strength and safety and we all wanted to see how it placed with aerobatic judges.

Biplanes like my Pitts had been well-proven and tested over time, but innovations were occurring. Manufacturers were producing aerobatic monoplanes that had previously only been home- or kit-built. The field of aerobatics was undergoing a metamorphosis every bit as exciting and wondrous as that of the caterpillar changing to a butterfly. I listened to discussions of the new clean monowing designs and rumors of roll rates that were significantly faster than those of the biplanes most competitors still flew. It made me aware that technology was at the cutting edge of the aerobatic scene.

I felt safe flying the Pitts, designed, licensed, and approved in the 1940s and flown by hundreds of pilots, national champions on down. Yet owning a monoplane was a lingering dream. I lusted after the 230, but I kept my cool. In truth, I really had no choice. And although I enjoyed giving rides in a two-seat Pitts on occasion, I liked that my airplane was a single-seater. I liked the feeling of taking off in my Pitts after a contest or an air show and being the Lone Ranger, all alone in the skies, making my own decisions, choosing my own fuel stops, my own altitudes. When the weather cooperated, those were peaceful times.

I had grown accustomed to shoehorning myself into a short, snappy airplane, but I found that the flying characteristics differed between the S-1S and the S-1T. Fighter pilots say, "If you can fly one airplane, you can fly them all." Yet I found that each aircraft seemed to have idiosyncrasies that needed to be explored, tested, and discovered. I also found that what others told me was true. That is, you don't get to really feel an airplane until you have fifty hours in it, and, when you have doubled that, you realize that you knew next to nothing at fifty.

The aerobatic season of 1986 brought me in touch with a host of competition pilots and a chance to know better some that I had already met: Tom Jones, Clint McHenry, Mike Stauter, Kirk Fulton, and Ole Olsen. Groups of people who lived in regions of the country traveled together. Aerobatic competition was like a family gathering. Showing up at most contests guaranteed that you were automatically welcomed and accepted by a friendly and outgoing group. These pilots were some of the most down-to-earth, fun people in the world, all sharing a good deal in common.

Bill McIntyre, for one, was a great friend. He coached me at Falcon Field in Phoenix, Arizona, as often as we could get together. Bill was fully dedicated to aerobatics, wanting to see that the sport itself was furthered rather than his own ego. And never asking to be paid, Bill met me at the airport and spent entire days coaching me. Taking to the air sometimes two and sometimes three times in a day, I flew maneuvers over the desert, connected to Bill's voice by radio as he stood on the ground below, squinting into the sun, critiquing and commenting.

When Bill said, "Crossing now!"—words that were cemented in my brain—he meant that I was at the center of the box. His advice was immediate and helpful. Sometimes he traveled to Avra Valley to repeat the process. A competition pilot must be coached from the ground as often as possible. It is invaluable and equally as important as the hours of solo practice a pilot puts in.

I started calling Leo Loudenslager in 1986. Leo left competition aerobatics behind in 1983 after dubious circumstances and confusion that arose over whether or not he had flown into a "hot box," an aerobatic box in which another competitor was still flying. He continued as an airline pilot and as an air show pilot. When I called to try to hire him to coach me, he was always very pleasant and gracious, but he was also very busy. It took several years to make it onto his schedule.

I spent most of the spring and early summer in Avra Valley, Bob and I commuting between Alaska and Arizona, generally never spending more than two weeks apart. I lived in a Tucson motel and spent my days at the airport. I trained every day three times a day and rarely took a day off unless I was in transit to or from a competition. As much as I adored flying aerobatics in my little Pitts, learning new maneuvers and tumbling around the skies, I was also driven by the realization that Bob had shown faith in my flying ability. I didn't want to disappoint him. My motivation was so intense that, if I took a day off, I felt guilty. A feeling of remorse persisted for years if I went to the mall instead of to the airport. I felt like a failure and sensed that Bob disapproved of my failure to practice.

As I flew in more contests and more people felt that I wanted to be a challenge to them, I heard more sexism creeping into conversations. I taxied out in my Pitts one day and a guy came running over to me, saying, "Watch out for that little airplane, honey! She'll swap ends on ya!" I smiled, wondering, "Would you say that to one of the guys?"

Another time, a guy put his arm around me and said, "Hey, babe, d'ya know what you're doin'? That little thing'll get ya!"

It slowly became apparent that I had to *show* people that I could be serious, capable, and dedicated while being my tolerant, friendly, and spirited self. Some people had a hard time fitting all those facets in one individual. I realized that in order to change perceptions of women in aviation, women in aerobatics, I had to initiate an education process—my own and that of others. This actually served to cement my goal to be the best pilot, not just the best woman pilot. I knew I could do anything in an airplane just as well or better than anyone else and I hoped that the time would come that I could be judged as a pilot, not as a woman pilot. It was my dragon to slay and I was lucky to have one.

I tried to keep a good sense of humor. It was the best antidote to sexism that I have found. With humor, I nudged people with a gentle education, a simple pointing out of the offensive behavior in question or maybe returning a taste of the same dose of medicine. I like to tease guys who slip up. And we all slip. We are all victims, men and women, of sexist thought and behavior. Do we say, he's a "male dentist"? And if we did, would it mean that he was unusual or different or better? To avoid sexism takes constant vigilance.

Some guys simply meant to be helpful, not even realizing that their concept of helpfulness accentuated sexism. I had to find a delicate balance to succeed in a "man's world." I could never give in to complacency because in the long run, it would hurt my efforts and those of other women to be taken seriously. Yet, getting too uptight about little things and being too brusque fails, too. [2]

When I first showed signs of the determination and focus toward my own goals in competition aerobatics—and made those goals known—I had little other than pure encouragement, especially from the men in the sport. Most of them pulled for me, genuinely wanting me to do well. One of my competitors in a contest said, "Patty, if you were to draw your lines a little longer, you'd get better scores."

Another said, "Your snap rolls weren't quite crisp enough, Patty. Try using more rudder in the entry."

I was surprised to discover that the women competitors, on the other hand, never went out of their way. After I started winning and beating men, the women's attitudes changed, too.

Equally important to my personal education was the challenge of my first aerobatic world competition (WAC 1986) to be held in South Cerney, England, that summer, my first international competition as a member of the U.S. team. The U.S. Aerobatic Team! I had pictured it, dreamed about it, and, once a member, let people know how delighted I felt to make it and be part of it.

I trained every day, went to regional contests, and flew in an air show as a volunteer pilot. I hung on every word of those who were willing to help me to improve, to push me beyond my limits.

I prepared and practiced with one goal for the year, to do well at WAC 1986. As a rookie, I held few expectations of the team training session in Springfield, Tennessee, in the spring of 1986. I arrived there with the optimistic idea that helpfulness and the we're-all-in-this-together attitude would prevail, that it would be a team. Competing with one another and then sharing the camaraderie of teamwork is easier to say than to do. I discovered, too, a good old boys' club made up of a group of those who had flown together for years. Members of the clique weren't inter-

---

[2] In my experience, unless there is an instance of blatant and base sexism, a woman who calls attention to certain behaviors is often lumped into the category of ball buster, or worse, *feminist*! That word has become linked with *radical* with its ugliest connotations. The word represents a stereotype of an ultraserious, resentful, unattractive woman or someone with a major chip on her shoulder. In reality, being a feminist has nothing to do with taking sides in a sexist issue, what you look like, or even your gender. I know a lot of men who are feminists; they're supportive of women.

ested in anyone new coming along to disturb their status quo, and the team manager seemed intent on perpetuating the club, as well.

I was on my own!

Brigette de Saint Phalle, a pilot who had competed on the 1984 team and qualified for that of 1986, opted not to participate. Brigette clued me in, telling me that one of the reasons she decided not to compete was because of negative attitudes and a lack of helpfulness on the part of some other pilots. I, too, got more criticism than encouragement and took a jet-propelled course on the rough, tough world of competition. I *expected* to compete with members of international teams. I was disappointed to find virulent competition between members of our own team.

Was I naive to think it should have been different? My first trip to practice in Springfield had been terrific. The contrast was dramatic.

I learned that although many people—the Clint McHenrys and Gene Beggs of the world—were very helpful, others were out solely and childishly for themselves, caring more about their own egos than the nature and the improvement of our sport. Other women on the team were especially difficult and I found myself wishing that Brigette de Saint Phalle had come along.

There had been no doubt that there was a lot to learn about aerobatics, but now I was challenged to learn about interpersonal relationships. Grateful for the training I received, I discovered that adversity could be helpful, too. My stubbornness flared as soon as I realized how nasty some competitors could be. But in a way I was grateful because, for the first time, they galvanized me into truly wanting to win. My first fiery desire to win was actually physical. Like a red-hot blush that reddens an embarrassed face, I felt the rush of adrenalin, and the sharp clutch in my gut, and I wanted to be the very best, to kick some butts. All I could think was, "There is no way that I'm going to let these people get the better of me. There is no way they are going to see me fail."

My only experience in sports prior to aerobatic conflict was to "compete" in horse shows. Team sports had never been offered in the schools I attended and little in my past prepared me to comprehend the sometimes vitriolic spirit of competition.

Our culture doesn't offer women many chances to discover the challenges *and* the joys of sports psychology, interpersonal antagonism, *and* teammate bonding. Male players on football, soccer, basketball, and baseball teams learn from their earliest days how to feel anger toward another only to, moments later, swat that person affectionately for a spectacular slam dunk or a flashy touchdown run.

I think that men learned to release competitive zeal in a different way toward women and that was a more complex subject. Some bonded and were supportive, tolerating competition with women. Some were passive and even patronizing about women's successes, while others enjoyed competing on an equal basis with women. Actually, I found that most men understood a team spirit that transcended individuality.

Sure, I got the round of sexist jokes like, "You sure fly good for a girl!" Laughed off with a good sense of humor, that was harmless. It was rewarding, in fact, to change a man's psyche a little, to jog his reality.

But the women on the team were another story. Are women unable to separate competition in the air from competition on the ground? Why is there this competition at all? Although generalizations are apt to be faulty, I believe that women find it difficult to be direct and honest while being combative. Perhaps it's nature; perhaps it's nurture. Men are raised with expectations that they will compete in business and sports. Women are not. They are taught to be sweet and compliant.

I got a message from the guys on the team that told me, "You're OK. We can deal with you like we've dealt with other competitors before."

I got a message from the women that sounded more like, "You threaten me. Your enthusiasm and your talent are troubling."

Few were encouraging and I was more often ignored and shunned than included. Most women carefully guarded their positions, their team rankings. Was it jealousy? I had a great husband, a good airplane, capability, and drive, and, no matter how hard I worked and practiced, I tried to get along and to find time to have fun. I felt as if some tried to undermine me. Perhaps they tried to beat me on the ground as they tried to beat me in the air. I looked at preparing for competition like a job. I worked hard during the day and, at night, I relaxed and enjoyed myself. A lot of people couldn't do that.

Some might have thought that I was born to compete, but nothing could be further from the truth. I had to learn to be competitive. [3]

In the beginning, winning wasn't important to me. I wanted to do well in order to fly and competition was a means to an end for me. Com-

---

[3] James E. Loehr, author of *Mental Toughness Training for Sports*, believes that mental toughness is learned. He wrote that there are mental attitudes that typically characterize tough competitors and that these are learned, not inherited.

petition taught me to be assertive, and the cold shoulder from some of my colleagues contributed to my own inner strength. I owe a great deal of thanks to those to whom I was a prime competitor. Whether they knew it or not, they pushed me to become a winner.

Prior to departure for England, I had good reason to be thankful to Steve Thompson for having given me some formation time. We flew in loose formation from Springfield, Tennessee, to Dover Air Force Base in Delaware following, like a gaggle of geese, lead pilots Bob Davis and Don Taylor in a well-equipped Beechcraft Baron.

The weather was much cloudier than we would have liked. None of our aerobatic planes had instrumentation for flying in inclement weather or descending through layers of clouds for approaches to landings. If we had gotten stuck "on top" with low fuel (and our little akro planes *always* had low fuel, even just after takeoff!), we knew that our choices were limited to parachuting out (and losing a perfectly good airplane!) or, my solution of choice, spinning down through the overcast (and hoping that there was sufficient room beneath the clouds to right the aircraft and get located!).

A pilot flying in the clear air above clouds has a pristine view of a whitewashed world. The heavy quilt of clouds forms a blanket that completely obscures the ground. Beautiful to see, the fluffy woolen white is dangerous to the hapless flyer who lacks sufficient instrumentation for cloud penetration and who has to descend into it as if into a morass. As we pressed on over the tops of the clouds, I radioed our lead pilots and told them that I had very little fuel left. I briefly considered breaking out of the formation and returning to an airport I knew to be accessible a few miles back but stuck with the group for a while longer.

It was a tremendous relief when the overcast layer finally broke up and the solid sea of clouds parted to permit isolated glimpses of the ground. Despite the tensions of formation flying and inclement weather,

---

His list included self-motivated and self-directed, positive but realistic, in control of emotions, calm and relaxed under fire, highly energetic and ready for action, determined, mentally alert and focused, doggedly self-confident, and fully responsible. Loehr noted that athletes with these qualities dominate the world of sports and show the reality of mental toughness each time they perform. Their inner strength makes all of the difference.

we reached Dover AFB, could see the runway stretching before us, and landed safely.

Our next task was to load all of our airplanes into a huge U.S. Air Force C-5A, a behemoth of an airplane, which we had chartered—thanks to generous sponsors and individual and corporate donors—for transportation to England. Our ten small airplanes, mostly biplanes, fit easily into the vast cargo area. Biplanes could be pushed straight into the larger airplane. Monoplanes, because of their longer wings, had to be placed on dollies and slid aboard at an angle—a tricky, crabbing maneuver.

Finally, we left at three o'clock in the morning. Our ten beautiful and colorful aerobatic airplanes were secured on the cargo deck, the C-5 pilots were tucked into their cockpit on the upper deck of the C-5A, and we fastened our seat belts for a flight across the Atlantic Ocean. At takeoff, we faced aft from the cockpit in the huge cavernous interior, and a single porthole near the forward galley gave us severely limited views of the ground or of the seemingly endless sea. We were assailed with the sounds of the inner workings of the huge airplane—levers cranking and hydraulically moving parts grinding as they slid in and out.

We were airborne, bound for Mildenhall Air Force Base, north of London, for the thirteenth World Aerobatic Championships, WAC 1986! I felt a surge of pride to be part of my nation's team, a feeling reminiscent of how it seemed as a kid in Japan to be a representative of America. Overwhelmingly, despite the motivations of individual team members, we all felt the challenge and the weight of proving ourselves and of doing our best for our country, for our team, and for ourselves.

Unfortunately, individual competition continued. I spent time with the team members that I liked and respected and kept my distance from those with whom I had little rapport. It was a distinct challenge to act as an individual who faced singular competition and who had to simultaneously compete as a member of a team.

After landing, we flew as a group to Strathallan, near Auchterarder, Scotland. I had never flown my own airplane in any foreign country other than Canada, and, though I had been to England, it was incredible to me to be flying low over the lush green of the Lake District, the Borders, the North Country's quaint villages. The British and Scottish accents in the speech of the air traffic controllers combined with the unique views of the ground to establish without a doubt that we were flying in the airspace of other nations.

Our world contest took place not long after the 1986 U. S. retaliatory military action against Libya, ordered by then-President Ronald Reagan in response to the barbaric in-flight bombing of a Trans World Airlines flight over Greece and the destruction of a discotheque frequented by Americans in Berlin, both of which resulted in American deaths. Just before we'd left, the news media of our country flashed grim reports of slaughters at European airports. I wasn't alone in feeling a bit paranoid about international travel.

Our Atlantic crossing and arrival in England went smoothly, although the excitement of global competition was exacerbated by the jitters of global tensions. Bob and I were assigned a room in dorms at the South Cerney Agricultural College, and, one evening, rooming next door to us, our team manager and his wife heard a knock on their door at about ten o'clock at night. The knock was quickly followed by a loud thump. They opened the door and were horrified to see that someone had dropped a gruesome and bloody severed horse's head! The next morning, another U.S. team member discovered a gory horse's leg in the communal bathroom. I had visions of terrorism, though no one claimed responsibility for such mindless, horrifying acts. Bob and I decided we had had enough of dorm life and took a room in a hotel in town.

My uncle Jack Combs, a fighter pilot during World War II, and his wife Hilary joined Bob's parents, Robert and Katherine "Kitty" Wagstaff from Kansas City, Kansas, as part of our cheering section for a few days of the competition. Unfortunately, the weather was abominable—chilly with low fog and misty rain. Inclement weather complicated the enjoyment for those watching and reduced the chances that competitors could get airborne.

At the beginning of the contest, we parked our airplanes in a semicircle, waiting for all contestants to arrive at the aerodrome. It was exciting to see aircraft designs I had only read about—the French CAPs built by Avions Mudry, German Extra 230s, and exotic homebuilt monoplanes. We were gathered in a large group when the Soviets arrived, demanding our rapt attention like Klingons aboard Federation starships. Built in the days of paranoid communism and KGB secrecy, Sukhois were not built for cross-country flight. To get to an international contest, the wings of each Suke were removed and the airplanes were reassembled at an airfield close to the contest site. Once reassembled, the pilots took off, closed in tight formation, and arrived at the contest en masse. Their bold, brassy arrival was a cleverly intimidating achievement.

The Soviet Sukhoi 26s clawed toward us from the distance, their engines growing progressively louder, more insistent, more *commanding*. Conversations stopped and all eyes turned upward to witness the impressive arrival that thundered overhead. Someone yelled, "The Russians are coming!"

Three formidable airplanes streaked across the field in a low, loud, distinctive pass. Their engines resonated with deep rhythmic pulses that differed greatly from the identifiable Lycoming engines of the United States. It was an entirely new experience to hear snarling growls of 360-horsepower Vedenyev M-14 engines; the Soviets had cowed their competition before the contest even began.

They landed on their springy titanium gear and slowly taxied over, their brakes emitting another distinctive Sukhoi sound, a high-pitched squeal. The airplanes seemed huge in comparison to the machines that were their competition. No wonder someone called them "aerobatic airplanes on steroids."

The pilots climbed out, their faces stern and serious, their bodies making no useless or wasteful motion. Like combat troops, they were instantly surrounded by protective and swarthy KGB types.

On closer inspection, the airplanes were outwardly rough, painted as if brooms had been the brushes, the lettering and signage slapped on. Outward appearances, however, belied the powerhouses under the engine cowls and the extremely strong structure beneath the skins. The Vedenyev engine, one of the most rugged and reliable radial engines in the world, was sophisticated largely because the Soviets never stopped building radial engines after the Second World War as did aircraft manufacturers of the western world. Also, the airplane was built almost solely with composite construction at a time when Extras, CAPs, and Pitts were all still made of wood and fabric. Lightweight and extremely strong, the Sukhois tested to an unheard-of twenty-three Gs! In the air they were performing monsters! Their roll rate was fantastic and vertical performance was mind-boggling—almost unbelievable. The pilots, though trained to perfection, were challenged to stop that incredible roll with precision. Obviously not lacking an energy management problem, Sukes could enter a routine at a low altitude, climbing handily. Most of the rest of us started at a high altitude, entering the aerobatic box from above and taking advantage of all the speed that we could muster from an entry dive.

It took a while for the ex-Soviet and Russian pilots to adapt fully to the capability of the Sukhoi airplane. Once accomplished, and because of the Soviet system of subsidized athletic teams and full government support, they have been responsible for raising the standards of unlimited competition aerobatics.

On a rainy morning before the competition began, the contest director asked for volunteers to fly an air show the following day at a nearby U.S. Air Force base. There isn't a lot of crossover between competition pilots and air show pilots. Many competition pilots feel very purist about their sport, simply don't enjoy air shows, and/or feel that air show flying is dangerous. I loved both forms of aerobatic flying and my hand immediately went up. As usual, my enthusiasm evoked a few raised eyebrows from my teammates.

Two other pilots also volunteered to fly the air show—Eric Mueller of Switzerland and Ian Padden of England. The next morning dawned with rain pouring out of the heavens with a vengeance. Despite the weather, Eric, Ian, and I flew because the base was only a ten-minute flight away and a huge, and evidently hardy, English crowd had gathered, complete with umbrellas. How could we disappoint them?

Ragged cloud bases hung only 500 feet above the ground, leaving us with little room for any maneuvers other than a few rolls. Ian Padden flew first. He departed from South Cerney, flew over the air base performing a few rolls, and, as he returned, I took off.

I flew toward the base thinking, "Wow, what a change from my last visit. Here I am in the air instead of just a street person." As I reached the base, rain started to pour. The ceiling was incredibly low, but the crowd was huge. I thought, "This is great! Only in England would you get a crowd this size to stand outside in weather like this!"

I flew my allotted four minutes, doing rolls, point rolls, rolling turns, more rolls and more point rolls, and departed the area. I was followed by Eric Mueller. I heard later that, although we were forbidden to fly in the clouds, Eric had done loops up into the clouds only to shoot out beneath them on the bottom part of the maneuver! He did half his routine in that weather! When he landed back at South Cerney, he climbed out of his Extra with a huge smile on his face. Eric looked at me, his face beaming, and said, "Wasn't it wonderful?" I liked him from that moment on.

On the ground at the contest, I felt as if I were an actor in the play of life. The flying was lousy because there wasn't much of it, but the people were fascinating. Tents that were fashioned in a circle around the center of the contest site were erected for the relaxation of the pilots of each country, and outside of each tent was a picnic table. The scenes were stereotypical. Soviets, dark and mysterious, serious and intense, played a lot of chess. The French, more carefree and outgoing, preferred to be cooking up an omelet and having lengthy, talkative lunches, loosely gathered at their picnic table. The Italians, friendly and scattered, were animated and vigorous, boldly waving their arms to punctuate their speech. The British were quiet, introspective, and rather subdued. The Americans? We spent a lot of time avoiding each other and practicing independence. Capable of speaking a little French, thanks to my year of school in Switzerland, I opted to hang out with the affable, outgoing French.

Each morning, more than seventy pilots from seventeen different nations woke eager to look at the sky. Invariably, it was clear, with promise of good flying weather. Then, well before noon, clouds rolled in, fog blanketed the area causing restrictions to visibility for most of each day, wreaking havoc with flight schedules and depressing already-tense flyers. Grounded aerobatic pilots do not make a happy group.

We were on an island in the North Sea. The poor weather shouldn't have surprised me. But after traveling halfway around the world and gearing up to be competitive, to be the best, to be prepared and psyched and in a Zen mode, I found it extremely difficult to find flying scrubbed day after day. My frustration level escalated, my sharp edge of control started to unravel. Doubts began to creep into my thoughts and I wanted to fly so badly I could taste it. I would have given anything for the chance to resharpen my touch, to *fly*.

By the last day, the entire competition was squeaked in. Everyone got a chance to fly, even though it meant flying the last of the unknown flights in near dark. South Cerney proved to be good practice for readying ourselves for subsequent competitions, like 1992 in Le Havre, France, where we were almost completely rained out and only completed one flight.

Many articles in 1986 sought to report our Olympic-style event, describing the site and discussing the athletes, but found little to discuss about the flying because of the weather. But most news articles superficially skimmed highlights and missed the undercurrents and behind-the-scenes machinations. I couldn't believe the politics! There were even some situations that turned downright nasty.

The management of our team seemed mired in two sets of standards. In the States, the team's elite were rewarded with the best rooms in the best hotels. In the UK, on our cross-country flights from England to Scotland and back to South Cerney, only a few pilots were given navigational charts, and they were proprietary about them.

On a personal level, a horrible pair of polyester pants and a shirt started a problem for me. This was a uniform, an outfit designed to identify us as members of the U.S. team, our country's representatives. Any knowledgeable pilot knows that it is dangerous to fly in plastic material. I thought, "I'm not going to have that kind of stuff melt on my skin if I'm in a crash!"

I spoke to the team manager. "I can't wear synthetic stuff. It's dangerous. Nobody should wear it. I'll buy something identical but made of cotton, okay?" It was a small thing, and with the team manager's approval I did it, but I took flak over it.

Some scuffles didn't involve me personally, but team cohesion was inevitably affected. It was exceedingly tough to compete as individuals, then pull together to compete as a team and to act like teammates. Perhaps it was best described as "antagonistic cooperation."

After several days and too many tense confrontations, I had about had it. So many of the complaints sounded like nothing more than whining, most were petty and snide. It reached a peak for me when, in the midst of bitching about something else, one particularly critical woman turned to me and sniped, "You—you didn't wear your uniform."

I retorted, "You know, the reason I didn't wear my uniform is because I didn't want to be associated with assholes like you. You don't represent our country. You don't show up at the tent where you are supposed to greet visiting Americans. You are nasty. It makes me sick."

Afterward, some slapped me on the back. "Way to go, Patty."

Others avoided me. In a sport that demanded such dedication, skill, grace, and timing, I thought I would see some of those qualities displayed on the ground as well as in the air.

Yet amidst vicious rivalry, there are moments of greatness, moments of shared delight. Those rarities were like oases in a desert. The men's contest was won by Petr Jirmus, a Czechoslovakian in a Zlin 50LS and the first and only person to win the overall world contest twice. Petr was wonderful to watch. He flew as smoothly and accurately as I had ever seen. Three U.S. team members finished among the top ten. Though I longed for the day that they would no longer say, "The women flew a separate contest," by the completion of the competition, Soviet team member Liubov Nemkova was first among the women in a Sukhoi Su-26M. I placed seventh in my Pitts S-1T.

Flying brings out the ego in all of us and aerobatic flying makes us tigers. Writer and photographer Budd Davisson wrote that a view of me contrasted wildly with the image of my air show routine. The show was frenetic and brutal, he said, but, once out of the airplane, I showed none of the visible savagery demonstrated in the air.

Some in England must have seen some indications of the aerobat that I was in the process of becoming and some saw a bit of that visible savagery. I hope they saw the genuine thrill that I felt to represent the United States in an international competition. I made a sincere effort to represent the country and my team well. I came home hoping to improve, hoping to represent my country again. I also came home with a new resolve to be better than anyone else on the team.

After returning to the States, I attended a team meeting and heard that there was an opening for U.S. Aerobatic Foundation President. I immediately thought of my husband, Bob. I knew that he would be outstanding and thought of the numerous positive changes he could make. The U.S. Aerobatic Foundation not only does all the fund-raising for the team, but it is in charge of policy with the board. Once he accepted the presidency, I knew that Bob would make valuable contributions.

I came home, too, deciding that I needed to fly more air shows to balance my competition flying. For one, I loved the positive energy of the crowd, the other pilots I had met, and their contagious excitement. For another, I felt that I would develop a poor attitude due to the conflicting personalities and petty politics if I were limited to competition. The politics of the air show business, or what I knew of them, seemed to operate on a higher and more democratic level.

I decided to attend the 1986 Convention of International Council of Air Shows (ICAS) in Las Vegas, Nevada. Bob returned to Anchorage, and, after dropping off my little Pitts, N200ST, in Avra Valley, I stopped in Las Vegas alone before continuing on to Alaska for the winter. My intent was to learn all that I could about the marketing of an act. I wanted to meet the people who were at the top of their performance careers and I luckily met several whom I had met previously and with whom I felt comfortable—the late Bob Herendeen, a couple of the members of the Red Barons, Brigette de Saint Phalle, and Lee Manelski. They were all very helpful, and, after the clamor of competition, the difference in the climate of the air show convention was genuinely delightful, a breath of fresh air.

I listened and tried to learn and spent time in the convention hall and in the bar at night getting to know promoters and performers. I had no idea how to make arrangements for appearing in a particular air show, but Tom Jones, who had already delved into the world of performance, generously shared a copy of his very simple, one-page contract for me to use as a template for my own.

I found Las Vegas's glitz a real trip and stayed up every night until the wee hours of the morning. One morning at about eleven o'clock, my hotel room phone rang. A voice told me, "I represent Quinte Air Force Base in Ontario, Canada. Could you come downstairs to talk with us? We would like to book you." All I could think was, "Book me? Had I done something wrong?" After showering and quickly dressing, I went downstairs and signed my first performance contract. Invited for an appearance at the Canadian military base in June of 1987, I returned to Alaska even more excited than ever about my next flying season.

The balance between performance and competition was what pleased me the most. In competition, flying was formal, structured like a triumphal march. I loved the perfectionism and the discipline of it in the same way that I loved the order of classical ballet. Air show flying moved more to the lyrical rhythm of modern dance and I loved that freedom. In competition, the climate was sometimes clouded with intensity and tension, while on the air show line during an afternoon's performance, the mood was often conscientious yet lightened with laughter. I knew the *joy* of arriving at a parking area for air show aircraft and joining a friendly group of air show stars.

Gathering with people of the entertainment industry who radiated the warmth and camaraderie that performance engenders reminded me of slipping into the river in Australia after a day of 110-degree heat. In contrast to the hot pressure of competitive flying, the ambiance of an air show was like a cool, refreshing dip into soothing water with green, feathery, overhanging branches.

I was finding the best of both worlds.

FOURTEEN

Gypsy Spirit

Though Bob had suggested my first air show performance in Gulkana in 1984, he was not supportive of my increasing involvement in air shows, initially. He felt that air shows were kind of a carny thing and that air show pilots lived a gypsy life. He suggested that I stick with competition.

But I wanted to do air shows. The few I had done proved a great break from other pressures—business details, practice, and competition. I planned to fit performances around contests, and if I was successful, I could offset some of the costs of competition with air show earnings. Performing appealed to me. And besides, no one had much more of a gypsy spirit than I.

Once he'd expressed his way of thinking, Bob respected my wishes. He saw to the legal ramifications and Patty Wagstaff Air Shows (PWAS) was incorporated on the day after Christmas 1986. [1]

I started on a venture that required a simultaneous juggling of my athletic talents, business acumen, and my skills in scheduling, marketing, public relations, and management as if they were so many brightly

---

[1] It was about this time that a local newspaper referred to Bob as Bob Beck in an article about flying. I hadn't changed my name to Wagstaff yet, and, after this incident, Bob suggested that maybe it was time I do so.

colored balls that had to be kept in the air. I had to discover the business of running a career, including managing the diverse facets of my public life and my personal life, keeping them on track and as well-balanced as possible. I started with a small room in Bob's law offices and tackled a small start that promised to quickly grow into a formidable network of work. We both gave it our all. Money did start to creep in, as I was paid for my air show performances, but, for a long time, the costs of my ambition far outpaced my earnings.

I traveled to Avra Valley in the spring, planning to fly my Pitts S-1T during the year of 1987. But knowing that new airplanes had pushed my accomplishments previously and knowing that I was outgrowing the T's capabilities, Bob and I bought Kirk Fulton's Pitts S-2S, N216JC. That funky, powerful machine became my favorite Pitts of all time. A fat little banana-shaped airplane, the S-2S was a great air show airplane, the best Pitts ever built—for fun!

Originally, we bought 216JC for the express purpose of having Steve Wolf make it into a "super" Pitts. In addition to being great with modifications, Steve is a superb air show pilot and master craftsman who built a replica of Curtis Pitts's large biplane, named *Sampson*, and the Gee Bee replica flown by Delmar Benjamin. He figured that he could streamline my slightly rotund Pitts and increase its roll rate by other methods.

Once I'd taken possession of it, I flew it at Avra Valley before getting it to Steve's shop, then in Idaho. I *loved* that airplane. I loved its six-cylinder engine and its big nose out in front of me. I flew the S-1T once more in comparison, then decided to sell it, putting the S-2S project on hold.

I took to the air in the red-and-white S-2S, N216JC, and used it for competition and air show performances, following the show circuit and chasing aerobatic contests around the country. Just as farming started in the nation's South in early spring and moved northward with the warm weather, so too did air shows, and I migrated to follow the action. I swung toward the coasts in clockwise fashion, reaching Minnesota and the Dakotas in July and August, then circled toward the other coast and back to the warmer climates as fall chilled the air and winter closed the shows.

In the early days of aviation, it had been common to give names to airplanes. Everyone has heard of Charles Lindbergh's Ryan, *The Spirit of St. Louis*. I had named my first little Pitts S-1S *Minnesota Fats*, figuring if *Fats*, the famed pool shark, could get the ball into the pocket with consistency and finesse, then I could do the same with my little airplane, as precisely as possible.

When I started flying the S-2S, I found a great sign painter who followed my instructions and created a beautiful freehand paint job on the fuselage—a skull bedecked with a biker bandanna. Next to the logo and straight out of the philosophy of *Zen and the Art of Motorcycle Maintenance*, it said, "Ride hard. Die free" and in tiny letters alongside it, "Bad news travels fast."

At my first competition in California, I heard, "Are you *nuts? 'Ride hard. Die free?'*"

I have always been adventurous but rarely reckless. I never liked the idea of hurting myself. Yet I was rarely frightened of living on the edge as long as when I was thinking rationally, I remained in control. But the comments of others got through to me. I rubbed out my biker skull and logo with a mixture of Ajax cleanser and rubbing alcohol. I realized that people truly look at our sport as dangerous.

To those of us who fly, flying aerobatics is what we *do*. We don't belabor the dangers or even think much about them.

By midsummer of 1987, Duane Cole helped to get me included as an air show performer at the prestigious air show held at Oshkosh, Wisconsin, at the annual Experimental Aircraft Association (EAA)'s Convention and Fly-In. Already a member of EAA, I had served as secretary and treasurer at different times in my local chapter in Anchorage. At my first Oshkosh performance, not only was it great exposure to fly in front of a crowd that numbers nearly a million during the five-day convention, but it was my chance to give something back to the organization that gives aviation so much.

Aerobatic activity in Avra Valley had revived by that year, after having been set back by the loss of Amos Buetell. I became friendly with a local bunch of pilots like Wyn and Jason Hayward, who each owned a Christian Eagle biplane, and with Fred Leitig and his wife, Sally. Fred, always helpful with advice whether the information was mechanical or aerodynamic, had ready answers and a set of tools that he knew how to use well. He flew a beautiful yellow Hiperbipe biplane that he had built. Unfortunately, we lost a great friend when Fred was killed with another pilot, Bob Keller, in our Avra Valley aerobatic box a few years later.

It was at Avra Valley that I had originally met Ole Olsen and Kirk Fulton, the man from whom we purchased the Pitts S-2S. I met Rory Moore and Chip Beck from Phoenix, or the Firebird Aerobatic Team, which, as Chip said, was a spiritual place to be rather than a real team. That "team" was, in reality, a group of aerobatic friends who shared a hangar and depended upon Harley Elmore, a mechanic and friend, to maintain their airplanes.

Aviation is a small community, despite its global network. Air shows and aerobatic contests brought us all together—friends, relatives, performers, competitors, significant others, appreciative crowds, sponsors, the media, but mostly other aerobatic pilots. If we failed to catch up with one another at our home bases, we crossed paths in the air. Because those involved in aviation form such a large, boisterous, extended family of dynamic individuals, you appreciate those who come into your life, never knowing when, where, or even if they will enter your life again. But all have something of value to teach, if you are open to listening and learning.

I began to hear, loudly, that the stock Pitts S-2S I loved wasn't presenting itself well enough at the competition levels I was trying to reach. The belly was so round that some said it looked like a football. Painted white, it was hard to see. (Aerobatic pilots like to paint their airplanes in dark colors to make them stand out against the blue sky.) Judges weren't impressed with it and lower scores attested to that. It was suggested that my airplane scored poorly in competition because it looked "like a grand piano hurtling through the air."

The more contests that I watched, the more opportunity I had to see what others were flying and to see how their airplanes presented visually. My aircraft wasn't impressive, but that wasn't entirely the fault of the Pitts.

I trained with a past national champion, the late Bob Herendeen, in Delano, California, in 1987. (He also traveled to Tucson to coach me in 1988.) A consummate and highly respected airline and aerobatic pilot, he helped me with Tail Slides, with inverted flat spins, and with my first Ribbon Cut. For the latter, he showed me the correct pole setup, width of the ribbon, how to piece the ribbon together, and inverted and close to the ground, how to maintain the concentration necessary for cutting the ribbon and maintaining a straight line.

Because I was having trouble getting my Pitts S-2S Tail Slides to go straight backward, I asked Bob for help. I blamed the rigging of the airplane for my having such a tough time keeping the aircraft straight to the vertical line. He generously offered to fly the airplane. I watched him climb into the sky, then start a series of Tail Slides. He slid backward down the vertical line, and every Tail Slide was perfectly straight.

I felt like a whipped pup, my tail between my legs. After he landed, I mumbled something like, "Guess it's not the airplane, eh?" Always the gentleman, he smiled gently and described more fully just exactly what it was that I had to do. [2]

Famous for his inverted flat spins, Herendeen's air show act generally started from high above show center and the crowds chanted the number of turns as his little airplane corkscrewed down toward them: ten, eleven, twelve . . . fifteen, sixteen . . . twenty-seven, twenty-eight. Sometimes he completed thirty, his tiny craft looming out of the hazy blue distance and growing more visible with each rotation.

I appreciated his invaluable help and I appreciated the help and moral support that I got from my husband, Bob, too. I flew to Anchorage about once a month and Bob took time off from his law practice to fly to Tucson every chance that he could. When he was in Tucson, he rode his motorcycle to watch me fly, parking on what we called the Hump, a small mountain situated in a curve in the road. Just glancing down and seeing him straddling his parked bike, often with a video camera in his hand, was a boost to my morale, and he also critiqued via radio, helping me a lot with my accuracy and my precision. Our competition and air show business was a joint venture, a growing commitment, and an expensive and time-consuming process. Bob put a great deal of time into its operations and its requirements. Yet he also expected me to perform and I was always wary of disappointing him lest he take my "toys" away. Some of that concern pushed me toward my success like tension fuels the bow before it releases an arrow.

---

[2] I asked Bob Herendeen how he got into flat spins and he told me that he rolled inverted, stalled the airplane and, when it was fully stalled and the nose started down, he kicked full right rudder (because it won't spin flat with left rudder) and let it turn a quarter to a half turn. Once established in a turning mode, he put in aileron on the same side as the rudder—*right* aileron. (When inverted, the aileron that flattens the spin is opposite the one that you'd use right side up!) Power added brought the nose up and the result was a flat inverted spin. Once established, he could reduce power, except for the smoke system.

Throughout my career, one constant need was aircraft maintenance. In addition to mastering aerobatics, consistently honing my talents with practice, and learning the intricacies of the business world, I had to master the care and feeding of a mechanical steed. Like every technical field, aircraft mechanics have changed a great deal as aircraft have become more sophisticated, as aircraft engines have become more complicated, as engineering has become more advanced, and as rules and regulations have become more stringent. A pioneer pilot of the 1930s like Nancy Hopkins Tier or Phoebe Omlie might have been able to make quick repairs with a screwdriver, a wrench, and some baling wire. My flying, my airplanes—and the Federal Aviation Administration—required much more.

I liked hanging around when I had an airplane repaired or in for its annual inspection. I changed oil, did my own refueling, and performed some of the minor adjustments. But I didn't (and couldn't) do major work myself. The government has established rules about the inspections, the maintenance and repair, and the technicians required with which I had to comply. [3]

When shop costs gobble $40 per hour, the cost of maintaining an aerobatic aircraft can be astronomical. Over the years, I've needed a mechanic at the damnedest times—at an air show or a competition on the opposite side of the country from my repair shop of choice, flying cross-country miles from anywhere, or, worse, just as I tried to start the engine to take off for a performance. There were times I depended on mechanics that I didn't know, some whose skill was a total unknown, and my plane was serviced in shops where my aircraft was the first they had ever seen like it.

I've gotten pretty good at troubleshooting, and as the engine is the heartbeat of the airplane, I know when it misses a beat. I recognize seri-

---

[3] Those that have studied the art of maintenance—and it is an art *and* a science—have passed required practical and written tests and are certificated as airplane and powerplant experts—A&Ps. Those mechanics qualified to work on aircraft and to judge the work of others are called authorized inspectors—IAs. I had added a lot of flying certificates to my list of credentials, but I never pursued the A&P. As my list of competitions and air show performances grew, I doubted I would. I had little time to apprentice or to even consider getting additional certificates and, as I purchased new and more sophisticated aircraft, I developed an even greater need for someone to turn to, a mechanic I could trust.

ous problems or minor problems quickly and learned to recognize early warning signs of impending engine trouble. As my experience grows, I've learned enough to supervise mechanics who work on my plane and I generally know what they mean in their explanations of problems.

When time allows, I watch closely when my airplane undergoes repairs because no matter how good a mechanic is, mistakes can happen. I once had my airplane repaired, took it up for an air show flight, and came close to becoming a statistic. Some screwdrivers had been left under the cowl, and, after a control jam, I lit on the runway as if I were landing on glass. An inspection of the tail section netted *eight* screwdrivers tangled in the control cables. The mechanic was mortified and terribly contrite. I learned to keep an eagle eye on all repairs and preventive maintenance. [4]

Maintenance has been my aerobatic jigsaw puzzle, a major concern of my career. My airplane *has* to be reliable. No matter how much better and stronger the aircraft are becoming, you can't fail to show up at a competition or an air show for which sponsors have advertised and into which a lot of money has been sunk on your behalf. Nor can you slide in and have your airplane break down immediately after you land (although

---

[4] One of my favorite A&Ps, New Hampshire's Dennis Sawyer, has not only been an expert with aerobatic machines, he is also an accomplished aerobatic pilot. I can ask him to fly the airplane after he is through working on it and ensure that everything is OK. It is terrific to be able to count on someone like that, to be sure the work will be done right.

My engine builder, Monty Barrett of Barrett Performance Aircraft, has taught me about engines, too. I went to his shop in Tulsa, Oklahoma, and learned by osmosis, by watching Monty and his guys at work. Monty modified my Lycoming engine by porting and polishing the cylinders, by flow-balancing everything, and by turning it into a super-smooth racing engine. He stands behind the engines on which he puts his mark and his name and says, "Here's the new engine, but remember it's not your engine, it's always going to be mine. Since I have built it, I'll stand behind it. Whenever you have a problem, it's my problem, too." Time and again Monty proved that he meant that and, when the engine work was finished, he played a mean blues guitar to boot.

Most aerobatic airplanes used the Lycoming engine, designed for inverted flight and for rigorous aerobatics. The number of Gs pulled on a daily basis multiplied by the number of flight hours on a machine reduces the total hours of engine life by a like amount. Leo "Looper" Loudenslager once said that all airplanes are progressive failures—add a few Gs and they progressively fail all the more quickly. I've needed to change my engines about every three hundred

202 FIRE AND AIR

that sometimes happens). Everyone knows everyone else in the networking of aviation and reputations can be dashed very rapidly. An air show pilot who is a no-show or a disappointment doesn't receive another invitation to perform and doesn't get paid. A competitive pilot who fails to arrive at the contest is a loser.

My newest airplanes have been strong and mechanically sound and have caused me very little grief in the mechanical department—with a great deal of deserved praise for the designer, Germany's Walter Extra. He has constantly improved his airplanes to withstand the weird and twisting things that we do to them. Like the high-tech world of which it is a part, aerobatic flying has changed dramatically, not only since it began but within its last decade, since his Extra 230 first came out in 1984. Torquing and tumbling maneuvers were then limited to a few lomcevaks—*lomcevak* translating from its Czechoslovakian roots as "headache." A maneuver that results in a tumbling, nose after tail of the airplane, a lomcevak was about the wildest of the maneuvers when I started competition.

Today we do some high-speed actions that push planes and pilots. Knife-edge spins on every axis and maneuvers that depend on the torquing moment of the propeller and engine combination get the planes to

---

to four hundred hours. I never count on it going to TBO, the factory-recommended time limit for overhauling an engine, which is typically about two thousand hours. Some modern maneuvers, vertical torque rolls, knife-edge parabolas, fishtails in knife edge, and such dramatically push machines. It doesn't matter whether the flying has changed the airplanes or the airplanes have altered flying styles. With the advent of the Soviet Sukhois, the French CAP airplanes, and the German Extras came maneuvers that had not previously been possible. Pilots stretch their own envelopes as they test to see the limits to which they can push their new and exotic machines.

Aerobatic planes are very tightly cowled, making it hard to properly cool engines in the air and on the ground. As a consequence, they often run at very high oil temperatures causing, among other things, magneto problems. Given the nature of the flying and the necessarily abrupt throttle applications, cylinders that heat and cool quickly are prone to shock cooling and the resultant tendency to crack. When I fly my airplane every day, I would be remiss if I didn't learn to read it like my own body. I'm a good troubleshooter. The engine is my heartbeat, my "mechanical extension," Lesley Hazleton would say, and I know when I have the slightest vibration. I know when something is wrong long before any mechanic will believe me or be able to find the problem, because it's sometimes so internal only I can feel it.

do wild things; there aren't even names for them all. Professional aerobatic pilots have to expect problems and emergency reactions have to be prepared and practiced for. The more constantly I flew, the more attuned to my aircraft I became. I found that airplanes generally warned me before problems got beyond my capabilities. I could never afford to be cavalier.

It is rare, but engines can spin bearings and quit, propellers can lose bolts and counterweights, and airplane fuselages, especially at the longerons, can break. I can attest to that; I've had a broken longeron. I have had landing gear problems and loose canopies. I have had exhaust stacks depart the airplane or crack open, leaving an open flame in my engine compartment.

Sometimes mechanical problems aren't gradual, but relatively sharp and sudden. I've blown jugs and had leaking fuel tanks. I've had fuel pump failures and more instrument failures than I care to count. I've had radios pop out of their trays and float around the cockpit during maneuvers. My foot has gone clear through floorboards, shattering the Lexan foot rails. I've described my control failures as due to loose debris floating around the airplane or frayed rudder cables. It has been important to learn to expect everything and nothing.

However, like a horsewoman who improves past the ability of her mount and searches for a better show horse, I have upgraded my equipment as my talent has improved. And I have improved with the machinery. As I demanded more out of my airplane, the hardware has improved, new designs have been created, and new and stronger materials have been discovered.

Looking back on my career as I wrestled with balancing my schedule, the rhythm of my life, in sync with its times, blended perfectly with aerobatics. I started competing on the leading edge of exciting new technology and have not only watched it develop, but been a participant in its creation and development. Composites were introduced in the mid-1980s and I have watched them work their magic.[5]

---

[5] Barring the wood stringers and some fabric on the fuselage, my Extra 300S, purchased in 1993, is made almost entirely of composite materials—carbon fiber, Kevlar, and fiberglass. The smoothness of its finish resembles marble. Its steel tube frame fuselage has an advanced design that includes a roll bar behind my head. The high-tech Hartzell propeller, made entirely of baked Kevlar with a foam core, is designed to go to high pitch in the event of an engine failure—to help the airplane maintain altitude.

The rhythm of my life easily took to being on the road. It suited me. Traveling teaches people a lot about themselves—what they can stand, how alone they can be, how likable they are, and how they can be their own best company. I learned early on how to deal with different kinds of people, how to gauge them, to size them up, and then how to trust my own judgment. I learned perspective. Freed from everyday chores and little necessities, I was free to pursue other aspects of life. Being on the road teaches the art of traveling through life with a light load. Materialists discover, when not surrounded by stuff, how little is truly needed. On the road, you dream of your own bed, your own closet, and you can't wait to get home, away from daily packing and unpacking. Then, adjusted to home, you become restless and start planning and dreaming about the next trip. Once you've chosen the road, you give yourself to it.

Once you've chosen your goals, too, it cements them to tell others what they are. In the admission of intention lies some strengthening of commitment. You can fool yourself, sometimes, but once you have told others of your plans, it becomes more imperative that you fulfill them. Although experience is known as a super-teacher, I hoped that several lessons would come from the experience of others. I hired champions and asked the best to help me become the best—not the best *woman*, the best. I wanted nothing less than to be the best because I knew that goal was within the realm of possibility.

In part, the success of my business depended upon the airplane that I was flying. I was part of the changing times in aerobatic competition, and no sooner had I reached a decently expert level with my Pitts than it became apparent that at the highest levels of competition, biplanes were losing ground rapidly to the new high-tech, strong, and sleek monoplanes. So in the summer of 1987, Bob and I entered aircraft brokerage once more. It was time to sell the biplane, and, having ordered one of Walter Extra's best, we bought an Extra 230, previously registered as 230 EX, Echo Xray. I made it mine by including my initials in the new registration of 444 PW—the fours because four is my favorite and lucky number and *Papa Whiskey*, according to aviation's phonetic alphabet, for Patty Wagstaff. I knew that once I'd mastered it, it would show beautifully in every contest. I could hardly wait.

It was beautiful—absolutely state-of-the-art. Its lines were straight and slender, and it looked fantastic as it sat on the ground, nose pointed skyward as if it were begging for the four-cylinder Lycoming engine to roar into life and the wings to carry it skyward. I imagined that it looked even prettier as it pirouetted through the sky. I took possession of it in the middle of the summer of 1987, a mere five weeks before the nationals. I set my sights at its mastery.

The late Wayne Fuller, a good friend who lived with his family in Tampa, Florida, had an Extra 230 almost identical to mine and registered with his initials as 230 WF, *Whiskey Foxtrot*. Learning to fly my new airplane in Tampa, I stayed with Wayne and his family so that Wayne and I could practice together, with Ed Potter critiquing us. Wayne was a nice guy, very hospitable and congenial. Our two airplanes looked great side-by-side on the ramp, two keen swords ready to slice into the air. They looked even better in the rare air-to-air photograph that was taken of the two in formation over the blue waters and white beaches of the Gulf of Mexico.

In less than a month it was time to practice for the nationals. I flew the Extra directly to Chickasha, Oklahoma, as I had in 1986, to prepare for the 1987 nationals with, among others, my special friend, the late Tom Jones. Tom was my good buddy, like the brother I'd never had. Laughing was our favorite communication.

The year before, I had been looking for a place—an authorized aerobatic box—in which to practice for the nationals and Tom had urged me to come to Chickasha. There, I joined a group of competition pilots buoyed by their talents and pushed toward greater mastery. This year, as we had in 1986, Tom and I flew in formation to and from the practice area, tumbling through the sky and laughing on the way. Sometimes we'd race each other. At the time, our skill levels were similar and our goals were identical. Tom's great sense of humor showed on the fuselage of his biplane on which he had painted a little bumblebee and the saying, "Nice guys finish last."

Ian Groom, a good pilot, very witty and very bright, was also at Chickasha with his Pitts. He, too, became one of my best friends. Ian practiced with Clint, Tom, and I.

I discovered that competition had its own spirit. Yeah, we were all buddies, drinking buddies and flying buddies. We critiqued and coached each other, flew together to and from contests, laughed with each other, and knew when we could joke and when to swallow our words. But when it came time for the competition, *everyone* wanted to win. *Everyone* wanted to beat one another. Then, for some, the good buddies routine turned tense and sometimes vicious. The best of friends withdrew into icy silences, refusing to talk to each other sometimes.

I went into the 1987 nationals with a top place on the U.S. Aerobatic Team in my sights. After the gray skies caused flags to droop along with the spirits in the world contest in England the previous summer, this year's Texas sun warmed the contestants and brightened the contest. The week of September 21 to the 26 was a week of weather ideally suited to aerobatic competition. The skies, splashed with snow-white cotton puff-ball clouds, were a background of pearlized, iridescent blue, and light winds teased the wind socks, fluttering them like the wings of a baby bird before its first flight. Against a backdrop of perfection, the aerial stage featured one of the most competitive and intense U.S. nationals in history.

By week's end, nearly one hundred pilots in a diverse array of airplanes vied for the coveted titles and places in four categories, and thirty-seven unlimited pilots battled for the prestigious national titles and a position on the team that would represent the United States at the World Aerobatic Championship scheduled for 1988 in Red Deer, Canada.

Chosen on the basis of four flights, Clint McHenry, flying his Extra 230, was named undisputed U.S. National Aerobatic Champion for the second year in a row. Kermit Weeks, Harold Chappell, Henry Haigh, Alan Bush, and Tom Jones composed the rest of the men's team. For the first time, ten women competed in the nationals for the six slots—five team members and an alternate. It was a far cry from the competition in 1968 when Mary Gaffaney had been the sole woman; and in 1972, one of only two. Four flights were required—compulsory, freestyle, unknown, and a four-minute or air-show sequence—and a second unknown was added for team selection.

I finished in sixth place overall, men and women combined. That was a gratifying indication that last year's rookie had improved sufficiently to rate being an alternate to the men's team. I was the top-scoring female pilot and that was a milestone in itself! Only two short years after having barely squeaked onto the team in 1985, I would lead the women to represent my country in Canada with nine others of the nation's top pilots. *What an honor!*

I returned to Alaska ecstatic about the Extra 230 and making the U.S. Aerobatic Team and eagerly looking forward. Yet the good news was laced with tragedy. Not long after the nationals, Wayne Fuller was killed.

During a performance at an air show, Wayne got too low and snap-rolled into the ground, a sad loss. I felt as if I had somehow failed in my responsibility to Wayne. I could have called him more often to share experiences; I could have called him to stay in touch. We might have discussed that multiple snap rolls on down lines at low altitude could be very disorienting and dangerous. If he'd shallowed them out, he might have been able to tell up from down, blue from green. I could have warned him about slides after torque rolls, slides that go the wrong way, slides that rip the stick right out of your hand. We could have talked about the seductive and dangerous temptations of flying in air shows. There are temptations to show off a little, to include in your act everything new that you had practiced but perhaps not perfected.

I knew that the announcer's having an Aresti card that diagrammed the expected flight sequence didn't mean that it absolutely had to be flown that way. Pilots have to be flexible; wind and weather conditions and sudden, unexpected situations interrupt the best and the most experienced performers. Knowledgeable, glib announcers have the gift of gab and they can always tailor their comments to the maneuvers being flown and ignore those written on the card.

Wayne was a champion, confident and aggressive. Most competition pilots are. Like Amos, he wanted to compete on the U.S. team, to be national and world champion, and I have no doubt that he could have been a contender.

Are these always the things you think about after a friend dies? Maybe that is part of my legacy—the learning experience, the knowledge I've gained, and information that I can share that might educate others and help them to live.

Many women pilots who flew before me left a legacy, too. From them and from my own experience, I learned that an airplane doesn't know or care the gender of the person flying it, nor is the allure of speed and motion limited to the realm of the male. One of the members of the Women Airforce Service Pilots, Vi Cowden, told me when I asked her about the women flying in the 1930s and 1940s, "Extraordinary women have always done what they have wanted to do, Patty. Remember that!"

Wherever pioneer women who opened aviation's doors are today, I hope that they're pleased that I took their legacy and ran with it. I have a unique opportunity to interface and to network with women involved in aviation at this time.

I hope they are happy about that.

FIFTEEN

Competition

My work ethic had been drummed into me from my earliest days by my family, but my parents and my grandparents never could have imagined the career I'd chosen. It consumed me by 1988 and I worked really hard. My professional life had become a juggling act and I had to manage the logistics of organizing a tight schedule of contests and increasingly more important air shows, search for sponsorship, and, with Bob's help, do our accumulating business paperwork that accompanied our growing enterprise.[1] Everything snowballed.

My personal life, like a piece of rose quartz, striated into several different levels and necessitated a balancing act between Arizona, Alaska, and all the far-flung sites where my airplane and I were programmed to be. Bob and I spent countless dollars on the telephone calls and travel necessary to stay in touch with one another and to arrange the locations and times that we could be together.

My flying completely absorbed me and was what I lived for. I increasingly felt that nothing mattered until it really mattered fully and *because* it took over my life. My flying became a venue at which I could be totally

---

[1] My attempt at finding a sponsor was paying off. I was lucky in that being a woman was unique in the male-dominated world of aviation.

successful. Where once I had the luxury of taking a couple of weeks at a time to go to Alaska, now I rarely had a weekend off. Although it would eventually put a strain on my marriage, flying became my reality, my being.

I practiced to achieve a cutting edge as I readied for my second world competition, practicing three times daily. The World Aerobatic Championship, WAC 1988, was planned to be in Red Deer, Canada. I was no longer a rookie, glad to have the first international competition behind me. Bob, who flew his Baron to air show and contest sites as often as he could, had become the president of the U.S. Aerobatic Foundation, and he brought just the breath of fresh air to the policy-making and fundraising group that I'd known he would. He installed some much-needed change to the structure of the organization and worked at ridding the U.S. team of some of the sources of petty quarrels and the cliques that had plagued it in the past. Personally, I was happy that he was involved. As a skillful attorney and negotiator, he brought competence to his role, and it was an opportunity for him to be involved rather than to be solely my supporter.

Happily, WAC 1988 proved a much more positive event than its predecessor. Not only was it well run by the Canadian aerobatic people, like Ron Innes and Grant Mackay, but Red Deer boasted weather that enhanced the contest and allowed pilots to fly three complete flights to determine the aerobatic championship of the world most fairly.

A typical *regional* aerobatic competition in the United States generally began with the arrival of the pilots on a Wednesday or Thursday. Pilots settled themselves in and immediately scheduled time to practice in the aerobatic box for familiarization flights and their corresponding critiques. A briefing prepared everyone for the contest, then, weather permitting, the competition started on Friday at noon and continued throughout Saturday. It was interrupted for a hangar supper on Friday and ended with an awards banquet on Saturday night. The contestants drew their own sequence of performance for each flight, and the flights followed one another: first compulsory, second freestyle, third unknown, and, if offered, a fourth separate trophy flight, the four-minute freestyle. The world contest was all of that and more. Starting with the arrival of pilots with their families and supporters, airplanes, and crew at a prearranged practice site, the WAC lasted for two intense weeks.

Tom Jones and I flew our airplanes to attend the precontest training that was held at Ponoka, north of Red Deer. We left Oklahoma, sent off in style by a going-away committee headed by one of Tom's avid supporters, Carl Whittle. Tom's highly modified Pitts S-2S had a single hour's range, so we bounced to Canada, landing each hour to take on fuel and making our trip a long one, but, as was typical of whatever Tom and I attempted, full of laughter and fun.

When it was time for the competition to get underway, we left Ponoka for Red Deer. Our ten aerobatic planes flew together and landed at Red Deer in the midst of an air show. Tom and I were invited to perform and we're both delighted.

As the competitors gathered, I was intrigued with what perestroika meant to the Soviet Union team pilots. Perestroika, or "restructuring," had been introduced by Mikhail Gorbachev in 1985 and contained as its most dramatic component glasnost, or "openness." The aim was to give Soviet society its voice. Under glasnost, the crimes of the Stalin era were disclosed, but so too were dimensions of a contemporary crisis in politics, in economics, and in foreign affairs. The changes that I detected only two short years later were astonishing. Although the Soviet Union itself still existed, new freedoms lavished on the pilots were obvious and warmly welcomed. Soviet pilots were able to communicate freely for the first time. We discovered how many of them spoke English! We could talk one-on-one, could get together socially, and were more able to create and to enjoy friendships. Glasnost also gave me a chance to get better acquainted with good friends Russian Nikolai Timofeev and Lithuanian Yurgis Kairis, and gave me my first opportunity to meet another good friend, Lithuanian pilot and member of the Soviet team Vitas Lapenas. [2]

---

[2] It was inconceivable at the time to consider, but less than a year later, Vitas was badly burned over most of his body in a fiery aircraft accident in his local airfield in Vilnius, Lithuania. He lost his right leg and badly damaged both of his hands, justifiably raising the fear that his flying days were over.

When Randy Gagne, a member of the Canadian Aerobatic Team, and I heard that Vitas was finally able to drive a car modified for his handicaps, we knew that he could fly an Ercoupe, an aircraft with no rudder pedals and also able to be handled by someone without the use of legs. Making flight possible to a severely wounded aerobatic pilot was accomplished in an effort that drew in generous individuals like my personal assistant, Karen Roberts, and others including Eric Fleming, Terry Hutter, Wayne and Audean Woolard, Mark Baldwin, Steve Dyer and his late wife Jan of Univair, Pat Fedorowicz, John

I asked a friend, Hal Goddard, a Tucson flight instructor and friend, to drive my new Corvette to Canada for me. Having access to those wheels and not having to ferry our airplanes to Europe made the world contest an even better experience.

I had my first glimpse of things to come when Swiss champion Eric Mueller flew the prototype of Walter Extra's 300S. Unlike my wooden-winged Extra 230, it was made of a completely composite wing and fuselage panels. The 300S was much larger than anything else Walter had built and it performed well for such a relatively large airplane. It caught the attention of all. Eric flew it brilliantly in the unknown flight and taught all competitors a lesson.

The unknown, always a sequence of difficult maneuvers that is not seen by competitors until twenty-four hours prior to its performance and that may not be flown prior to competition, can be one of the most important flights of a contest. It has to be memorized, walked through on the ground, and it has been called "the great separator." His or her performance of it could make or break a competitor's championship po-

---

Dobberpuhl, Ed Turner, Bill Koons, Del Smith of Evergreen Airlines, Steve Wilson of BFGoodrich Aerospace, and many others. Additional assistance came after notices were printed in periodicals including *Sport Aviation, Sport Aero-batics, Ercoupe Owners Club, Pacific Flyer, Private Pilot,* and *General Aviation News and Flyer* and from companies like Thomason Aircraft, the Executive Committee of Aerospace America in memory of Tom Jones, the Southern Arizona Aerobatic Club, Skywords Aviation, and Hooker Custom Harnesses. Mechanics and technicians of the Emily Griffith Opportunity School in Denver, Colorado, created one restored aircraft out of two damaged ones and preparations were made to present the airplane to Vitas and to deliver it to Europe for him. There, additional friends Klaus Schrodt and Walter Extra saw to it that the airplane was picked up and stored until it could be flown across Poland to Vilnius.

For a time, it seemed the lengthy project would never end, yet we weren't sure that we wanted it to. The project was for Vitas, but once he received the airplane and began flying again in 1993, we discovered that by sharing in this group project, we were the lucky ones. The project drew its lifeblood and energy from good intentions and developed a momentum of its own. Randy and I may have originally conceived the idea, but he, Bob, and I took only a small part of the credit for its success. We appreciated those who rallied to the effort and provided the necessary energy to see Vitas fly. Wayne and Audean Woolard, who had been involved in many other community projects, said it was the first project in which they were involved that had absolutely no ulterior motives.

sition. For example, in 1994 Patrick Paris had flown beautifully and had accumulated scores that led the field by a wide margin. In his unknown, he rolled the wrong way, messing up one single maneuver, and, though he entered the flight in first place, his mistake dropped him to sixth among all of the competitors.

The unknown requires a superb combination of planning and execution on top of the memorization of the maneuver sequence. Energy management, wind drift, and following the exact format are crucial and are exacerbated by the pressure inherent in competition. Good competition pilots memorized their unknown flight sequences the day before flying them and sketched their various sequences in the Aresti code on a "flimsy," a card that is secured on the instrument panels in their cockpits. To indelibly etch a sequence in my mind, I lay in bed the night before competition and mentally flew the entire routine. Sometimes I imagined myself in the cockpit and added a wind to complicate the flight. Other times I imagined myself on the ground, an observer watching the airplane flying overhead.

The morning prior to the flight, all competitors visualized the sequence on the ground. Once it had been a widely held belief or superstition that a pilot could *not* win the third flight, the unknown, if he or she was the first to fly. The order is drawn by the pilots themselves. As names are called, each pilot draws a number from a box of randomly numbered slips of paper. Normally, drawing number one was equivalent to drawing the queen of spades in the card game of Hearts.

But at WAC 1988, Eric Mueller, the author of *Flight Unlimited*, shattered any mysticism about drawing that first slot. When Eric drew number one and held it for all the contestants to see, the entire crowd erupted in catcalls, whistles, laughter, and lusty clapping, Eric included. Everyone nodded knowingly to one another, "Eric doesn't have a chance now!"

But Eric had the last laugh. Eric flew first. He flew best, and then he relaxed to watch the rest of the competition. After more than seventy-five pilots had flown, Eric Mueller won the gold medal for the unknown. I watched as Eric was awarded that coveted medal. The medallion hung ceremoniously around his neck and I knew that all had received a great lesson in the power of belief and confidence and in the importance of shattering myths.

By the end of WAC 1988, in a real plus for the United States, Henry Haigh won the Aresti Cup and received the coveted gold as Men's World Champion. The U.S. men's team reigned as team champions and this feat was matched by the American women. For the first time that the Soviet women's team had been defeated in over twenty years, our U.S. women's team won the women's world championship! With medals and a handsome trophy, we had some valuable hardware to deliver to the United States. That would please our private contributors and our corporate sponsors.

When I flew, I felt that I had to perform something spectacular, something that would truly get attention. In my freestyle I did something that no one had done before and to date, no one has done since. I included a double vertical snap roll in my sequence. They are so hard to master and are so difficult to nail precisely that most competitors don't even include a single vertical snap in their freestyle program.

It worked. It captured everyone's imagination.

On the other side of the coin, the unknown flight at Red Deer ate my lunch! Although I cared little about winning a women's title, I had made up my mind that were I to be first, I would graciously accept the trophy in the interest of sportsmanship, but I wouldn't claim it, use it in advertising, or list it on my airplane. As the contest progressed, I moved into a good position to capture the women's gold medal, but in meteorology and the pressure cooker of contests, highs are accompanied by lows. During my unknown, like Patrick Paris, I zeroed a maneuver. It was a maneuver that I didn't really have a handle on—a one-half outside vertical snap roll. I was to climb directly upward, stalling the aircraft into a rapid half turn that held the vertical line, but I entered it too aggressively and over rotated, turning too far. Instead of stopping at the half turn, I made something like a three-quarter turn and earned a big fat zero. The title itself hadn't been important to me, but the zero cost me the gold medal, which deservedly went to French pilot Catherine Manoury, who was truly happy. The title had been her goal.

I understand why women's teams and men's teams are separated on the international level, though I've always had a hard time with it. In Eastern European countries, the aero clubs are fully subsidized by their governments and required to include women to receive the subsidies. Women from those nations recognize their part in the composition of the team and the monetary aspects involved. Women from France and England told me that they truly didn't want to compete with men. In the United States, our national team, with no governmental financial support, is not constrained by such an edict. Since 1972 the men and women had competed with one another in our country and that policy led directly to my opportunity to win the title of U.S. National Aerobatic Champion.

I thought that it stunk that women and men had to compete separately internationally. It was my dubious pleasure to aim for the *women's* world title. Yet, and this must be the feeling of every Olympic athlete who climbs onto the trilevel boxes to be awarded gold, silver, or bronze medals, it was a distinct honor to be one of three women to represent our country when the United States won the women's world championship, the top team in 1988. The women's team trophy, which was donated by the Soviet Aero Club, was a large, beautiful silver trophy, appropriately, a sterling woman with wings.

Before leaving Red Deer, I talked with Walter Extra, who competed for his native Germany. I asked Walter about the possibility of his building me a six-cylinder, single-seat monoplane as opposed to the two-seat Extra 300. It was time for me to move from the four-cylinder-engine-powered Extra 230 to a more powerful machine. Seeing Eric Mueller fly the Extra 300 had been a catalyst in my desire. Walter said that he would get back to me.

Bob and I flew in formation—I in the Extra and he in the Baron—directly from Red Deer to Paine Field, in Washington, where I was to perform in a large air show. The ambiance of the show was such a contrast to that of competition that it reminded me once again of the pleasure of combining air show flying with the contests.

I sailed into 1989 in high gear, and, after the season started in April, I performed at air shows in Washington, Arizona, California, Ohio, Wisconsin, and Florida, ferrying my Extra 230 over the distant states, zigzagging back and forth. I lived on the road until September. Then, as September lured the Cleveland Air Racers, the first hint of leaves taking on their fall colors heralded the return of aerobatic pilots to the national competitions in Texas following, for me, a practice stop in Chickasha, Oklahoma.

I learned a valuable lesson there. Always friendly with Tom Jones, I had a falling out with him. Our friendship was strained first because Tom had survived a number of incidents that worried me. I told him, because of a recent forced landing that damaged his airplane, that I didn't want any more emotional investment in him. I was sick of it. It was a protective mechanism, I'm sure, to prevent my being too devastated were he to have a fatal accident. The second reason for the strain was caused by a dispute over an unknown flight. Each of us as competitors had submitted one difficult maneuver to those officiating over our contest practice for them to weave into an unknown sequence. Though I knew the maneuver was very difficult, I didn't tell Tom which one I had submitted, and, when we competed, he zeroed that maneuver and was angry with me because he zeroed it and because I didn't tell him ahead of time.

I devised a difficult one—a roll and a half to inverted, a push to upright in a half loop, followed by an outside snap and a half to inverted—because I wanted to win the unknown. I wanted to beat everyone including Tom. I had put so much effort into my flying by this time that I'd become more and more competitive. I didn't win the unknown either, but I had some fences to mend with a good friend.

In a major turning point in competition for me, I received some great advice from a friend. During a previous contest, my airplane developed a gradually failing rudder cable, an insidious failure that hampered my flying but was so gradual that it wasn't instantly apparent. My scores were not what they might have been, and when I landed and discovered that the cable was down to only a few meager strands, I asked for and was granted a reflight. A hue and cry went up immediately and barbed criticism flew at me from a variety of directions—mostly charges of "Unfair!" from my own teammates.

It was decidedly fair to let me refly after correcting a problem that affected the control of the aircraft and was beyond any pilot's ability to correct. But I decided to be the good guy and opted not to take the second chance after the rudder cable was repaired and retightened. I thought I could win anyway, but I didn't. I came in second, and in retrospect, it made me angry.

I told Steve Conn, a good friend from Alaska, "I'm really pissed at myself! That's what I get, I guess."

Steve replied, and his words made a lasting impression on me, "Patty, if you want to compete with men on their own turf, then stop trying to be popular. If you want to go head-to-head in their own game, then you have to learn to be as ruthless as they. That is the only thing that they understand and the only thing that they respect." I realized that none of the guys would have turned down a reflight. I had to learn to compete before I could win.

At the nationals, I pushed and finished fourth overall, earning the highest score among all the women competitors, and once again made the U.S. team. This time I would represent the U.S. in Switzerland at

WAC 1990. I had made mistakes and somehow I didn't think I could win but had performed well-enough to place respectably.

Two Soviets flew at our U.S. nationals, invited by Brian Becker of Pompano Air Center (PAC) in Florida to exhibit the Russian Sukhoi. Excitingly, I finished ahead of both Soviet champions, and, when the scoring was complete, Clint McHenry led the U.S. men's team and I led the women's. For the second time I received the Betty Skelton First Lady of Aerobatics trophy. [3]

After the nationals and before the first snow fell in the lower forty-eight, I headed to Alaska for the winter. In Anchorage, I received a call from Walter Extra, who said, "You spoke to me about a six-cylinder monoplane at Red Deer. Are you still interested in having one?"

"You bet!" I answered. Bob and I were thrilled at the idea of having a one-of-a-kind airplane. We already had a trip planned to Dublin for a fall meeting of the International Organization of Aerobatics (CIVA) meeting. I told him, "We'll arrange a trip to Germany to see it and to watch it fly."

From Dublin, Bob and I flew to Germany and traveled to Walter's hangar and shop in Dinslaken to see his 260 put through its paces. I had fallen off my bicycle and crushed a major muscle in my leg. My leg was still black-and-blue so I couldn't fly the airplane, but it was awesome to see. I told Walter that I wanted mine to be just like it with minor changes

---

[3] Betty Skelton Frankman flew Curtis Pitts's first design, *Little Stinker*, which was first flown in 1944 and was then the smallest aircraft in existence. Betty won what was titled the Feminine Nationals and promptly flew to three consecutive victories, the first woman to win the title of International Feminine Aerobatic Champion three times. She contributed greatly to the Pitts's rapid rise to become, for its time in the sun, the most famous aerobatic airplane in the world.

Betty donated her beautiful trophy for permanent display in the EAA museum in Oshkosh and in 1988 saw to it that on an annual basis, it could be awarded to the highest-placing woman at the U.S. nationals. She was on hand at the awards banquet to give it to me, a very special honor for me.

Receiving the trophy reminded me that in May at the Redding Air Show in California, I had been the second woman to do the inverted Ribbon Cut. That low-level, upside-down maneuver had been first performed by Betty Skelton Frankman, a great lady in whose footsteps I was proud to walk.

for overall stability and strength. We arranged to purchase the airplane through PAC.

Walter estimated that we could take delivery in March of 1990. That would leave barely enough time to feel solid about competing with the 260 at the fifteenth World Aerobatic Championship in Switzerland, but I eagerly anticipated moving from the Extra 230 to my new 260.

However, construction took longer than planned. I was told "It's almost done," but I knew that I needed the new airplane well in advance of the world contest to adequately prepare to compete with it.

While I waited, I celebrated a decade of flying and six years of having competed by flying the socks off of my Extra 230 and loving every minute of it. My focus on my goal to become overall national champion was laser clear. When April turned to May and the plane wasn't delivered to PAC, I knew I'd have to fly the Extra 230. I practiced hard, improving daily. I set my sights on WAC 1990 and a triumphant return to a beautiful country that I had left so differently when I was a high school–aged kid. I was primed to do well. The judges knew me, I was flying the aircraft with which I was completely familiar, and having put the double vertical snap roll into my routine, I now focused on opening my freestyle with that challenging maneuver. I would get some attention with that.

The time to depart for Switzerland and the 1990 world contest came almost before I realized it. I was again proud to be representing my country and I looked forward to the competition. I had been flying the 230 for three years and knew all of its idiosyncrasies. I had made it my own.

Team training was held in El Dorado, Kansas, and then we flew together to the East Coast, Dover Air Force Base, Delaware. With thanks to supporter Paul Erdmann, who made the arrangements, we loaded another C-5A Galaxy with our airplanes and climbed aboard. This time our destination was Yverdon-les-Bains, Switzerland. A pall traveled with us, for our good friend and much-admired competitor, Tom Jones, was killed at the Oklahoma City Air Show just prior to the team's arriving at El Dorado, Kansas. [4] It made things very difficult. We all missed him acutely.

After landing and unloading our rare cargo at Ramstein Air Force Base in Germany, we flew to Colmar, France, in the Alsace region, for

---

[4] Tom had zeroed an unknown maneuver at the nationals and hadn't made the WAC team this year because of it.

our precontest training. Alsace was a beautiful location in its own right, and we had a treat in store after training—a flight to Yverdon-les-Bains over the breathtaking scenery of France, Germany, and into Switzerland. To the far eastern horizon of the airfield at Yverdon, the spectacular Matterhorn rose like a majestic guard of the perimeter. The "airport" was a grass field lined with flowerpots filled to overflowing with beautiful, colorful flowers. I thought again of my school year at the beautiful chalet La Chatelainie near Neuchâtel and the shores of Neuchâtel Lake. There was such a strange feeling of quiet triumph deep inside as I wondered what the nuns would say if they saw me arrive in their country once again, this time as a valued representative of my own. I wondered if the school officials would have attended if they had received an invitation to the World Aerobatic Championship competition!

After two weeks of good weather and good competition, Pete Anderson was the top U.S. male pilot; our women's team captured a second place—the silver medal; and the Soviet Union took the gold, with top honors going to Natalia Sergeeva, who later was tragically killed in the crash of a Yak 54 at a Moscow air show. The scores were close. Our U.S. team lagged behind the Soviet women's team by only 640 points, both teams receiving more than 29,000 points. As I'd planned, I opened my freestyle with the double vertical snap roll and pulled it off.

Yet, I faced a major disappointment. A new scoring system was being used, in which the judges fed the raw scores into a computerized program that was designed to eliminate bias in judging. The complex program threw out my six highest scores. It changed my position radically and my rating tumbled to a second place among the women. Though my raw scores were the highest overall, man or woman, I finished in second place in the women's division.

Walter Extra flew my new six-cylinder plane to Colmar, France, during practice for WAC 1990, and some confusion ensued. Walter's first use of composites for the ailerons and the tail was in his Extra 260. He hadn't wanted to sell the prototype 260, and I had ordered another *based on* the 260. He had finally finished what was to be my Extra 320[5] and he flew to France to show me the airplane we had ordered, the one for which

---

[5] My dream had been to fly the craft we planned to call the Extra 320, named for the horsepower that our engine builder Monty Barrett promised to extract from the engine.

we'd already paid. I was disappointed. I wanted a smaller, sleeker aircraft and I told him, "This can't be my airplane. It's too big."

I flew it once and was even more convinced. I knew it wasn't the plane for me. I had to wear my airplane, not just fly it, and I had to love it to wear it.

Although Walter hadn't wanted to sell his prototype 260, we eventually worked a deal. Brian Becker, Bob, Walter, and I sat on the grass at Yverdon and agreed that Bob and I would trade the 230 and the already-purchased 320 for Walter's original 260. The 260, built solely for aerobatic competition, had a lot of mystique about it. Intended as Walter's personal competitive airplane, the prototype 260 was powered by a Lycoming AEIO 540 engine and a wood-fiberglass-metal-composite MT propeller. Like the 230, its wings were very strong and flexible. Built with Polish pine box spars and solid Polish pine ribs, they were covered with aircraft mahogany plywood and coated with fabric for a smooth finish.

That Extra 260, which now is part of the collection of the Smithsonian Institution's National Air and Space Museum, became the machine that I flew to the national championship one year later in 1991, and then again in 1992. It wasn't an *easy* plane to fly: the center of gravity range was narrow, I had to work hard at maintaining a line because the weight and balance and trim were in a constant state of flux, and the ailerons had a snatch or pull to the right during high-speed rolls. The 260 was surrounded with intrigue because it was a one-of-a-kind design, it was considered the most beautiful akro plane ever built, and only one other pilot had ever flown it (Eric Mueller, Walter's best friend).[6] It wasn't like anything I'd flown to that time.

It was great. It was going to be mine. It was a rocket! I was going to the moon!

---

[6] Walter also knew that the plane was difficult to fly and because of a few strange (but not dangerous) flying characteristics, it was not designed or built for an inexperienced pilot. Walter also felt it was underbuilt because the layer six-cylinder engine was put on a fuselage designed for a smaller, less torquey, and less powerful four-cylinder engine.

SIXTEEN

Ride Hard, Die Free

Actors and actresses have to stifle sorrow and inner turmoil to get through their starring performances with a smile. It isn't all that different for those of us who perform on the aerial stage, those of us who must take to the air directly after something terrible happens, or, worse, after the death of someone who is very familiar and special. Perhaps you were just joking together before the fated flight. Perhaps you were the best of friends. It can be heart-wrenching, fearful, numbing; it can exact the whole gamut of emotions. To fly while smoke still rises from the crash of a friend requires the most professional detachment one can summon. Military pilots face that horror in training and in war, forced to fly over the smoldering remains of friends who flew into the face of death. Embedded in the training of these pilots is the ethic of compartmentalization—the ability to separate personal feelings and emotional stress from the job at hand. Small plane aerobatic pilots, however, have to teach themselves how to deal with such situations through trial and error and experience.

It all adds to the mystique of the pilot, but we're anything but superhuman. We're definitely not immortal. But there's something about the beauty, the pull, and the freedom of flight and the need to fly that keeps pilots in the air against the overwhelming odds of gravity and, on occasion, against a background of death or destruction. It makes us tough and pragmatic. Perhaps the more we fly, the greater the price we pay.

Had I come to terms with death? Even by 1990, I had lost too many friends, way too many. Yet life had a way of moving ahead. Like soldiers who carry on when buddies are cut down at their sides, pilots keep flying. A friend's death had to eventually be accepted, sometimes felt acutely and always deeply.

I knew that sooner or later it would be one of my best friends, and after the loss of several who were close to me, I had to decide whether or not to go on. I had to come to terms with loss, with danger, and I needed to confront mortality. Life is short and life is hard, but still, every day is precious as time runs out. I kept thinking of the motto I had painted on my Pitts—*"Ride hard. Die free."*

I began to think fatalistically, to believe in inevitability, that it was only a matter of time before I, too, would make a mistake. I wondered, "If so many others, those better than me, had somehow lost control or had things happen that were beyond their control, what separates me from them?"

I knew that fatalism was one nail in my coffin; it was dangerous, something—another challenge, I suppose—to overcome. I shook the feeling every time it raised its ugly head, but it lurked in the recesses of my mind for some time.

Howard Pardue, a war bird and air show pilot from Breckenridge, Texas, told me that you get callused, despite the way you react to a friend's death. You *need* to.

I asked Air Force–retired brigadier general Robin Olds how to deal with the dangers of flying and the loss of friends. Robin, one of history's most colorful aces and an unquestioned legend as a combat leader, told me that sometimes you have roommates and then, suddenly, they're gone. He said "Don't identify with those that don't return from combat. Don't let yourself believe that it will happen to you."

So you shelve it, parking it away in deep corners of your mind and heart. You try to keep your perspective after a few glasses of wine or when a particularly familiar song suddenly triggers a long-forgotten emotion. But the traumatic deaths of close friends can trigger symptoms of posttraumatic stress disorder and I felt some of the classic ones. I had to deal with a sense of pointlessness, survival guilt, and loneliness that went beyond bereavement and grief. I found that these feelings contributed to stress in my relationship with Bob.

Aircraft accidents are always reported by the media and pilots tend to analyze every aspect of an accident, to dissect it and learn from it. We gain and we lose by another aviator's death. If we're lucky, we gain by learning as much as we can and seek to prevent it from possibly happening again. We lose because most of the time it didn't need to happen. We lose because aviators are the type of dynamic people who contribute so much to life by living it to the fullest.

A friend's death affects people in different ways. Some quit flying after a good friend gets killed. Some go on. Some gain more focus and determination. Some give up. Some get drunk. Others sober up. Losing someone teaches you something deep about yourself—your philosophy, your reactions, how tough you are, and the substance and the depth of your emotions.

I guess there was a glimmer of an instant in which I questioned why I continued flying after losing so many friends in so short a period of time. But it is easier to say that you will fortify yourself against irrational fear than to actually do it. For a few years after some of my very best friends had been killed, I felt blanketed by a low-grade depression that I couldn't shake. Some of the joy of aerobatics—of doing what I loved to do—was gone. I knew that I still had feeling, a passion for it, but that was hidden by an overall dampening of feeling, a shroud that stifled the emotions. The joy was harder and harder to reach.

Lee Manelski had been a friend, a teammate. I knew him well. He was killed when the aerobatic airplane in which he was flying with a student was in a collision with a helicopter. Lee and the student had just taken off from an airport in California and the helicopter swung up from its pad into the path of his airplane. The newspaper writers made a big deal out of the fact that "Kirk Douglas, movie star, was in the helicopter." I have admired Kirk Douglas forever and was truly sorry he was in an accident, but Douglas wasn't badly hurt and the news reporters hyped, Kirk Douglas this, and Kirk Douglas that. What was discouraging and insulting was that the media statement, "A stunt plane crashed into them," implied that aerobatic pilots are automatically in the wrong. Was the helicopter pilot doing the correct departure procedure from the proper place with clearance? Was he looking for other traffic on the taxiway or runway? People of the media never asked the question. Right or wrong, Lee never had a chance.

Aviation seems to contribute to my intuitive voice. A pilot is more in tune with his or her senses when around airplanes or when flying. There is more going on. There is more at risk. Once, when I was flying my bright-red Pitts, a showy little airplane that should have been highly visible, I returned from a contest and landed. I was rolling out to the end of a runway, a rollout that would have meant turning around to taxi back on the active runway. A guy was parked, his engine running, waiting to take off after I landed. Generally, the pilot holding waits until the runway is clear before starting a takeoff run. Surely, he saw me! But just before turning my airplane on the ground, I had a weird feeling. The hairs on the back of my neck started to stand on end. I glanced over my shoulder and said, "Holy shit!"

The airplane was barreling straight toward me and I was just seconds away from having turned into what would have been his path. In a blink of an eye, he, his passengers, and I were inches away from being killed! I gunned to the edge of the runway and was astounded that the other pilot never got off the ground. He just shot past and out into the sand and sagebrush. I never learned the cause of this near miss.

What gave me the spine-tingling, intuitive feeling that made me glance over my shoulder? Whatever it was, it saved my life and perhaps the lives of all involved.

There have been other airplanes that have provoked strong and strange feelings in me after being invited to fly them. Joe Frasca and I were at contests in Salem, Illinois, two years in a row, and both years Joe invited me to fly his homebuilt Lazer. I put him off and disappointed him, I know.

A superb pilot and real natural, Joe had done a great job with his homebuilt. I had watched him fly and it seemed to fly well. I liked Joe a lot and would ordinarily have been happy just to please him, but I had a strong feeling that I couldn't explain. Then, less than a month later, something inexplicable went wrong with that airplane in flight. It must have been out of control because Joe had to bail out. He opened his canopy and jumped. But Joe never made it. His chute was hooked over his shoulders, but his leg straps had not been fastened, and, when he pulled the rip cord, Joe shot right out of his harness. It was a tragedy in the greatest sense. Everyone who knew him felt his loss keenly.

It wasn't only competition pilots who were getting killed. Compared to the high of performing in my first Roswell Air Show in New Mexico, I later had to deal with a dreadful loss at the same airfield. I was one of the last to talk with Frank Sanders before he took off from Roswell's runway for what proved to be his last flight.

Just before he departed, I enjoyed having lunch with Frank. He was in rare form that day, a witty, life-of-the-party kind of guy. He loved being the center of attention and was so proud of his family, so proud of his kids. Frank had taken a fatherly attitude toward me, too, and was free with good advice. He'd say, "Now, you gotta change that flight suit, Gypsy. You can't look like a race car driver!" Then he'd add, "Why don't you change your name to Gypsy for air show performances? That name suits you."

Frank, with his passenger, Tony Lucero, a local radio personality, took off for a press ride in the T-33 jet, *Red Knight*. I had arrived that morning in my 230, having flown from Tucson, and was taxiing out to practice.

No sooner had I gotten to a practice area when I discovered that my thermos was still in the airplane, so I turned back to land. I couldn't do aerobatics with a thermos flopping around.

As I returned to Roswell, I heard chatter on the radio about helicopters going out to search. The messages were clipped and vague. When I landed I noticed that Frank hadn't returned and found it unusual. Press rides are generally quite short.

I went to taxi back out and heard more chatter on the radio. I called Ground Control to ask what was happening.

The controller told me, "Contact tower." I switched frequencies and repeated my question. When put off by the controller, I insisted on having him tell me what was going on. The controller suggested that I taxi back in and not take off.

I never had the same feeling before or since, but as I got out of the airplane, I could barely walk. My feet were like lead. I knew Frank had been killed and I slogged as if I were walking in cement. I had trembled and had my knees shake like crazy before, but this was an entirely different physical manifestation.

It was shocking that Frank died, but he was a happy guy that day. It was like everything was OK with him.

Aviation is a web, an interconnecting network of people, and it is a huge loss to the whole community when something happens to any one of us.

The show had to go on and I had to fly my routine, sign autographs, smile and sparkle for the spectators and sponsors. That was the first time

I was involved with an air show where an accident occurred and I felt as if I were in a fog. I took my routine to higher than normal altitudes to allow for lack of focus and I flew as if I were strangely out of touch with my airplane. My feel was gone. The sounds of the engine and airframe didn't compute like they should, like I was in a tunnel. Nonetheless, I felt that being in the air was the best place for me to be. No matter what had happened to Frank, it was where I belonged.

The first time I met Rick Brickert, fighter pilot, prize-winning air racer, and air show pilot, was when he was in Prescott, Arizona, flying his first air show with the *Red Knight*. After Frank, one of the partners in the T-33, was killed in the first *Red Knight*, Rick got a second one. He suggested that I fly it in air shows for him. I flew the jet with him several times and rode through his air-show routine, but I told him that before I made the transition, I needed some T-6 time, something in between the Extra and the jet. [1]

Little did I think that at the Evergreen Airshow five years later, I would fly the Missing Man in the backseat of the *Red Knight* (T-33) in honor of Rick after he was killed flying the *Pond Racer* at the National Championship Air Races in Reno, Nevada. I was criticized for missing his funeral, but it was during the nationals and I couldn't be there. I knew Rick would understand. I had spent time with him when he was alive and then paid my own private respects.

Later, I flew down to see Rick's dad, George, a retired United Airlines captain, who was justifiably heartbroken. We went out to Rick's grave and George swept his hand toward the grave and said, "What a waste! Look at this. He was the best pilot I had ever seen. I know a father might say that about his son, but he was so much better than me that it wasn't even funny."

Rick would have agreed that it was the time spent when we are alive that is important. People don't attend funerals for the person who died; they go for their families. Rick's mother had died three years before, and after Rick's funeral was all over, George welcomed the chance to spend a little quiet time showing me pictures of Rick when he was a kid making

---

[1] Thanks to the Evergreen group, Mike Smith and Bill Muszala, I later started flying a T-6 and a T-28 at their base in Marana, Arizona.

model airplanes, and talking about his wife and his son. I comfort myself with thinking that George had an opportunity to talk more freely than he would have been able to at the funeral and it made me feel better, too.

Tom Jones and his wife, Kathy, who lived in Oklahoma City, were among those that I met the first time that I practiced for the nationals at Chickasha. Tom taught me a lot about showmanship. He was a real public relations man, a master at charming the press. In his warm and humorous way, he could charm anybody and everybody—TV crews, other air show acts, nosy reporters. I learned a great deal by watching and listening to him. From Tom I learned what it meant to be an entertainer, the other all-important ingredient for an air show pilot.

While Tom organized and flew his Sukhoi, *Rushin' Rage*, in what was fated to be his last Oklahoma City Air Show, Aerospace America—a show he started and ran—I performed at one at the Hillsboro, Oregon Rose Festival Air Show. Afterward, I left and headed south and east, aiming for practice in Oklahoma City prior to a competition in Denton, Texas. I had looked forward to seeing Kathy and Tom, and hoped to mend our friendship.

En route from my Hillsboro air show, I stopped in Boise, Idaho, to spend the night. I'd heard the sad news that a friend, Steve Van Eck, had been killed. I called Pete Anderson to tell him about the crash. Steve had been practicing in his Rebel 300 and he either got too low or something went wrong with his airplane. I'll never know.

Pete sighed heavily and told me that Eric Mueller had just died of a heart attack!

"Shit, Pete. What *is* it with this year?"

Pete paused, and then he asked, "Where are you?"

"I'm in a hotel room in Boise."

He said, "Are you alone?"

"Yes."

"Aw, shoot. Well, I gotta tell you something. . . . Uh . . . Tom got killed today."

"Oh, God! No!" I felt completely numb.

I put through a call to Kathy and several other people. I got on the phone and started talking, partly to find out what had happened and partly to reach out and make contact with those who were still alive. I hardly slept that night, and the next morning, already on my way to Oklahoma City, I flew, but I found it almost impossible to concentrate. I flew in a daze.

The next morning, Randy Gagne and I walked to the accident site. Beside the oily hole in the ground, we looked at each other, and Randy said, "You know, I have the feeling that Tom's spirit got out of here really quickly. He didn't hang around and haunt the place. He said, 'I'm outta here!'"

Randy and I stayed for the funeral and spent every evening in a local bar with Brian Becker and the Russian group who had been at the show—drinking, talking, and consoling each other. A few days later I flew the lead in the Missing Man formation at Tom's memorial service. As the rest of us, Rick White, Joe Underwood, and I held formation, Randy Gagne, flying a Sukhoi 26 like that in which Tom had died, pulled up and broke to the west.

It wasn't easy, but it was simpler being up there, flying, living, hanging in tight and close with others. My nerves would have been ragged if I were on the ground, watching others fly and having to hear the mournful sound of taps.

The chief designer of the Sukhoi 26, Boris Rakitin, was at Tom's funeral. After Tom was killed and we were on our way over to pay our respects to Kathy, Boris looked at me, held his hand to his heart, and said, "My heart hurts."

My heart hurt, too.

These few tragic losses are representative of the many—too many—that I have known. I discovered that my grieving process followed a predictable pattern: initial shock turned into feelings of anger, then there was deep sadness, sometimes depression, and finally acceptance. Life went on, and while there was life, I had to live it. I could remember fondly . . . and then I had to move on. We are on our own as aerobatic pilots. I had to learn to compartmentalize, to find a place to put grief, and to carry on despite it.

Time—a great healer—allowed all things to pass. I found ways of dealing with the acute pain of loss. I found ways to rationalize, paths to take toward the bigger philosophical, metaphysical, spiritual picture; I eventually found reason where there seemed to be none. I came to the conclusion that in the eternal quest for understanding, it's not in our power or our limited lifetime on earth to comprehend the big picture or the reasons why life is shorter for some than for others. Death is the only inevitable and is often beyond our control. I talked to a lot of people and I finally shook the numbness, the lack of luster, that these deaths brought to my life. When my emotional fog finally lifted, my love of flying remained.

The joy slowly returned. Deep inside, I felt that flying was truly fulfilling; flying gave me the greatest happiness and made the most sense—sometimes the only sense—in my life.

People sometimes ask me if I have a death wish because I fly so low to the ground. I tell them it has nothing to do with death but instead that it's the ultimate in living. In searching for the meaning of my life, I decided that whatever way I best expressed myself meant that I was fulfilling my individual purpose on earth. I wanted to create my best work possible, for only through my highest expression would I be able to share my energy and light with others.

SEVENTEEN

Combat

I had wanted to win the nationals in 1988, in 1989, and in 1990. I knew that I had been ready and that my flying was good enough, but everything hadn't come together. I was, in part, a victim of the erroneous belief that it wasn't my time, that I had to pay my dues, that I couldn't be so new to the sport and be challenging those at the top so quickly. Also, the title eluded me due to my own mistakes and my less-than-perfect competitive flying.

Some people blame failure on the judges and on the degree of subjectivity in the scoring in this sport, but I knew that wasn't the only problem. My errors were my own—either the wrong maneuvers, going out of the box, or any number of minor faults—and they lowered my scores from perfect tens to sevens or eights. I knew and I told myself that with continued dedication and training, my time would come. My goal was fixed and it didn't waiver. But it took more than a goal; it took incredible focus to face the pressure of competition. That was key. If I could be cool in the face of pressure, I could win anything. I was on a mission.

I discussed competition with Clint McHenry, and Clint talked with me about excellence, consistency, and persistence. He told me that if I kept putting excellence in front of the judges, eventually it would be impossible for them to deny me the scores I deserved. I believed that if there were ever a year in which to aim those words straight to heart, it was 1991. It was a year in which I had won almost every contest I entered, and before the nationals in September, I had to psyche myself up for the top, drive toward that excellence, and then *show* it. I could not waiver. It was only through constant, daily mental and physical preparation and training that I knew I would have the self-confidence to pull it off.

I created a mantra for myself: "Prepare. Memorize. Visualize. Sequester yourself under the plane and ignore any and all that seek to divert and disturb. Mentally rehearse each flight! (Remember that the harness ratchet was not working when I climbed into the airplane! Remember that the headset strap came off while practicing the freestyle. Should I wear a headset at all?) Prepare early!"

While watching others have good flights, I talked to myself, "Don't let it shake your confidence. Tell yourself that you are the *best*! Fly into the box saying, 'Just get the job done!'"

Marriage, stepchildren, sponsors, and Patty Wagstaff Air Shows demanded attention, but the flying was always of utmost importance. Flying made life worthwhile. There was nothing like being able to take a beautiful, highly specialized, incredibly smooth and powerful machine up into the vertical, seeing the horizon whirling by over my shoulder as I nail the line; nothing like being able to complete a perfect loop with a snap roll on top, an Avalanche, from an entry speed of 200 miles per hour; nothing like floating weightless or hanging from my straps looking at the fields below mesh into a patchwork of green and brown and knowing that I was *in* the bluest of blue skies; *nothing*.

I realized how lucky I was to have the Extra 260, N618PW. Originally an elegant light gray with dark gray-and-red stripes, it was repainted an eye-catching navy blue and gray-white and striped with red. The paint scheme and clean lines of the craft emphasized the precision of maneuvers; the vertical lines made it a true competition paint scheme. I was lucky, too, to have earned the support and sponsorship of II Morrow Inc., an Oregon-based manufacturer that designs and builds navigation equipment. Using their Apollo 618 Loran (long-range navigation instrument), the registration number was an advertisement in itself. The aircraft looked beautiful when flown cleanly. All I had to do was to master it.

Mastery, however, was not to be taken lightly. As sleek and slippery as the 260 was, its control surfaces were lighter and its roll rate faster. With its cantilevered tail, it lacked the support wires of the 230 and behaved quite differently, especially in elevator control. The airplane had very little lateral stability, making it a challenge to hold a straight line, and that was complicated by a very narrow center of gravity range that meant making constant trim changes to the controls while I was flying. I sat farther back in the cockpit than I had before and my sight gauges had to be realigned. I had the airplane flutter tested by Carl Pascarell of St. Augustine, Florida, a former Navy pilot, because the original ailerons were heavy in weight which meant that the roll was difficult to stop. The ailerons also had no "centering" or neutral position to return to. Walter Extra had built new, lighter-weight ailerons for me and I noticed a big improvement. The spades, extensions to the ailerons, on the 260 had a "snatch" to them, almost ripping the control stick out of my hand when I rolled at high speed to the right. Although I tried various combinations of spade designs, I could never get it just right, so I put up with it.

Adjustments finally took hold and it took the entire season to truly begin to wear my newest airplane, a season of daily practice and fifteen air show performances.

No sooner had I taken possession of the 260 from Brian Becker and his father, John, in February of 1991, than I went off to Argentina to fly in the International Aerobatic Masters (IAMA), one of the few contests with a monetary prize. Pitts biplanes were provided for the aerobatic pilots. A privately sponsored event, it combined a daily air show flown over the beach at Mar del Plata with a competition that was similar to an Olympic contest in that the judges displayed score cards immediately at the completion of the flight. [1]

The Argentinean Masters, which brought together twelve competitors from all over the world, was a great opportunity. Travel has deepened my appreciation for the freedom we have in aviation and for my own country. After two weeks away, I couldn't wait to get back to my rocket

---

[1] I flew and came in a close third in a later masters contest hosted by Breitling in Oshkosh, Wisconsin, to which only the top dozen aerobatic pilots of the world were invited. Breitling, manufacturers of world-famous watches, did much to advance the sport of competitive aerobatics and elevate it to a spectator sport by including it in their wonderful series of global events. In addition to prize money, the masters provided visibility and a different format that was more along the lines of performance—we could use smoke as well as music—and the limited number of contestants meant that the entire competition was more interesting.

of a 260. I hoped that I would rush toward new levels of competence, the razor-sharp edge that I'd sought.

My intriguing airplane drew attention from the press. Writer Budd Davisson put it through some of its paces and said that because of its leading-edge performance, flying it was a challenge in that fewer than twenty-five pilots in the world could adequately evaluate it. He said that my attitude toward life, especially toward competition, was placarded on my instrument panel, "Kick ass!" and correctly assessed that I hated to come in second. To be the best, he reported, I chose to fly the very best airplane in the world—a sacrifice because of its expense and the fantastic hours of practice time it required.

He was right. I *lived* flying, and, after competing at the world level three times, the nationals six times, and devoting my entire psyche to flying, I really wanted to win. When I wasn't practicing akro, I was flying cross-country between contests and shows, generally at speeds that averaged 200 miles per hour and gobbling up miles of sky in minutes. I flew in a direct line, navigating with my loran instead of meandering along on the labyrinthine highway system.

I, who love the solitude of travel, the differing scenes of sky and land, and a peripatetic existence, was made for this life.

I found that my commitment to aviation reached a turning point with two new truths about myself. One was there was no turning back. Two was stick with what you do well. Jimmy Franklin, an award-winning air show pilot, gave me some good advice. I was becoming restless and searching for new things to accomplish and I asked him whether I could try stunt work—fire-wall crashes or something equally dramatic. Jimmy told me to stick with what I do well. He knew that the more I attempted, the more I fragmented my goals, the less successful I would become. It was like being a jack of all trades. Jimmy made good sense and as I thought about it, he was a catalyst in keeping me directed. I never wanted to be master of none.

I was somewhat surprised to find an ego attachment tied up in what I do. Perhaps most careerists have known that from the start. Lose a career position, be fired, or in today's vernacular, "be downsized," and you suddenly don't *do* anything anymore. You lose your identity and your ego suffers a beating. I don't know if my total commitment was the go-ahead for my ego to become very much a part of what I do, but I knew it was a necessity for winning.

Every day during 1991 from the onset of training in early March, I focused on one goal—winning the U.S. nationals. Whether I was traveling cross-country, preparing for an air show, or facing a regional competition, my sights were focused.

By late September, I wondered if I was ready. If I ever had an airplane that could carry me to the top, I knew the Extra 260 was the one that could give me the chance to become National Aerobatic Champion. I prepared myself physically and mentally. I had to put faith in myself and become a "warrior athlete," a term coined by author Dan Millman.

Although the national championship had proved elusive for several years, I always knew that I could fly well enough to win. In the past, what had stood between my dream and actually winning was being unprepared mentally. I had allowed nerves and pressure to get the better of me. I had to make the connection that flying well was only half the battle. I had to face pressure with self-assurance. Self-confidence had always been a problem for me, but with my competition successes, it was getting stronger.

There were many motivational books available and most advocated the same words of advice: "Don't worry about what other people think; this is *your* game," or "Pretend that this is the last event in which you'll ever compete. What results do you want?" or "Exude confidence!"

Dan Millman's *The Warrior Athlete* became my bible. Dan's philosophy was that we are all *born* as natural athletes. He suggested that we allow societal pressure and other outside influences to get in the way of superior athletic performance. He urged that we deny those who would pressure us to be less than we are capable of becoming. I read his book until the pages were torn and returned to it time and again as the nationals neared.

In choosing competition aerobatics, I had chosen, without a doubt, the most challenging, difficult, and complex sport known to man. In a class alone, it combines more variables than any other sport. Ice skating is difficult, complex, and intensely physical. Motor car racing is expensive and dangerous, requiring acute hand-to-eye coordination skills and highly developed organizational skills from the driver and the team. Baseball, basketball, and football games are highly structured, competitive, rough, and demanding on a mental level as well as physical. But competition aerobatics encompasses all of those and more. At the unlimited level, it requires an expensive, specialized aircraft that is exceedingly strong and has a powerful and expensive engine, to boot. The airplane and the power plant have to be impeccably maintained in the same manner as any racing vehicle but unfortunately don't offer as much protection to the pilot as racing rigs do to the driver. In addition, and unlike the racing rig, the aerobatic airplane has to be able to withstand incredible twisting and torquing to its basic structure. There is little margin for error at the most difficult levels of competition in which the pilots fly as low as 300 feet above the ground.

Aerobatics is intensely physical. What other sport requires that a competitor develop a tolerance to intense positive and negative G forces? Marathon running requires that a runner maintain a proper diet and challenging daily workouts. Aerobatics demands much of that as well as the arduous development of a tolerance to having the body's blood thrown to the head and toward the feet in repeated spinning, turning, and rugged twisting movements. To develop proper G tolerance in my body by June required that I begin serious training in March, and even then there could be serious side effects. I worked out at gyms wherever and whenever possible. I rode a bicycle, hiked and/or walked vigorously, and lifted weights regularly to sustain necessary upper body strength. I watched my diet, taking care to keep hydrated, and generally ate whole grains, potatoes, fiber-rich vegetables, and brown rice washed down with water during the day and wine in the evenings. I never lost sight of the fact that the most important regimen for the rigors of akro is to fly every day.

I had to deal with some of the side effects of aerobatics. Wild gyrations and up to ten positive and eight negative Gs bring on swollen and reddened eyes, inner ear reactions, earaches, sore hips, backaches, tendonitis, and bursitis. Using heating pads on my neck every night eased the pulled neck muscles and ice packs from the refrigerator handled edema and sore joints.

I developed the muscle memory and timing necessary to finesse such complex maneuvers as vertical snap rolls and rolling 360-degree turns only by spending hours and years of practice at the aircraft controls. But after any layoff, I've had to virtually start over again to recapture G tolerance, a sensitive feel and precise timing.

Aerobatic competence and ability are not necessarily age-related, nor are they particularly for the young. Physically, older people have better G tolerance because their arteries are harder. Interestingly, in the last decade, the U.S. has had national champions ranging from ages twenty-seven to sixty-two.

I knew it was possible to "peak out." I had seen some of our best pilots show up in top shape before a world contest only to exhaust themselves by the end of the training session. A champion has to master pacing and learn to manage time and energy very carefully. At the bottom line, too, there is always luck—luck of the draw, luck of the weather, lucky winds, and luck with the machine.

Although I try not to focus on the danger inherent in aerobatic competition and although the International Aerobatics Club (IAC) is proud to point out that there has never been an accident at an aerobatic competition, danger cannot be completely dismissed. The pilot whose aircraft is not well maintained, who screws up, who has a cavalier attitude, who forgets a modicum of humility, or who is, perhaps, merely unlucky is asking for trouble. I have tried to stay on top of all the possible problems associated with my airplane and depend on excellent mechanics for support.

Because I wanted to balance all aspects of my life, I have tried to make time and money available for both competitive and air show aerobatics. Having made aerobatics my vocation, I am one of the rare competitors who is also a full-time air show pilot. Inclement weather and physical health notwithstanding, as an unlimited aerobatic pilot, I have had to hone my ability to make instantaneous decisions based on being able to see all the minute details while keeping the big picture in sight.

I wanted to be the first woman to win the U.S. National Aerobatic Championship and I considered myself lucky to have something to prove. I trained with Clint McHenry in El Reno. He gave me a few pep talks and sent me off to the 1991 nationals in Texas.

Grayson County Airport had hosted thirty-three nationals since 1949 and time had changed the scene. When Duane Cole, former U.S. National Aerobatic Champion, was competing, the nationals featured fairly common general aviation aircraft like his own Taylorcraft. The highest number of competitors that he faced was twelve. In 1991, there were more than one hundred competitors, the unlimited contenders flying in high-performance aircraft with fantastic roll rates and unbelievable vertical penetration. Plus it was a U.S. Aerobatic Team selection year, so unlimited competition was more intense because more people had more invested in doing well, needing to be in the top ten to qualify.

The competition started well for me. It was important to start strong and I won the first flight, the compulsory, generally my worst flight. Then, just after beginning my freestyle routine, which is generally my best flight, the Lexan floorboard broke under my left rudder pedal. I immediately broke the flight off.

As I rocked my wings to signal my problem, a wayward single-engine training plane took off and wandered into the aerobatic box. The Cessna came into view after the floorboard broke and I had already stopped the routine. Yet I was lucky to see that airplane. That pilot would have been in the wrong, had we had a mishap—the worst scenario being a midair collision. But whether another pilot is wrong in entering specially designated airspace or not, there's no comfort in being dead right.

Contest officials ruled my floorboard failure a mechanical malfunction that was out of my control and allowed a reflight. The reflight was relegated to the end of the rotation, and, although it is best to have a break between flights for proper mental preparation, it meant that I would be flying two competition routines on the same day, separated only by a couple of hours. [2]

Even though I had prepared mentally for months—reading sports psychology books and thinking about focus, becoming mindless, and how to complete the athletic task without letting pressure get the best of me—I still didn't know if I would be completely in control of my nerves as I entered the box for each flight. [3]

While holding, I told myself repeatedly, "Shut everything else out. Fly this like one more practice flight. Just get the job done!" It became my mantra and seemed to work. It also helped me to be a little angry. I almost had to *find* anger and work it to my advantage. I had talked about

---

[2] I have Gerry Molidor and Mark Peteler to thank for seeing me through the incident and helping to repair the damage to my plane.

[3] Each competitor takes off and holds at 3,000 feet above the judges, waiting for the colored panels to signal that the box is open and ready.

this with my thirteen-year-old stepson Dylan, who seemed to have a lot of youthful male anger as an energy force. I knew that he was highly competitive in life and in sports, and watching him, I saw that he held one of the keys to my success. I wanted to maintain the anger of a youthful eighteen-year-old—anger that I had once felt, anger at being alive, a young-and-restless type of anger. I wanted to maintain the anger that, after a beer, makes you want to drive too fast, play too hard, smash into a wall with your fist or with a car. I knew if I could find that anger I could do anything!

Despite the regimen that I had chosen for myself, I felt that parts of my life had become too easy, that I was too cared for. I needed to be hungry and independent. I needed to be angry at the world for leaving me alone in it, tired and defensive, and I used the anger to my advantage in competition.

Anger was fueled in sometimes surprising encounters. After I had flown one time, a woman experienced in aerobatic competition said to me, "I saw you fly. You flew like shit."

I tried to talk about the bumpy air and the high-density altitude, but she insisted, "No. It wasn't the conditions. It was you. You really flew like shit."

She was wrong. I had to prove myself, as my friend Ian Groom said, "with substance."

By the end of the 1991 nationals, my scores reflected twenty-eight perfect tens to my nearest competitor's seventeen. I was on a roll. Each flight was better than the last and this alone gave me the confidence to stay focused. I won the gold medal in each flight: compulsory, freestyle, and unknown. I fulfilled my goals and achieved just what I had known I could accomplish.

By mastering the challenge, cultivating the anger, coaxing myself to believe I was the best, I reached the top. For me it was a hard-fought, hard-won battle, but for the first time in the United States, a woman was victorious. I became the first and only woman to win the U.S. National Aerobatic Championship. It felt great!

In the past, when I hadn't won, I felt that I had disappointed others—those who had believed in me, encouraged me, coached me, listened to me, and anguished over the competition with me, especially Bob. He was almost speechless when I called to tell him the good news. He was very happy but disappointed that he was involved with a trial and couldn't come to the awards banquet.

In the past, I had learned that losing took grace. Now in one elated, excited moment, I knew that winning took grace as well. It was one of the greatest moments of my life; at the same time, it was good for other people, too. It was another door being opened, another chance for women to hear, "You have a choice!"

Kermit Weeks, who had won twice previously and certainly had hoped to win again, was one of the first to congratulate me. Kermit and I had never been the best of buddies, so I really appreciated his sincerity.

Don Johnson, someone to whom I will always be grateful, encouraged me and helped me by videotaping each of my flights so that I could see for myself how my flying looked to observers on the ground.

Clint McHenry wrote, "Mere congratulations are not enough. I'm almost as happy for you as I would be if I had won myself. I'm really proud of you. I also think it is great for the sport."

Leo Loudenslager wrote a long letter in which he said in part, ". . . you must know how proud I am of you. You are walking very tall now and you deserve every bit of pride that you have in yourself and what you have accomplished. You have worked long and hard for it. I suppose you will be taken aback a little by members of the aviation community who do not fully grasp the depth of the accomplishment. Those of us who know you and the sport do, however, and we are indeed proud of you. Make sure that you also understand how much of life has been given to you in the way of support that other women have not had. You have a new respect from people. You are also a leader. I'm sure you will shoulder that well and use it to the best of your ability to advance the sport."

After she had won a prestigious air race in Cleveland, Ohio, in 1948, Grace Harris wrote of the moments of ecstasy created by the thrill of competition. Her happiest triumph was having pushed to a new frontier knowing full well how difficult and long the road to triumph.

My friends, John and Martha King, co-owners and founders of the King Schools, a successful company based in southern California, came to the awards banquet. John wrote, "When Patty became the first woman ever to win the U.S. National Aerobatic Championship in 1991, Martha and I joined the celebration and later several of us flew off together in our Citation to Branson, Missouri, to see some shows. During a quiet moment that evening, Patty looked at us seriously and asked, 'You don't think I'm a trophy wife, do you?' We were stunned. In our opinion, Patty's success was something Bob and Patty had done together over the years and this was just the culmination. But Patty felt vulnerable. She wanted to make sure no one could ever own her."[4]

Each of us has insecurities. Even at the apex of my achievements, small niggling doubts had a way of rising unbidden in my thoughts. I brushed them off. What was important was the tremendous success, the icing on the cake, the absolute joy of having done it. I recalled Jay Hanna "Dizzy" Dean's saying: "If you really done it, it ain't braggin'!"

I really done it. . . .

Like any other major goal achieved by someone with high aspirations and dedication, I found that I relegated this achievement immediately to one more stepping stone. I knew that I had achieved one goal, but I knew instantly that it wasn't enough. I knew that I had to do it again. I had to return to prove that I was even better—a smoother, more accomplished, and *more* successful aerobatic champion.

I felt that I had not flown my best. Most competitors never fly their best at a contest due to pressure. I wanted to show that I'd learned to fly my best in front of judges.

I had not always been an exemplary loser. I had pouted and had a hard time talking to Pete Anderson when he won the nationals in 1990, just as he pouted a little when I won. I had been happy for him and knew that he had deserved to win, but I had wanted the championship that was his.

Winning makes it easier to dedicate yourself to excellence and harder to defend your position. You are on the top and it is as if a bull's eye were painted on the middle of your back. You become the one that everyone else wants to beat!

I decided what to do, saying to myself, "I have to win the nationals again. I'm not ready to retire or quit and I know I can fly even better!"

Navy captain and F-14 driver Dale Snodgrass said, "Dominance in the air and in its ultimate form must be measured over time. The path to achievement is simple . . . sustained superiority fueled by competitive fire."[5]

---

[4] King, John and Martha King, The King Schools, personal interview, 1995.

[5] Snodgrass, Dale, personal statement, 1996.

I was willing to take the time. I wanted to sustain superiority. But competitive fire is hard to maintain. It is hard to stay hungry. Like a race car driver, I wanted to lead the pack, drive hard, and come in first, again and again.

EIGHTEEN

Caviar

After the intrigue of first seeing Soviet team pilots surrounded and protected from any communication with Westerners by members of the KGB during WAC 1986, it was a unique opportunity five years later for some of us on the U.S. team to go to Borki, Russia, to participate in what had been the Soviet Team Training Camp. Now it was the Russian Aerobatic Team Camp. The prospect of flying the Sukhoi SU-26M for two weeks was a terrific lure, but the bigger thrill was the anticipation of meeting my international competitors on their own soil and flying their airplanes in their airspace. It was difficult to equate the new openness with my original conceptions of secrecy and separation.

Pete and Sara Anderson and I arrived at the huge, sprawling, and dark structures of Shermetevo Airport in Moscow. Sounds of a guttural and unfamiliar language surrounded us and signs on the wall bore the Cyrillic letters that dated to the ninth century. We knew immediately that we were in a strange and different land. I had never been to Eastern Europe and the airport was distinctly foreign, a vast area of drab buildings bathed in dreary blackness.

U.S. team pilots Peter Anderson, Ellen Dean, and I were the three Team pilot guests of the Russian Aerobatic Team as part of an exchange program. Bob, president of the U.S. Aerobatic Foundation, had worked out the details of the exchange with Kasum Nazhmudinov, the longtime coach and manager of the then-Soviet team, and now it became a reality.

Upon arrival, we were welcomed by Elena Klimovich, a member of the Russian Women's Aerobatic Team, with colorful and generous bouquets of fresh flowers, although it wasn't until later that I realized how precious those carnations were. During our entire stay we saw little fresh anything—fruit, vegetables, nor other flowers—and we realized that we had not fully appreciated the significance of the kind gesture. I learned that in Russia, besides the wonderful spirit of the people, not much else was available.

From the airport we journeyed north-northeast by bus from Moscow to Borki, near Dubna on the Volga, shaking along on rutty, gravel-strewn two-lane roads, our only opposing traffic a few oxcarts. Once in Borki, the bus stopped at a three-story dormitory where we were greeted by Kasum, a paternal figure with a great deal of pride in his crew. Kasum elicited respect from each of us.

"It is time," he said, "to eat."

When Kasum spoke, we listened, and all of us followed his directions.

A communal cafeteria in the town of Borki, with its 1,000 residents, was the building in which we took most of our meals. Bright and cheerful, the tables were clean and well laden with butter, dark and white breads, potatoes, and a lot of meat. It appeared a lot of strenuous training was planned judging from the carbo loading that began that night.

When dinner was over, we returned to the dormitory and tried to get some sleep in Borki's early autumn. Borki, in a steppelike, subtundra environment, bordered on northern woods. On our first morning, the hardest freeze was still to come, but frost sprinkled the window panes and the sky was tinged with yellow as sulphur-crested hills of clouds hung in low stratus layers across the horizon. We breakfasted and then, en masse, attended our first scheduled briefing in a room that had been installed sometime during World War II.

Once the early fog evaporated, we were treated to a line of airplanes, seven colorful Sukhois, poised with their heavy noses pointing skyward on a concrete ramp that paralleled the runway. The runway extended 4,500 feet in an east-northeast to west-southwest direction to favor the prevailing winds. The seven Sukhois were flanked with tan-and-red Yak 52s and a Yak 55, all powered by the same engine, a Vedenyev 360-horsepower workhorse that rarely seemed to break or require maintenance.

Kasum conducted the briefing surrounded by his Russians, healthy and physically fit and dressed in team gear: paramilitary camouflage pants or blue jumpsuits, green khaki jackets, tennis shoes, and bad haircuts. Kasum read from various schedules and announced that the Americans would fly twice daily after initiation flights in the Yaks. I elected to go last and awaited my turn. Ellen and Pete came back from their flights laughing and shaking their heads—not so much from amusement, but from the differences in the airplanes. All felt a new respect for the abilities of the Russian pilots.

My turn came and Victor Smolin, a former World Aerobatic Champion, was my Yak 52 host. We climbed into the Russian airplane under an overcast sky and I couldn't help but wonder, "How will we do aerobatics under such a low cloud ceiling?"

We took off, climbing over the wide, meandering Volga River, and Victor started to describe the sectors in which we would be flying—he called them zona one, closest to the runway, and zonas two and three. In all honesty, I was so blown away by the magical scenery and the awe of being airborne in a Russian plane with a Russian pilot that I didn't pay much attention to the locations of zona two and zona three.

Victor pointed the way to Dubna, a quaint town fifteen kilometers from Borki, and explained that A. N. Tupolev, the famous aircraft designer, was a native of that village. Tupolev's name graces Russian aircraft that first appeared in the 1920s and continued on into the age of jets and to modern supersonic transports. An aircraft was mounted in the center of Dubna as a monument to him.

All of a sudden, I felt myself cringing in instrument conditions as Victor climbed into the clouds. I wondered when we would break out into sunshine above just as we popped into a beautiful clear Russian sky. Victor used the cloud layer as a base and a horizon line for aerobatics and did a couple of vertical rolls, loops, and snaps before giving me the controls. Painted by the yellow and pink northern light, the clouds were salmon-colored and in perfect puffballs below us.

After having flown the Extra, the Yak 52 felt a bit mushy, and I discovered that it took a lot of rudder pressure to keep the Yak headed in a desired direction. In getting acquainted with the rudder, I did some overcontrolling yet finally began to get the feel of the Yak 52 and started to truly enjoy what I was there for. I was sure that we both were filled with awe—he thinking, "I'm here with an American team pilot!" and I thinking, "Wow! I'm in Russia flying with a Russian!" We were amazed at the changes in our governments that gave us this opportunity.

When our flight time was nearly over, we punched down through the clouds again, and burst out directly over a tiny village that was cut geometrically into small, tidy, identical garden dacha plots. We were just sightseeing and it was so cool.

Skimming just over treetop level and rocketing along following the contours of the winding Volga River, Victor treated me to a unique view of his country. We waggled our wings at the occasional fishing boat—the Volga boatmen of legend and song?—and from our vantage point a few feet above the water, we looked up at the onion-domed minarets, and the grays, blues, and whites of a mosque. We created a blurring view of an interesting landscape and etched permanent memories into our minds' eyes. Aviators are brothers and sisters and now we transcended time and place.

When flying was over for the day, mechanics put the airplanes away. They postflighted, preflighted for the next day, refueled, and oiled each craft. Because the aircraft weren't hangared, they saw to it that heavy canvas covers were secured over the fuselages, canopies, and wings. They were outdoor beasts in stark contrast to our hangar queens.

For dinner there were generous servings of hearty meat and potatoes, bread and butter, bulgur or white wheat that to me, was somewhat less appealing drenched with ladles of butter, and we washed it down with hot tea. The cafeteria rang with the clink of utensils against the plates, but dinner conversation was kept at a minimum, and as soon as Kasum was finished, he stood up and dinner was over. Dinner was clearly not a social event; there was no lingering over after-dinner coffee or cigarettes.

On day two I was slated to solo the single-seat Yak 55. Prior to that, however, Kasum demonstrated the Yak in zona one and showed the control of a master. Incredibly welded to his familiar aircraft, he flew as if he were a man-machine, as if they were one.

Then my turn came and I found that the Yak 55 was hot! It wasn't quite the Sukhoi 26 that waited on the ramp to tempt us, but the Yak's 360-horsepower engine provided plenty of power and commensurate torque. At the controls and headed down the runway, my Yak lifted off in 500 feet with energy to spare. Cleared over the radio to zona one, I turned to the right and thought, "Here I go, cleared to fly alone over the Volga River in Russian airspace. Amazing!"

The Yak 55, the aircraft used for the Russian national contests, was fun to fly and a good transition to the Sukhoi. The propeller rotated in an opposite direction to those in the United States, which resulted in an aircraft that rolls better to the right than the left and in a need for more left rudder pressure than right—important changes to pretty well-ingrained habits. The roll rate was moderately fast and the plane had fairly good vertical performance, but oh, that rudder. I knew that if I could stop overcontrolling, I could master the airplane.

I enjoyed my time in the air and treasured the experience of rolling, looping, and generally cavorting around the sky, but it was magical to actually be in the Russian sky. Time flew past and soon I heard, "Patty, end flight." Then, "Patty, return."

I did as I was told.

The seat in the Yak 55 was not as reclined as in the SU-26, but nevertheless, more reclined than in my own airplane. My legs were more nearly level with my eyes, and though the low-slung style was a bit awkward on the ground, it proved very comfortable in the air. The controls were heavier than those of a Pitts, an Extra, or even a Cub, with ailerons that tended to overcenter slightly. That made it hard to stop rolls precisely but would have taken only a short time to overcome. I was sure that the secret to flying that airplane lay in the correct use of the rudder.

After the morning's flying, we were bussed to the cafeteria to another filling lunch—another meal of meat and potatoes that was accompanied by a choice of borscht or milk soup, more bread, pickled cabbage, pickled fish, and tea—and went back to work. Victor and Elena Klimovich, two of the few who spoke English well, briefed us on the starting procedures for the Sukhois. Thanks to Brian Becker at Pompano Air Center in Florida, I had flown a Sukhoi, but it had been a while and I was grateful for the transition time in the Yak 55. Each of us was assigned to a particular airplane; Ellen and I to a pink Sukhoi with a seat modified for smaller people, while Pete to a blue-and-white one.

Flying the Sukhoi was a thrill! I was sitting up high feeling every one of the 360 pulsating horses up front, raring to go. The wings were in line with my sternum and my knees stared back at my eyeballs. A voice from the portable control tower said, "Patty, take off."

As I put power to the Sukhoi, or according to the Russians, the Soo (or Suke to the U.S. pilots), it jumped off the runway and into the air—all three wheels at once. The propeller whirred so close to the ground that there was no gentle raising of the tail wheel prior to takeoff. At no time, in fact, could one forget that huge, whirling, two-bladed metal fan.

I entered the aerobatic box. Everyone could see me, but I knew that I could handle that. We were all in the same boat, so to speak, and we could all make fun of each other, if need be. I concentrated on verticals, rolls, and some snap rolls. I tried to get a feeling for the Suke.

It felt good! It rolled like a maniac and had a lot of energy in the vertical. The Sukhoi was an honest and eager airplane, a fantastic airplane. There has never been another quite like it. It was neither easier nor harder to fly than other planes. It just took the hand of experience to get the best out of it.

I was told not to fly below 300 feet and was given twenty minutes of solo time. I took advantage of my opportunities.

With great ailerons, the Sukhoi's roll rate was really dazzling. The snap rolls required techniques that had to be explored. They were, to me, the key to learning to fly the airplane.

With no provisions for it, a bit of coaxing was required before any of us wanted to critique one another. Elena, Victor Shmiel, and Alexander Liubarets were the least shy, and they eventually were convinced to offer critiques of our flights. The realization that we were American pilots training in a former Soviet training camp made us all incredulous; it was a totally new concept. A feeling of brother- and sisterhood began to develop and we began to laugh at the same jokes, to understand the same internal politics.

We were well-cared for at the highest of standards. We were made to feel part of the group and were in company with the best of the Russian pilots. All good and well-trained, their team was chosen by aptitude and personality. It held four training sessions a year lasting for approximately three weeks to one month each time, in dramatic contrast to that of the U.S. team members, who trained for two weeks every two years! Fully subsidized by the Russian government, their team has astounding depth and many good pilots.

We saw Nikolai Nikitiuk, Nikolai Timofeev, and Vitas Lapenas, who drove from Vilnius, Lithuania, on his way to Moscow in his little red Lada. It was great to spend some time with those I had gotten to know in previous world contests.

When fog canceled our flying, training continued in the form of athletics at the local gymnasium and track. I have an aversion to games played with balls that become airborne missiles, so I ran laps around the outside of the building while many of the group played volleyball. The Russians were good at it. Kasum provided knee pads and everyone wore bright satin shorts. There wasn't an ounce of fat on any of the Russians' athletic bodies. It was no wonder they fly so well.

We slowly became part of the scene, a group of gentle, quiet, and thoughtful people who seemed to care for each other and for each other's needs. One night we made popcorn, and as we Westerners dug our fistfuls into the bowl, we looked greedy in comparison to the locals who ate it one kernel at a time. They'd never seen it before! They offered us some good beer and vodka appeared on occasion, generally accompanied by jars of exotic caviar and brown bread and butter.

Members of the Russian team wanted to discuss the rules and regulations of the world competition aerobatics and I wondered, "Am I in Star Trek? Do I trust the Klingons? Are they for real or just trying to feel out our ideas?" Good sense prevailed and we had a substantive, positive exchange on judging, boundaries, the scoring system, men's and women's teams, and plans for the world championship to be held in France in 1992.

Their economy was in disaster, with many citizens not knowing where their next meal would come from much less how to support a national aerobatic team. [1] I credited the Russians with having raised the level of our sport a great deal and having been instrumental in bringing the sport to the respected level at which it is today. I hoped that they would continue to be financed.

One of the strengths of the Russian team is their depth and experience. Any reduction in the effectiveness of the Russians would be a deep loss to the world aerobatic community. And those of us fortunate enough to train with them gained some of their experience.

After a few days and a few flight hours in the Sukhois, we truly began to fly them. We began to do takeoffs and landings consistently well and we no longer felt quite as shy about flying in the box in plain sight of everyone at the training camp. I was impressed and proud of the quality

---

[1] When we were there, we understood that financing would continue for only one more year. But Kasum Nazhmudinov sent a message in February 1992 that the sport club of the former USSR had been renamed and restructured and was to receive continued support from the Sukhoi Design Bureau. I had never believed that it would be in the best interests of the Sukhoi Design Bureau to allow the Russian team to go without support. The bureau's biggest advertising tool is the national team.

of flying achieved by my teammates. I enjoyed seeing them fly. They did masterful jobs.

When it came time to leave, Nik Timofeev drove me to the airport. We crept slowly through the thickest fog I had ever seen, leaving at one in the morning in order to be in Moscow for a six o'clock departure. The road to Moscow was narrow with almost no traffic whatsoever.[2] Suddenly, out of the fog, a police box loomed and Nik slowed the car to a stop. A black-booted officer in a greatcoat appeared in the doorway. He stepped out, his hand outstretched for our papers, his coat frosted by the damp foggy air. Despite having nothing to hide, we both felt nervous. Movie scenes flashed through my head—black-and-white oldies, film noire. Our papers were in order, so we moved forward slowly following the sweep of his dark arm and mittened hand. Wisps of fog curled over the sleeve of his coat and added to the surreal experience.

The scene darkened to a nightmare once inside Shermetevo Airport. There were no ticket counters, no computers. Miles of sleepy and sleeping people drooped with only their luggage supporting them. I was told to get in the custom's line two hours before my flight. Finally, a bored young immigration and customs agent fingered his papers, looking around absently before eventually waving me through.

After this two-hour wait, I reached the front of the line only to be told by a heavily made-up woman that I was not listed for the flight. I was incredulous. I couldn't believe this was happening to me. I protested vigorously, wanting to grab the woman by the collar to shake her until her teeth rattled. "No! You cannot do this. You will let me on that airplane! I'll pay for a first-class ticket with my credit card or with cash that I brought especially for an emergency such as this." *Allowed* to purchase a ticket at an exorbitantly higher price, I later heard that this was not an unusual circumstance. It smelled of scam. Actually, it just smelled.

But not even a scam could dim my pleasure at having been able to participate in this historic exchange. I was warned that it would be like camping indoors but found that the accommodations were more than

---

[2] Nik and I had a lot of time to talk about funding and air shows and what the Russian team would do. The U.S. team had never been subsidized by its government, depending completely on sponsorships and individual contributions. I assured him that we in the United States struggled for funding every year and our future seemed just about as uncertain as theirs. We guessed it best to keep trying and to keep the faith in what we do.

satisfactory. I was warned that Sukhois were not user-friendly, and, while I believe one has to respect them for the awesome machines that they are, they are just airplanes. I had some expectations, but like the rest of my team members, I tried to fit in and keep an open mind. We were treated exceptionally well by gracious hosts, and though we have different training techniques, we found that we are all in similar circumstances. With both of us struggling for the funding to continue our programs, each of us, Russian and American, was left with the feeling that the sport of aerobatics and aviation in general had bridged another gap.

It struck me that one universal mode of communication in Russia is playing chess. Chess, like aerobatics, is a sport with champions that have a history and a structure for competition, and it brought us together.

We had an exciting, wonderful time. In our own small way, by working together and gaining mutual respect, we transcended our countries' tensions. The world scene changed dramatically not long after our visit, but that one foray into a microcosm of aerobatic excellence is etched in my memory. I relegated to memory my fantastic opportunity to take to the controls of a Russian aerobatic airplane and fly solo above the Volga River, sweeping to the curves of the rippling waters and slipping over the steppes, dachas, and mosques in aerobatic antics.

NINETEEN

Performance

Looking back, right from the start, I was eager to get into air shows after watching my very first at Abbotsford in 1983. I knew air shows were where I wanted to be. The performers looked trim and fit and moved with casual intensity; they looked confident and competent, and a bit excited with preshow anticipation. I enjoyed the obvious camaraderie between the pilots and the coordination between the crews. I knew I was watching the best and I wanted to fly like that, to perform like that, to be part of their scene.

I figured that it must be a rush to tear at 200 miles an hour in front of the crowd, to blur individuals into streams of glorious colors, to turn the runway into a licorice ribbon. I wanted to take my airplane to the edge of its performance, fly low enough to dust the ground with my smoke, roll the airplane into the sky, and show off the beauty of flight. I knew it would be a toss-up as to whether it was the crowd or I that would be the most thrilled.

I knew, too, that it was important to generate income to offset some of the costs of competition aerobatics. By flying as a professional air show performer, I could continue to fly aerobatics. Above all, I appreciated the balance that I found between the intensity of competition and the joy of performing on an aerial stage in a freer, less emotionally charged atmosphere.

From 1985 on, I flew a combination of competition and air shows all summer long. The two meshed well, though scheduling took a great deal of creative logistics. I was eager to learn what it took to be a professional air show performer and was intrigued by the business aspects of it. Initially, Bob was particularly concerned about the danger of flying air shows. I talked with Duane Cole who assured me that any aerial performance is only as dangerous as the performer makes it. Not incidentally, Duane had tragically lost his son flying in an air show due to a mechanical failure. He urged me to pursue it if it was truly what I wanted to do, and that was all I needed to hear. Once Bob heard that, he never mentioned the risks again.

Patty Wagstaff Air Shows, (PWAS), was Bob's and my baby. Bob prepared corporation papers and assisted me greatly with the creation of the business, and we poured time, energy, and money toward its success. I bought myself an electric typewriter, managed my own accounting by hand, and started advertising. I mailed out a black-and-white flyer to interest possible sponsors and started learning the intricacies of marketing myself.

Bob was a huge help in sending out press releases and keeping sponsors informed of my activities, but he had a law career and I couldn't expect him to do my accounting, answer my phone, and attend to all of the things that cropped up. Besides, he was in Alaska a good part of the time that I was in Arizona.

As I booked more air shows, I spent increasingly more time in Arizona. To prepare for the seven- or eight-month show season, I moved into my hangar office. It was ironic. The more I searched for sponsors and booked air shows in order to pay for bigger, better, and more expensive competition aircraft, the more the business side of PWAS kept me from my main purpose—flying!

Karen Roberts, my personal assistant, started working with me part-time in 1989. I met Karen, a friendly woman with a great sense of humor, at the Avra Valley Airport in 1987.

After we started hanging out together, I asked her to help me in the office and it soon escalated to her traveling to local air shows to act as my helper and crew member. As time went on, the job required everything from answering the phone to waxing the airplane. Karen, who also came from an aviation family, brought the right combination of skills to PWAS and she quickly made herself indispensable. [1]

As PWAS became a success, it was, as Karen said, "like pushing something weighty uphill, then cresting the top of the hill and thinking, 'What happened? This is neat! *This* is what the effort was all about.'"

Air show flying got into my blood. Shy about greeting crowds at first, I gradually learned to wave, to smile, and to cheer. I especially learned to enjoy the kids that flocked around. There is a dichotomy between being a pilot—secure in the cocoon of a cockpit, senses alert and mechanically meshed with the machine in its every tumbling attitude—and being an entertainer. Like most air show pilots, I had to learn to be an entertainer, with little guidance or direction.

Being an air show performer was hard for me, but it is actually painful for some otherwise shy, introverted pilots. Drawn by the common bond of the love of flying, normally retiring pilots often have to make the big sacrifice to come out of their comfort zones. Although I am in tune with the entertainment aspects of the air show business, my flying has always been a very personal thing to me. Air show pilots learn a bravado. We learn to greet strangers, give good interviews, smile for television cameras, and sign autographs and publicity materials that are designed to be self-promoting but, at the same time, try not to believe our own press. We want to walk the tightrope of confidence and humility, competence and sincere awe. We do whatever it takes to keep sky dancing.

---

[1] Handling a large share of the office work in Tucson, Karen has ferried airplanes for me. She performed preflight checks and kept the airplane clean. Karen inspects the plane so often in the process of keeping it clean that she is good at troubleshooting. She knows the plane as well as I do and she notices every little screw, small hole, and incipient crack, appreciating how serious they all can be. Karen, who's gregarious and gets a kick out of being with people, drives our van and travels untold miles without complaint. We get along well and it has worked out better than I would have imagined. I've been lucky. Karen has not only been a big part of PWAS, but she has also been my most loyal friend.

When you are around guys all the time, it is fun to have a woman's perspective. Karen and I are not in competition with one another and we are different enough that there is never a problem that we can't work through. Most importantly, having a good, dependable friend on the road helps make life bearable, even during the longest hauls.

In searching for a major sponsor, I was responding to reality. I couldn't continue to be the financial drain on Bob's and my resources without finding a way to contribute. In Anchorage, my cousin Cindy's husband, Greg Bombeck, helped to design beautiful color press kits, and we sent them to approximately one hundred companies. Rejection letters raced back before I could believe that the press packages had arrived, but I learned to take rejection letters in stride. I also learned to pursue when a company hesitated briefly or even tolerated my foot in their door.

I knew I could find a sponsor if I persisted. I wanted sponsors who were involved with and understood aviation, who truly appreciated what my kind of flying was all about, whose vested interests were with mine, and for whom I could perform the best marketing and advertisement service. In 1988, I was flying my Extra 230, 444 Papa Whiskey, and I wanted a company to sense my excitement about my beautiful, responsive airplane and to have that enthusiasm spill over to their product.

Bob Dilger of II Morrow, the company that manufactured navigational equipment in Salem, Oregon, was the first to notice the potential and obvious connection between salesmanship and having his product well-displayed for the public at air shows. After getting my toe in the door, I followed up by sending numerous press releases, information, clips of articles in which I appeared, and contest results. After a time, Tim Mackey, in marketing, showed definite interest in my program, and I arranged a meeting with him, flying from Anchorage to Salem without knowing exactly what to expect.

Tim took me on a tour of the small company in its modernistic manufacturing and office complex on the east side of the Salem airport, McNary Field. Halfway through the tour, Tim smiled and told me, "We will be meeting with the owners and managers in the board room in a short while." Gulp.

I hadn't really prepared for a formal presentation, but knew I couldn't blow the opportunity to give one. I had press kits and a promotional video ready and hoped that I could answer any questions that they asked of me.

Eight businessmen in crisp shirts, ties, and conservative suits were seated around the large mahogany table. They looked at me expectantly, their faces noncommittal. I introduced myself and thanked them for their time before plugging in my videotape and letting the action and the color demonstrate what I had to offer them, far more graphically than I could have on my own.

They watched the video with interest, which was an encouraging sight, and when it came to an end, I took about ten minutes to tell them some of the truths about the marketing venue of an air show, how I could benefit their advertising, the potential I intended to demonstrate as a competitor and on the air show circuit, and the goals that I had established for myself. I showed them brochures of several other air show personalities who had been sponsored by other companies and saved my trump card for the finale. The husband and wife team Montaine Mallet and Daniel Heligoin, who fly as the French Connection, were ambassadors of one of the major competitors of the II Morrow businessmen I faced. I could almost hear the collective "Aha!" Thanking them for their consideration, I left and flew back to Anchorage.

I was thrilled two days later to hear the phone ring and to hear, "Yes. We would like to sponsor you!" That generosity and faith in me guaranteed that I would be able to compete and to fly air shows for one more season. They featured my picture in their ad for their navigational equipment on the back page of the highly visible *Trade-A-Plane*, a popular tabloid that reaches hundreds of thousands in the aviation community.

II Morrow generously sponsored me from 1988 through 1991. When I began to negotiate my 1992 contract with them, I realized we'd come to the limit of what they could afford to pay. I decided to take a year off from sponsorship to assess other, larger opportunities that might be available to me. But a single year without a sponsor brought home to me quickly that it was impossible to maintain PWAS, to pay my crew, fly competition, and even perform in air shows, without major financial backing. Air shows pay respectable fees, but not enough to cover combined travel, maintenance, and crew management costs. Although I tried to fit in as many as fifteen air shows a year, weaving them into a network of five or six regional competitions, the nationals, necessary training sessions, and a variety of other commitments, being an air show performer wouldn't work without financial assistance. [2]

It takes preparation to be ready to take advantage of the opportunities that come along. Sometimes opportunities are of your own making. They're always a combination of timing, luck, and preparation. So I just continued working and flying, confident that all those things would gel.

---

[2] I maintain my friendship with II Morrow and to date, II Morrow provides me with GPS, a state-of-the-art navigational system.

Air show performers' lives, from March to November, are those of showmen—a modern repeat of the lives of itinerant barnstormers, the nation's travelers of the 1920s and 1930s who bounced their biplanes from farmer's field to farmer's field, arousing folks who otherwise wouldn't have had an inkling about flight and coaxing them to take enough in the way of paying rides so that the fuel and the repair bills would be met. We have become modern barnstormers—more encumbered with the complicated info-tech world of machines, phone calls, modems, multimedia opportunities, and other demands than a single person can handle—still gypsies of the air, free, within reason, to be paid for doing what we love to do.

Over the years, I've had many memorable air show experiences. I flew in the same air show in 1987 as the headline act, the legendary and awesome Bob Hoover. He was so charming. When I landed after my ten-minute performance, he congratulated me, saying, "Good job. Welcome to the air show world!"

In 1989, when Dave and Mary Lou Sclair's *General Aviation News and Flyer* held a reader's choice favorite air show performer contest, Bob Hoover and I were selected for the honors. That was a special thrill for me.

By 1989, I was no longer a rookie at the ICAS convention[3] nor at air shows around the country. I was soon to be invited to fly in bigger, more prestigious shows, and as with movie credits on a marquee, that meant my name was climbing higher on the program. I was getting to be a female headliner and getting to know more performers and promoters. Admittedly, being a woman in the air show industry—a bit of a rarity—didn't hurt. There aren't many of us. In addition to Suzanne

---

[3] As a member of the air show industry, I always make time in my calendar for the annual International Council of Air Shows (ICAS) convention. Designed to facilitate the union of performers with organizers and interested sponsors, the ICAS convention has developed over time into a slick promotional, marketing city of booths with high-tech enhancements like videos, computer displays, holography, rock music, posters, photographs, and colorful brochures, all of which clamor for attention—and bookings. Since I, too, go there to book shows for the following air show season, I produce videos, create handouts, and like a debutante, seek to fill up the following year's dance card with as many performances as my competition schedule will allow.

Asbury-Oliver, Julie Clark, Joann Osterud, and Montaine Mallet, good friends and leading women air show pilots, there are other well-known performers: Pat Wagner, a pilot who has celebrated more than twenty-five years of riding the wing of her husband Bob's Stearman; Cheryl Littlefield, who works on the wing with her husband, Gene; Theresa Stokes, a talented aviation artist who walks Gene Soucy's Ag Cat wing; and Ruthie Blankenship, another pilot who met her husband when applying for the job as his wingwalker. Ruthie billed herself as Wonder Woman of the Skies and dressed the part.

Like many of the others, I choreographed my routines to music and designed them to be exciting, a constant blur of motion. I flew directly in front of the crowd, smoke billowing as I circled and returned with Half-Cuban Eights and Hammerheads, reversing maneuvers that kept the airplane visible at all times. I choreographed an aerial ballet, combining precision of competition with the excitement of air shows. I kept twirling, rolling, and spinning in maneuvers designed to thrill the crowd *and* me.

When I moved from the Extra 230 to the Extra 260 in 1991, my routines also moved forward. They became more intricate and more challenging, always designed to show off my airplane to the max. From the 260, I moved to the Extra 300S in 1993 and again my routines changed, and, on new wings, my capability soared. Each new airplane encouraged more challenging and exciting routines.

At one air show, air-show great Sean D. Tucker and I were asked to fly with others in circles around colorful parachute jumpers signaling the start of an air show. What an honor it was to fly with the best formation team in history, the Eagles, led by the late Charlie Hillard, with aerobatic champions Gene Soucy and Tom Poberezny as wingmen. Sean and I bounced off the end of the five-ship formation, then joined the trio for an impromptu formation routine after all the jumpers were safely on the ground. It was an entertainer's cameo, a walk-on part, unrehearsed, and a blast for me and Sean.

Sean and I are great friends, but when we fly, the sparks of competition are real. We were performing at the El Toro Air show in California as solo performers when the organizers dreamed up a dual act—a mock duel between the two of us that was to be billed as the Duel of Champions. Sean is a terrific pilot, which inspires me. He and I agreed that we would put an act together and the promoters really hyped it! Ads were on television and in the newspapers, there were posters and invitations, and neither Sean nor I realized how much they counted on us.

Our good intentions went awry. Sean's airplane had been damaged and we didn't practice. We never even choreographed a routine. Before the show, we both tried to beg off, but the officials would hear none of it. They told us that they'd advertised, the crowd was waiting, and they wanted to see that duel.

Sean and I got together on the ground and sketched a scenario, fast. We opposed each other—Sean diving in from the right, corkscrewing around into a maneuver, and climbing out as I dove into show center, both of us avoiding closing in on each other and doing tricky, tight formation. We flew about eight showy maneuvers before Sean did his Harrier Pass, a slow pass with his airplane hanging on its prop, while I buzzed him at warp speed. We enhanced the act with the most challenging maneuver of all, a formation, inverted Ribbon Cut. Both of us, side-by-side, were upside down just feet above the ground, the tails of our airplanes slicing two ribbons strung between four different poles and held by eight people on the ground. We ended by flying in tight formation, Sean in knife-edge flight close beside me and my airplane upside down over the ground. That flourish proved to be a dramatic photo finish. As close to the ground as I flew, I had to trust that Sean was watching my airplane as I monitored the straight track and the distance above the crowd and from the the ground (about 50 feet). I caught peripheral glimpses of his black biplane but more *felt* its presence and heard its engine roaring and growling a few feet from my left ear. [4]

As we performed the duel at more air shows, we got better and more in tune with each other. If a jet car or jet truck performed, we challenged it, flying in inverted formation and racing the rig—a modern conversion of the races between an early biplane pilot chasing auto racer Barney Oldfield around an oval auto track. If Rich Gibson of Rich's Incredible Pyro were around, we'd ask him to set off dramatic flares, making our Ribbon Cuts as showy as the fireworks on the Fourth of July. Announc-

---

[4] Sean is one pilot with whom I will fly in such close proximity. There aren't many. Flying a formation routine with inevitable times in which you momentarily lose sight of one another requires intense concentration, practice, and, at the base, a close bond and special relationship of complete respect. But, even then, Sean isn't surprised to hear me shout at him over the radio, "Talk to me, Sean. Where are you?"

ers got into the act, too. They played "Dueling Banjos" over the P.A. system and made a big deal of the boy versus the girl, the black biplane versus the white monoplane, X versus Y chromosome.

Air shows that feature military jets and their precision exhibition teams are larger and more prestigious. Being booked to fly for such shows has also marked my progress and sparked them with excitement. The Canadian Air Force's Snowbirds headlined the first large air show in which I performed and put on their usual stirring performance. Because of the Snowbirds and their enormous popularity, the show itself rose to be classed as a "big show," and the popularity of the Snowbirds trickled down to the rest of us on the playbill. At that time I assumed that it would be a long time before I would be an air show headliner, but I was delighted to be included in a schedule that featured a military jet team.

I have since performed many times with the U.S. Navy's Blue Angels (the Blues) and with the U.S. Air Force's Thunderbirds.

In 1993, Captain Greg Wooldridge was lead pilot of the Navy's Blues. When I was performing at Aerospace America, the annual Oklahoma City air show, one of the Blues members asked if I would like to fly in an F-18 with the precision team. He said as long as I could make the briefing at noon, they'd take me for the ride of my life. I glanced across the flight line at the straight, formal, commanding row of gleaming fighters with their familiar butterfly tails and spotless glossy blue paint jobs. I laughed at my good luck and jumped at the chance.

The briefing was an event all its own and one to which very few people are invited. It was hushed, quiet, completely organized, and efficient. I could have sworn that I was in the sanctuary of a church.

After marching toward the jets, they strapped me in an F-18, sans G suit or oxygen, which surprised me. My pilot, Doug Thompson, number four, slot position, climbed in and shut the canopy. We taxied out onto the runway in a clean formation with three other jets only inches from one another. At take off, with the unbelievable burst of raw horsepower, I knew this would be a ride I would never forget; I almost experienced sensory overload! Barely comprehensible chatter between the pilots squawked on the radio and I was in the midst of a tumultuous drama in which thousands of tons of metal hurtled within a hair's breadth of one another. Although the F-18 pilots didn't put as much G on the airplane as I do in a normal flight, the sustained Gs in tight turns and the steely wings' nearly touching gave me new appreciation for their skill and precision. It was a symphony of color, sound, rhythm, and motion.

I agree with Danny Clisham, noted air show announcer, philosopher, and raconteur, who said that air show performances are the only form of entertainment that goes on week after week without a single rehearsal. A credit to the skill and dedication of modern air show performers, the four- or five-hour demonstration has to be perfect the first time, every time; and no other form of entertainment boasts that discipline.

Professionals in any sport are so good that they make the difficult look easy; however, flawless performance comes only with faithful and arduous practice. To advance beyond a local level, air show performers require hours and hours of flight for every ten- to fifteen-minute performance. First-timers are limited in how low they can fly, given minimums that they are required to maintain. But to be a marketable air show performer, a pilot has to learn to descend lower and lower, closer and closer to the ground.

Like all beginners, I started into air shows as a fly speck in the stratosphere, relegated to the higher altitudes by inexperience. Thanks to hundreds of practice hours, I descended into the atmosphere, my limit the ground. I learned with absolute certainty what my combined woman-machine would do and how it would do it. I learned maneuvers at altitude and brought them closer and closer to the ground, always connected mentally and physically—a mechanical-metal-flesh-and-blood combination—until I was one with my machine. [5]

When I began flying at the lowest altitudes of the air show stage, ground zero, I increased my vigilance on safety. If a few weeks elapsed

---

[5] In the United States, regulations prevent air show airplanes from flying closer than 500 feet to the crowd and the more powerful military jets from flying a more distant 1,500 feet from the crowd, stipulating that energy may not be directed toward spectators. Safety is paramount and aerial displays are closely monitored by officials of the FAA. In addition, ICAS administers the Aerobatic Competency Evaluation (ACE) program. ACE evaluates performers and decides on their suitability for receiving low altitude waivers. In a graduated-level process, a performer might qualify to perform aerobatics at a minimum of 1,000 feet above the ground, then, with added experience and evaluation, at 800 feet, then 500 feet, and ultimately at ground zero, the most demanding of skill and the most difficult level to achieve. As much as good judgment is heralded, however, it cannot be legislated, and dangers inexorably creep in.

I eventually became an ACE, one of the evaluators who recommends altitude limits to the FAA for budding air show performers.

between doing inverted Ribbon Cuts, I practiced before I attempted them; if I hadn't flown a "low show," designed for low ceilings, I practiced prior to performance. Knowing that complacency can kill, I practiced to achieve the fine line between thrilling the crowds and frightening them. I fostered in myself respect toward fear and have even tasted its sour, acrid flavor in my mouth when I had a momentary lapse of focus. To this day, when I perform, all of my senses respond.

Aerobatic pilots who want to become air show pilots must have or develop the extroverted nature of entertainers to show spectators what they can do and to share the beauty of flying with others. In an interesting inverse relationship, I felt an innate desire to achieve the highest level of air show aerobatics, which meant flying as low as possible, daring the ground to ever come too close. As any mountain climber responds, "Because it is there," when asked why he or she tried to get to the top, when asked why I flew so low, my response was "Because the ground is there!" I wanted to barely skim the surface, to feel the ground rush and see raw speed as all outside references blurred into formless streaks.

Over time, I've become increasingly involved in the air show world, enjoying the people with whom and for whom I perform. Air shows and competition differ greatly, but the air show pilot has to apply some of the same training techniques as a competition pilot, that is, practice, watch other performers, and ask for advice. In contrast to the world of competition, the politics of the air show world seem cleaner and less self-serving, genuinely targeted for the good of the industry as a whole. Air shows, still a relatively small industry, have the warmth of family reunions. I like that. Besides, I get along with other performers really well and have fun with people like Sean Tucker, Steve and Suzanne Oliver, Daniel Heligoin and Montaine Mallet, Bob and Maryellen Bishop, members of Team America, Big B and Little T Beardsley, and a *lot* of others.

At Pratt, Kansas, I met Lori Lynn Ross, a well-known stuntwoman in Hollywood, who was especially adept at mountain and rock climbing. Lori, who at one point turned her agility to wingwalking, nominated me as the first pilot member in the prestigious United Stuntwomen's Association. At Pratt I also met Jimmy Franklin and Eliot Cross, on whose biplanes Lori wingwalked along with wingwalking legend, stuntman Johnny Kazian.

I enjoy air shows in part because they are such a contrast from the insanity of competition. Yet life hasn't always been upbeat at air shows. A few years ago, I performed in Lafayette, Louisiana, at a show to which my cousin Theresa Syversen brought her five children. She had invited her neighbor, who declined because she didn't want her kids to see any accident that might happen. That particular answer really hit me. People *don't* want to see accidents. Despite the curious fascination with accidents that is encouraged by the media's sensationalism of them, I don't think tragedy is what most people want to see.

I thought about my cousin Theresa again after Jim Gregory was killed in a crash at the El Toro air show in California in 1993. Jim's F-86 fighter smashed into the ground. The crowd was utterly silent. Shock registered on people's faces. Jim's airplane exploded in a fireball, a hurtling mass of twisted flaming metal that careened a full mile down the runway. It seemed to keep on going forever—an unspeakable horror. The spectators, a mass of humanity 600,000 strong, became a mindless entity surging toward the crash site, only to be stopped by young Marine guards.

After a respectful length of time, Sean Tucker and I went to talk with people along the crowd line, trying to distract those who were justifiably distraught. When I looked at kids, all I could think was, "That child won't want to learn to fly," "There's one that won't like aviation," or "There's one that will never want to come to another air show." It was very traumatic, for everyone. The faces of the kids who witnessed that crash haunt me.[6]

When asked if air show flying is dangerous to a pilot, I answer that it can be seductive and, yes, it is dangerous. I have known too many to lose their lives as air show performers. Ego involvement, impressing others, peer influence, media demands, unforeseen weather, mechanical difficulties, and a myriad of factors compound the pressure cooker called performance that is in and of itself a demanding challenge. There are ways to mitigate the hazards, but it takes skill, good judgment, prior planning, successful practice, experience, and a dose of good fortune and humility to be safe.

---

[6] We later discovered that the parents, concerned about dealing properly with the tragedy, were grateful that we talked to the kids. The announcers, Gordon Bowman-Jones and Bill Bordeleau, did a masterful job of keeping the crowd soothed and quieted and, later, a write-up in the local paper dealt with issues that linked kids and tragedy.

When asked if air show flying is dangerous to spectators, I answer an unequivocal "No." Governmental rules and regulations prevent performers from directing any energy toward the crowd. Air shows are great family entertainment.

Inevitably, to this day, I spend the greatest amount of my time between air shows rather than at them. Travel and the logistics of scheduling mean that most of my flying is from air show to air show, to a competition, or toward my hangar in Tucson. Every air show ends and begins with a cross-country flight. Some performers dread cross-country flying, feel it is a bore. I have always loved it as a relatively relaxing break in an otherwise intense series of events. Although my airplane is well endowed with high-technology navigational equipment and a decent stereo system plugged into my noise-canceling Bose headsets, when I leave an air show, I fly with my eyes on the roads, the rivers, the gullies, the outlines of the states etched in fields. I fly with ease and I fly free.

Had it not been for air shows, I would have missed meeting hundreds of interesting people and a generation of terrific kids. Pleasing the crowd is the intrinsic joy in entertainment, but I especially love reaching the kids, turning them on to aviation, and convincing them that they can be anyone they want to be, and do anything they want to do. While it is true that they have to work at it, that they have to create their own opportunities, that anything worthwhile takes determination and sacrifice, my greatest joy as an air show pilot is inspiring children and having them respond to me. You never know when you will inspire one person with the desire to learn to fly or at least to appreciate aviation.

TWENTY

Centering Gravity

O nce I had won the National Aerobatic Championship in 1991, I knew that I had to do it again. It wasn't something that had even occurred to me prior to winning, but as soon as I saw the scores posted that listed me as number one, I knew once wasn't enough. I felt an exhilaration and a deep satisfaction, but it was accompanied by momentum that I had never known. Not only did I recognize that I was on a roll and that I had the support of a lot of people, but I had the airplane and I had the desire.

At an air show in early 1992, Sean Tucker said, "You're planning to win again this year, aren't you?"

I looked at him questioningly and he continued. "I hope so, because if you don't, they will say it was a fluke. They'll say, 'Yeah. Sure a woman can win it once, but she lucked out!'"

That completely cemented my goals. I knew then that I had no choice but to win again. I made winning the championship three times in a row my goal.

Little did I know then that a particularly unusual hazard faced me. Eliot Cross ferried my Extra 260 for me from Florida to Tucson in the spring of 1992, and, after his arrival, he suddenly said, "God, I am sick! I don't know what's wrong with me, but I feel so nauseated. I'm so tired, I can't keep my eyes open."

267

We figured that his trip had been long, but his eyelids drooped uncharacteristically and he went to bed exhausted. Soon thereafter, I flew the 260 from Tucson to Tulsa, Oklahoma. The vents were taped to prevent cold air from seeping through to the cockpit and I suffered in the same way as Eliot. Safely on the ground (fortunately), I was overcome with a wave of nausea. I started experiencing double vision and I became nauseous and violently sick. I extended my stay in Tulsa to recuperate. Finally, after I flew the airplane to perform at the EAA's Sun 'n' Fun Fly-In in Lakeland, Florida, the illness recurred. Then I realized that Eliot and I had been poisoned by carbon monoxide![1]

I fanned vents on the airplane's belly and opened all of them. That helped by expelling the engine exhaust out and away from the airplane rather than allowing fumes to seep into the cockpit. It took me six to eight months to fully recover. Months passed before I could walk down a city street without feeling waves of nausea from exhaust fumes.

I kept on flying and worked through much of 1992 as hard as usual, with my combination of training, air shows, competition, and practice centered on a singular goal—winning the nationals. Like a universe of planets that whirled around one bright magnetic sun, a constellation of other goals and commitments circled on the periphery. Many opportunities opened because of the national championship and I was flattered to receive invitations and to be asked for interviews. Yet the more I pursued a variety of interests, the more I was subjected to. I had to work very hard to remain focused and to remember my purpose.

I sought a balance. I couldn't accept an interesting opportunity and fail to see the commitment through, but I didn't want to refuse any exciting events in which I was invited to participate. Luckily, my Virgo side makes me organized. I got more compartmentalized, more focused.

Invited by Hollywood's well-known aerial coordinator and stunt pilot, Jim Gavin, to fly in my first major motion picture, *Forever Young*, I flew my airplane to Long Beach, California, to the Los Alamitos Naval

---

[1] Carbon monoxide poisoning is insidious. It is an odorless, tasteless, innocuous gas that has been accused of killing pilots in the past. Now that I have felt its symptoms, I watch for early signs and am especially careful during the winter months, when I am trying to keep myself warm inside a snug and tightly closed cockpit.

Base for a week of work. Working with Hollywood stunt pilots Jimmy Franklin and Craig Hosking, I absorbed all that I could about movie flying. Jim later gave me a couple of great jobs, including the movie *Drop Zone*. A great guy, he was good to work with despite the fact that my story echoed that of a lot of starlets: my part in *Forever Young* hit the cutting room floor!

Once the air show season started, I had to weigh the expenses of performing against the income. To make a profit without sponsorship, I would have to perform at thirty air shows a year, yet to do that would cost commensurably more. The more shows, the more expensive it became because of more time spent on the road, more flight time on the aircraft, and increased maintenance costs. I had to figure closely the income versus the outgo, a classic catch-22. Plus I would have no hope of continuing competition flying and training.

I flew in the 1992 Cleveland National Airshow in Ohio and met Bob Judson, a clever and talented photographer who was working for BFGoodrich (BFG) Aerospace. [2]

Bob said he would like to attach a video camera to my airplane and use the film footage for public relations. I called on my business acumen and told him, "Well, you are going to have to pay me, Bob. I can't let you have that for nothing. BFGoodrich might want to sponsor me someday. If this is free, what am I worth?"

Bob introduced me to BFGoodrich Aerospace president David L. Burner. I invited Dave to look at my airplane and he delighted me with the comment that BFGA sponsored Bob Hoover, currently sponsors Bill Leff, and would be interested in sponsoring another air show performer.

Excited with the possibility of being sponsored by such a prestigous aerospace company and aware of what nailing another championship might mean, I focused even more on a second championship at the nationals. I made a mental note to set up a meeting with Dave as soon as I had won the contest.

---

[2] BFG, with corporate headquarters in Akron, Ohio, owns divisions and subsidiaries across the country that manufacture aerospace products for many facets of aviation: landing gear, wheels and brakes, flight instruments and avionics, and safety-related equipment such as deicers and collision avoidance systems. BFGoodrich also manufactures a cockpit weather-mapping instrument, Stormscope.

My fourth World Aerobatic Championship loomed on the horizon and would take place prior to my attempt to win a second nationals in Texas in September. The sixteenth world contest, WAC 1992, was to be held in Le Havre, France, on the murky, misty shores of the English Channel. I told Daniel Heligoin, air show performer and a former aerobatic champion of the French Air Force, that WAC 1992 was going to be held in Le Havre. [3]

Daniel slapped his hand down on the bar with a loud whack and laughed hysterically! He said, "Vell, Patty, you know, there weel not be a contest! Eet ees not possible to have a contest in Le Havre. Zee weather steenks!" I should have known that with his Gallic charm, Daniel spoke the truth. It was a mistake for the organizers of the competition to hold the contest in such an unsuitable location.

We began our WAC odyssey at a weeklong training camp at Rickenbacker Field in Columbus, Ohio, from which our ten airplanes flew in formation to Dover Air Force Base, Delaware. One of the greatest expenses of fielding a team on the world scene is the cost of the transport, paid for out of money raised by the U.S. Aerobatic Foundation from individuals and through sponsorships like that of Sporty's Pilot Shop, Ohio, and Aeroshell Oil. But many times U.S. pilots have had to dig deeply into their own pockets.

On the ramp at Dover, dozens of behemoths—C-5A Galaxies—dwarfed our tiny airplanes. It looked as if one of the great beasts had given birth to a litter.

---

[3] Between thirty and forty pilots generally compete in the unlimited category at the national level, and, while some competitors are better than others, most of us have similar styles, presentations, and expectations. At the world contest, up to one hundred unlimited pilots generally fly. The ten judges, some of whom have judged only one contest, sometimes the world contest, are from ten different countries; their stylistic and presentational expectations differ from those of judges in the United States. With so many pilots competing, it is highly unlikely that all competitors will be able to fly in the same weather conditions and with the same variables of wind and cloud cover. The draw for order of flight is also important. The worlds require a great degree of luck.

The winning team at the World Aerobatic Championship, the most prestigious aerobatics competition, is awarded the Nesterov Cup. The Nesterov Cup is named for the Russian pilot who completed the first loop in 1913. The Aresti Cup, named for the designer of the aerocryptographic code for aerobatics, is traditionally awarded to the single individual who has the highest overall score and is therefore the World Aerobatic Champion.

Ten pilots, five men and five women, comprised the U.S. Aerobatic Team, and we were joined by an eager ground crew. It consisted of a manager, a trainer, a judge, an assistant judge, a video technician, and several mechanics. With numerous helping hands, we faced the harrowing experience of loading our airplanes without damage into the yawning jowls of the "kneeling" transport. All extraneous parts—wheel pants and sight gauges—were removed and stashed inside cockpits or tied down with other items. Turtle decks were jammed with tool bags and suitcases, and pallets loaded with tools, spare parts, spare engines (courtesy of Lycoming), and personal baggage were loaded last.

When the wheels left the ground, we popped the corks of our contraband iced champagne and celebrated the start of a grand adventure. Nine hours later, we arrived in Ramstein, Germany, in a rain shower, a harbinger of things to come. Eventually we were able to fly our planes to the training site at St. Valery.

Our first attempt to get into Le Havre was foiled by weather. We returned to St. Valery and watched and waited. When we finally returned to Le Havre, it had been transformed into a virtual mud hole. Opening ceremonies were held in the rain and just getting from our cars to the airport was an exercise in good sportsmanship. During welcoming

---

Competition aerobatics, the sport of champions, has a long way to go before it will draw huge crowds, an outpouring of monetary support, and inevitable hordes of media reporters that follow other competitive sports. This is a mixed blessing. We are not bombarded by microphones being shoved into our faces at strategic moments that need desperately to be kept private, the time necessary for us to be alone to get psyched for competition. But unfortunately, when the flying is over and interviews could be conducted, we are often largely ignored by the media. Because there is little publicity, the people who might watch aerobatics and support national teams do not get information to feed this enthusiasm. Things are beginning to change, however, with coverage from ESPN and Speedvision. Only special-interest magazines, videos, and books regularly feature aerobatics' innovative machines, leading technological modifications and their ramifications, and pilots, who are superior athletes at the leading edge of their sport. Although sport aerobatics attracts athletes of great skill with leading edge equipment in a most beautiful activity, it is still basically a "club" sport, run primarily by volunteers and lacking the infrastructure and leadership to make a significant difference to our press opportunities. Perhaps this will change over time.

speeches, those of us who had met competing pilots in prior years let our eyes wander, smiling and winking as we met the eyes of friends. The Russians arrived with Yurgis Kairis, who was flying for the Lithuanian flag for the first time.

On day one of the compulsory flight, good weather prevailed—finally! It was windy and cold, but a pleasure to watch the best aerobatic pilots in the world. After the compulsory, the Americans were in second place overall in men's and women's team standings. That early, second was a good place to be.

Seventy-four pilots from twenty nations competed over the two-week championship, although between contest flights, arriving and departing private and commercial flights stopped the action with alarming regularity. We spent a lot of time in the large white tent furnished with tables, chairs, a cafeteria assembly line, and a coffee machine. The weather deteriorated with each passing day, and, though we gathered in the briefing tent daily, the weather was never good enough to complete a flight. The very few who took off were hampered by strong winds, scud, and rain.

The decision was made to terminate the contest on Friday and we departed, our participation trophies in hand. I carried the women's silver medal home from Le Havre.

After two weeks of sitting around and eating *pommes frites* in the mess tent and having seen only one and a half flights with no champions declared, I found WAC 1992 so depressing that I had to take some time off to recharge my batteries. I wondered how such a beautiful sport, featuring so many talented, devoted pilots who spend an inordinate amount of time and effort to fly beautiful, expensive, and specialized machinery, could be at the mercy of such poor organization and lack of leadership. Unfortunately, four years later at the Oklahoma City WAC 1996, similar problems interfered with the success of the competition.

Ironically, it is an akro pilot who gets rustiest at world contests. Too much time elapses between flights. I *needed* to fly, to focus mentally on my goals, to keep my G tolerance. Above all, I had to stay focused on my goal of winning the nationals, pitting myself not only against myself, but against all the other well-trained team pilots and contenders. I read and reread *Zen in the Art of Archery*, listening to the audiotape of Eugen Herrigel's words as I lay down at night to go to sleep, as I prepared a meal, as I hiked, or as I drove in my car. I knew I was good, but while some people have the innate self-confidence to go into competitions knowing they will win, I had to find ways to convince myself. Perhaps I was looking for ways to get "in the zone" to focus, or perhaps I was only scared and whining! Whichever it was, I had to find ways to prepare and psyche myself up for success, to win.

As I prepared the concentration necessary for some of the toughest competition of my life, I discovered that it is only rarely that a pilot—or an athlete in any discipline—has one of those performances that is totally in "flow," in controlled and slow motion. Only after such a flight, one in which I was in total control, one that took months of effort to perfect, and one in which I was not shaken by nerves nor affected by external or internal pressures, may I recall its most minute details. I can replay it in my mind in the same slow motion as I flew it. Conversely, when a flight is *not* in "flow," and I am not in control, it seems to rush past, and, at its end, I can barely remember what I accomplished and what I might have missed. It was (*and* is) hard to capture that feeling of "flow," and it takes me months to perfect the mental process.

Herrigel pursued the "artless art" as he learned from his Zen master and described an immediate reaction "that is devoid of conscious purpose." I tried to add that concept to my flying. I tried to concentrate on motion that sought a specific reaction but was outside of purposeful thought. Herrigel asked about attaining the state of detachment, generally something I'm good at and one of my favorite topics. [4]

That state requires practice, and although air show performance was important—a release valve of sorts—I practiced detachment and kept my mind focused on competition.

I loved competition flying. There was nothing like it. Like the lyrical mysticism of a Richard Bach search for perfection, the structure, the achievement of perfect lines and precise angles, the physical intensity of pulling and pushing so many Gs, and the ability to execute exactly puts competition aerobatics into a world all its own, a detached world of beautiful precision. Because I had spent so much time as a leaf in the wind, it was ironic that I so loved the discipline of being confined to one finite box of air like a tiny bird captured in an invisible cage, tumbling and spinning with obvious joy, content with its severe, unyielding limits. The

---

[4] One manifestation of detachment is the condition of ceasing to think about what is being done and simply doing it, the Zen state in which a person ceases to be distracted by outside influences and performs without conscious thought.

challenge of winging my way faultlessly through that cage, never letting my ethereal wings touch the sides, never allowing myself to burst higher or farther from the limits of the cage that only takes seconds to cross, and controlling every movement in unblemished precision—that was my idea of perfection. In exacting timing and technique, I wanted to avoid even the smallest mistake, the least bobble, the most imperceptible of errors. These were flying's challenges that pushed me to excel, that gave me pure delight. Their mastery made it all worthwhile.

I knew that combining spectacular flying with a mastery of the mental game meant not only succeeding but dominating. And dominating meant overcoming fears of inability; a lack of self-confidence; pressure from judges, real or perceived; pressure and mental psych games from other pilots; and all the what-ifs in the world that enter my mind. A match of one-on-one, mastery of the flying and mastery of the mind require equal amounts of effort and time. Mastering flying means simply gaining an athletic skill, but mastering the mind is equivalent to trying to hold a dollop of quicksilver.

I begged Clint McHenry to coach me again for the 1992 National Aerobatic Championship and he reluctantly agreed. He didn't mind coaching, but he was trying to retire from competition and from all that it entailed. Clint had more than given of himself; he had been on every board and every committee that the aerobatic scene could offer. He had paid his dues. Clint had donated enormous amounts of time to others. He was ready to enjoy his new home and to play golf, his other passion.

To my good fortune, I finally coaxed him to El Reno, Oklahoma, for the week prior to the nationals. I lured him with the promise of a good bottle of wine, a good meal or two, and that I would win!

Clint warned me, "Winning once is hard, but winning twice or three times is much harder. You are going into this competition with a different mind-set than you had in 1990 or 1991. Then, you had the attitude, 'I want to win!' Now, you are on the top and your attitude will be, 'I don't want to lose.' There is a big distinction between those and you have to be aware of it. Now, let's get to the flying. Let's pin down that perfection you're striving toward."

Leo Loudenslager talked with me, too. He said, "When you're the underdog trying to make a name for yourself, you have a lot of support. Once you're no longer the underdog, the psychology changes. People don't have the same encouraging thoughts about you and many almost want to see you fail. It won't be too bad the second time, but it gets much more difficult by the third and fourth times. You'll find, too, that when you're on top, the great scores will be harder to get because the judges expect so much more. Sometimes what they expect is unreasonable and out of bounds, but it's human psychology."

The cover of the official program of the 1992 nationals depicted my Extra 260 and me bursting straight up above a cloud layer of white. When I saw it I hoped it was a sign of good things to come.

We who were competing that year had one major plus. The Texas weather was a huge improvement over the weather conditions at the last world competition. The competitors all had a decent chance to fly, the competition went without any major hitches, and as I watched the scores, I knew I was on a roll. I came in third on the first flight, but instead of sabotaging myself and allowing any lack of self-confidence to enter the picture, I went back to my hotel room and told myself I could do it, that indeed, I was the best. I returned the next day and won the second flight (freestyle) as well as the third (the unknown). I won the contest with a total of 517.67 points. I had shown them that I could overcome my fears and dominate the competition.

Veni, vedi, vici! I received the Mike Murphy Trophy, awarded to the National Aerobatic Champion for the second time, and as highest-placing woman competitor, I received the Betty Skelton First Lady of Aerobatics Trophy for the fourth time! (It eluded me one time, in 1990, when my longtime rival Russian Elena Klimovitch flew at our nationals as a guest and beat me.) At the awards banquet, I didn't get the standing ovation that I did in 1991 and I thought, "This is good. They're getting used to women winning."

I retained my place as U.S. National Aerobatic Champion and I knew I was on my way to a third win.

Just as I had promised myself, I contacted David Burner of BFGoodrich Aerospace and asked for an appointment. [5] When I finally walked into

---

[5] My advice to people who are seeking sponsors smacks of the advice one would give on the subject of friendship: cultivate, cultivate, cultivate! You never know where a relationship is going to lead. A company may start by giving you a product, but a couple of years down the line (like with II Morrow), a marketing person might come along who sees your potential. Stay in touch. Keep them

his Akron office, I wore a business outfit and was prepared with bro-chure material, a nice proposal, and a second national championship. I was (and continue to be) the only woman to become U.S. National Aero-batic Champion and I was one of only a handful of aerobatic pilots who had won the championship more than one time. I knew that my visibil-ity and my accomplishments would make me a good marketing tool for their company, and my presentation helped them to see this, too.

I lucked out. Dave Burner agreed to my proposal and I was grateful and delighted that BFGoodrich Aerospace elected to sponsor me for 1993, 1994, and 1995. The company has continued to generously spon-sor me to date. It has been, I hope, a mutually satisfying and beneficial relationship. [6]

---

apprised of your activities via press clippings, brochures, and videos, and let them get to know you. Show them that you are a dependable, trustworthy per-son and be ready when and if the moment comes that they want to get involved in air shows and, specifically, with you.

[6] I am proud to have the BFGoodrich Aerospace's support and to fly with their name on my wings.

In subsequent years I have asked, "Are you happy with everything? Is there any more I can do for you guys?"

All I hear is, "You just keep flying air shows and winning those trophies, Patty."

TWENTY-ONE

Fusion

In choosing a career that combined competition with air shows, I had to assess which airplanes presented well at air show center and which paint schemes had enough impact on judges to place high in competition. I upgraded my aircraft to push *my* skills. I also knew the importance of having a beautiful, showy airplane—an airplane on the cutting edge. As a woman in competition, I knew I was under more scrutiny and had to perform better to score well. I had to have every advantage in skill and equipment. We competitors may have gotten rained out of WAC 1992 in Le Havre, but it wasn't a complete fiasco. In a rare moment of flyable weather, I watched Walter Extra fly his new design, the single-seat, all-composite Extra 300S, with typical Teutonic vigor. Christine Genin of the French team flew one aggressively as well. The airplane was larger and stronger than my prototype Extra 260 and it looked damned good in the air with a roll rate that was lightning fast. I realized it was time to move up. I wanted to be flying an Extra 300S, too. When I told Bob, he simply groaned (I couldn't blame him).

At about the same time, I received a letter from Dorothy Cochrane, a curator at the Smithsonian Institution's National Air and Space Museum (NASM). Dorothy, a private pilot, and I had met when she invited me to speak about aerobatics at NASM's Langley Theater for the General Electric Lecture Series. Her letter astounded me. She wrote that were I to get a new airplane to replace my hand built Extra 260, the Smithsonian would like to have the 260 as part of their collection. It was an amazing honor to be considered.

I remember my first visit to the museum and the awe I felt. Bob took me there in 1980. I remember reaching out and touching the airplanes in the collection. And as amazing as it would have seemed in 1980, in 1992 my plane joined the airplanes that had been flown by the Lindberghs, Jimmy Doolittle, and Amelia Earhart and air show pilots like Art Scholl, Bevo Howard, Betty Skelton, and Roscoe Turner.

I reread Dorothy's letter and laughed. I said to Bob, "Isn't this incredible?" I was eager to purchase a 300S, but we couldn't afford to simply donate the 260. But this was an opportunity that I wasn't willing to let slip through my hands. I thought of contacting sponsors but felt it was too personal an honor to be commercialized. Bob and I approached Bob's mother, Kitty Wagstaff, of Kansas City, who we thought might be interested in making a donation in memory of her deceased husband, Bob's father, Robert Wilson Wagstaff.[1] Kitty considered it and then generously agreed. As a patriot and community leader, we knew this was something Bob's father would have greatly appreciated. In this way, I realized two dreams—to buy an Extra 300S and to exhibit the Extra 260 for all the world to see.

After the aircraft was officially pledged to the museum, Dorothy worked hard on finding a place for it to be exhibited and not simply stored. We discussed possible locations for it and kept our fingers crossed that it would be displayed in the Pioneers of Flight Gallery the following spring of 1994. The knowledge that my unique Extra 260 might be exhibited in its new home in Washington, D.C., pumped me even more for competition and for winning. I was more motivated than ever to spend 1993 in hot pursuit of a third title at the U.S. nationals. So few pilots had successfully defended their championships twice, but when my airplane was unveiled in 1994 in the Pioneers of Flight Gallery, I wanted to be among that elite. I felt driven to win, but I had to gear up for my tough-

---

[1] Robert W. Wagstaff was a respected lawyer and businessman in Kansas City. He was also at one time a president of the Kansas University Alumni Association and a major contributor to projects for his alma mater, which was Bob's alma mater, too.

est competition yet, an internal battle and a battle of wills and talents with every other aerobatic pilot who wanted to beat me. [2]

I took possession of the best airplane I had ever flown, the Extra 300S, N328PW, in March of 1993. It was the right move. For the first time in history, the six-cylinder Extras, Sukhois, and CAPS, all production aircraft, were stressed for limits that exceeded any pilot's. My 300S was designed to withstand plus or minus twenty G's and actually certified to plus or minus ten, an amount of Gs that is brutal to the pilot and to the aircraft. In the past, a pilot would strap on a 180-horsepower Pitts and be able to withstand more stress than the airplane. Modern airplanes are so strong and so sophisticated, they can withstand amazing G forces. Also, pilots can fly them for a longer length of time without breaking them or growing out of them. Having a new and stronger airplane built with today's remarkable fusion of metals and composites gave me confidence in my equipment and that trust enabled me to improve my flying. [3]

---

[2] Sandwiched into a busy summer was an opportunity to become a better pilot. Bill Muszala, who ran Evergreen Ventures in Marana, Arizona, for owner Del Smith of McMinnville, Oregon, and his son Mike, president of Ventures, made me the offer I couldn't refuse. Bill introduced me to war birds and gave me the chance to spread new wings. I think anyone can fly the same airplane every day and do a good job. I knew that I was getting stale just flying my plane all the time. I needed a fresh challenge. I needed my enthusiasm for flight to be renewed by stretching my limits and my transition into different aircraft.

Bill checked me out in a T-28 and I immediately began to earn my keep by flying with the Evergreen International Airlines pilots. Then I moved into the T-6. While I gave unusual attitude training to other pilots in that World War II trainer, I got my type rating in the TBM Avenger, a huge airplane capable of carrying a 2,200-pound torpedo bomber. (This was the same plane flown by former president George Bush.) My confidence level in my piloting skills increased and flying this airplane opened up a whole new door to aviation for me.

[3] Only a prototype, the Extra 260 was somewhat under built. I knew it wasn't designed to withstand many more years at the G levels I was flying. I'd broken a longeron by the end of the 1992 season and I worried about stressing it more. I'd cut down the chord of the elevator to lighten its pitch, so I had put 12 Gs on the G meter more than once. When volunteers at NASMs Garber Facility took the wings off the airplane, they informed me that the wings were difficult to remove because the main spar bolts were slightly bent.

The year 1993 proved to be a stellar and grueling year. It was somewhat easier to focus on winning the nationals a third time with a new and more powerful airplane, but with a full air show season and the Breitling Masters competition in Oshkosh, I had a lot on my plate. After Oshkosh in early August I flew in the IAC Championship in Fond du Lac, the contest where I got my start but where first place had always eluded me for one reason or another. I not only won the contest but won every flight, which gave me the confidence to go to the nationals knowing I was still on the roll, that I still had the confidence and support of the judges. Still, I couldn't afford to take a day off from training between air shows and flew harder than ever. I kept Clint McHenry's and Leo's words in mind, "It's *much* harder the third time. Your competitors will be out to get you, most hoping to see you fail. The judges won't give you the scores you deserve."

Winning the second nationals had felt satisfying. I knew no one could ever call my first championship a fluke, but to win an auspicious third time had only been accomplished by a handful of men: Clint McHenry, Gene Soucy, and Leo Loudenslager. As well as I knew I could fly, I knew mind control would be key. I was glad I had an entire year to prepare. It was going to take all the preparing possible to hone my cutting edge and not let myself be distracted.

I still had the eagerness that I felt so long ago when my mother took me for my first roller coaster ride; all I wanted to do was to get back on and do it again. But competence takes awareness, a mastery of skill and of the mind. I tried to make each day of training better than the last because I knew I would only have the self-confidence to win if I were flying my best. And I believed that in wanting this so much, I could create the energy around me that would make it happen and inspire the support of others—the support that is essential in a sport with so much subjectivity. I wanted to win so that I could continue to fly. In a complex way, winning was my goal, but winning was truly a means to this other end.

In an even bigger picture, it was my goal to finally fly my best. The key, I felt, was to be able to fly as well in front of the judges as I could fly in practice. I needed to have the perfect, in-flow flight that not only scored higher than everyone else, but that demonstrated to me that I had attained complete mastery.

I had to fly with the same surge of energy, electric excitement, and joyful abandon we see in the ice skating of an Oksana Baiul or a Katerina Witt. Katerina glides, she twirls, she choreographs her entire program to the rink in which she performs, sometimes harshly slicing into the ice and sometimes airily spinning above it, her landing crucial to every performance, and all with a smile. My sequence had to contain the same joy the skaters show—the delight and exuberance I felt had to translate through my fingers to the stick, through the push rods to the ailerons. And like an actor portraying deep emotion, regardless of her true feelings, my joy had to be shown to those watching from the ground. Squelching nervousness and fear, I had to fly with true ecstasy while maintaining precision and discipline.

I couldn't convince Clint to come back to El Reno for a third time. The wine and food just weren't good enough to lure him away from his beautiful new home in Florida. He just said to me over the phone, "Patty, you don't need me! You're flying better than anyone else. There's no question about it. Just go and kick ass!"

I asked Don Taylor, a longtime contributor to and judge of sport aerobatics, to critique me for the 1993 nationals. Don put on the televised Hilton Masters of Aerobatics competitions in the early 1980s and knew a lot about the sport. He traveled from his home in Illinois to spend the week at El Reno, and we went to work, flying three times a day. I had Karen videotape every flight, which Don and I watched and studied.

Finally, I flew to the U.S. National Aerobatic Competition on September 18, 1993. On September 20, all the competitors in the unlimited category flew compulsories. I took first place. I was off to a good start, but the next day in the freestyle I won a silver medal in the flight instead of a gold. I was devastated. I went back to my hotel room and felt a huge tension. I sat down and psyched myself up. Was it happening? Was I already not getting the scores I thought I deserved? Or was my flight just not good enough to win the gold medal? I was used to winning. I was confused and really upset, but this was what all the mental practice and training I had put myself through was for—not to let it get me down, not to let it destroy my self-confidence. I went into the third flight, a particularly difficult unknown, and won first place, putting me in first place overall, the 1993 U.S. National Aerobatic Champion. In my new airplane and with an accumulated total of 11,039 points, I won my third title.

I knew this was what I had worked for, yet even as I accepted the trophy, I thought, "What now?" I was prepared for that feeling of let-down. I knew I had to look to the future. Betty Stewart, twice a winner on the international level, stopped competing after her second title. She had warned, "When you achieve your goals, it can send you into a state of depression. You work so hard for so long and all of a sudden there is nothing to work toward."

I heard that loud and clear and knew I had to keep the future in focus. I had to look forward to another step, another goal.

TWENTY-TWO

Air and Space

By 1994 I had reached goals that never would have occurred to me a scant dozen years before. The best part of it, though, was the feeling that it was all just beginning, that there were roads to new adventures, new journeys. I had a vision of widening expanses beyond the window of focus I'd been drawn into.

I wondered if all the discussion of being "in the zone," the focus I had to develop to win, and the Zen in the art of aerobatics was just to overcome being scared. Bob had told me more than once to stop whining and get the job done and perhaps he was right. But the more I thought about it, the more I knew focus was required for success in my sport, in any sport. The distractions of other competitors, jealousies, greed, and competitive nature, especially in a sport with a degree of subjectivity and politics, make it imperative to develop tunnel vision, focusing on the perfect sequence, the perfect flight. I had to train my mind as well as my body.

I once asked Gene Soucy, one of four who won the U.S. nationals three times and won them back-to-back, how he dealt with the mental aspects of winning.

He said, simply, "I was just plowing on through. I didn't have any problems with nerves. Hell, I was twenty-one years old! I didn't even *think* about nerves."

Clint McHenry was older than Gene when he won his titles. I doubted that age had anything to do with it, but Clint admitted he had to work hard to not let pressure affect his style of flying. Graceful and fluid in his aerobatics, Clint could put ten on a G meter in a most aggressive flight and do it so smoothly it looked like six. So popular and so sought-after by other pilots seeking advice on the ramp at a contest, Clint found he had to stay away from the airport until moments before it was his turn to fly. He needed solitude and others wouldn't leave him alone. And even Clint, always willing to help another pilot and always seeing the best in people, was dealt his fair share of grief from jealous pilots.

"That's what happens when you're good," Clint told me, and laughed. "Remember our motto: don't let it get to you; *screw 'em!*"

Before a flight, I tried to remain friendly and accessible, yet I had to give myself room to focus on the upcoming flight. Leo Loudenslager isolated himself as well. He often escaped the airport in order to concentrate. He had to distance himself from other competitors and as a consequence had to deal with people calling him stuck-up, or aloof. He said, "I was there to win, not to make friends or to influence people."

Of course, Leo did make friends and influence a lot of people, including me. I called him dozens of times over the years when the pettiness of the competition scene got me down. His words often kept me going. He once said, "Patty, there are three things you'll never been able to deal with or rationalize: jealousy, hatred, and greed. You'll find all three in competition. You can't change that. Just ignore it and let it go. Don't let the bastards get you down."

Monty Barrett, my friend and engine builder, said, "Patty, if they can't get you in the air, they'll try to get you on the ground. Ignore the backstabbing and jealousy and just fly your best."

Leo and Monty were right, but it was not only aggressive competitors that got me down. In a sport subject to a number of variables and complexities, not the least of which is weather, there was always the unexpected to deal with.

At WAC 1994 in Debrecen, Hungary, I was to represent my country again for the fifth time as a member of the U.S. Aerobatic Team. Before the first flight, the compulsory, my time in the box was just ahead. Our airplanes—their brilliant reds and blues, stripes and chevrons shown polished to a sheen—were lined up on a flat grassy area beside the runway. Alone by mine, I was psyched; I was in a nice little Zen mode and feeling really good. We had beautiful weather and calm winds. I knew I could nail the flight and even felt good about my draw—number eighteen out of eighty pilots.

Performing my preflight, I divorced myself from everything else around, something I was getting good at. The airplane and I were all that existed. But then, the unexpected happened. Almost in a trance, I walked right into the prop! It wasn't moving, of course, or my head would have been cut in half, but the blow stunned me and knocked me flat. I saw stars. I was flat on the ground for a few seconds. Everything blended into a hazy gray. Blood trickled down my face. I touched it with the back of my hand and grimaced to see it. It really threw me and I got inordinately upset.

No one was close by. People had purposely left me alone, aware that I was readying for a flight. But when I was on my way back to the tent, a team member saw that I needed attention and immediately called the team doctor, Brent Blue. He calmed me down and pressed cloths against my head, applying pressure to stop the bleeding. He asked, "Do you want to fly?"

"Oh, yeah, I want to fly. I'll be all right. I feel fine. I have a good draw. I don't want to lose that. And I *don't* want to fly last!"

It probably didn't matter when I flew, but drawing a slot was part of the ritual and we all wanted to fly somewhere after first and prior to eightieth. We got the bleeding stopped and I decided to compete. My turn came and I took off. I dived into the box when the red panels on the ground turned to white, waggling my wings to let the judges know I was starting my flight. The routine began. It wasn't until I pushed some hard negative Gs about halfway through the flight that I knew I was in trouble. The blood rushed to my head. I'd known that it would, but I hadn't expected what followed. Tossing my head back to look up at the canopy as I started an outside loop, I saw the horizon behind me, badly spattered with blood. The bubble canopy was painted with large drops of crimson. Blood was everywhere!

I cursed, wondering what to do. I knew if I landed, people would see the mess for themselves. But I wasn't sure if I would be granted a refly. It wasn't in my nature to quit. I had to be tougher than anyone else, especially as a woman. Besides, I still had something to prove.

Once I had entered the box, the ten judges began calculating the value of every maneuver I flew, every move I made. If I landed for reasons clearly out of my control—if sudden bad weather forced me down, or if something mechanical went wrong and I landed early enough in the flight—a reflight could have been arranged. But if *I* interrupted my flight, the judges might believe it was because of something that I could have prevented. Would they say I should have used better judgment and excused myself because of banging my head on the prop? What if they decided that I could have selected not to go and refused a reflight? It could have been two years of training down the drain.

So I went for it. What a nightmare! I finished the flight and brought the airplane in for a landing. There was blood all over everything. I looked as if I'd been in some sort of wreck. As I taxied up to the fuel pump, people gawked at me! Although it took only three stitches, the head wound bled heavily. It was very dramatic.

Was my flight affected? Yes. It was a good flight, but not up to my stringent standards.

I had to chalk it up to bad luck, but things didn't get much better. As I took off to fly my freestyle, a piece of plastic surrounding the throttle broke in my hand. Again, I went ahead and flew, but the mishap affected the quality of my flight, distracting me. I felt like I was behind the airplane, instead of on top of it or in front of it.

Then, to cap things off, I took off for the third flight, the unknown, and found the winds to be extremely strong. I flew the routine but the maneuvers were greatly distorted by the wind. I had two "outs," costing me sixty points, or any shot at a gold medal and first place. After landing I asked for a wind measurement and found that, as I thought, the winds were out of limits, stronger than the rules allowed. The international jury hadn't checked them as required by the rules. They granted me a refly, but I declined. I didn't want to make waves. I regretted not taking the flight anyway. After ten years of competing, I wanted to win, but even more, I wanted the U.S. team to be well-represented.

It was always discouraging to see the lack of cohesiveness in our team. It did nothing to further the sport. Sure, there were bound to be personality conflicts in any group, but it was a shame that ego and personal motivation often overrode the best interests of the sport. I had to blame it on a basic lack of leadership. People sometimes blamed our team's problems on the fact that the competition was run by volunteers, but so are a lot of the air shows that I fly, and the volunteers put on wonderful events.

The ground crew, the combined group of mechanics and helpers, was always wonderful and dedicated, however, and watching them work kept my faith in the system.

Regardless of politics, at WAC 1994, after watching the wind snap flags straight away from their poles and the clouds lower and darken until they burst into torrential rain, reality set in. With unpredictable weather conditions and the diversity of individuals, airplanes, languages, foods, and schedules, I felt elated to finish among the top ten pilots in the world—the real goal I had set for myself.[1] I also went home the top-placing American pilot. This was a feat I repeated at WAC 1996 and, that time, it was even sweeter.

I had won the nationals three times. I was ready to branch out and look toward my future. Some people involved in competition aerobatics have nothing else to look forward to, so they stay in it too long. As much as I had put into it, I made it simply my job. I made sure that I had things to look forward to, that there was more to my life.

I wanted to stretch myself in aviation. I had begun flying helicopters, Bell 47-Gs, in Alaska in 1984 and completed my private helicopter rating in a Hughes 300 a decade later in Arizona. Bell Textron of Fort Worth, Texas, generously offered me a Jet Ranger transition course and commercial check ride, which I completed in February 1996. My friend Craig Hosking, well-known Hollywood aerial coordinator, stunt pilot, and helicopter pilot, let me tag along and assist on some of his commercial and film jobs, enabling me to build helicopter ferry time.[2]

Sometimes I struggle to get in the air, for I've become like every other business executive in the 1990s and joined the high-tech world of computers, faxes, and E-mail. I started in the 1980s as a free spirit in Alaska, into gardening and exploring the mountains and never wearing a watch, but I had grown into a modern businesswoman. I have hosted a videotape of the life stories of women in aviation, flown in television shows

---

[1] It is generally thought that any pilot in the top ten is capable of winning overall. From there, it's a combination of weather and luck of the draw.

[2] Helicopters aren't much for long cross-countries, but for their true applications they are fantastic. Used extensively in the film industry as camera ships and for stunt work, they're exciting to watch and to fly close to the ground. I enjoy the feel and the finesse required to fly them; it's a little like the light touch, the seat-of-the-pants feel, and the outside orientation required to be a good aerobatic pilot.

and feature-length movies, done commercials, and explored contributions I could make to the high-tech world of computers. I contracted
with Microsoft to appear on their World of Flight CD-ROM, and my
airplane, the BFGoodrich Aerospace Extra 300S, is featured on the new
Microsoft Flight Simulator for Windows '95.

I am a member of the Screen Actors Guild (SAG), I am the first pilot
member of the United Stuntwomen's Association (USA), I acted as an
aerial coordinator for the film *Up Close and Personal*, and I flew as a stunt
pilot in the television shows *Fortune Hunter* and *Lois and Clark*. Movie-
goers saw me in costume, blonde wig and pink jacket, in the Paramount
Pictures *Drop Zone*. I was doubling for actress Grace Zabriskie, playing
Winona, and I logged about one hundred hours of turbine Pilatus Porter time doing it. I loved the movie business. In an industry that is so
competitive, only the best at what they do survive in it.

In 1995 I was greatly honored by the International Council of Air
Shows (ICAS) with the industry's top award, the ICAS Sword of Excellence. The award recognizes outstanding service and personal contribution
to the industry. Past recipients include Bob Hoover, Tom Poberezny, Leo
Loudenslager, T. Allan McArtor, and Danny Clisham. When Clisham
received the award, he said, "This feels as if I have won an Oscar!" I
could relate to that.

Two points of my life stand out, inextricably linked: becoming the U.S.
National Aerobatic Champion and having my airplane and my experience displayed in the Smithsonian Institution's National Air and Space
Museum (NASM). Like some sports champions, winning was never the
only piece of my game plan, but victories tasted sweet and winning
brought with it interesting and sometimes unexpected opportunities.

Thanks to the generous donation of my mother-in-law, Kitty Wagstaff,
the Extra 260 was placed in the permanent collection of the Air and
Space Museum in March 1994. As part of the Pioneers of Flight Gal-
lery, I'm humbled and thrilled to see my airplane placed beside Amelia
Earhart's bright-red Lockheed *Vega*, next to the Lockheed *Sirius* in which
Charles and Anne Lindbergh pioneered the Great Circle air routes to
Asia and Europe. It is exhibited below the Curtiss Schneider Cup racer
flown by James H. "Jimmy" Doolittle, the incredible leader in World
War II who was the first pilot to successfully complete an outside loop
and fly strictly by instruments. My little 260 is in mighty good company.

Bob worked with Dorothy Cochrane of NASM to find a spot for the airplane in the gallery, and museum staff began to disassemble the airplane for its eventual reassembly inside the museum on Independence Avenue. Patty Woodside of NASM and Bob Judson of BFGoodrich Aerospace created a video that highlighted my flying and story, and three panels on which my career and sport were illustrated were placed on the wall. My flight suit, first U.S. National Aerobatic Champion trophy, and three gold medals were also attractively displayed. I couldn't help but think, "Not bad for a hippie from Australia (Alaska, Japan . . .)!" I had to pinch myself to make sure I wasn't dreaming the whole thing up. This was the answer, I thought. You *do* get the things you wish for, the things for which you dare to dream. If you focus on what you really want, you can get everything you wish for and more.

For the official donation to the Museum's Director, Martin Harwitt, I flew a private air show for the Smithsonian staff and volunteers at Andrews Air Force Base, just outside of Washington, D.C. I wanted them to see the airplane before it was retired, disassembled, and relocated to the Paul Garber Facility.[3] As I had already begun my 1993 aerobatic season with the new Extra 300S, I arrived at Andrews a day or two early to train and readjust to the 260 for its final aerial ballet.

I had mixed feelings, but it was poignant to know what the airplane had meant to me and that I was flying it for the last time. But I also knew it was time to retire the prototype airplane and that it was going to an incredible new home.[4]

In March of 1994, in coordination with the celebration of Women's History Month and sponsored by BFGoodrich Aerospace, we held a gala champagne reception in the Pioneers of Flight Gallery. We invited as many friends and family members as the gallery would hold. Many of my aunts and uncles were there, and my father was there with Anna

---

[3] That site, a vast array of nine or ten large buildings housing an unbelievable collection of rare and historical aircraft, is also a restoration center for the museum's aviation treasures. It was to be the Extra 260's home for several months until the exhibit space in the gallery was ready for it.

[4] I have loved flying each of my airplanes better than the last, holding some part of each in a special place of appreciation. But it is important to move on and I've always moved up to better and stronger equipment. There can be a challenge in change, but I try to detach myself from any regrets I may have and look at the next step as an opportunity; the last, a learning experience.

Lies. He had come so far in getting his life back on track and I was very proud of him for overcoming so much. My mother, then living in Los Angeles, didn't make it, but I was proud of her, too, for making an effort in her life to work and remain sober. Her life had been a long struggle for her.

It was gratifying to participate in a program that highlighted women's achievements in the world of aerospace. I appreciated that a Smithsonian report reiterated my own thoughts ". . . that the term 'women in aviation' will be regarded as a positive historical term, referring to a time when a few women followed a different and difficult dream. We hope these lives challenge and inspire both young women and men alike, showing that the opportunity to participate and excel is open to everyone." Amen.

In an introspective moment one morning, I sat and looked at my airplane under the lights in its exhibit and wondered what it meant to me on a deeply personal level. I realized that it gave me a sense of history and a sense of place I had never known in my gypsy existence. I felt as though I had given birth, that my flying and my airplane were my babies and my genes would carry on. I'd found a home in the aviation community, but more importantly, I hoped I'd contributed something to the sport and industry I loved.

In September 1994, I was notified that I had been nominated for and would be honored with the prestigious annual National Air and Space Museum Award for Current Achievement. Prior to my selection, this award had been presented to such luminaries as Dick Rutan and Jeana Yeager, for flying their homebuilt Voyager nonstop around the world, and to Kathleen Sullivan, the astronaut.

At a black-tie awards ceremony in Washington, D.C., in December 1994, I was awarded a small edition of the large sculpture, Web of Space, commissioned from artist John Safer. The sculpture is placed in a prominent location in the museum and the smaller version is placed in a prominent location in my hangar and office in Avra Valley, Arizona. Walter Boyne, former NASM curator and bestselling author, initially created the award for the museum. The trophy and award commemorate those persons who are, in Boyne's words, "current leaders in the world of air and space—pilots, engineers, designers, manufacturers—whoever might have accomplished in recent times a feat worthy of a major award."[5]

---

[5] Walter Boyne, *Art in Flight: The Sculpture of John Safer*, (New York: Hudson Hills Press, 1991),pages 54–56.

With the thrilling new opportunities I received came lows that mirrored the highs. It wasn't until I actually had a chance to sit down and think about all the things that were happening that I discovered a distance between Bob and me. We had achieved our goals together, but, to do it, we had to spend a great deal of time apart. I knew he gained personally from his presence in aviation and his reputation as an aviation attorney was enhanced, but I also knew he'd sacrificed a lot of his own career as a lawyer to chase me around the country. I felt he needed to spend more time on *his* life. While we continued to believe in Patty Wagstaff *Air Shows*, we had drifted apart on other issues in our life.

I think a feeling of independence crept in because we spent too much time apart. Issues important to the relationship that should have been dealt with were either put aside or not addressed so that we wouldn't ruin what little time we had together.

I stopped going to Alaska. I needed time alone and had difficulty with the idea and concept of relationships, showing some classic symptoms of post-traumatic stress disorder. Perhaps I had allowed the stress of my competitive life on the edge to take its toll.

Sadly to me, Bob and I split up in 1994. I don't know if it was a good thing or bad. I still haven't figured it out.

I appreciated being given the two NASM honors. They came at a time when I was committing myself to two more years of competition because WAC '96 was scheduled to be held in Oklahoma City. This was the first time in many years that this competition was held in the U.S. and I wanted to fly. I felt it was important for me to compete there because it would be the first international contest held in the United States since 1980 and probably the last in the Western Hemisphere for some time to come.

Also, my last two nationals, 1994 and 1995, had come at a time when my marriage was breaking up. In 1994, my motivation slipped; I came in a close second to Phil Knight. I would have liked to win, but failing to didn't freak me out. The title also eluded me at the 1995 nationals; Mike Goulian, coauthor of the book *Basic Aerobatics*, deservedly won. My lack of focus and a clear goal made a difference both years. I simply didn't care if I won the title four or five times; three had proved my point. I knew, too, that without Bob, competition aerobatics would never be the same for me.

It was time to focus more on my vocation, air show flying, and give my body a break from the intense and unusual physical demands of competition flying. Even though I knew I had incredible stamina, maintaining my G tolerance was a full-time job, leaving little time or energy for anything else. Developing a G tolerance for unlimited competition was grueling and my body reflected the pain. On the morning after a good day of training, my eyes were swollen, and while I've never had "the wobblies," or vertigo, that unlimited competitors sometimes face, my inner ears began to throb and ache. I had calluses on my hipbones from the harness that tethered me to the airplane when outside loops were trying to force me out of it. While I have developed my arm, shoulder, and back muscles through my flying, I have aches and clicks in my muscles and ligaments. There is a price to pay for anything worthwhile, but the more I yanked and banked, the more I felt each maneuver in my bones and muscles. Still, each day I trained I reached new levels of competence and ability, so the punishment was joy rather than pain. Besides, I would do almost anything in order to continue to fly. The rush of zero-G flight, the feeling of weightlessness at the top of a loop, made it all worthwhile.

While they have to fly lower than competition pilots and have to develop their own creative routines, air show pilots aren't required to push as many negative Gs. Therefore, air show flying is less physically demanding.

Air shows are the second largest spectator event in North America, so I continued flying in front of millions of people a year at venues across North America. By 1995 I knew I had inspired others to learn to fly. One of them was Jan Jones.

I left the El Toro Air Show in April 1995, intending to meet Jan at the Poughkeepsie Airshow in New York. Jan was a high-energy person, a force to be reckoned with. She took flying lessons after having seen me fly at Oshkosh a few years prior and credited me with having inspired her. I had stopped for the night in Wichita, Kansas, when I heard she had crashed. On her way to the show, Jan, struggling with a rough engine, tried to make a forced landing in a field in Ohio. The engine quit before she could get positioned for landing; she stalled and spun in. I flew all day in horrible weather to get there before she died, but didn't quite make it. I paid my respects to her in the hospital just after she passed away.

It took me a long time to sleep without a light on at night. Jan wasn't the first friend I'd lost, but her death made me rethink what I was doing. If I inspired people to learn to fly and then they got killed, what was I doing? Where was the sense in it? I talked with a lot of people on the subject and eventually came to terms with it. Just because you inspire someone or plant a seed in her mind doesn't mean that she has to go all the way with it, or to extremes like Jan did or I did. A lot of people will learn to fly, have successful flying careers, and never get to the point where they are pushing themselves in experimental airplanes and engines. It was her choice.

I found ways to deal with and go on with life. My salvation, whether as a student pilot in Alaska, a flight instructor, a cross-country pilot, or an Olympic-level international aerobatic pilot, was and always has been flying. Aviation, to me, has never been a waste of my time and that is important.

Speed is life. Speed is fun, and so is tumbling and floating. One essential to all who fly aerobatics is a love of cutting through the air in a way that most never experience, seeking a freedom in release, in motion for its own sake. Reactions have to be split-second in timing, demanding the most from the person in control. Being tuned to the inner melody, the heartbeat of the airplane, the engine, gives us the quality of being in the moment. In the midst of an aerial performance, I am elevated into the dimension of space, and I feel more than a person, an integral person-machine with powers greater than I possessed on the ground—a bird, a winged human—in reality, a fusion of fire and air. When I am strapped tightly inside and the machine roars to life, it takes on a feeling—a pulse, a heartbeat, and combined physical and mental activity that would not be possible to either one of us without the other. It gives me power, it gives me life, it gives me freedom. And it is much more than mere sensation and experience; it has a greater purpose when performed for others. Perfect!

To share the beauty of flight, once I have taken off, one with my machine, I am no longer tethered emotionally or mentally to the earth. I am an entity with fire in my belly and fuel in my veins, a rolling, tumbling, smoking, winged creature. Mortals are rooted to the ground, cheering my performance, and, because my flying has been very personal to me, I temporarily lose my kinship with them. But I look forward to renewing the acquaintance when the cacophony of the throaty engine quiets down, the wheels once more touch the pavement of the runway, and I roll toward the crowd, reentering their world and anticipating their approval and joy.

I may not perform as an aerobatic star forever. I'll go wherever my goals and interests lead me, but I'll continue to fly. Flying has always kept me intrigued and challenged, and it's never wasted my time. Some people simply crumble, losing their sense of identity and self-image, if they suddenly change from what they did well and for which they received adulation and praise. I say, "Stay hungry! Stay hungry for experience, for growth, for new roads, for new journeys. Don't get too comfortable wherever you are."

Aviation has a dynamic of its own and it's what you do with it that counts. A unique career field, aviation has room for everybody. I plan to continue to develop my air show routine. I don't have to compete with my sister, Toni, who flies a commercial airliner. I enjoy the friendship of aviation writers, aerospace engineers, and other flight instructors. There is room in aviation for everyone to create his or her individual niche and that's what is so neat about it, plus, it attracts people with energy and drive, the winners. There's no room or tolerance in aviation for energy vampires, people who don't carry their weight. There are war bird pilots, instrument pilots, and weekend pilots; mechanics, engineers, and air traffic controllers. We can all enjoy aviation and the sharing of it with others. And as diversified as the career field is, we can continue to grow. We can move on.

People ask me what it's like to be a woman in aviation. I don't know, really. I fly with my head, I fly with my heart, I fly with my hands. I don't fly with my genitalia. I suppose it feels the same for me as it would feel for a man to fly. I feel like a pilot. And although I didn't believe in them when I first started flying, I do feel that there is still a need for women's aviation organizations to educate women about the opportunities available to them and to keep the historical perspective of women's contributions to aviation.

Someday I will assess the word success, but my accomplishments in aviation are nothing if I have failed to make aerobatics more widely respected by the public. I want aviators and sports enthusiasts to recognize the athletic prowess and efforts of what has been an almost unseen and unknown national sport and international event.

Some people are born to live for challenge and adventure. I want people to know they have a choice. I would tell another, "Don't worry about where something is going to go or how far it is going to go. If you really want something to happen, you can create the energy around you to *make* it happen. Don't worry about the outcome, just go for it."

In 1996 the aviation world lost one of its icons, Charlie Hillard. Charlie, a renaissance man in aviation and the first American to be the World Aerobatic Champion, had completed twenty-five safe years of flying as the leader of the Eagles Aerobatic Team. He announced, after the team retired, that he would fly a Sea Fury the following season. After his second performance, he landed, the brakes locked, and the aircraft flipped onto its back tragically, killing Charlie instantly.

My heart went out to his wife, Doreen, and to his children, Ryan and Heather. My heart went out, too, to his good friends and longtime teammates Tom Poberezny and Gene Soucy. It was a great loss, but, as they say in aviation, he died doing what he loved to do.

As the top-scoring U.S. pilot at WAC '96 in Oklahoma City, I received the first Charlie Hillard Trophy. In a poignant moment, Doreen Hillard presented the trophy. Prior to that contest I had announced that this would be my last aerobatic competition. To have had that moment so brilliantly enhanced by the memorial to a pilot of such talent, scope, and accomplishment was a great honor. I couldn't have appreciated anything more.

I've wondered what lies ahead, but I have learned that we can only take the path that feels right. We have to have open hearts and open minds to be ready for opportunities that come our way. But I know that timing and good luck play a part. I suppose it's the time wasted that shelters any regrets I may have, but who knows? Maybe everything we do, short of hurting others, is time well spent. Maybe everything is somehow perfect and meant to be.

I have been lucky. I found a passion and I found people who believed in me even when I didn't believe in myself. There is an age-old theme in literature of redemption through love. For me it's been redemption through faith, the faith that others have shown in me. I owe thanks to those who gave wings to the hope I had. That became faith in myself.

Ten-year-old Wylly Marshall sent me the following poem. She became the voice for hundreds of kids that I have met. [6] Wylly's poem helps me to remain inspired and completes a circle.

I Love Flying
by Wylly Marshall

I love flying.
I love to be in the clouds,
close enough to touch them,
if you actually could.
Sometimes it looks like a painting.
The loud noise of the engine,
yet I feel quiet and alone.
The lifting of the plane lifts my soul
and my spirit skyward.
Places to visit,
possibilities limitless,
always an adventure.
I feel the warmth of my father who loves it, too.
No borders
No barriers
No limits.

---

[6] Wylly is the granddaughter of Mary Travers of Peter, Paul, and Mary folk-singing fame, one of my favorite singing groups of the 1960s.

Aerobatic Shorthand

The Aresti Key, Maneuver Key, the Aerobatic Box, and a Flimsy

Aresti Key

An aerobatic competition pilot fits a snappy routine into a cubic chunk of air, a defined space called a "box." This differs from the air show performer's more loosely defined space, an aerial stage, which is directly in front of and parallel to a crowd of spectators. In both cases, however, the aerobatic performers utilize an aerocryptographic code—the Aresti Key.

The Aresti key has been modernized and altered to fit the capabilities of the newest generation of aircraft, but it is based on the thousands of maneuvers cataloged and described by Spain's J. L. Aresti.

Just as all flight consists of straight and level, climbs, turns, and descents, all aerobatics start with the loop, spin, and roll that form the building blocks of a myriad of complex maneuvers. At every competition, a copy of a pilot's planned maneuvers, in Aresti Key code language, is given to the judges. The competitor or air show pilot mounts a copy, or "flimsy," on the control panel of his or her aircraft.

The Aresti Key has been used extensively and successfully, although air show and competition pilots have been known to devise additional individual symbology to clarify particular subtleties of their routines. According to the key, a dot indicates the beginning of a maneuver and a slash indicates the completion. Solid lines indicate normal flight and dashes indicate inverted flight.

Time and timing are vital. Some air show organizers allow a pilot to fly a long routine, and other times, organizers ask the pilot to perform a six- or seven-minute routine.

Competition and air show aerobatics can differ, but the basic Aresti Key is widely accepted. I start with the Aresti and embellish my diagrams to sharply focus particular points of the routine.[1] A page from my Aresti Key shows, typically, that I will roll to inverted flight, and do three climbing rolls, an Inside-Outside Horizontal Eight, a half loop, a half roll, and two inside snap rolls to the left. Then, I will again roll inverted and do two outside snap rolls to the right, a Hammerhead turn, a one-and-one-half turn inside spin, a Half Cuban Eight, a Tail Slide, another Half Cuban Eight with two points of a four-point roll, tumbling double lomcevaks, inside loops, a half roll, a half loop, and a Humpty Bump. And finally, I'll end with a snap roll, outside loop, square loop, rolling 360-degree circle, and eight-point roll. My flimsy also will indicate particular and important altitudes.

I try to have my routine look as fiery and gyrating as that of a flamenco dancer, and it takes many hours of timing, practice, and experience. During my flight, I may glance at the Aresti Key to confirm a maneuver or sequence the way a concert pianist glances at a memorized score. Whether air show flying, stunt flying, or in competitive aerobatic flight, my routine is exacting and precise. The Aresti Key is my cue card, the written score, the shorthand that is behind the scenes in every performance.

Maneuver Key

Aerobatic figures historically can be traced to the earliest days of flight and many were specifically developed as combat tactics for use in the First World War. As a general rule, all aerobatic figures, upright or inverted, start and end from horizontal lines. The altitude at entry to the figure does not have to be the same as the altitude at the exit except in the Cuban Eight and all loops.

Elemental to the figures are horizontal, vertical, and 45-degree lines. Loops have to have the same radius in all parts of a figure. Rolls have to be centered on the horizontal, vertical, or 45-degree line.

---

[1] Refer to the flimsy at the end of this appendix for an example.

Rolling on the longitudinal axis, an imagined straight line from the nose of the aircraft through to the tail, is controlled by the ailerons. Pitching on the lateral axis, an imagined straight line from wingtip to wingtip, is controlled by the elevator. Alternating from side to side on the yaw axis, an imagined straight line perpendicular to the first two at their point of intersection, the aircraft rotates from side to side and is controlled by the rudder.

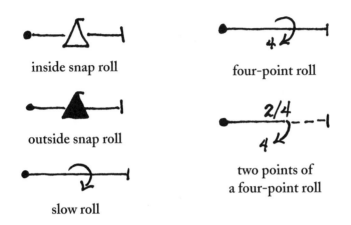

inside snap roll

four-point roll

outside snap roll

slow roll

two points of
a four-point roll

Roll: To circle the aircraft around its longitudinal axis. There are two basic types: the "slow roll" and the "snap roll" (or "flick roll" to the Europeans). In a slow roll, the rate has to be constant and the longitudinal axis of the plane has to be straight. "Hesitation rolls" include stops at certain roll angles; there are two-, four-, and eight-point rolls. The snap (flick) roll also has to be flown on a straight line and is similar to a horizontal spin, an autorotation with one wing stalled more deeply than the other. In an inside snap, the plane has to be stalled by applying positive G forces. In an outside snap, the plane is stalled by applying negative G.

Loop: One of the basic maneuvers. The exit and entry must be at the same altitude and the figure has to be perfectly round, a difficulty that is affected by the direction and speed of the wind. Variations to the loop are the Avalanche, square loop, and eight-sided loop.

Avalanche: A basic loop with a roll, generally a snap (flick) roll that is centered at the top of the loop.

Square Loop: A loop in which two vertical lines and the horizontal line on the top are of the same length.

Eight-Sided Loop: A loop in which the two vertical lines, the 45-degree lines, and the horizontal line on top are of the same length.

Immelmann: The aircraft completes a half loop to inverted flight, reversing the direction. Then a half roll results in horizontal upright flight.

Split S: The opposing figure to the Immelmann. The aircraft starts in level flight, rolls to inverted, and completes the second half of a downward loop, reversing direction.

Half Cuban Eight: Starting the figure in upright, level flight, the air-craft completes five-eighths of a loop to a 45-degree down line inverted. Centered on this down line, the aircraft does a half roll from inverted to upright, reversing direction.

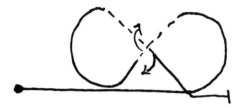

Cuban Eight: This figure combines two Half Cuban eights. The aircraft starts upright, completes five-eighths of a loop to a 45-degree down line inverted. The aircraft rolls to the upright, begins the second loop, and completes five-eighths of the second portion of the loop to form a figure eight. The aircraft exits at the same altitude it enters the figure.

Reverse Half Cuban Eight: Starting with a pull to a 45-degree up line, the aircraft does a half roll from upright to inverted centered on that line. Five-eighths of a loop completes the figure and restores the aircraft to horizontal flight.

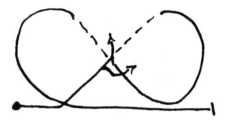

Reverse Cuban Eight: Like the Cuban Eight, the Reverse Cuban Eight combines two Reverse Half Cuban Eights.

Inside-Outside Eight: Similar to a Cuban Eight, this figure does not contain any rolls. The first loop is an inside loop and the second is an outside loop. The loops have the same radius and are flown at the same altitude.

Hammerhead: The aircraft does a one-quarter loop into a vertical climb with a pivoting maneuver around the aircraft's vertical axis (that is now horizontal). The nose of the aircraft points straight up, pivots point straight down. The maneuver ends with a quarter loop to horizontal flight.

Humpty Bump: Starting with a quarter loop to a vertical climb, the aircraft does a half loop at the top to a vertical down line and then another quarter loop to horizontal flight.

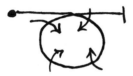

Rolling Turn: In this difficult maneuver, the aircraft flies at a constant altitude and does a complete circular (360-degree) turn with rolls throughout the turn.

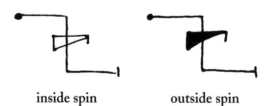

inside spin   outside spin

Spin: The autorotational movement of the aircraft around the longitudinal axis and the result of stalled wings, one wing stalled to a greater degree than the other. During spin entry, the plane has to show a stall break and the autorotation to an exact and specified number of turns. In a crossover spin, the plane first stalls upright, the nose pushes forward so the plane enters an inverted spin, and then the plane recovers from inverted flight. An accelerated spin is a spin that the aircraft enters and completes at a faster rate of rotation, generally with the addition of power.

Tail Slide (stick forward): The aircraft climbs on the vertical line until forward momentum ceases. After it has begun to slide backward, the pilot uses the elevator to prevent the trailing edge of the wing from developing an angle of attack. The aircraft recovers through the pilot's prompt forward or backward movement of the control stick.

Wingover: The pilot notes a position at 90 degrees to the aircraft on entry, and pulls up the nose of the aircraft and banks it steeply at the same time. When the bank exceeds 45 degrees, the nose starts to drop and the aircraft continues turning. Halfway through the maneuver, the plane has turned 90 degrees (toward the point originally noted), the fuselage is level with the horizon, the nose continues to drop below the horizon. The plane keeps turning, and the pilot shallows the bank. When the bank drops below 45 degrees, the pilot pulls the nose up toward the horizon, the plane reaches horizontal flight with wings level and having completed 180 degrees of turn. The aircraft should be at the same altitude as it was on the entry.

Lazy Eight: Two wingovers flown in succession. It is as if the nose of the aircraft has a paintbrush sticking straight out of it and is painting an eight on its side on the horizon. The aircraft turns 180 degrees and then reverses to end up in the direction where the maneuver began.

Knife-Edge Flight: At the completion of the first quarter, or 90 degrees, of a slow roll, the aircraft assumes a vertical bank attitude with no turn involved as the pilot neutralizes the elevator and uses the rudder to keep the aircraft nose up.

The Aerobatic Box

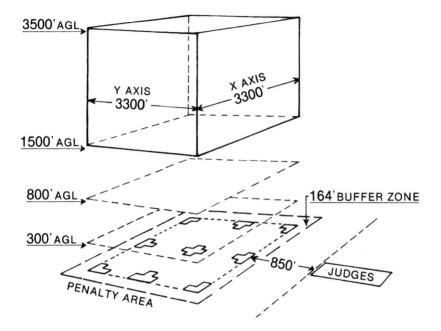

All competition flying should be done inside the "aerobatic box," which is a block of air 3,300 feet long, 3,300 feet wide, and with its top 3,500 feet above the ground. The bottom of the box is set for safety, with the less skilled pilots required to stay higher. It's 1,500 feet for sportsman pilots, 1,500 feet for intermediate pilots, 800 feet for advanced pilots, and 300 feet for unlimited pilots. Anyone who flies outside the box during his or her performance will be assessed penalty points. Positioning judges sitting on the corners of the box determine when a contestant has left the box. This is then called in to the chief judge by radio and recorded.

A Flimsy

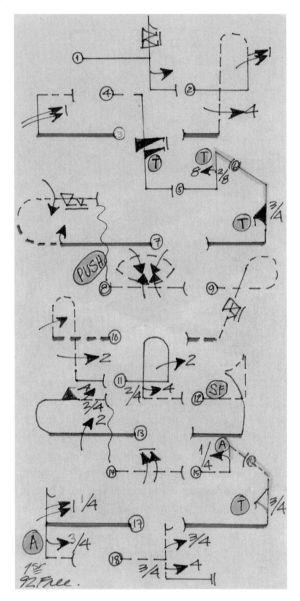

This is the diagram, or flimsy, of Patty's freestyle performance at the 1992 U.S. National Aerobatic Championship. She flew this sequence in her Extra 260 and scored the highest number of points among all competitors. She went on to win the national championship.

Highlights of Patty Wagstaff's Career

Aerobatic Aircraft

1984-85:

Super Decathlon, N1118E, flown in 1984.

Pitts S-1S, N8078, flown throughout the 1985 season. I purchased one-half interest in the S-1S from Ron Fagen in 1984 and purchased the other half in 1985.

1986:

Pitts S-1T, N200ST, flown throughout the 1986 season.

1987:

Pitts S-2S, N216JC, flown until August 1987.

Extra 230, N444PW, flown for U.S. National Aerobatic Championship 1987 and during the 1988, 1989, and 1990 seasons.

1991-92:

Extra 260, N618PW, flown in 1991 and 1992.

1993:

Prototype Extra 260, N618PW, donated to National Air and Space Museum, Smithsonian Institution, Washington, D.C.

Extra 300S, N328PW, flown at U.S. National Aerobatic Championships of 1993, 1994, 1995, and 1996 and at the World Aerobatic
Championship in 1994 and 1996.

Organizations

Airplane Owners and Pilots Association (AOPA)

Antique Airplane Association (AAA)

Experimental Aircraft Association (EAA)

Fédération Aeronautique Internationale (FAI)

International Aerobatic Club (IAC)

International Council of Air Shows (ICAS), ACE and Safety committees

International Women's Air and Space Museum (IWASM), former ad-
visor

Midwest Aerobatic Club, IAC Chapter 1, Illinois

National Aeronautic Association (NAA)

National Association of Flight Instructors (NAFI)

Ninety-Nines (organization of women pilots)

Ohio Aerobatic Club, IAC Chapter 34, Columbus

Professional Air Show Performers Association (PAPA), director

Phoenix Aerobatic Club, IAC Chapter 69, Phoenix, Arizona

Screen Actors Guild

Southern Arizona Aerobatic Club, IAC Chapter 62, Tucson

United Stuntwomen's Association (USA), first pilot member

West Texas Aerobatic Club, IAC Chapter 71, Midland, Texas

Whirly-Girls, National Association of Women Helicopter Pilots

Women in Aviation International (WIAI)

Women's Sports Foundation

Awards and Honors

1983:

Interior and Arctic Alaska Aeronautical Foundation Farthest Travel
Award, Carl Ben Eielson Air Race, Fairbanks, AK

1984:

Participant, first air show, Gulkana Air Show, Gulkana, Alaska

Cessna 185

Second place, Intermediate, Tequila Cup, Southern Arizona Aerobatic
Club, IAC Chapter 62, Tucson, AZ

First aerobatic competition, IAC Championships, Fond du Lac, WI

1985:

First place, Unlimited, International Pilot at Canadian National Aerobatic Championships, Gimli, Manitoba

First place, Sportsman, IAC chapters 1 and 70, Marengo, IL

Second place, Advanced, Minnesota Cloud Dancers, IAC Chapter 78,
Princeton, MN

Third place, Unlimited, Midwest Aerobatic Club Championships,
Clarinda, IA

New member, U.S. Aerobatic Team

New member, International Council of Airshows (ICAS)

1986:

Harold Neumann Award for Aerobatic Excellence, IAC Chapter 15,
Lawrence, KS

Third place, Unlimited, Lone Star Aerobatic Championship, Dallas, TX

Third place, Unlimited, IAC 49er 12th Gold Cup Regional Aerobatic
Contest, Taft, CA

Medal winner, World Aerobatic Championship, South Cerney, England

1987:

Rolly Cole Award, for contribution to sport aerobatics, awarded by Duane and Judy Cole, ICAS Convention, Las Vegas, NV

First place, Unlimited, IAC 49er 13th Gold Cup Regional Aerobatic Contest, Taft, CA

Third place, Unlimited, North American Aerobatic Championship, Red Deer, Manitoba, Canada

Top U.S. female pilot for the first time, unlimited, U.S. National Aerobatic Championship

1988:

Third place, Unlimited, U.S. National Aerobatic Championship, Sherman-Denison, TX

Betty Skelton First Lady of Aerobatics Trophy, U.S. National Aerobatic Championship, Sherman-Denison, TX [1]

Triple medal winner, World Aerobatic Competition, Red Deer, Manitoba, Canada

Second place, Unlimited, Rocky Mountain Aerobatic Championship, Longmont, CO

Judge, 49er IAC 14th Gold Cup Regional Aerobatic Contest, Taft, CA

1989:

First place, Unlimited Four-Minute Freestyle Program, Northern California Aerobatic Club, Chapter 38, Paso Robles, CA

First place, Unlimited, Salem Illinois Regional Contest, IAC Chapter 61, Salem, IL Open

First place, Unlimited, Tequila Cup, Southern Arizona Aerobatic Club, IAC Chapter 62, Tucson

First place, Unlimited, Okie Twistoff, Stillwater, OK

Second place, Unlimited, Northern California Aerobatic Club, Chapter 38, Paso Robles, CA

Second place, Unlimited, IAC Championships, Fond du Lac, WI

Third place, Unlimited Four-Minute Freestyle Program, IAC Championships, Fond du Lac, WI

---

[1] This is awarded to the highest-placing woman competitor in the unlimited category. This was the first time this trophy was awarded and presented by Betty Skelton Frankman herself.

SIT   SIS

Third place, Unlimited, IAC 49er 15th Gold Cup Regional Aerobatic
Contest, Taft, CA

Betty Skelton First Lady of Aerobatics Trophy, U.S. National Aerobatic
Championship, Sherman-Denison, TX

Readers Choice Award, Favorite Female Performer, *Western Flyer*, Tacoma,
WA

1990:

Top overall U.S. medal winner, World Aerobatic Competition, Yverdon-
les-Bains, Switzerland

1991:

First place, Unlimited, U.S. National Aerobatic Championship, Sherman-
Denison, TX

First place, Unlimited, IAC Chapter 15 Regional Contest, Lawrence,
KS

First place, Unlimited, Salem Illinois Regional Contest, IAC Chapter
61, Salem, IL, Open

First place, Unlimited, Robert L. Heuer Classic Aerobatic Contest, IAC
Chapter 1, New Lenox, IL

First place, Unlimited, Midwest Aerobatic Club (MAC) Championship, Harlan, IA

First place, Unlimited, Okie Twistoff, Stillwater, OK

Third place, Unlimited, IAC Championships, Fond du Lac, WI

Betty Skelton First Lady of Aerobatics Trophy, U.S. National Aerobatic Championship, Sherman-Denison, TX

Mike Murphy Trophy, U.S. National Aerobatic Championship, Sherman-Denison, TX [2]

Participant, International Aerobatic Masters, Mar del Plata, Argentina

Participant, joint training with the Soviet Aerobatic Team, Borki, USSR

Readers' Choice Award, Favorite Overall Performer and Favorite Female Performer, *General Aviation News and Flyer*, Tacoma, WA

Lecturer, aerobatic flying, General Electric's Series on Flight, National Air and Space Museum, Smithsonian Institution, Washington, D.C.

1992:

First place, Unlimited, U.S. National Aerobatic Championship, Sherman-Denison, TX

Medal winner, World Aerobatic Championship, Le Havre, France

Betty Skelton First Lady of Aerobatics Trophy, U.S. National Aerobatic Championship, Sherman-Denison, TX

Mike Murphy Trophy, U.S. National Aerobatic Championship, Sherman-Denison, TX

1993:

First place, Unlimited, U.S. National Aerobatic Championship, Sherman-Denison, TX

First place, Unlimited, IAC Championships, Fond du Lac, WI

First place, Unlimited, IAC Chapter 15 Regional Contest, Lawrence, KS

First place, Four-Minute Freestyle Program, Arizona State Championship, Chandler, AZ

First place, Unlimited, Okie Twistoff, IAC Chapter 59, Stillwater, OK

Second place, Unlimited, Four-Minute Freestyle Program, U.S. National Aerobatic Championship, Sherman-Denison, TX

Major Achievement Award, EAA #200806, for outstanding service to sport aviation, Oshkosh, WI

---

[2] This is awarded to the U.S. National Aerobatic Champion.

S2S

Tom Jones Award for Excellence in Aerobatic Flying, presented to aerobatic pilot who achieved the highest percent of possible points in all categories of competition, Okie Twistoff, Stillwater, OK

Harold Krier Cup, awarded to IAC unlimited champion, Fond du Lac, WI

Betty Skelton First Lady of Aerobatics Trophy, U.S. National Aerobatic Championship, Sherman-Denison, TX

Mike Murphy Trophy, U.S. National Aerobatic Championship, Sherman-Denison, TX

Aerobatic Competency Evaluator (ACE), for evaluating air show pilots, ICAS, Jackson, MS

Honorary Chairperson, Annual Fund for Excellence, Experimental Aircraft Association (EAA), Oshkosh, WI

Final aerobatic flying demonstration in the Extra 260 Championship Aircraft, prior to its donation to the National Air and Space Museum, Smithsonian Institution, Andrews Air Force Base, Washington, D.C.

1994:

National Aeronautic Association Certificate of Honor, Fédération Aeronautique Internationale, for extraordinary individual competitive achievement at the national level, National Aerobatic Championship, Sherman-Denison, TX[3]

National Air and Space Museum (NASM) Trophy for Current Achievement, miniature of original John Safer sculpture at NASM. Inscription reads "Her exceptional piloting skills and achievements have made her an outstanding leader in aerobatic flying, December 9, 1994," Smithsonian Institution, Washington, D.C.

Second place, Unlimited, U.S. National Aerobatic Championship, Sherman-Denison, TX

Professional Pilot of the Year, *Professional Pilot* magazine

Betty Skelton First Lady of Aerobatics Trophy, U.S. National Aerobatic Championship, Sherman-Denison, TX

Silver Medal, highest-scoring U.S. pilot, and placed tenth in the world, World Aerobatic Championship, Debrecen, Hungary

Airplane Owners and Pilots Association (AOPA) Project Pilot, Washington, D.C.[4]

Rating, Private helicopter, Phoenix, AZ

Participant, first air show in Hermosillo, Mexico, as guest of the Mexican government

Host, Aviation Forum, attended by 7,500 people, America Online Computer Network

Rules Committee Member, IAC, Oshkosh, WI

Aerobatic Competency Evaluator (ACE), evaluating air show pilots for low-level waivers, ICAS

Type rating, TBM-3E Torpedo bomber, Evergreen Airlines, Marana, Arizona

Instructor, SNJ4, Evergreen Ventures, Marana, Arizona

Featured, *Nova* documentary "Daredevils of the Sky Take Flight with the Aerial Acrobats," PBS, February 1

Featured, *World of Wonder*, Discovery Channel

---

[3] This certificate is presented in the United States with the National Aeronautic Association representing Fédération Aeronautique Internationale. This was the first time that a woman had won the National Aerobatic Championship three consecutive years.

[4] I joined astronaut Senator John Glenn and noted aviation author Barry Shiff to help AOPA launch their project to involve and interest others in aviation.

| Extra 260 | Extra 300 |

Judge, *Professional Pilot* magazine's 21st Annual Fixed Base Operator (FBO)/Flight Support Contest, Alexandria, VA

1995:

Sword of Excellence, highest award given by the International Council of Airshows (ICAS)

Member, ICAS Aerobatic Competency Evaluator (ACE) and Safety committees

Featured in cover story, *Parade Magazine*, August 20

Cohost, "Women in Aviation" segment of Experimental Aircraft Association television series *Ultimate Flights*, ESPN2, July 15, Oshkosh, WI

1996:

Medal winner, World Aerobatic Championship, Oklahoma, OK

Featured on CBS Television, 150th Birthday of the Smithsonian Institution, Aug. 10

First Annual Charlie Hillard Memorial Trophy, presented by Doreen Hillard and Tom Poberezny to the top-scoring U.S. pilot at the World Aerobatic Championships, Oklahoma City, OK

Rating, Commercial helicopter, Fort Worth, TX

Readers' Choice Award, Favorite Female Air Show Pilot, General Aviation News and Flyer, Tacoma, WA

1997:

Inductee, Arizona Aviation Hall of Fame

U.S. Aerobatic Team Member

1986–87: Rookie, 13th World Aerobatic Championship, South Cerney, England

1988–89: Member, winning women's team, 14th World Aerobatic Championship, Red Deer, Canada

1990–91: Top U.S. medal winner, 15th World Aerobatic Championship, Yverdon-les-Bains, Switzerland

1992–93: Top U.S. medal winner, 16th World Aerobatic Championship, Le Havre, France

1994–95: Top U.S. medal winner, 17th World Aerobatic Championship, Debrecen, Hungary

1995–96: Top U.S. medal winner, 18th World Aerobatic Championship, Oklahoma City, OK

International Aerobatics Club: Experimental Aircraft Association

The International Aerobatics Club (IAC), of the Experimental Aircraft Association, (Oshkosh, WI), has many programs under way to foster and promote the sport of aerobatics in the United States and worldwide, including all of the following:

Sport Aerobatics Magazine: The only publication of its type in the world, IAC's monthly magazine is read by members in fifty countries as well as by all the members of the FAI International Aerobatics Commission (CIVA), who are provided with complimentary copies.

Achievement Awards Program: This program is for pilots who wish to be recognized for reaching various skill levels in aerobatic flying. Awards are given at ten different levels—five competition levels and five noncompetition levels. More than three thousand pilots have qualified for the awards since the inception of the program in 1971.

Human Factors Program: In its fourth year, this program emphasizes the physiological aspects of aerobatic flying and through applied technology, focuses on the special problems associated with the role of the human in the aeronautical system.

Technical Safety Program: The IAC's is one of the finest technical support and safety programs in the aviation industry. The program provides technical tips for members every month in *Sport Aerobatics Magazine*. Periodically, Tech Tips manuals are published and made available to the membership. Thanks to this program, accidents that are due to mechanical problems with aerobatic aircraft have virtually disappeared. Identification of the types of problems that occur with aerobatic airplanes has been accomplished through effective member communication.

Chapters: By promoting the formation and organization of chapters, IAC has brought aerobatics to the grassroots level that did not exist prior to its own formation in 1970. Nearly every chapter organizes a regional aerobatic competition in its area, and in several areas, multiple chapters sponsor state championships.

Judges Program: IAC sponsors schools and certification programs for judges to promote knowledgeable and quality competition judging. Within the program, IAC periodically sponsors instructors' seminars for the purpose of training and improving the skills and knowledge of the instructors of the judges' schools.

Aerobatics Hall of Fame: In 1987, IAC formed the International Aerobatics Hall of Fame and has inducted several aerobatic luminaries since that first year. The inductions take place every two years.

Fédération Aeronautique Internationale Representation: IAC represents the United States at the international aerobatics commission.

The IAC Aerobatic Pavilion located at the Experimental Aircraft Association (EAA) convention and fly-in site in Oshkosh, Wisconsin: Dedicated just prior to the 1991 event, this pavilion has continued to be an ideal facility from which to promote aerobatics during the world's largest aviation event. Plans for future structures include the addition of an aerobatic wing and hall of fame at the EAA Aviation Center in Oshkosh.

For more information, contact the International Aerobatics Club, EAA Aviation Center, P.O. Box 3086, Oshkosh, WI 54903-3086. Telephone at (414) 426-4800 or fax at (414) 426-4873.

Our Energy Will Travel Together Again: A Tribute to Lost Friends

One quiet evening, another aerobatic pilot asked, "How do you deal with the loss of friends—their accidents, . . . death?"

I answered, "Every day that I drive to the airport along the desert highway that passes our aerobatic box, my Porsche clicks the miles away smoothly. I have a cup of coffee in one hand, the other on the wheel, and with every fiber of my being I can feel the car making contact with the ribbon of road. I play music on the radio, and, as the turbocharger kicks in, I turn the sky of Arizona purple through my blue sunglasses and I take in the beautiful dusky mountains, soaring birds, and crop dusters spraying the cotton fields. I say out loud, '*I'm Alive!* Yeah!!'"

I believe that there's a certain tenor of justice, a certain journey of the soul that carries me on. I do know that *I'm still alive*. Nothing and nobody is going to change that.

I came to grips, through the years, with losing close friends. I have stared death in the face myself. But, as if their lives are a stage show, aerobatic competitors are actors and actresses. The show goes on. The friends I've lost were not the first to die, nor would they be the last.

I hope that I've learned from my friends' lives and from their deaths. I feel their parents' and loved ones' loss, but I'm still here. One day our energy will travel together again.

320 FIRE AND AIR

Andy Anderson
Mike Anderson
Shane Antarp
Jim Batterman
Rick Brickert
Timothy "T. J." Brown
Mike Brundage
Amos Buetell
Chuck Carothers
Harold Chappell
Maurie Davidson*[1]
Jan Dyer*
Ron Elton
Rick Fessenden
Scott Finagin*
John Fitzgerald
Jerry Fowler
Joe Frasca
Wayne Fuller
Brian Furstenau
Lynn Getshel
Jim Gregory
Joe Hartung
Carl Henley
Bob Herendeen
Charlie Hillard
Herb Hodge
Dave Hoover
Bob Humphries*
Mike Ilyin
Jan Jones
Tom Jones

Bob Keller
Dean Kurtz
Doug Lanam
Fred Leitig
Dick Lewis
Alexander Luibarets
Don Madonna
Lee Manelski
Rick Massegee
Ray Mabrey
Anne Marie Morrissey
Eric Mueller*
Al Pietsch
Frank Sanders
Bob Sears*
Natalya Sergeeva
Karen Shelley
Ron Shelley
Will Shepherd
Flip Smith
Mike Smith*
Clancy Speal
Ed Stanley
Drew Stephens
John Taylor
Steve Van Eck
Mike Van Wagenen
Marty Vavra
Charlie Wells
Moon Wheeler
Bruce Wilbur
Phillipe Wolf

---

[1] People with an asterisk beside their name did not die in an aviation accident.

Mandala
by Patty Wagstaff

I was looking for strength
and my spiritual center,
    healing my soul.
I find talking is strength.
Communicating with an
    open heart and mind
    is my spiritual center.
Honesty is release from fear.
In my pain of discovery,
in shedding my skin,
    questioning my place in the world,
Pandora's box of emotion,
    raw and untamed,
    is spilled all over the ground.
And you have tried not to tread
but softly, over the shells
    of fragments I've left lying there.
In the chaos of sabotage
we create fear and anger,
    fear of loss,
    anger at the power of fear.
And because we don't honor
the fear, the doubts, the
    unsettled circular motion in our guts,
    in our Ki,
We realize that the
world is not linear.
It is circular,
it is a mandala,
    and that which is at the beginning
    is also at the end.
In the genesis of trying
to figure it out,
it's easy to see, it's hard to do,
but we have to return
    to the source
    and the healing which honors our souls.
We have to embrace our fears,
to love our souls,
    to be at peace.

Bibliography

Ackerman, Diane. *On Extended Wings: An Adventure in Flight.* New York: Charles Scribner's Sons, 1987.

Beck, Emily Morison, ed. *Bartlett's Familiar Quotations.* Boston: Little, Brown, 1980.

Blyth, R. H. *Zen and Zen Classics.* Vol. 1. Tokyo, Japan: The Hokuseido Press, 1960; Rutland, Vermont: Charles E. Tuttle Company, 1988.

Boyne, Walter. *Art in Flight: The Sculpture of John Safer.* New York: Hudson Hills Press, 1991.

Camus, Albert. *The Plague.* Paris, France: Librairie Gallimard, 1947.

Cernick, Cliff. "Cape Smythe Air Says No 'Glass Ceiling' for Women Pilots." *General Aviation News and Flyer,* vol. 48, no. 12, June 21, 1996.

Chapin-Carpenter, Mary, and Don Schlitz. "I Take My Chances," *Come On Come On.* EMI April Music Inc./Getarealjob Music, Compact disc, 1992.

Cole, Duane. *The Flying Coles.* Milwaukee, Wisconsin: Ken Cook Transnational, 1974.

Cole, Duane. *Conquest of Lines and Symmetry.* Milwaukee, Wisconsin: Ken Cook Transnational, 1970.

Cole, Duane. "Report from the U.S. National Aerobatic Championships: Patty Wagstaff Steals the Show." *Flight Training,* vol. 4, no. 1, January 1992, 58-60.

Corroone, Debra. Personal letter, 1996.

Davisson, Budd. "Flight of the Bumblebee." *Private Pilot*, vol. 30, no. 12, December 1995, 60-64.

Davisson, Budd. "Something EXTRA!" *Air Progress*, vol. 54, no. 1 (January 1992): 40-45, 63, 67.

Dylan, Bob. "If Dogs Run Free," *Lyrics, 1962–1985*. Big Sky Music, 1970; A. A. Knopf, New York, 1985.

Earhart, Amelia. *Last Flight*. New York: Crown Publishers, 1988.

Editors. *Mirabella*. "One Hundred Fearless Women." Special Fifth Anniversary Issue, June 1994.

Gann, Ernest K. *Ernest K. Gann's Flying Circus*. New York: Macmillan Publishing, 1974.

Gann, Ernest K. *Fate Is the Hunter*. New York: Simon and Schuster, 1961.

Gonzales, Laurence. *One Zero Charlie: Adventures in Grass Roots Aviation*. New York: Simon and Schuster, 1990.

Goode, Katie. *Fliers: In Their Own Words*. Renton, Washington: Aviation Supplies and Academics, 1994.

Gose, Frank. "Grassroots Aerobatics." *Private Pilot*, vol. 30, no. 12 (December 1995): 32-39.

Goyer, Robert. "Breaking Through to the Other Side." *Air Progress*, vol. 54, no. 12 (December 1992): 53-57.

Halberstam, David. *The Amateurs*. New York: William Morrow & Company, 1985.

Harris, Grace McAdams. *West to the Sunrise*. Ames, Iowa: Iowa State University Press, 1980.

Hassilev, Alex, Glenn Yarbrough, and Lou Gottlieb. "Have Some Madeira," *The Limeliters Reunion—Volume 2*. San Bruno, California: West Knoll Records. Audiocassette, 1989.

Hayward, Justin. "Nights in White Satin," *Moody Blues*. Audiocassette, 1967.

Hazleton, Lesley. *Confessions of a Fast Woman*. New York: Addison-Wesley Publishing, 1992.

Herrigel, Eugen. *Zen in the Art of Archery*. New York: Vintage Books, Random House, 1989.

Holden, Henry. "Sport Aviation," In *Ladybirds II*. New Jersey: Black Hawk Publishing Company (1993): 125-129.

Hyams, Joe. *Zen in the Martial Arts.* New York: Bantam Books, 1982.

Jacobs, Bruce. "A Wing and a Dare." *The Discovery Channel Magazine,* vol. 7, no. 4 (July 1991): 20-29.

Jones, Mel R. *Above and Beyond: Eight Great American Aerobatic Champions.* Blue Ridge Summit, Pennsylvania: TAB Books, 1984.

Kershner, William K. *The Student Pilot's Flight Manual.* Ames, Iowa: Iowa State University Press, 1977.

King, John, and Martha King, King Schools. Personal interview, 1995.

Krishnamurti. *You Are the World: An Authentic Report of Talks and Discussions in American Universities.* New York: Harper & Row, 1989.

Langewiesche, Wolfgang. *Stick and Rudder: An Explanation of Flying.* New York: McGraw Hill, 1944.

Lillberg, John. "Walter's Magnificent Aircraft." *Sport Aerobatics,* March 1993.

Loehr, James E. *Mental Toughness Training for Sports.* Lexington, Massachusetts: Stephen Greene Press, 1982.

Loh, Jules. "Looping Loop Second Best, Patti Says." *The Daily Olympian* (Washington), July 14, 1977.

Lowe, Larry. "Ballet Among the Clouds." *Air & Space,* vol. 6, no. 3 (Aug/Sept, 1991): 72-80.

Medore, Art. *Primary Aerobatic Flight Training with Military Techniques.* 4th ed. Banning, California: Banaire Enterprises, 1992.

Milles, Billy. Quoted in a photographic exhibit; photographs by Don Dill. Dayton, Ohio: Dayton Museum of Natural History, 1995.

Moll, Nigel. "Patty Wagstaff Hangs It Up." *Logbook* in *FLYING* (September 1993): 100.

Moolman, Valerie, and the Editors of Time-Life Books. *Women Aloft.* Alexandria, Virginia: Time-Life Books, 1981.

Morris, Steve. Official Program, U.S. Aerobatic National Championship, Sherman-Denison, Texas, 1992.

National Aeronautic Association, National Aerobatic Club of the United States. *World and United States Aviation and Space Records and Annual Report.* Arlington, Virginia: United States Representative Fédération Aeronautique Internationale, 1994.

Nevin, David, and the Editors of Time-Life Books. *The Pathfinders.* Alexandria, Virginia: Time-Life Books, 1980.

Nicks, Stevie. "Docklands," *Street Angel*. Audiocassette, 1994.

Pirsig, Robert M. *Zen and the Art of Motorcycle Maintenance*. New York: New Age Edition, 1981.

Poberezny, Tom. "Predictions." *Homebuilders' Corner: Sport Aviation*, February 1996.

Reynolds, Malvina. "Little Boxes." *Gonna Sing My Head Off! American Folk Songs for Children*. Arranged by Kathleen Krull. N.Y.: A. A. Knopf (1992): 69.

Schaare, Harry J. Personal telephone interview, 1994.

Shaffer, Jan. "Upside Down." *Indy Car Racing*, vol. 9, no. 4 (April 1992): 22-23.

Smith, Brian. "Britain Hosts the Ultimate Test." *Flight International*, July 1986.

Sorg, Jean, ed. "Aerobatic Profile: Meet the Sole Rookie 1986 U.S. Team Member—Patty Wagstaff." *Sport Aerobatics*, vol. 14, no. 12 (December 1985): 18-19.

Szurovy, Gesa, and Mike Goulian. *Basic Aerobatics*. Pennsylvania: TAB Books, McGraw-Hill, 1994.

Thomas, Stanley G. "A 'Coupe for Vitas Lapenas." *Sport Aviation*, March 1993.

Toplikar, Dave. "Barrel Rolls, Loops Are All in a Day's Work." *Lawrence* (Kansas) *Journal World* (September 1993): 1A.

Venkus, Robert E. "Mission Improbable: The 1986 Raid on Libya." *Friends Journal*, Spring 1996.

Vos Savant, Marilyn. "Ask Marilyn," *Parade Magazine Dayton Daily News*, January 7, 1996.

Wagstaff, Patty. Journals, 1971–1995.

Wagstaff, Patty. Personal Interviews, 1988–1996.

Wagstaff, Patty. "Russia." *Sport Aerobatics*, 1991.

Wagstaff, Patty. "Mr. Show Biz." *ICAS News*, third quarter (1993): 44-53.

Wagstaff, Patty. "With His Wife's Permission," *ICAS News*, second quarter (1993): 42-63.

Wagstaff, Patty. "The Morning After a Good Day." *Flight*, summer 1996.

Whyte, Edna Gardner, and Ann L. Cooper. *Rising Above It: The Autobiography of Edna Gardner Whyte*. New York: Crown Publishers, 1991.

Williams, Neil. *Aerobatics*. 10th ed. Shrewsbury, England: Airlife Publishing, 1991.

Wright, Bill. "From Depths of Despair to Ultimate Success." *Pacific Flyer*, August 1991.

Woytowich, Judy. Lifestyle, "Women at Work." *Pacific Daily News*, February 25, 1991.

World Airshow News. Oshkosh, Wisconsin, A press release, July/August, 1993.